T0260514

Garbage Collection

Garbage Collection
Algorithms for Automatic Dynamic Memory Management

Richard Jones

University of Kent at Canterbury, UK

Rafael Lins

Universidade Federal de Pernambuco, Brazil

JOHN WILEY & SONS

Chichester · New York · Weinheim · Brisbane · Toronto · Singapore

Copyright © 1996 John Wiley & Sons Ltd, The Atrium, Southern Gate, Chichester,
West Sussex PO19 8SQ, England

Telephone   (+44) 1243 779777

Email (for orders and customer service enquiries): cs-books@wiley.co.uk
Visit our Home Page on www.wileyeurope.com or www.wiley.co.uk

Reprinted February and November 1997, January 1999, June 2000, January 2003
May 2004, July 2006, October 2007

All Rights Reserved. No part of this publication may be reproduced, stored in a retrieval
system or transmitted in any form or by any means, electronic, mechanical, photocopying,
recording, scanning or otherwise, except under the terms of the Copyright, Designs and
Patents Act 1988 or under the terms of a licence issued by the Copyright Licensing Agency
Ltd, 90 Tottenham Court Road, London W1T 4LP, UK, without the permission in writing of
the Publisher. Requests to the Publisher should be addressed to the Permissions Department,
John Wiley & Sons Ltd, The Atrium, Southern Gate, Chichester, West Sussex PO19 8SQ,
England, or emailed to permreq@wiley.co.uk, or faxed to (+44) 1243 770571.

This publication is designed to provide accurate and authoritative information in regard to
the subject matter covered. It is sold on the understanding that the Publisher is not engaged in
rendering professional services. If professional advice or other expert assistance is required,
the services of a competent professional should be sought.

Other Wiley Editorial Offices

John Wiley & Sons Inc., 111 River Street, Hoboken, NJ 07030, USA

Jossey-Bass, 989 Market Street, San Francisco, CA 94103-1741, USA

Wiley-VCH Verlag GmbH, Boschstr. 12, D-69469 Weinheim, Germany

John Wiley & Sons Australia Ltd, 33 Park Road, Milton, Queensland 4064, Australia

John Wiley & Sons (Asia) Pte Ltd, 2 Clementi Loop #02-01, Jin Xing Distripark, Singapore
129809

John Wiley & Sons Canada Ltd, 22 Worcester Road, Etobicoke, Ontario, Canada M9W 1L1

British Library Cataloguing in Publication Data

A catalogue record for this book is available from the British Library

ISBN-13: 978-0-471-94148-4 (H/B)

To Robbie
& Carmo

Contents

List of Algorithms

List of Diagrams

List of Tables

Preface

This book is about garbage collection: the automatic reclamation of heap-allocated storage after its last use by a program. Memory is and has always been a scarce and precious resource. In the early days of computing, before the advent of very large scale integrated circuits, memory was expensive and even a time-sharing operating system like Unix was expected to run in just one 64-kilobyte segment. Today, although SIMM memory modules are comparatively cheap to buy and easy to install, programs are increasingly profligate in their consumption of this resource. Microsoft Windows'95, an operating system for a single-user personal computer, needs more than twelve megabytes of RAM to operate optimally. Thus main memory alone may account for half the cost of a PC. As with all precious resources, memory needs to be carefully managed and recycled when no longer needed.

The storage requirements of many computer programs are simple and predictable. Allocation and deallocation of memory for such programs can be handled by the programmer or the compiler, and indeed is best done so. Other programs have grown enormously in size and complexity. Languages like Lisp and Prolog typically manipulate large data structures with complex inter-dependencies. Functional and logic languages have complex patterns of execution. The result is that the useful lifetimes of many data structures can no longer be determined before execution, either by programmer or by compiler. Automatic storage reclamation is essential.

One reflection of the growing importance of garbage collection is the level of debate on this subject within the computer science community. As well as individual papers in journals and conferences, there have been workshops on garbage collection at the 1990, 1991 and 1993 Object-Oriented Systems, Languages and Applications OOPSLA conferences, as well as international workshops exclusively devoted to the topic in 1992, 1995 and 1998. Garbage collection is also a perennially popular subject for extended argument on Usenet news groups.

Object-orientation is the strongest growing area of interest in analysis, design and programming today. The key to good software engineering is the control of complexity. One of the ways that object-oriented design achieves this goal is the encapsulation of abstractions into objects that communicate through clearly defined interfaces. Programmer-controlled storage management inhibits this modularity. For this reason, most modern object-oriented languages, such as Smalltalk, Eiffel, Java and Dylan, are supported by garbage collection. Today, even languages used in part for systems programming, such as Modula-3 and Oberon, provide garbage collection for these sound but pragmatic reasons. Garbage collecting libraries are also available for such uncooperative languages as C and C++.

The audience

The literature on garbage collection is enormous. Well over a thousand journal articles, chapters in books, presentations to conferences, technical reports and postgraduate theses have been written on the subject. Despite this many myths about garbage collectors prevail. 'They are only necessary for Lisp and functional languages; they can only be used with interpreters rather than for compiled code; they place an intolerable overhead on programs' — and doubtless they have cloven hooves and forked tails as well! Two corollaries follow. First, garbage-collected solutions are often ignored where they could profitably be applied. Second, where the complexities of the data structures involved demand garbage collection, the experience provided in the literature is often unfamiliar so a wheel is reinvented.

The aim of this book is to draw this wealth of experience together into a single, accessible and unified framework. State of the art techniques are described and compared for declarative and imperative programming styles, for sequential, concurrent and distributed architectures. Each of the most important algorithms is explained in detail, often with illustrations of its characteristic features and animations of its use. Its complexity, performance, applicability and relationship with other related algorithms is also discussed.

We believe that this survey should prove useful to postgraduate students and researchers working in Compiler Construction; Functional, Logic and Object-oriented Programming and Design; Software Engineering; and Operating Systems. The book should also be of interest to students taking advanced courses in these areas. We hope that professionals developing programs — from simple software tools to complex real-time systems — will find this book valuable. In particular, the rapid growth in popularity of object-oriented systems over the past few years makes a thorough understanding of garbage collection methods essential for any programmer in this area.

Organisation of the book

The first chapter begins with the evolution of computer memory management and the need for automatic storage reclamation. We then describe the representation of objects in our heap, and discuss the yardsticks by which different strategies of garbage collection may be measured. The chapter ends with a description of our pseudo-code notation.

Chapter 2 introduces the three 'classical' techniques for garbage collection: reference counting, mark-sweep and copying collection. Readers with some experience of these techniques may wish to skip this chapter.

The next four chapters cover these styles of collection — and mark-compact collection — in more detail. Chapter 7 introduces generational garbage collection, a paradigm that has proved effective at reducing garbage collection pause times and overall costs in a wide range of applications, and Chapter 8 describes how garbage collection can be finely interleaved with the rest of a computation. Chapters 9 and 10 extend garbage collection to environments in which there is no support from the language compiler, C and C++ respectively. The next chapter of the book discusses a relatively new research area, the interaction of garbage collection with hardware data caches. Finally, Chapter 12 briefly surveys garbage collection for distributed systems.

We have included a summary of issues to consider at the end of each chapter. These summaries are intended to offer guidelines to the reader on the questions that should be answered about the collectors, the client program and the operating system and architecture before a garbage collector is chosen. These questions are designed as prompts to the reader. The summaries are certainly not a substitute for reading the appropriate chapter, and we have not attempted to provide 'pat' solutions. Moreover, strategies of garbage collection (such as reference counting, mark-sweep or copying) introduced in earlier chapters are revisited in later ones. The characteristics and performance of naïve implementations should not be mistaken for those of state of the art implementations of the same garbage collection strategy. Nevertheless we hope that these summaries will provide, rather than a 'cook book', a focus for further analysis.

We should also declare what is missing from the book. The most effortless form of memory management is to do none at run-time. A considerable amount of research has gone into compile-time techniques to discover when objects can be discarded or reused. Most of this work has been theoretic and, as yet, we believe that there has been little evidence of substantial performance gains. We have omitted this material. Some techniques and tricks are language specific. While we have chosen to cover C++ because of its increasing popularity and growing realisation by many of its practitioners that garbage collection is sorely needed, we have concentrated in the main on generally applicable methods. Techniques that are specific to certain styles of programming, for example pure functional programming or logic programming, are only mentioned briefly.

Finally, energetic researchers who trawl through on-line bibliographic databases will discover papers on other garbage collection techniques and issues in their catch. We were intrigued by, but chose to ignore, burying garbage in landfills, incineration and dumping it at sea. The question of public health and garbage collection is also often raised — but language wars are another ball game altogether!

The Bibliography and the World-Wide Web

We mentioned earlier that over a thousand papers have been published on this topic. The bibliography at the end of this book is considerably shorter. However a comprehensive database is available electronically from

`http://www.cs.ukc.ac.uk/people/staff/rej/gc.html`

This bibliography also contains some abstracts and URLs for electronically available papers. Richard Jones will endeavour to keep his bibliography up to date and would be most grateful to receive further entries (preferably in BibTeX format) as well as URLs for existing papers (and any corrections).

We have endeavoured to eradicate any errors from the code fragments presented in the book. While not having the courage to repeat Donald Knuth's offer of cash for errors reported, a list of any errors found is maintained at this web site. Reports should be sent either by email to `R.E.Jones@ukc.ac.uk`, or by post to Richard Jones, Computing Laboratory, University of Kent at Canterbury, Canterbury, Kent, CT2 7NF, UK.

Acknowledgements

This book would never have been completed with the encouragement, assistance and patience of many people. I would like to thank the Theoretical Computer Science research group at the University of Kent at Canterbury for cheering from the side-lines. In particular I am indebted to Simon Thompson for patiently reading and commenting on drafts of this book, and for all his encouragement. I would also like to thank Hans Boehm, Jacques Cohen, Keith Dimond, and David Turner for their comments and suggestions. I would also like to thank Martin Broom, Tim Hopkins, and Simon Thompson for their advice on how to wrestle LaTeX into submission. The two term study leave granted to me by the University of Kent and visits to the Federal University of Pernambuco, Recife, Brazil (and the caipirinha), funded by the British Council and CNPq-Brazil, were invaluable.

I am also grateful to Rafael Lins who originally conceived the idea for the book and wrote the chapter on Distributed garbage collection, as well as contributing to some other chapters. Acknowledgement must also be paid to all those — too numerous to mention — who have worked on garbage collection over the last thirty-six years.

Finally, and above all, I must thank Robbie, Helen, Kate and William without whose support and forbearance none of this would have been possible. For more than two years you have put up with me occupying the dining room claiming that it was my study; you have forgiven my bad temper; and you have graciously accepted that I could not come out to play. I thank you from the bottom of my heart.

Richard Jones
Canterbury
February 1996

I am most grateful to the many people who contributed in many different ways to make this book possible, and in particular to David Turner, Simon Thompson, Jon Salkild, Rosita Wachenchauzer, Alejandro Martinez and Marcia Correia. I am grateful to the Universidade Federal de Pernambuco, Recife, Brazil, for granting sabbatical leave, funded by CAPES-Brazil, and several visits to the University of Kent, funded by CNPq-Brazil and the British Council. The many friends at Kent made those visits ever so pleasant! I am also grateful for all the support and love I have received from Carmo, Gilka, Maria Teresa, Rilane and Silvia.

Rafael Lins
Recife
February 1996

Revisions

This reprinting has given me the chance to make some small improvements to the book. The index has been extended to allow easier discovery of algorithms from the names of their authors. Errors in the 1996 and 1997 printings have been corrected. Those observant enough to spot bugs and kind enough to point them out to me include: Andrew Appel, Nick Barnes, Stephen Bevan, Matthieu Blondeau, Hans Boehm, Thomas Burri, Morris Chang, Sid Chatterjee, Peter Dickman, Alex Garthwaite, Tim Geisler and Pekka Pirinen. I am also grateful to Gaynor Redvers-Mutton, my editor at John Wiley & Sons, for her continuing encouragement and in particular for the opportunity to make these improvements.

Richard Jones
Canterbury
November 1998

1

Introduction

"One of LISP's most lasting contributions is a non-language feature: namely the term and technique *garbage collection*, which refers to the system's method of automatically dealing with storage."

Jean E. Sammet
Programming Languages: History and Fundamentals, 1969

Over the last dozen years, garbage collection has come of age. Whereas it was once confined to the realm of Lisp and functional languages, today garbage collection is an important part of the memory management system of many modern programming languages, imperative as well as declarative. Although garbage collection has had a reputation for sloth and for disrupting interactive programs, modern implementation techniques have reduced its overheads substantially, to the point where garbage collected heaps are a realistic option — even for traditional languages like C.

Despite the rapid growth in memory sizes of even the most modest computers, the supply of storage is not inexhaustible. Like all limited resources it requires careful conservation and recycling. Many programming languages today allow the programmer to allocate and reclaim memory for data whose lifetimes are not determined by lexical scope. Such data is said to be *dynamically* allocated. Dynamic memory may be managed explicitly by the programmer through invocations of built-in or library procedures that allocate storage and that dispose or *free* that storage when it is no longer needed.

Manual reclamation of dynamically managed storage is often unsatisfactory. The alternative is to devolve responsibility for dynamic memory management to the program's run-time system. The programmer must still request dynamically allocated storage to be reserved but no longer needs to determine when that memory is no longer required: it is recycled automatically. *Garbage collection* is precisely this — the automatic management of dynamically allocated storage. Some authors prefer to distinguish between *direct techniques*, such as reference counting, and *indirect*, tracing techniques. However the term garbage collection is widely used to refer to all forms of automatic management of dynamically allocated storage, and we shall use it to refer to both reference counting and tracing methods. We shall need to distinguish between the garbage collector and the part of the program that does 'useful' work. Following Dijkstra's terminology, we shall call the user program the *mutator* since, as far as the collector is concerned, its sole rôle is to change or mutate the connectivity of the graph of active data structures in the heap.

In this introduction we seek to answer three questions. What problem does garbage collection solve? How costly is garbage collection? By which parameters may different garbage collection algorithms be compared? We also outline a taxonomy of garbage collection techniques and explain the notation used in the rest of the book. Let us first briefly review the history of programming languages, and in particular the implementation of storage management, from the 1940s to the present day.

1.1   History of storage allocation

The history of the development of programming languages can be considered to be an account of the provision of greater support for abstraction and the automation of actions that were previously manual or explicit.

In the early days of computing all communication between programmer and machine was on a bit-by-bit basis, with simple switches for input. Shortly afterwards, the introduction of simple input and output devices made the exchange of hexadecimal values between operator and machine easier. The next step was to allow programmers to use mnemonic codes that were mechanically translated into binary notation. Nevertheless, users were responsible for every detail of their program's execution. For example, special attention was needed to count the number of words in the program and to find the absolute address of instructions in order to determine whether there was enough space available to load the program and in order to specify the destination of jumps.

By the late 1940s and early 1950s, this book-keeping burden had been transferred to macro codes and assembly languages [Metropolis *et al.*, 1980]. Symbolic programs are easier to write and to understand than machine-language programs primarily because numerical codes for addresses and operators are replaced by more meaningful symbolic codes. Nevertheless the programmer must still be intimately concerned with how a specific computer operates, and how and where data is represented within the machine. The large number of small machine-dependent details continues to make assembly language programming an exacting task.

To overcome these problems, ideas for high-level programming languages, intended to make the programming task simpler, appeared during the mid to late 1940s. By 1952 the first experimental compilers had appeared, and the first Fortran compiler was delivered in early 1957. A compiler for a high-level language must allocate resources of the target machine to represent the data objects manipulated by the user's program. There are three ways in which storage can be allocated.

Static allocation

The simplest allocation policy is static allocation. All names in the program are bound to storage locations at compile-time: these bindings do not change at run-time. This implies that the local variables of a procedure are bound to the same locations at every activation of the procedure. Static allocation was the original implementation policy of Fortran, and it is still used by Fortran 77, for example. Static allocation has three limitations.

- The size of each data structure must be known at compile-time.
- No procedure can be recursive since all its activations share the same locations for local names.
- Data structures cannot be created dynamically.

Nevertheless, static allocation does have two important benefits. Implementations of statically allocated languages are often fast since no data structures, such as stack frames, need to be created or destroyed during the program's execution. Since the location of all data is known by the compiler, storage locations can be accessed directly rather than indirectly. Static allocation also offers a safety guarantee: the program cannot fail by running out of space at run-time since its memory requirements are known in advance.

Stack allocation

The first block-structured languages appeared in 1958 with Algol-58 and Atlas Autocode. Block-structured languages overcome some of the constraints of static allocation by allocating storage on a stack. An *activation record* or *frame* is pushed onto the system stack as each procedure is called, and popped when it returns. Stack organisation has five implications.

- Different activations of a procedure do not share the same bindings for local variables. Recursive calls are possible, thereby greatly enhancing the expressivity of the language.
- The size of local data structures such as arrays may depend on a parameter passed to the procedure.
- The values of stack-allocated local names cannot persist from one activation to the next.
- A called activation record cannot outlive its caller.
- Only an object whose size is known at compile-time can be returned as the result of a procedure.

Heap allocation

Unlike the last-in, first-out discipline of a stack, data structures in a heap may be allocated and deallocated in any order. Thus activation records and dynamic data structures may outlive the procedure that created them. Heap allocation has a number of advantages.

- Design is about creating abstractions to model real-world problems and many of these are naturally hierarchical; the most common examples are lists and trees. Heap allocation allows the concrete representation of such abstractions to be recursive.

- The size of data structures is no longer fixed but can be varied dynamically. Exceeding built-in limits on the size of data structures, such as arrays, is one of the most common sources of program failure.
- Dynamically-sized objects can be returned as the result of a procedure.
- Many modern programming languages allow a procedure to be returned as the result of another procedure. Stack-allocated languages can do this if they prohibit nested procedures: the static address of the returned procedure is used. Functional and higher-order imperative languages may allow the result of a function to be a *suspension* or *closure*: a function paired with an *environment* of bindings of names to locations. These bindings will therefore outlive the activation of the function that created them.

Today many if not most high-level programming languages are able to allocate storage on both the stack and the heap. Many languages, such as Pascal and C, have traditionally managed all data on the heap explicitly. C++ is one recent language that remains committed to this approach. Functional, logic and most object-oriented languages use garbage collection to manage the heap automatically. Examples include Scheme, Dylan, ML, Haskell, Miranda, Prolog, Smalltalk, Eiffel, Java and Oberon. Other languages, notably Modula-3, offer both explicitly and automatically managed heaps.

1.2   State, liveness and pointer reachability

The values that a program can manipulate directly are those held in processor registers, those on the program stack (including local variables and temporaries), and those held in global variables. Such locations holding references to heap data form the *roots* of the computation. Automatic heap-memory management demands that certain rules be followed by the programmer. Dynamically allocated data should only be accessible to the user program through the roots, or by following chains of pointers from these roots. In particular, the program should not access random locations in its address space, for example by picking an arbitrary offset from the base of the heap. This restriction is not unique to garbage collection. It is also enforced by strongly-typed languages such as Pascal. Safe use of C's explicit `malloc`/`free` allocation mechanisms also demands that the user program does not access unallocated regions of memory.

An individually allocated piece of data in the heap will be called, interchangeably, a *node*, *cell* or *object*[1]. The rules above imply that the storage mechanism's view of the liveness of the graph of objects in the heap is defined by *pointer reachability*. An object in the heap is live if its address is held in a root, or there is a pointer to it held in another live heap node. More formally, define $\rightarrow$ as the 'points-to' relation: for any node or root M and any heap node N, $M \rightarrow N$ if and only if M holds a reference to N. The set of live nodes in the heap is the *transitive referential closure* of the set of roots under this relation, i.e. the least set[2] *live* where

$$live = \{N \in Nodes \mid (\exists r \in Roots.r \rightarrow N) \vee (\exists M \in live.M \rightarrow N)\}$$

---

[1] It will be made clear where the latter term is meant in the object-oriented sense.

[2] Mathematical note: such a least set exists by Tarski's theorem, which states that any equation of the form $S = f\,S$, where f is a monotonic operation on sets, has a least fixed point.

For the moment, we note that this view of the set of live cells in the heap is only a conservative estimate of the actual set of cells that are potentially accessible to the program. It may include cells that analysis of the program text or data flow analysis by an optimising compiler would reveal to be dead. Typical examples include a local variable after its last use in a procedure, as yet uninitialised slots in a stack frame, or an obsolete pointer left in a register (to avoid the cost of clearing it). We shall return to this question later in this chapter and also when we consider techniques for conservative garbage collection in Chapter 9.

A node's liveness may be determined either directly or indirectly. Direct methods require that a record be associated with each node in the heap, of all references to that node from other heap nodes or roots. The most common direct method is to store a count of the number of pointers to this cell, its *reference count*, in the cell itself. Direct algorithms for distributed systems may instead keep lists of the remote processors that contain references to each object. In either case, these records must be kept up to date as the mutator alters the connectivity of the graph in the heap.

Indirect or *tracing* collectors typically regenerate the set of live nodes whenever a request by the user program for more memory fails. The collector starts from the roots and, by following pointers, visits all reachable nodes. These nodes are considered to be live and all memory occupied by other nodes is made available for recycling. If sufficient memory has been recovered, the user program's request is satisfied and it is restarted.

1.3   Explicit allocation on the heap

A simple example

Traditionally, most imperative languages have placed the responsibility for the allocation and deallocation of objects on the heap with the programmer. In Pascal, memory is allocated in the heap by the new procedure. Given a pointer variable p, new(p) causes p to point to newly allocated storage for an object of the type to which p is declared to point. The object is deallocated or *freed* by calling dispose(p). The program fragment in Algorithm 1.1 on the following page creates a list [1,2,3].

Garbage

Dynamically allocated storage may become unreachable. Objects that are not live, but are not free either, are called *garbage*. With explicit deallocation, garbage cannot be reused: its space has *leaked* away. We could generate a space leak in the program in Algorithm 1.1 on the following page by adding a line

```
myList↑.next := nil;
```

after the list is created (Diagram 1.2 on page 7).

Now only the first element of list is accessible to the program; the memory containing items 2 and 3 is out of the program's reach and can neither be used nor recovered. Automatic storage management can recover inaccessible memory: this is the subject of this book.

```
program pointer(input, output);
type ptr = ↑cell;
     cell = record
                   value : integer;
                   next  : ptr
             end;
var  myList : ptr;

function Insert (item : integer; list : ptr) : ptr;
var  temp : ptr;
begin
     new(temp);
     temp↑.value := item;
     temp↑.next := list;
     Insert := temp
end;

begin
     myList := Insert(1, Insert(2, Insert(3,nil)))
end.
```

Algorithm 1.1   Dynamic allocation of a list in Pascal.

Dangling references

Memory can also be deallocated while there are still references to it. Suppose we replace the
new line in Algorithm 1.1 by

```
dispose(myList↑.next);
```

to return item 2 to the heap manager. Again, item 3 has become garbage: this small leak will
not harm our tiny program (see Diagram 1.3 on the next page). However, the next field of
item 1 refers to memory that has been deallocated. A *dangling reference* has been created.

The program has no control over the use to which the disposed storage is put. It may
be cleared, used to store book-keeping information or recycled by the heap manager. If
the program follows the dangling reference, the best that can be hoped for is that it will
crash immediately. If the heap manager had reallocated the disposed memory to another of
the program's data structures, a single location would represent two different objects. If we
are lucky, the program will eventually crash at some future point. If we are unlucky, it will
continue to run but produce incorrect results.

Diagram 1.1   The list built by Algorithm 1.1.

Diagram 1.2 `myList↑.next := nil` creates a space leak.

Sharing

Garbage and dangling references are the two sides of the same coin of explicit allocation. Garbage is created by destroying the last reference before an object is deallocated. Dangling references are created by deallocating an object while references to it remain. It might appear that the solution is that both actions — destruction of the last reference and deallocation of its target — should be co-ordinated, but this is not easy in the presence of sharing.

Suppose two lists share a common suffix (see Diagram 1.4 on the following page). A well-behaved list disposal routine will recursively deallocate each item of a list when the pointer to the head of the list is destroyed. However, if either cat or mat were destroyed in this way, the other would consist of a single item and a dangling pointer. This was the problem that led to interest in automatic storage reclamation techniques in the late 1950s [McCarthy, 1981].

Failures

Dynamic memory in complex programs is hard to manage correctly with explicit allocation and deallocation, and examples of failing programs are common. Programs crash unexpectedly and servers run out of memory for no apparent reason. The effect of such programming errors is indeterminate, particularly in multi-threaded environments. Dangling references may be benign if the heap manager does not reallocate that particular object. Space leaks may lie dormant under testing and even under normal conditions of use. Failures commonly only surface when the program is put under stress or left running for long periods. For example, the input to a compiler may be machine generated and violate assumptions about the shape of code that a programmer might reasonably be expected to write. Space leaks may remain undiscovered when the code is run on the development machine. However, when executed on a machine with a smaller memory or on a long-running server, the leak may exhaust the memory. Debugging under these conditions is extremely difficult as failures are often unrepeatable.

Diagram 1.3 `dispose(myList↑.next)` creates a space leak and a dangling pointer.

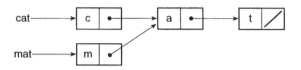

Diagram 1.4   Two lists may share a common suffix. `mat := Insert('m',cat↑.next);`

1.4 Why garbage collect?

Language requirements

Garbage collection may be essential or merely highly desirable. It may be a language requirement: heap allocation is required for data structures that may survive the procedure that created them. If these data structures are then passed to further procedures or functions, it may be impossible for the programmer or compiler to determine the point at which it is safe to deallocate them. The prevalence of sharing and delayed execution of suspensions means that functional languages often have particularly unpredictable execution orders. Garbage collection is mandatory.

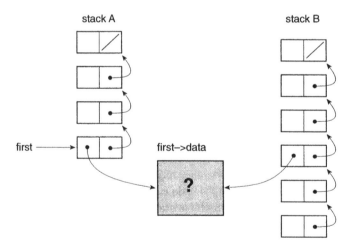

Diagram 1.5   Should the data object be deallocated when the stack is popped?

Problem requirements

Garbage collection may be a problem requirement. Boehm and Chase offer a helpful illustration [Boehm and Chase, 1992]. Suppose a general stack data type is to be implemented in C as a linked list. Each node on the stack contains two pointer fields: `data` and `next`.

The `Pop` operation is to deallocate the top of the stack, call it `first`, and return a pointer to the remainder of the stack. Should `Pop` deallocate the data referenced from the top element, `first->data`? If the data is statically allocated, the answer is 'no'. Otherwise, if this is the last reference to the data, the answer is 'yes'. If the data may be pushed on to more than one stack — it is in Diagram 1.5 on the preceding page — the answer is 'maybe'. Some convention is required for deallocation even for such a simple abstraction. This will either complicate the interface to the stack, reduce its applicability or force unnecessary copying (so that deallocation decisions can be made locally).

Software engineering issues

Software engineering is most succinctly described as the management of complexity in large-scale software systems. Two of the most powerful tools available to the software engineer are abstraction and modularity. We strongly believe that explicit memory management cuts against these principles. Automatic memory management gives increased abstraction to the programmer. The model of memory allocation is less low-level and programmers are relieved of the burden of book-keeping detail: their time is better spent on higher-level details of the design, and implementation of the programming problem at hand. Memory management by the run-time system is adopted by all high-level programming languages for static and stack-allocated data. Abstracting away from such low-level issues is universally recognised by designers of high-level programming languages to be essential for global and lexically-scoped data. Programmers do not have to worry where to place global data, or how to set up or take down procedure activation frames on the stack. We believe that the case for abstraction applies equally strongly to heap-allocated data in complex programs.

Reliable code is understandable code. At the level of the module, this means that a programmer should be able to understand its behaviour from the module itself, or, in the worst case, a few neighbouring modules. It should not be necessary to understand an entire program before being able to develop a single module. This is clearly essential for large-scale projects involving teams of developers. In contrast, explicit allocation can allow one module to cause the failure of another through space leaks or premature reclamation of storage. The behaviour of the module is no longer independent from the context in which it is used.

The oft-cited goal of allowing software components to be combined in the same way as hardware components requires that interfaces should be simple and well-defined. Modules that are extensible may be composed more easily with other modules: the module is reusable in different contexts. Increasing module cohesion also makes programs easier to maintain. Meyer suggests that every module should communicate with as few others as possible, and if any two modules do communicate, they should exchange as little information as possible [Meyer, 1988]. Wilson correctly observes that 'liveness is a *global* property' [Wilson, 1994]. Adding book-keeping detail to module interfaces weakens abstractions and reduces the extensibility of modules. Modifications to the functionality of a module might entail alteration of its memory management code. Since liveness is a non-local matter, changes to book-keeping code might radiate beyond the module being developed.

While global explicit dynamic memory management may be efficient and appropriate for monolithic systems built from hierarchical designs by stepwise refinement, this approach to design seems at odds with the philosophy of object-orientation. It conflicts with the principle of minimal communication and clutters interfaces. If objects are to be reused in different contexts, the new context must understand these rules of engagement, but this reduces the freedom of composition of objects. One author has suggested that the problem of memory management in complex systems may only be solvable without garbage collection if programs are designed with correct memory management as their *prime* goal [Nagle, 1995]. Garbage collection, on the other hand, uncouples the problem of memory management from class interfaces, rather than dispersing it throughout the code. This is why it has been a fundamental component of many object-oriented languages.

A further indication of the extent of this problem is the range of tools available to assist with checking correct usage of heap memory: the best-known examples include CenterLine [CenterLine, 1992] and Purify [Purify, 1992]. The very existence of tools of this kind reveals the importance of correct memory management and the difficulty of getting it right. However, such tools are only practically useful as debugging aids since they impose a considerable run-time overhead on programs (the CenterLine interpreter by a factor of fifty, the Purify link-time library by a factor of two to four [Ellis, 1993]).

Although these tools are often very useful for tracking down programming errors, they do not address the heart of the problem. Debugging tools do nothing to simplify the interfaces of complicated systems, nor do they enhance the reusability of software components. Considerable effort still must be devoted to correcting an implementation or, even worse, a design after a leak or a dangling reference is discovered. Debugging tools tackle the symptoms rather than the disease itself. Garbage collection, on the other hand, is an effective software engineering tool because it relieves the programmer from the burden of discovering memory management errors by ensuring that they cannot arise.

Work by Rovner suggests that a considerable proportion of development time may be spent on memory management bugs [Rovner, 1985]. He estimated that forty percent of the time developing the Mesa system was spent on memory management[3]. Today, object-oriented programming languages are increasingly commonly used. Programs written in these languages typically allocate a greater proportion of their data on the heap than their conventional procedural counterparts. The data structures generated, and the problems tackled, by object-oriented programs are often more complex. These factors can only increase the intricacy of explicit storage management.

Designers and programmers are tempted to be over-defensive in order to overcome the complexities of explicit dynamic memory management. Data is allocated statically or copied between modules rather than being shared: each module is then free to destroy its copy of the object at will — the global liveness decision is transformed into a local one. Unnecessary copying and static allocation are, at best, wasteful of space since cautious overestimates of memory requirements must be made. If used on larger problems, however, static limits may prove inadequate and the programs will fail.

A commonly used alternative is to build a domain-specific garbage collector. Domain-specific collection often fails to take advantage of advances in garbage collection techniques. Because their applicability is by definition limited, the costs of development of such collectors cannot be amortised over a wide set of applications. This means that testing is likely to be

---

[3] There is a real need for more research to be published on the cost of memory management bugs to development time.

less thorough. Wilson notes that the very existence of such weakly engineered collectors is testimony to the importance of garbage collection [Wilson, 1994]. The solution is to make garbage collection part of system rather than a 'bolt-on' extra.

No silver bullet

We do not argue that garbage collection is a mandatory requirement for the solution of every problem in every language. Programs with straightforward dynamic memory requirements may be supported at lower run-time cost by explicit deallocation[4]. However, beware solutions to simple problems that are reused in more complicated programs: the short-term gain may have a longer-term cost. Problem specifications may make demands that garbage collection may not be able to satisfy. Hard real-time systems demand guarantees that memory requests will be satisfied and that the upper bounds on the time spent serving such requests be small. The problem of garbage collection for hard real-time programming has yet to be solved without the use of special hardware.

Nor do we argue that garbage collection is a panacea for all memory management problems. Garbage collection has its own costs, in terms of both time and space, and we introduce these in the next two sections. Furthermore, although garbage collection removes the two classic bugs of explicit storage management — dangling pointers and space leaks — it is still vulnerable to other errors, and moreover raises debugging problems of its own.

Garbage collection has no solution for the problem of data structures that grow without bound. Detlefs and Kalsow report that such data structures are 'surprisingly common', with one example being the caching of intermediate results to avoid recomputation [Detlefs and Kalsow, 1995]. Such growth is often benign in programs under test or used in a short-lived context, as the program is likely to terminate normally and exit before it runs out of memory. However, if the size of the problem is increased or the code is used as part of a long-running server, the program may crash.

We argued above that one of the major strengths of garbage collection is its support for abstraction leading to simpler interfaces between software components. Unfortunately this abstraction may hide another source of errors if the concrete representation of an object references heap data that its abstract representation does not. The most common example of this behaviour is a stack of references to heap-allocated data implemented as an array. What should Pop do? The choice suggested by the abstract representation of the stack is to return a reference to the heap object pointed at by the top of the stack, and then decrement the top-of-stack pointer. However, this leaves the heap data still accessible from the concrete representation of the stack, the array (see Diagram 1.6 on the following page). The safe solution is that Pop should null the pointer held at the top of the stack before it returns a reference to the heap data.

Tracing garbage collectors identify live data by following pointers from the roots of the computation, including the program stack. Unfortunately the stack can become polluted by obsolete pointers: if these pointers are traced, a space leak might occur. One source of stack-frame pollution is failure to null local variables after their last use. However, one frame may inherit obsolete data from another frame after that frame's death. Suppose a procedure A calls

---

[4] But note that this is not necessarily always true.

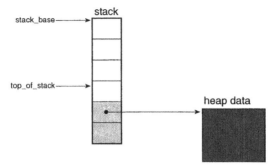

Diagram 1.6   The concrete representation of a stack may hold references (in the array elements shaded grey) that its abstract representation does not.

procedures B and then C, and that B stores a pointer x to heap data in its stack frame. If B returns without clearing its frame — and this would be expensive and so is never done — and C then reserves work-space that overlaps x in its stack frame, again without first clearing this work-space, the heap object will become reachable again — it has been resurrected! Although this problem is well known to implementors of conservative garbage collectors (see Chapter 9), Detlefs and Kalsow point out that it is more widespread since x is a perfectly valid pointer [Detlefs and Kalsow, 1995]. Normally, this kind of error is not too severe since the work-space holding x is likely to be used before the next collection. However, Detlefs and Kalsow suggest that multi-threaded environments are particularly vulnerable to leaks caused by stack-frame pollution since, in the example above, the thread executing C may be blocked, and several collections may occur before x is overwritten.

   Detlefs and Kalsow have produced tools to help to diagnose these problems in Modula-3 programs. Modula-3 is a strongly typed language in which each heap object is tagged with its type. Their tools allow heap allocation to be viewed by type, and heap usage to be viewed by type and call-site (since some types are ubiquitous). The tools also allow the programmer to identify every object reachable from a single chosen root and to assert that an object is unreachable: if the assertion is false then the tool will print a path from a root to the object.

1.5   How costly is garbage collection?

Garbage collection has a reputation for placing a large overhead on the execution of programs. In the past this was certainly true for some applications though its costs are highly system-dependent. For example, studies from the 1970s and early 1980s found that large Lisp programs were typically spending up to 40 percent of their execution time in garbage collection [Steele, 1975; Foderaro and Fateman, 1981; Gabriel, 1985]. In the cases where they were comparable, programs written in garbage-collected languages often run slower than equivalent ones written in conventional languages: garbage collection was an obvious scapegoat. However, implementations of these languages often ran slowly for reasons other than garbage collection, such as less efficient parameter passing mechanisms, or support for higher order functions or delayed evaluation of expressions.

Modern techniques have reduced garbage collection overheads substantially to the point where even languages used for systems programming, such as Modula-2+ and Modula-3, are supported by garbage collection. The cost of automatic memory management is highly application- and language-dependent so it is not possible to give simple prescriptions for its overhead. For example, the garbage collection overhead may be a much smaller proportion of overall execution time for an interpreted language than for an implementation of the same language that uses a highly optimising compiler. The style of test program used (for example, whether it is written in a largely functional style) and language implementation details (for example, whether procedure activation records are heap- or stack-allocated) will also have a profound effect. Costs of collection will also be affected by object demographics such as the distributions of object lifetimes and sizes. Finally, it is usually possible to trade space for speed. Certainly collection frequency can always be reduced by increasing the size of the region being collected.

Given these caveats, the overall execution time for garbage collection typically ranges between a few percent to around 20 percent. If a ball-park figure had to be chosen, 10 percent would not be unreasonable for a well-implemented system [Wilson, 1994]. However, simple headline figures for garbage collection overhead need to be treated with care.

1.6 Comparing garbage collection algorithms

It is difficult to compare different garbage collection algorithms, either in principle or in practice. While formulae for algorithmic complexity can be determined, their constants and implementation details often have substantial impact on actual performance. In this book we survey a wide range of different techniques for garbage collection. The most obvious cost to be considered, in terms of both time and space required by the collector, is that of reclaiming cells. However, this is not the only factor. Allocation costs are equally important — an efficient collection algorithm that exacts a heavy price for the allocation of new cells is unlikely to be effective. Some algorithms also impose a tax on user program operations such as pointer reads or writes (reference counting being a prime example); this also needs to be considered. The user program may be suspended while the collector runs: garbage collection delays will be important for certain classes of application.

Unfortunately, these are not independent parameters. Moreover, results presented in the literature for different methods are often acquired on different machines, with different processors and under different operating systems. The way algorithms are implemented may have subtle and possibly unexpected effects on overall performance. The execution time of a collection cycle depends in part on the topology and volume of live data in the heap. Even simple issues, such as minor changes to the size of the heap or the layout of objects, can cause collections to occur at different intervals and hence with different live graphs. Different data access patterns interact with the memory sub-system hierarchy of disk, main and cache memory in different ways. The order in which a graph is traversed or copied may affect the virtual memory behaviour of a program. It is desirable to be able to discuss the effects of a single design decision, 'all other matters being equal', but in practice they rarely are.

However, we can elaborate the principles and factors that might be taken into consideration when choosing an algorithm for garbage collection. Garbage collection must be *safe*. Live data must never be erroneously reclaimed. However, there is a risk that some collectors may be compromised by aggressive optimising compilers that disregard pointer-reachability invariants. We discuss this further in Chapter 9 where we consider conservative garbage collectors.

Garbage collection should be *comprehensive*: garbage should not be allowed to float unreclaimed in the heap. However, collectors vary in their approach to comprehensive collection. Most collectors based on reference counting cannot reclaim linked data structures of garbage if the structures are circular. Rather than collecting the entire heap, some collectors may concentrate their efforts in a collection cycle on just one region of the heap. It is reasonable to ask when other regions of the heap are collected and at what cost. Alternatively, a single collection cycle may be interleaved with the execution of the client program. The most comprehensive collection policy would be to ensure that any data that became garbage before the collection was complete is reclaimed in that cycle. However, such a policy might be expensive to implement. The collector may relax its view of the heap by collecting such data in the next cycle.

The programmer will wish to consider the overheads of garbage collection on the program's execution time. One factor is the overall time spent by the program in the garbage collector. For interactive programs it will also be important to consider whether the user program is suspended during garbage collection and, if so, what is the extent of these pauses. If the collector is able to reclaim the heap region by region, the pause time for the collection of a single region will be considerably less than that required for the collection of the entire heap. The relative frequency of these minor and full collections may be significant.

Incremental collectors do not suspend the mutator program while garbage collection completes. However, it may be necessary to halt it briefly at the start of each collection cycle while the collector is initialised. For example, it may be necessary to take a 'snapshot' of the state of the program by examining the roots. Non-concurrent incremental collectors will also suspend the mutator briefly at each step of the collection algorithm while a small amount of work is done by the collector. This might vary from processing a single node to scanning a virtual memory page of nodes. A further factor for incremental collection is the cost of determining whether a collection cycle has terminated. This might again require the suspension of the mutator.

Overall garbage collection time and pause times are not the only time factors to be considered. For good interactive or real-time response, it is not sufficient simply to limit pause times. It is also important that bounds be placed on the proportion of time spent in the garbage collector in any period of time in order that the mutator may make sufficient progress.

The cost of allocation of new data in the heap is as important as the time spent reclaiming garbage. In general, it will be more expensive to allocate in a fragmented heap than in a compacted one, since it may be necessary to search the heap for a contiguous area of free memory sufficiently large to accommodate the new object. Fit-finding will be easier if all data is the same, fixed size than if objects of varying sizes are to be allocated. The problem of the allocation of variable-sized data in a fragmented heap is not unique to garbage collection but is shared by all heap management systems, both explicit and automatic.

Automatic memory management may impose a direct overhead on mutator operations such as pointer writes. The simplest reference counting systems require that cell reference counts be updated whenever a pointer to a heap cell is created or deleted. More sophisticated collectors may relax the reference count invariant in order to reduce this overhead. Incremental and generational collectors perform partial collections of the heap. Incremental collectors usually guarantee to reclaim any garbage created before the start of the collection cycle in that cycle; generational collectors collect only a part of the heap, a *generation*, at each collection. Both place a time overhead on the mutator. Incremental collectors require the mutator to report any changes that it has made to the connectivity of the graph while the collector is running. Generational collectors require the mutator to keep a record of any references to cells in one generation stored in cells of other (usually older) generations.

The rôle of the garbage collector is typically to reclaim memory when the mutator has exhausted the heap. However, the collector may require additional memory for its own purposes and these space overheads must be taken into consideration. Collectors may require space in each cell in the heap to store reference counts, mark-bits to indicate that the cell is live, or the address of the cell's new location (if a moving collector is used). A collector may also require information to be stored in each cell that allows it to determine the location of any pointers stored in the cell (although this information is often also required by the mutator and, in this case, should not be counted against the collector).

A collector may also employ its own auxiliary data structures, such as a stack for recursive traversal of heap data structures. Copying collectors also require extra address space compared with non-moving collectors as all live data is picked out of the region of memory currently occupied by the heap and copied compactly into a fresh region. Depending on heap layout and collection strategy, copying collectors may require up to twice the address space of non-moving collectors.

The cost of a particular collection algorithm cannot be determined by simple analyses of asymptotic complexity, such as whether it is proportional to the size of the heap or to the volume of surviving data. The constants in complexity formulae are also important. Equally, counting the number of instructions performed by the allocator and collector does not provide a complete answer. The effects of a program's locality of reference will be important. Recent studies have also shown that different styles of garbage collection have different performance at both the virtual memory and the data cache levels. It may be possible to tune the behaviour of the collector to improve both. In particular, it is worth spending some extra CPU effort to reduce paging in a virtual memory environment. More seductively, it may be possible to use the collector to improve the locality of reference of the mutator and thereby enhance performance.

The heap occupancy, or *residency*, of a program is unlikely to remain constant. Collection algorithms may or may not be affected by residency. For reference counters, residency is not an issue but tracing collectors will be invoked more frequently if the occupancy of the heap is high than if it is low. How gracefully the performance of the memory management systems degrades with occupancy will be important.

Finally, garbage collection algorithms may be general purpose, or their applicability may be restricted to particular styles of programming language (for example, to pure functional languages or to logic languages), or restricted to particular programming idioms (for example, the manner in which circular data structures are created and accessed may be constrained).

Many of these factors will weigh against each other. Trade-offs between time and space are commonplace in computer science and different applications will wish to prioritise different factors. For instance, an interactive application would stress low pause times whereas overall execution time would be more important to a non-interactive one. A real-time application would demand small upper bounds on both garbage collection pauses and on the proportion of time spent in the collector in any period. Good paging behaviour would be important for a program running on a workstation in virtual memory while low storage overheads might be the main concern of an application running in a small personal computer or embedded system.

Portability of a collector between different architectures, compilers or application programs may also be a significant consideration. Ease of maintenance should also be weighed, as in any design. Storage managers, like reference counting, that are tightly coupled with compilers will be harder to maintain than those with a simpler interface, for example tracing collectors.

Inevitably there will be trade-offs between these constraints, and we compare some of the methods that have been proposed. We do not provide 'pat' solutions to the question of which collection strategy to use but we do hope that this book identifies the right questions to raise and suggests approaches that might be profitably explored. The slogan of garbage collection must be 'know the requirements of your system and understand the demographics — the volume, type, topology and lifetime — of the data that it generates'. This is not a suggestion unique to garbage collection: it applies equally to explicit allocators. It is clear that performance of programs with explicit memory management can often be improved with better understanding both of the allocation behaviour of the program and of the allocator being used [Zorn, 1993; Wilson et al., 1995].

In summary, we argue that garbage collection is a useful tool for the software engineer. We believe that it is essential for certain problems and styles of programming and at least a feasible and realistic alternative for others. Experience of garbage collected systems has shown that their use can lead to reduced development time. At the very least they are worth considering as an alternative to explicit memory management — the development time spent chasing memory management bugs could be more profitably spent concentrating on other areas in which performance or functionality could be enhanced.

1.7 Notation

We complete this introduction by describing the assumptions that we shall make in the rest of the book about the organisation of the heap and the layout of objects within it. We also describe our pseudo-code notation for describing garbage collection algorithms.

The heap

The heap may be a contiguous array of words or it may be organised into set of discontinuous blocks of words. User data within the heap will be described interchangeably as *cells*, *nodes* or *objects*. It will be made clear whenever the latter term is used in its object-oriented sense. A cell is assumed to be a contiguous array of bytes or words, divided into *fields*. A field may contain a pointer or a non-pointer value: the latter is an *atomic* field. By extension, an object that contains no pointer fields will be called an atom. The data in the heap reachable from each root of the program forms a directed graph whose nodes are the data cells and whose arcs are references to heap objects. References are stored within pointer fields of heap cells. These graphs may overlap or they may be disjoint.

Often we shall treat the heap as a contiguous array of slots, which we denote by Heap. When we are considering algorithms for fixed-size objects, the size of a slot will usually be one object. Otherwise the size of a slot shall be one word. We denote the bottom of the heap by Heap_bottom and its top by Heap_top.

Pointers and children

In general, we shall refer to a cell by the memory address of its initial word. Given a cell N, we denote the list of (addresses of) pointer fields that it contains by Children(N). On occasion we shall wish to refer to arbitrary fields of a cell — which may or may not contain pointers. In this case, we shall treat the cell itself as an array. Thus the ith field of a cell N will be denoted N[i]. We also choose to count fields from 0.

To refer to the immediate descendants of a cell, it is necessary to dereference the pointer field. We shall use a notation borrowed from C. Thus, given a cell N, its descendants are the *p where p is a member of the list Children(N).

In Diagram 1.7, the root cell has address n and its children are the two fields shaded grey. The cell also has a header and a non-pointer data field. Each of the four fields is one word long. The children of n point to two further cells whose addresses are *(n+2) and *(n+3).

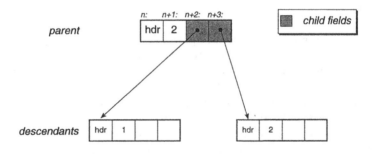

Diagram 1.7   A heap cell.

Pseudo-code

We shall use a common framework to describe garbage collection algorithms. We have chosen to use a pseudo-code rather than a real programming language for four reasons. First, pseudo-code reduces clutter (such as variable declarations) that does little to aid comprehensibility of short fragments of code. Second, the consequence of using a real programming language is that these fragments would become very large. Third, our algorithm fragments are intended to be illustrative rather than definitive. Coding a real garbage collector is a complex language- and architecture-dependent undertaking. A short code fragment should not be mistaken for a fully polished implementation. Finally, using real-code runs the risk of biasing descriptions of algorithms towards a specific language. Wherever possible, we have tried to avoid language-dependencies.

The instruction set of the mutator has two operations: New and Update. New acquires a new object from the heap manager and returns a pointer to the start of the newly acquired object. New may take the size of the storage to be allocated as an optional parameter. This parameter will be omitted where the algorithm under consideration only handles fixed-size objects or the size does not contribute to an understanding of the algorithm.

Values in cell fields may be modified with Update. Update is a generalisation of the assignment operator and takes two arguments: the field to be modified and its new value, which is usually a pointer or the distinguished value nil.

The extent of procedure bodies and the scope of control statements is denoted by indentation. The assignment operator is = and we often use multiple assignment. Thus

$$a,b = b,a$$

swaps the values of a and b. Again, after C, the equality operator is == but we use mathematical symbols for the other relational operators, such as $\leq$, $\geq$ and $\neq$.

Where appropriate, we use procedures returning a *l*-value to read and modify the fields of a cell. For example, the reference count of a cell N is given by RC(N) and a cell's reference count is initialised by the statement

$$RC(N) = 1$$

1.8 Notes

A good reference for the history of early computers and programming languages is by Donald Knuth and Luis Trabb Pardo in [Metropolis *et al.*, 1980]. The earliest versions of Lisp used an explicit deallocation function, *eralis*, but this was soon superseded by garbage collection [McCarthy, 1981].

General descriptions of techniques for storage allocation in fragmented heaps can be found in [Knuth, 1973; Standish, 1980; Bozman *et al.*, 1984; Aho *et al.*, 1986]. Paul Wilson, Mark Johnstone, Michael Neely and David Boles offer a particularly thorough survey of explicit allocation techniques, and especially of the shortcomings of some analyses of the behaviour of allocators [Wilson *et al.*, 1995].

2

The Classical Algorithms

In this chapter we introduce the three classical methods of storage reclamation: reference counting, mark-sweep and copying. As the techniques and ideas behind these algorithms form the basis of many schemes covered later in the book, it is important to understand clearly how they work. For this reason, the algorithms presented in this chapter are described in simple recursive terms. In later chapters more efficient ways of implementing these methods of garbage collection are examined.

2.1 The Reference Counting Algorithm

The first algorithm is a direct method, based on counting the number of references to each cell from other, active cells or roots [Collins, 1960]. Its virtue lies in its simplicity of keeping track of whether cells are in use or not. It is also a naturally incremental technique, distributing the overheads of memory management throughout the program. Algorithms based on reference counting have been adopted for many languages and applications, for example, early versions of the Smalltalk object-oriented language [Goldberg and Robson, 1983], InterLisp, Modula-2+ [DeTreville, 1990a], and the Adobe Photoshop program. It is also the method used by many operating systems (for example, Unix) to determine whether a file may be deleted from the file-store.

The reference counting method operates under a fundamentally different strategy from that of tracing garbage collectors. Each cell has an additional field, the *reference count*. The storage manager must maintain the invariant that the reference count of each cell is equal to the number of pointers to that cell from roots or heap cells. The starting point for this algorithm is that all cells are placed in a pool of free cells, which is usually implemented as a linked list — a chain of cells linked by one of their pointer fields, which we shall call next — along with a free_list pointer to the head of the chain. The next field need not be used exclusively for this purpose. Typically it is the same field as the reference count field — free cells do not need explicit reference counts. Alternatively, one of the cell's user data fields may be used.

The algorithm

Free cells have a reference count of zero. When a new cell is allocated from the pool, its reference count is set to one. Each time a pointer is set to refer to this cell, the value of the cell's counter is increased by one; when a reference to the cell is deleted, the counter is decreased by one. If this causes the reference count to drop to zero, the reference counting invariant implies that there are no remaining pointers to this cell. Furthermore, because the location of the cell has been 'lost', there is no (legitimate) way of re-establishing contact with this cell. The cell is no longer required by the computation and it can be returned to the list of free cells.

```
allocate() =
    newcell = free_list
    free_list = next(free_list)
    return newcell

New() =
    if free_list == nil
        abort "Memory exhausted"
    newcell = allocate()
    RC(newcell) = 1
    return newcell
```

Algorithm 2.1   Reference counted allocation.

Let us look at the algorithm in detail. In each algorithm considered, allocate will be a general purpose mechanism for reserving space in the heap. In this case it pops the first element from a free-list. In other algorithms its implementation will be different. New returns a fresh cell acquired from the free-list, after setting the value of the new cell's reference count to one (see Algorithm 2.1). If the free-list is empty the computation is aborted — the alternative would be to expand the heap — otherwise allocate removes the head of the free-list and returns it to New. For safety, the pointer fields of the new cell, Children(newcell), could also be cleared although this would be unnecessary if its fields were initialised as soon as the cell was acquired. In this case, New might also remove a number of arguments from the program stack and install them in the cell's data fields. For simplicity, we shall assume for the moment that all cells have the same fixed size.

Update overwrites the word in the heap that is its first argument, R, with its second argument, S (which we assume to be a pointer) — see Algorithm 2.2 and Diagram 2.1 on the next page. The reference count of S is incremented to take account of this new reference. The update has also removed the original pointer from R to its target, *R, so the reference count of *R must be decremented too. By incrementing the count of the new target before decrementing that of the old, we handle the case when the targets are identical. Suppose the pointer at R originally referred to node T. If this pointer was the last reference to T, delete can return T to the free list. But before it does so, any pointers from T must also be deleted recursively[1].

---

[1] A more efficient coding of delete might leave the reference counts of free cells at one, thereby saving a couple of instructions in both New and delete.

```
free(N) =
    next(N) = free_list
    free_list = N

delete(T) =
    RC(T) = RC(T) - 1
    if RC(T) == 0
        for U in Children(T)
            delete(*U)
        free(T)

Update(R, S) =
    RC(S) = RC(S) + 1
    delete(*R)
    *R = S
```

Algorithm 2.2   Updating pointer fields under reference counting.

An example

As Update is more complex, an extended example is useful. In the structure shown in Diagram 2.2 on the following page, the pointer right(R) is overwritten (say with nil). Since this is the only pointer to S, delete is now invoked recursively on both pointers from S before S is added to the free-list. Delete(right(S)) in turn generates a call to delete(right(U)) before U too is added to the free-list, and so on.

Strengths and weaknesses of reference counting

The strength of the reference counting method is that memory management overheads are distributed throughout the computation. Management of active and garbage cells is interleaved with the execution of the user program. This contrasts with (non-incremental) tracing schemes

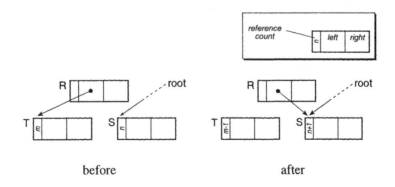

Diagram 2.1   Update(left(R),S).

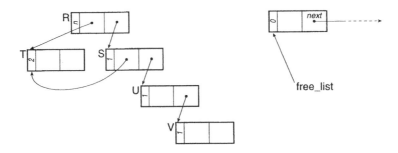

Diagram 2.2   Before `Update(right(R), nil)`.

such as mark-sweep in which useful processing is suspended while the garbage collector runs. Reference counting may therefore be a suitable method if a smoother response time is important, for example in a highly interactive or a real-time system. However, the simple reference counting algorithm given above distributes processing overheads 'lumpily': the cost of deleting the last pointer to a sub-graph depends on its size. We consider how to ameliorate this in Chapter 3 when we discuss reference counting in more detail.

A second benefit of reference counting over garbage collection schemes is that its spatial *locality of reference* is likely to be no worse than that of its client program. A cell whose reference count becomes zero can be reclaimed without access to cells in other pages of the heap (other than its descendants, but again see Chapter 3). This contrasts with tracing algorithms which typically need to visit all live cells before reclaiming dead ones. However, note that Update alters the reference counts of both the old and the new targets of the pointer field being updated. If either of these fields are paged-out (on a machine with virtual memory) or not held in the data cache, a page fault or cache miss will occur.

Thirdly, although empirical studies are implementation and language dependent, a wide range of language studies suggest that few cells are shared and many are short-lived (for example, Lisp [Clark and Green, 1977; Stoye *et al.*, 1984; Zorn, 1989], Cedar [Hayes, 1991], Standard ML [Appel, 1992], and C and C++ [Barrett and Zorn, 1993b]). The standard

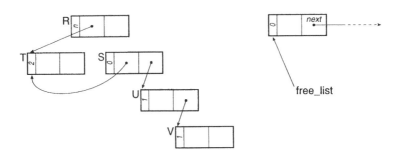

Diagram 2.3   `delete(right(R))`.

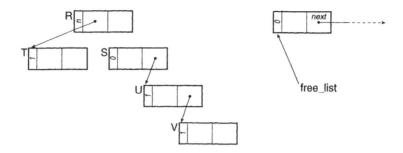

Diagram 2.4 `delete(left(S))`.

reference counting method allows these cells to be reused as soon as they are discarded, in a stack-like manner, whereas under a tracing scheme dead cells remain unallocated until the heap is exhausted, at which point the garbage collector would be invoked. Immediate *reuse* of cells generates fewer page faults in a virtual memory system, and possibly better cache behaviour, than simple tracing garbage collection methods that acquire *fresh* cells from the heap, unless the entire heap can be held in main memory or the cache. We return to this issue in Chapters 7 and 11 when we consider generational garbage collection and the cache behaviour of garbage collection respectively.

Immediate knowledge of when a cell can be reclaimed also brings other advantages. If a modified copy is required of an object to which there are no other references, the cell can be copied by borrowing the pointer to it and updating its contents destructively or 'in-place', instead of allocating a fresh cell, copying the data word by word and then freeing the old cell. This useful optimisation for purely functional languages is used in the Glasgow Haskell compiler [Peyton Jones, 1992]. Reference counting can also simplify 'clean-up' or *finalisation* actions, such as closing files, by invoking the finaliser immediately an object dies (see Chapter 10 where we discuss garbage collection for object-oriented languages).

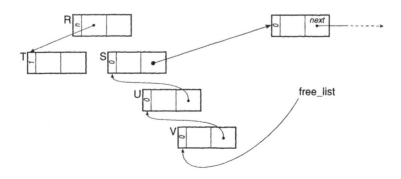

Diagram 2.5 After `Update(right(R), nil)`.

On the debit side, reference counting suffers from a number of disadvantages which have led many implementors to reject it as an efficient method of memory management. The most serious disadvantage is the high processing cost (using today's conventional hardware) paid to update counters to maintain the reference count invariant (see, for instance, [Hartel, 1988]). Each time a pointer is overwritten, the reference count in both the old and the new target cells must be adjusted. In contrast, pointer updates have no memory management overhead under a simple tracing regime.

Reference counting storage management is tightly coupled to the client program or its compiler. Every time a pointer is updated or copied, reference counts must be adjusted. For example, in its simplest incarnation, this means that reference counts must be incremented when a pointer is passed to a sub-routine and decremented on its return. A single omission can spell disaster. This fragility of reference counted systems makes them harder to maintain than memory management systems that are more loosely coupled to the mutator.

Reference counting techniques must also use extra space in each cell to store the reference count. In the worst case, this field would have to be large enough to hold the total number of pointers held in the heap and in the roots: it must be as large as a pointer. In practice reference counts will not become this large and a smaller field (possibly just a single bit) can be used in conjunction with a strategy to handle overflow (see Chapter 3 where we consider reference counting in more detail).

Cyclic data structures

However, the major drawback of simple reference counting algorithms is their inability to reclaim cyclic structures. Ability to recycle such graphs is an important requirement for many systems. Cyclic data structures are more frequently used than might be immediately apparent. Common examples of cycles include doubly-linked lists, and 'trees' in which leaf nodes contain a pointer back to the root node. Also, many implementations of lazy functional languages based on graph reduction use cycles to handle recursion. As an example, consider the structure shown in Diagram 2.6 on the next page and suppose that the pointer right(R) is deleted. In the call delete(right(R)) the reference count of S remains non-zero after it is decremented and so control is returned to the user program. Unfortunately, rather than pushing S, T and U onto the free-list, an island has been created, disconnected from the rest of the graph. This island is not required for subsequent computation, but the cells S, T and U cannot be reclaimed. An area of heap memory has effectively leaked away — it is not required for computation but it cannot be recycled either.

Fortunately other garbage collection techniques handle cyclic data structures without difficulty, and several authors have suggested combining reference counting with tracing garbage collection [Weizenbaum, 1969; Knuth, 1973; Deutsch and Bobrow, 1976; Wise, 1979]. Reference counting would be used until the heap was exhausted at which point a tracing collector would be invoked. The collector starts by resetting the reference counts of all cells to zero. The count of each active cell is then restored by incrementing it by one each time the cell is visited in the marking phase. Since the marker visits each cell exactly once via each pointer to it from another live cell, the reference count of each cell will be set to be the number of references to it from active cells by the end of the marking phase, which is just what the reference counting invariant requires. This method offers two gains. Firstly, circular

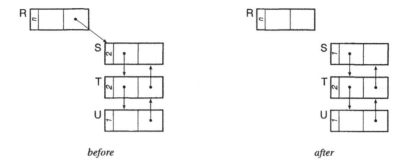

before   *after*

Diagram 2.6 Reference counting cyclic data structures: after `delete(right(R))` the cycle STU is neither reachable nor reclaimable.

structures can be reclaimed by the tracing collector. Secondly, small reference count fields can be used (thus reducing storage requirements). Counters that reach the maximum value that can be stored in this smaller field are no longer modified by Update; instead, responsibility for their management is passed to the tracing collector. In Section 3.5, we shall pursue other approaches to the problem of cyclic reference counting.

2.2   The Mark-Sweep Algorithm

The first algorithm for automatic storage reclamation was a tracing garbage collection technique: the *mark-sweep* or *mark-scan* method [McCarthy, 1960]. Under this scheme, cells are not reclaimed immediately they become garbage, but remain unreachable and undetected until all available storage is exhausted. If a request is then made for a new cell, 'useful' processing is temporarily suspended while the garbage collector routine is called to sweep all currently unused cells from the heap back into the pool of free cells. Mark-sweep relies on a global traversal of all live objects to determine which cells are available for reclamation. This trace, starting from root, identifies all cells that are reachable and hence, by definition, active. All other nodes are garbage and can be returned to the pool of free cells. If the garbage collector is successful in reclaiming sufficient memory, the user program request is satisfied and computation can be resumed.

```
New() =
    if free_pool is empty
        mark_sweep()
    newcell = allocate()
    return newcell
```

Algorithm 2.3 Allocation with mark-sweep.

The algorithm

Let us look at the algorithm in more detail. New acquires a new cell from the pool and returns a pointer to it (see Algorithm 2.3 on the preceding page). Again, we do not specify how allocate operates but we use the abstraction of a free_pool to describe the set of free cells. One possible implementation is to link free cells into a free-list exactly as in the reference counting algorithm (see Algorithm 2.1 on page 20) but there are other more efficient alternatives. We consider these in Chapter 4 when we discuss more efficient techniques for mark-sweep garbage collection.

Updating a pointer requires no additional effort other than the write. This is in marked contrast to reference counting which required several extra instructions to manipulate reference counts (see Update in Algorithm 2.2 on page 21). The cost of reference counting is even greater if it leads to cache misses, or worse, if either of the pages that contain the target cells are currently paged out.

```
mark_sweep() =
    for R in Roots
        mark(R)
    sweep()
    if free_pool is empty
        abort "Memory exhausted"
```

Algorithm 2.4   The mark-sweep garbage collector.

Mark-sweep garbage collection is performed in two phases (see Algorithm 2.4). The first phase, known as *marking*, identifies all active cells. The second, *sweep*, phase returns garbage cells to the free pool. If the sweep phase fails to recover sufficiently many free cells, the heap must be expanded or the computation aborted.

```
mark(N) =
    if mark_bit(N) == unmarked
        mark_bit(N) = marked
        for M in Children(N)
            mark(*M)
```

Algorithm 2.5   Simple recursive marking.

A bit associated with each cell is reserved for use by the garbage collector. This *mark-bit* is used to record whether the cell is reachable from the roots. As mark traverses all cells reachable from the roots, the mark-bit is set in each cell visited (see Algorithm 2.5). For clarity, we give a simple recursive algorithm but we show how this can be replaced by more efficient code in Section 4.2.

Termination of the marking phase is enforced by not tracing from cells that have already been marked. When the marking phase has completed, all cells reachable from root will have had their mark-bits set. In this respect, the mark procedure is a simple transliteration of the definition of *live*, the set of reachable cells, given in Section 1.2. An example of marking is shown in Diagram 2.7 on the next page; cells that have been marked are indicated by shading their mark-bits, those left clear being unmarked. Any cell that is left unmarked could not be reached from root, and hence must be garbage.

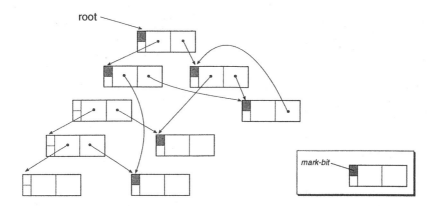

Diagram 2.7   The graph after the marking phase. All unmarked cells (with unshaded mark-bits) are garbage.

It is safe to return these unmarked cells to the pool of free cells. This is the job of the sweep phase. The collector sweeps the heap linearly from bottom to top, returning unmarked cells to the free pool and clearing the mark-bits of active cells, in preparation for the next garbage collection cycle. Again we do not define free other than to state that it returns its argument to the free pool for recycling. For example, if the free pool were implemented as a free-list, the code given in Algorithm 2.2 on page 21 would suffice.

```
sweep() =
    N = Heap_bottom
    while N < Heap_top
        if mark_bit(N) == unmarked
            free(N)
        else mark_bit(N) = unmarked
        N = N + size(N)
```

Algorithm 2.6   The eager sweep of the heap.

Strengths and weaknesses of mark-sweep

Mark-sweep has two advantages over reference counting that have led to its adoption by some systems (for example, by the functional language Miranda [Turner, 1985] and by conservative garbage collectors [Boehm and Weiser, 1988]). Cycles are handled quite naturally, no special precautions need to be taken, and no overhead is placed on pointer manipulations. On the other hand, mark-sweep is a stop/start algorithm: computation is halted while the garbage collector runs, and the pauses engendered by the mark-sweep algorithm may be substantial. For example, in the early 1980s, Fateman [Foderaro and Fateman, 1981] found that, as memory sizes grew faster than processing speeds, some large Lisp programs were spending 25 to 40 percent of their time marking and sweeping, and that users were waiting for an average of 4.5 seconds every 79 seconds. Non-interruptible, globally traversing mark-sweep algorithms are not practical for real-time, highly interactive or distributed systems. It would certainly not be acceptable for a safety-critical, real-time system or even a video game to pause for lengthy periods during a garbage collection. One solution may be to disable the collector in critical sections. We investigate other methods of reducing pause times in Chapters 7 and 8 where we discuss generational and incremental techniques respectively.

However, if response time is not an important consideration, mark-sweep does offer a better performance than, for example, incremental methods such as reference counting. Nevertheless, the costs of garbage collection are high. Every active cell is visited in the marking phase, and all cells are examined by the sweep. Thus the asymptotic complexity of this algorithm is proportional to the size of the entire heap rather than, say, just the number of active cells[2].

The simple algorithm for mark-sweep presented above also tends to fragment memory, scattering cells across the heap. In a real memory system the effect on performance may not be great although benefits of caching could be lost. In a virtual memory system such fragmentation may lead to loss of locality between associated cells of a data structure and result in 'thrashing', excessive swapping of pages to and from secondary storage. In either case, fragmentation makes allocation more difficult as suitable 'gaps' must be found in the heap to accommodate new objects.

Tracing garbage collection also requires some head-room in the heap to be efficient. Assuming that the rate of allocation is constant and that fragmentation is not an issue, the interval between collections depends on the amount of free space discovered at each collection. Garbage collection will therefore become more frequent as the heap occupancy or *residency* of a program increases, and so the mutator's share of the processor will be reduced. In other words, the garbage collector will thrash. The performance of reference counted systems, on the other hand, does not degrade with heap occupancy (although fragmentation may affect allocation behaviour).

2.3 The Copying Algorithm

The final class of tracing algorithm that we consider in this chapter is that of copying garbage collectors. Copying collectors divide the heap equally into two *semi-spaces*, one of which contains current data and the other obsolete data (see `init` in Algorithm 2.7 on the next page). Copying garbage collection starts by *flipping* the rôles of the two spaces. The collector then traverses the active data structure in the old semi-space, *Fromspace*, copying each live cell into the new semi-space, *Tospace*, when the cell is first visited. After all active cells in Fromspace have been traced, a replica of the active data structure has been created in Tospace

---

[2] This measure of complexity is too simplistic. We shall return to this matter in Chapters 4 and 6 where we discuss mark-sweep and copying collectors in more detail.

and the user program is restarted. Since garbage cells are simply abandoned in the old semi-space, Fromspace, copying collectors are often described as *scavengers*[3] — they pick out worthwhile objects amidst the garbage and take them away.

A natural and beneficial side-effect of copying garbage collection is that the active data structure is compacted into the bottom of Tospace. Compacting collectors can allocate objects much more efficiently than collectors for which fragmentation is a problem. All New must do is check for sufficient space and then increment the next free space pointer, free. Since the active data is compacted into Tospace, the space check is simply a pointer comparison (see Algorithm 2.7). Copying collectors handle variable-sized objects naturally so we give New the size of the object to allocate as a parameter, n. Like mark-sweep, copying collection imposes no overhead on mutator operations such as pointer updates.

```
init() =
    Tospace = Heap_bottom
    space_size = Heap_size / 2
    top_of_space = Tospace + space_size
    Fromspace = top_of_space + 1
    free = Tospace

New(n) =
    if free + n > top_of_space
        flip()
    if free + n > top_of_space
        abort "Memory exhausted"
    newcell = free                               —allocate()
    free = free + n
    return newcell
```

Algorithm 2.7   Allocation in a copying collector.

The algorithm

First, the rôles of Tospace and Fromspace are swapped by flip, which resets the variables Tospace, Fromspace and top_of_space (see Algorithm 2.8 on the next page). Each cell reachable from a root is then copied from Fromspace into Tospace. For clarity, we use a simple recursive algorithm [Fenichel and Yochelson, 1969]; more elegant iterative algorithms are covered in Chapter 6 where we discuss copying collection in more detail. Copy(P) scavenges the fields of the cell pointed at by P (see Algorithm 2.9 on the following page). Care has to be taken when copying data structures to ensure that the topology of shared structures is preserved. Failure to do so would lead to multiple copies of shared objects, which at best would increase the heap residency of the program but may also break the semantics of the user program (for example, if it updated one copy of a cell but then read the value from another). Copying cyclic data structures without preserving sharing would also require a lot of room!

Copying collectors preserve sharing by leaving a *forwarding address* in the Fromspace

---

[3] This term is due to Ungar [Ungar, 1984].

```
flip()=
    Fromspace, Tospace = Tospace, Fromspace
    top_of_space = Tospace + space_size
    free = Tospace
    for R in Roots
        R = copy(R)
```

Algorithm 2.8   The flip in copying garbage collection.

object when it is copied. The forwarding address is the address of the copy in Tospace. Whenever a cell in Fromspace is visited, Copy checks to see if it has already been copied. If it has, the forwarding address is returned, otherwise memory is reserved for the copy in Tospace. In this recursive copying algorithm, the forwarding address is set to point to this reserved memory *before* the constituent fields of the object are copied — this ensures termination and that sharing is preserved.

The forwarding address might be held in its own field in the cell. More generally it can be written over the first word in the cell provided that the original value of the word is saved beforehand. In Algorithm 2.9 we assume that the forwarding address field of cell P is P[0], and we use forwarding_address(P) and P[0] interchangeably.

```
— Note: P points to a word, not a cell
copy(P) =
    if atomic(P) or P == nil              —P is not a pointer
        return P
    if not forwarded(P)
        n = size(P)
        P' = free                         —reserve space in Tospace
        free = free + n
        temp = P[0]              —field 0 will hold the forwarding address
        forwarding_address(P) = P'
        P'[0] = copy(temp)
        for i = 1 to n-1                   —copy each field of P into P'
            P'[i] = copy(P[i])
    return forwarding_address(P)
```

Algorithm 2.9   Fenichel–Yochelson copying garbage collection for variable-sized cells.

An example

As an example of copying garbage collection, let us look at how the infinite list [0,1,0,1,...] might be collected. The list can be represented in finite space by a cyclic data structure (see Diagram 2.8 on the facing page). To help clarify the example, we shall name the cells in the graph A, B, C, D and their Tospace replicas A', B', C', D' respectively. Initially the single root points to A.

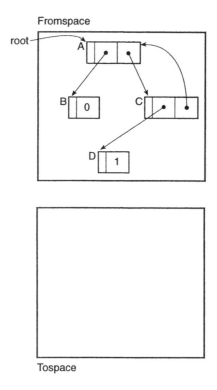

Diagram 2.8   Copying the list [0,1,0,1,...].

Garbage collection starts by flipping the semi-spaces. The root is copied: space is reserved for A in Tospace and its forwarding pointer is set to A′ (see Diagram 2.9 on the next page).

The next two invocations of copy reserve space for B and update the left field of A′, and then copy the contents of B. Since this is an atom, its value is simply returned (see Diagram 2.10 on page 33).

The collector then copies A's right sub-tree. C and D are scavenged in the same way that A and B were. Finally, copy follows C's right pointer, which points back to A. Space has already been reserved for A in Tospace (in fact it has been completely copied), so the right-pointer of C′ is updated with the forwarding address A′ stored in A, and the collection cycle is complete (see Diagram 2.11 on page 34).

Strengths and weaknesses of copying collection

The advantages of copying garbage collection over reference counting and mark-sweep have led to its widespread adoption. Allocation costs are extremely low: the out-of-space check is a simple pointer comparison; new memory is acquired simply by incrementing the free space pointer; and fragmentation is eliminated by compacting the active data into the bottom of

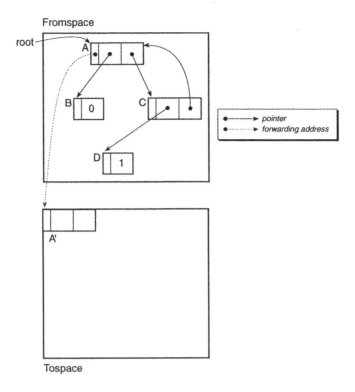

Diagram 2.9   First, the root node is copied.

Tospace. The cost of allocation in non-compacting algorithms is much higher, particularly if variable-sized cells are required. It is hard to see how one could allocate more cheaply.

The most immediate cost of copying garbage collection is the use of two semi-spaces: the address space required is doubled compared with non-copying collectors. It is often argued that this is not a problem for virtual memory machines since the pages of the inactive semi-space will be evicted to secondary storage, but this argument ignores paging costs. Compare the behaviour of mark-sweep and copying over two garbage collection cycles for a fixed size of heap. In this period, the copying allocator will touch every page of the heap regardless of the residency of the user program. Unless both semi-spaces can be held simultaneously in physical memory, copying collection will suffer more page faults than mark-sweep, as it uses twice as many pages.

On the other hand, this has to be traded against the benefits of compaction. Data in the simple mark-swept heap is likely to be more fragmented leading to an increase in the size of the program's working set of pages. This will also tend to increase the rate of page faults if the working set cannot be accommodated in main memory. Poor locality of reference will also affect cache performance but this will have very much less impact on overall execution than poor paging.

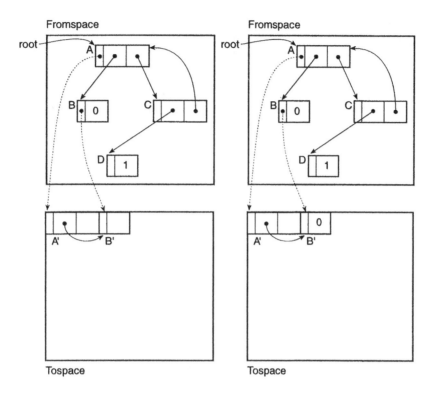

Diagram 2.10 Space is reserved for B; then it is copied completely.

2.4 Comparing mark-sweep and copying collection

The chief drawback of copying collectors is the need to divide the available memory into two semi-spaces. As the residency of a program increases the performance of the collector degrades, as less free space is recovered and so collections become more frequent. Programs with memory requirements larger than the semi-space size will fail. Virtual memory can alleviate these symptoms: the semi-space can be as large as (or larger than) the physical memory and the heap can be expanded if necessary. On the other hand, the performance of mark-sweep collectors degrades with heap occupancy only half as quickly as that of copying garbage collectors.

The asymptotic complexity of copying collection is less than that of simple mark-sweep collection: it is proportional to the size of the active data structure rather than the size of the heap (semi-space). Furthermore, if the majority of cells do not survive until the next collection cycle — this is typical for many functional and object-oriented styles of programming — only a small proportion of the heap must be copied. Let us compare the asymptotic complexity of the simple mark-sweep and copying garbage collectors described in this chapter. We do not take allocation costs into account for the moment, nor do we consider locality effects upon

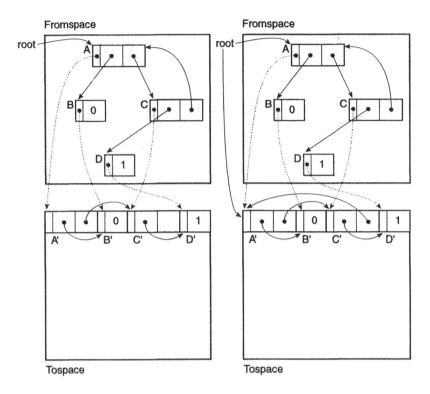

Diagram 2.11 left(C), D and right(C) are copied, and the collection is complete.

the virtual memory subsystem and the data cache. Let M be the size of the heap and R be the amount of live memory.

The copying collector described in this chapter must trace and update every pointer in the root set and in the active data graph, and evacuate those objects to Tospace. The time complexity of a copying collector to perform a garbage collection can therefore be approximated to R:

$$t_{Copy} = aR$$

The mark-sweep collector traces pointers to live data structures in the mark phase, and sweeps linearly through the entire heap in the sweep phase. The time complexity of the mark-sweep collector can be approximated by:

$$t_{MS} = bR + cM$$

The amount of space recovered by a garbage collection is

$$m_{Copy} = \frac{M}{2} - R$$
$$m_{MS} = M - R$$

Define the efficiency, e, of an algorithm as the amount of memory reclaimed in a unit time

$$e_{Copy} = \frac{1}{2ar} - \frac{1}{a}$$

$$e_{MS} = \frac{1-r}{br+c}$$

where $r = R/M$ is the residency of the program.

Looking at the efficiency graphs in Diagram 2.12, we observe that copying collection appears to be arbitrarily more efficient than mark-sweep collection provided that the heap can be made large enough. However, beyond a certain residency $r*$, the mark-sweep collector is more efficient.

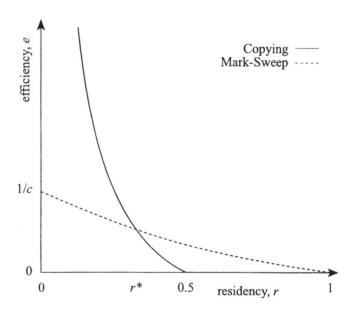

Diagram 2.12   The efficiency of mark-sweep and copying collection.

However, the matter is more subtle than this. *The collectors described in this chapter are very simple and inefficient.* The behaviour of these collectors cannot be automatically ascribed to their more sophisticated variants. The cost of copying an object is likely to be more expensive than simply testing and setting a mark-bit, particularly if the object is large. Although mark-sweep must sweep the entire heap, in practice its real cost is dominated by the mark phase. Linearly scanning the heap will generally be less expensive than tracing data structures even using the simple technique shown above. Thus, $a > b > c$, in the argument above. Furthermore, more sophisticated methods can substantially reduce the cost of the sweep (see Chapter 4 where we discuss advanced techniques for mark-sweep collection). Although copying garbage collectors have predominated in the past, recent studies suggest that the choice between mark-sweep and copying garbage collection may well depend as much on the behaviour of the client program as on the inherent properties of the garbage collection algorithm (see, for example, [Zorn, 1989; Hartel, 1990]).

2.5   Issues to consider

At the end of each chapter we include a summary of points to consider when comparing the collectors reviewed in the chapter with other collectors. We urge the reader to treat these summaries with some caution. While it is appealing to make comparisons with 'all other things being equal', they rarely are. The aim of these summaries, therefore, is to provide a focus for analysis of the behaviour of the collectors in different environments rather than to provide a cook book, which would be necessarily simplistic. We first examine how well each collector satisfies any requirements that client programs may place on a storage manager, and then we consider the performance of each one.

   This chapter introduced three strategies for automatic storage management — reference counting, mark-sweep and copying collection — and discussed a simple implementation of each one. We now summarise their relative merits under different conditions. We emphasise that these are naïve implementations and that the performance and behaviour of each cannot be assumed to apply automatically to the more sophisticated implementations that are covered in later chapters.

Requirements

The first issue that we consider is the client program's tolerance of interruption by the storage manager. Both the mark-sweep and copying collectors were stop–start algorithms: the client program was suspended while the collector ran to completion. The delay to complete a garbage collection of a large heap with these simple algorithms may last from a fraction of a second up to a few seconds. This behaviour is clearly not acceptable for a wide range of applications from interactive programs to those with hard real-time requirements. Reference counting operations, on the other hand, are interleaved with mutator instructions, giving a smoother response in general. There is one exception: the simple algorithm in this chapter recursively frees garbage structures eagerly: the user program is suspended until the entire garbage structure has been returned to the free-list. In Section 3.1 on page 44 we show how this delay can be avoided.

Immediacy

A consequence of the interleaving of reference counting operations with mutator instructions is that (non-cyclic) garbage is detected as soon as it becomes unreachable. For certain applications and styles of programming this is either desirable or an essential requirement. First, it allows space known to be garbage to be reused immediately, which may enhance performance. For functional languages in particular, it means that destructive assignment may be used, for example to update arrays in place rather than copying. Second, object-oriented languages often support finalisation, whereby a user-defined procedure can be invoked upon the death of an object. The canonical example of finalisation is causing a file to be closed after the last reference to the file is destroyed. If finalisation is used to release scarce resources held by an object, it is important that the finaliser is called as soon as possible after the object becomes garbage. Reference counting can ensure that the finaliser is called as soon as the object's reference count falls to zero. Tracing garbage collectors, such as mark-sweep and copying, cannot provide this guarantee since an object's death is not detected until the next garbage collection. Nevertheless, there has been considerable successful experience of tracing garbage collection and finalisation. By far the most common finalisation action is simply to return the object's space to the storage manager, a rôle accomplished by the garbage collector. We consider finalisation further in Section 10.9 when we discuss garbage collection for object-oriented languages.

Cyclic data structures

Many programs need to use cyclic data structures. As well as structures that may have obviously cyclic concrete representations, such as circular buffers, other common data structures, such as doubly-linked lists and 'trees' whose leaves contain a back-pointer to the root, are also cyclic. As we saw in Section 2.1, simple reference counting cannot reclaim cyclic data structures. In Chapter 3 we explore variants of reference counting and constraints on programming style that allow cyclic garbage to be reclaimed by storage managers based on reference counting. Tracing collectors, on the other hand, can manage cycles correctly without need for any special action or restrictions on coding style.

Roots and pointer finding

Tracing garbage collectors do need to be able to find all the roots of a computation, and possibly all the pointers in the active data structure. Moving collectors, such as copying collectors, must be able to locate all the roots so that the active data can be traced, and all pointers in the active data structure so that they can be updated with the new location of their referee. The set of roots and the set of pointers must be determined precisely: an underestimate would cause a pointer not to be updated; an overestimate would risk updating non-pointer data with an incorrect value. A copying collector cannot be used unless these requirements can be met (although we shall see in Chapter 9, where we discuss conservative garbage collection, how a copying collector that is tolerant of overestimation of the root set can be constructed). This means that non-conservative copying collectors need cooperation from the compiler.

These requirements can be relaxed somewhat for non-moving, tracing collectors. An overestimate is not dangerous since objects are not moved and hence pointers are not updated. Heap data need not be modified if mark-bits are stored in a separate table to the side of the heap. Furthermore, it is not necessary to trace all live pointers; it is sufficient to ensure that at least one pointer to each live object is followed by the marker. Hence mark-sweep collectors can be used with less cooperation from the compiler than copying collectors need. Again in Chapter 9, we shall see how a conservative, mark-sweep collector can be used with little support from the compiler other than knowledge of the extent of the run-time stack and the location of global data.

Reference counters relax these requirements even further. All that is necessary is that every pointer in a reference counted object can be found when an object is deleted. For this reason, reference counters can be implemented as a library, and used without any support from the compiler. For example, Christopher's reference counting system is designed to provide automatic management of dynamic memory for Fortran (see Section 3.5, page 67).

Implementation

As well as conformance to requirements imposed by client programs and environments, performance will be an important factor in choosing between different garbage collection algorithms. Performance can be measured in terms of the time overhead on mutator operations, the time cost of both allocation and collection, and both the space overheads incurred directly by the collector and those added to user data.

Processing cost

Reference counting is tightly coupled to the mutator, and this has two consequences. First, reference counting imposes a tax on each mutator operation on a pointer. Many adjustments to reference counts can be optimised away although this risks precisely the storage management errors that garbage collection is designed to avoid. Herein lies the second consequence of reference counting's tight coupling to the mutator: program maintenance and development is made more difficult as reference counting invariants must be preserved across any changes to the program. Simple, non-generational, tracing collectors on the other hand impose no processing overhead on client program operations. Well-designed tracing collectors therefore have lower overall execution time overheads than reference counters.

Both reference counters and mark-sweep collectors typically use a variant of a free-list to manage the available pool of free space. Consequently fragmentation of the heap is an issue for these collectors. Fragmentation not only dilutes the locality of active data but also makes the allocation of variable-sized objects more difficult and hence more expensive of processor cycles. In contrast, copying collection compacts the active semi-space of the heap. Allocation is done linearly, making it equally cheap to reserve space for any size of object.

Space overhead

Storage managers have a space, as well as a time, overhead and garbage collection is no exception. In the case of the garbage collectors discussed in this chapter, storage may be required to direct the traversal of the graph as well as for management of heap-allocated data. All three collectors used recursion — mark-sweep and copying to trace active data, and reference counting for delete — which requires space for the recursion stack; in later chapters we shall see how recursion can be avoided.

Reference counting requires space for a reference count in each heap object. Since an object may, in the worst case, be referenced by every other object in the heap and all the roots, the reference count field should be pointer-sized (although in practice a smaller field could be used, and we examine safe methods of reducing the size of the reference count field in the next chapter). For small objects like *cons* cells, this imposes a fifty percent space overhead. Mark-sweep garbage collectors also require extra space in each heap object for a mark-bit. The amount of space required for the mark-bit is architecture- and implementation-dependent, determined by the smallest unit of data that can be addressed, and whether the bit can be smuggled into a word used for other purposes, such as a tag field or an unused bit of a pointer. Copying collectors require an address space twice the size of the maximum residency of the client program in order to accommodate both semi-spaces.

Heap occupancy and collector degradation

For any given level of efficiency, copying collectors are easier to implement than mark-sweep collectors. Linear allocation is fast and the complexity of copying collection is proportional to the number of live pointers in the heap (and hence approximately to the volume of live data) whereas the complexity of simple mark-sweep collection is proportional to the size of the heap. The performance of both types of tracing collection degrades with heap occupancy. Reference counting, on the other hand, suffers no such degradation for collection although fragmentation may make allocation harder.

However, some caveats are in order when comparing the complexities of mark-sweep and copying collection. First, copying collection only has a clear asymptotic advantage over *simple* implementations of mark-sweep collection. Even so, this advantage diminishes as the residency of the client program increases. As the residency increases beyond a certain point (typically around one-third of the size of the heap), copying collectors start to thrash and the advantage turns in favour of mark-sweep collection (see Diagram 2.12 on page 35). Second, the constants in the complexity formulae are as important as its asymptotes. The cost of copying an object depends on its size but will be greater than that of simply setting its mark-bit. Furthermore, long-lived data will be repeatedly copied from one semi-space to another by a copying collector. The choice between mark-sweep and copying collectors will be influenced by the size and longevity of heap data, and whether garbage collection or allocation dominates storage management costs.

2.6 Notes

Mark-sweep collection

The mark-sweep and the reference counting algorithms were both developed for implementing Lisp. They were also both published in the same year, 1960: mark-sweep by John McCarthy in April [McCarthy, 1960] and reference counting by George Collins in December [Collins, 1960]. The very earliest versions of Lisp required the programmer to handle erasure of lists explicitly with a built-in operator called *eralis* [McCarthy, 1981]. Lisp was developed on the IBM 704 computer. This machine had 15-bit index registers and 36-bit words, made up of four parts: the *tag* part, the *decrement* part, the *prefix* part, and the *address* part[4]. Hence, *car* is *c*ontents of the *a*ddress *r*egister and *cdr* is *c*ontents of the *d*ecrement *r*egister.

The address and decrement parts were each 15-bit quantities, the tag and prefix parts each 3 bits. Because the latter two bits were separated by the decrement, they could not easily be combined into a single quantity. This made the architecture unsuitable for reference counting. Furthermore introducing reference counting rather than mark-sweep garbage collection would have meant a complete rewrite because of the close coupling of reference counting with the user program. It is interesting to note that McCarthy implemented recursion in Lisp by entering labels, i.e. new copies of function definitions, which does not generate cycles. In fact, he prohibited cyclic data structures even though his mark-sweep method was capable of reclaiming such structures.

Reference counting

The first, though cumbersome and error-prone, reference counting technique was described by H. Gelernter, J.R. Hansen and C.L. Gerberich [Gelernter *et al.*, 1960] but the standard reference counting algorithm is due to George Collins [Collins, 1960]. Collins was working with the CDC 1604 which also had 15-bit addresses. However, the CDC had a 48-bit word, enabling him to use reference counting. Interestingly, he described McCarthy's mark-sweep algorithm as 'elegant yet inefficient', claiming that reference counting outperformed mark-sweep by a factor of three in a typically half-full heap memory. This surprising claim may be an early example of how closely the performance of an algorithm is tied to the machine on which it is implemented. The inability of the reference counting algorithm to collect cyclic structures was first noted by Harold McBeth [McBeth, 1963].

Copying collection

The first copying collector was Marvin Minsky's garbage collector for Lisp 1.5 [Minsky, 1963]. Instead of having two semi-spaces in primary memory, secondary tape storage was used. The live data were copied out to a file, and then read back into a contiguous area of the heap. Minsky's algorithm did not use a stack, but required one mark-bit per Lisp cell. In the early days of virtual memory architectures, Daniel Bobrow and Daniel Murphy combined mark-sweep as the primary method of garbage collection for their implementation of Lisp on a DEC PDP-1, with a variant of Minsky's copying collector to compact the heap when necessary [Bobrow and Murphy, 1967].

D.T. Ross's AED Free Storage Package used the concept of 'plex programming' as a generalisation of list processing [Ross, 1967]. His system generalised copying in a number of interesting ways. It was the first copying algorithm for variable-sized cells; the heap was split into an arbitrary number of spaces; and, whenever a space became full, its objects were copied into a different space. Similar ideas are used today for generational garbage collection (see Chapter 7). The generality of the Ross copying collector made it hard to understand and this is possibly the reason why it has been poorly acknowledged. Wilfred Hansen described a variant

---

[4] Notice that the order is the reverse of Lisp's *car-cdr* list structure which reflected the 704's assembly language rather than the machine itself.

of Minsky's algorithm that was similar to Ross's algorithm [Hansen, 1969]. His algorithm also linearised lists so that the spines of *cons* lists were stored contiguously. The algorithm required two marking bits in each cell, and live data were scanned twice in a recursive process. A fix-up table was used to handle circular lists.

Robert Fenichel and Jerome Yochelson devised the copying algorithm presented in this chapter for Lisp *cons* cells [Fenichel and Yochelson, 1969]. The chief motivation for their scheme was to provide a collector for enormous address spaces (potentially billions of *cons* cells in a Multics system) — an eager sweep phase that visited each cell in the address space would not suffice. Copying was recursive with explicit mark-bits stored in the *car*-field of each copied cell in the same way as forwarding pointers were stored in the *cdr*-field. The best-known copying algorithm is due to C.J. Cheney [Cheney, 1970]. His elegant algorithm is iterative rather than recursive and so runs in constant space (see Chapter 6 where copying garbage collection is discussed in more detail). General algorithms for copying lists in constant workspace can be found in [Lindstrom, 1974; Fisher, 1975; Clark, 1975; Clark, 1976; Robson, 1977; Clark, 1978; Lee *et al.*, 1979; Lee, 1980].

3

Reference Counting

Chapter 2 introduced a simple algorithm for reference counting. This technique had a number of advantages. It was simple to implement; it identified garbage cells as soon as they died, allowing immediate reuse; storage reclamation had good spatial locality of reference, only the cells involved in a pointer update needing to be accessed; it did not require additional headroom in the heap to avoid thrashing the garbage collector; and its overheads were distributed throughout the computation, making reference counting suitable for interactive programs and other applications that cannot tolerate garbage collection delays. Counts of references to each object may also have other uses, for example, in profiling and for systems that can take advantage of run-time sharing analysis.

These virtues have led to reference counting being adopted by several systems (for example, early versions of Smalltalk [Goldberg and Robson, 1983] and InterLisp; Modula-2+ [DeTreville, 1990a]; SISAL [Cann *et al.*, 1992]; and the Unix utilities awk and perl [Aho *et al.*, 1988; Wall and Schwartz, 1991]). Reference counting has also been adopted for memory management in distributed systems, where its good locality of reference implies reduced communication overheads (see Chapter 12).

Chapter 2 also identified several deficiencies in the simple reference counting algorithm. The cost of removing the last pointer to an object is unbounded since any descendants reachable only from that object must also be freed. Although the cost of reference counting may be amortised over the entire computation, the total overhead of adjusting reference counts is significantly greater than that of tracing garbage collection. Despite operating successfully in more tightly confined heaps, reference counting also has a substantial space overhead, requiring space for counters in each cell. A further and major drawback for many applications is its inability to reclaim cyclic data structures. In this chapter, we examine methods for overcoming, or at least ameliorating, each of these shortcomings.

3.1   Non-recursive freeing

In the simple reference counting algorithm introduced in Section 2.1, Update decremented the reference count of an object whenever a pointer to that object was overwritten. If this caused the count to become zero, any pointers that the object contained were also deleted recursively before the memory occupied by the object was returned to the free-list. Consequently, simple recursive freeing distributes processing overheads unevenly: the cost of deleting the last pointer to an object is not constant, nor even proportional to the size of the object, but depends on the size of the sub-graph rooted at that object.

The algorithm

Weizenbaum proposed a method to smooth freeing by using the free-list as a stack [Weizenbaum, 1963]. When the last pointer to a node N is deleted, N is simply pushed onto a free-stack. No recursive freeing is done. Instead, when N is about to be reallocated from the top of the free-stack, any pointers in N are deleted by New, and any immediate referent which would have a reference count of zero is pushed back onto the free-stack (see Algorithm 3.1). It is important that the cell is pushed onto the stack without destroying its pointer contents. The only field that is guaranteed not to be needed, and hence can be used to chain the free-stack, is the reference count field (since it must be zero if the cell is free). To make freeing 'lazy' in the sense of delaying tests for garbage, the definitions of free and Update are unchanged from those given in Algorithm 2.2 on page 21 of Chapter 2, other than to use the RC field rather than an unspecified next field to link the free-list. New and delete must be modified, however. For reasons that will become apparent in Section 3.3, we use incrementRC and decrementRC to abstract away from low-level details of the operations to adjust the reference count fields.

```
New() =
    if free_list == nil
        abort "Memory exhausted"
    newcell = allocate()
    for N in Children(newcell)
        delete(*N)
    RC(newcell) = 1
    return newcell

delete(N) =
    if RC(N) == 1
        RC(N) = free_list
        free_list = N
    else decrementRC(N)
```

Algorithm 3.1   Weizenbaum's lazy freeing algorithm for reference counting.

Costs and benefits of lazy deletion

This lazy method is as efficient as the original eager method — the same instructions are used but have moved from `delete` to `allocate` — but the algorithm is not so vulnerable to delays caused by cascades of cell releases. Unfortunately this does not entirely solve the problem of uneven processing. If an array is freed, for example, all its pointers must still be deleted when it reaches the top of the free-list (albeit to a depth of only one level); the delay to delete the pointers and manipulate the free-stack may or may not be noticeable, depending on the size of the array. The laziness of Weizenbaum's algorithm also loses some of the benefits of immediacy of standard reference counting. The memory occupied by components of a garbage data structure remains inaccessible until the data structure is removed from the top of the free-stack by New. Suppose a type of object is represented by a small header pointing to a large body, and that such an object is deleted — the header of the object will be pushed onto the free-stack. If several other objects are also deleted and pushed onto the free-stack, the memory occupied by the large object's body will no longer be immediately available.

3.2   Deferred reference counting

The overhead of maintaining reference counts is high on conventional hardware. This has made reference counting a less attractive option for storage management than tracing methods (see, for instance, [Hartel, 1988]). Overwriting a pointer typically requires a dozen or so instructions to adjust the reference counts in both the old and the new target cells. Reference counts must also be manipulated when pushing a pointer onto, or popping it off, the system stack. Even non-destructive operations like traversing a list require that the counter of each element in the list must be incremented and then decremented as that element is passed over. In a modern architecture with a data cache, instructions to fetch counts may cause lines to be brought into the cache that otherwise would not be touched. These lines would be 'dirtied' and would have to be written back to heap memory even though their values were identical to those that were brought into the cache [Baker, 1994]. Worse still, reference count manipulations may cause pages containing the remote objects to be paged in [Stamos, 1984].

This overhead can only be reduced by taking every safe opportunity not to adjust counts. One technique commonly used in hand-crafted reference counting systems is to avoid incrementing and decrementing counts of arguments to sub-routines on entry and exit. This is safe only if it is known that the execution of the sub-routine will not cause the arguments' reference counts to drop to zero. Manual reference count optimisation is likely to trade reduced CPU time for increased debugging time. More reliably, the optimiser can be placed in the compiler; this has proved to be very effective at eliminating reference counts in parallel implementations of SISAL [Cann and Oldehoeft, 1988; Oldehoeft, 1994]. Unorthodox type systems may also be used to identify singly-threaded objects, rendering reference counts unnecessary. Baker advocates use of a type system based on linear logic [Girard, 1987] as an effective technique, although others have found it disappointing in practice [Baker, 1994; Wakeling, 1990]. The functional programming language Clean uses a similar system of *unique types* [Brus *et al.*, 1987]. Although these systems require programmers to identify singly-threaded objects, the correctness of their type assertions can be checked by the compiler.

The Deutsch–Bobrow algorithm

Rather than attempt to eliminate reference count manipulations through compile-time analysis, Deutsch and Bobrow devised a systematic run-time method of deferring reference count adjustments [Deutsch and Bobrow, 1976]. The majority of pointer stores are made into local variables; with modern optimising compilers for Lisp or ML, the frequency of other pointer stores may be as low as one percent [Taylor *et al.*, 1986; Appel, 1989b; Zorn, 1989]. *Deferred Reference Counting* takes advantage of this observation by treating operations on local variables and stack-allocated compiler temporaries specially: no reference count book-keeping is done when they are modified. Pointer writes to local names therefore use simple assignment rather than the Update instruction (see Algorithm 3.2). Reference counts now only reflect the number of references from other heap objects: references from the stack are not counted. This means that objects can no longer be reclaimed as soon as their reference count drops to zero since they might still be directly reachable from a local or temporary variable. Instead cells with a reference count of zero are added to a *zero count* table (ZCT) by delete. The ZCT is typically implemented as a hash table or a bitmap.

```
delete(N) =
    decrementRC(N)
    if RC(N) == 0
        add N to ZCT

Update(R,S) =                          —R and S are heap objects
    incrementRC(S)
    delete(*R)
    remove S from ZCT
    *R = S
```

Algorithm 3.2   Deferred Reference Counting: updating pointer values.

Entries in the ZCT are deleted and the reference count incremented when a reference to the object is stored in another heap object. Periodically the ZCT is reconciled to remove and collect garbage. Any object with a reference in the ZCT that is not also found by scanning the stack must be garbage and can be returned to the free-list. Reconciliation works in three phases: first all objects directly accessible from the stack are marked, then unmarked objects with entries in the ZCT are freed and finally all marked objects are unmarked.

One way to mark and unmark objects is to increment and decrement their reference counts respectively (see Algorithm 3.3 on the next page). An object in the ZCT can only have a zero reference count after the reference counts of all objects directly accessible from the stack have been incremented if it really is garbage. These objects can be freed after their component pointers have been deleted. Finally the reference counts that were inflated in the first phase — scanning the stack — must be decremented.

An example

Let us look at an example to see how deferred reference counting works in practice. The function gcd(x,y) calculates the greatest common divisor of its non-negative integer

```
reconcile() =
    for N in stack                          —mark the stack
        incrementRC(N)

    for N in ZCT                            —reclaim garbage
        if RC(N) == 0
            for M in Children(N)
                delete(*M)
            free(N)

    for N in stack                          —unmark the stack
        decrementRC(N)
```

Algorithm 3.3   Deferred Reference Counting: reconciling the ZCT.

arguments. If we assert that its first argument must always be greater than or equal to its second, gcd can be written as:

```
gcd(x,y) =                                  —assert: x ≥ y ≥ 0
    if y == 0
        return x
    t = x - y
    if x > t
        return gcd(y,t)
    else return gcd(t,y)
```

Algorithm 3.4   Greatest common divisor.

Let us suppose that we have a system in which all objects are allocated in the heap, and that expressions are represented by graphs whose nodes are heap objects. Suppose further that the system stack also contains pointers to heap-allocated data[1]. The first step in a hand evaluation of gcd(18,12) would be to rewrite it to gcd(12,6). Let us see how the system would do this.

First the graph of gcd(18,12) is created and unwound, leaving R, the two arguments and a pointer to the function gcd on the stack. For convenience, we name atomic objects by their value. At this stage all nodes have a reference count of one (except R which might be shared) and the ZCT is empty (see Diagram 3.1 on the following page).

The first test fails as y is not zero, so the local variable t is set to 6. A new cell is acquired from the free-list and filled with the value 6. As there are no heap references to the new cell 6, it is added to the ZCT. Our compiler is also smart enough to realise that x is no longer used in this call to gcd, so it reuses its slot on the stack for 6. Although 6 has a reference count of zero, it is safe from reclamation as it is accessible from the stack (see Diagram 3.2 on the next page).

The next two steps are to link 6 into the graph with Update(right(R),6), and to acquire a new application cell, B, and Update(left(R),B). Linking 6 to R increments 6's count and

---

[1] Graph reduction, used by implementations of lazy functional languages, is an instance of such a system.

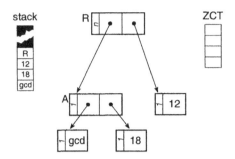

Diagram 3.1   The graph gcd(18,12).

deletes its entry from the ZCT. Let us suppose that overwriting left(R) causes the pointers to A, gcd and 12 to be deleted recursively. At this point the ZCT contains 12, 18, A and gcd (see Diagram 3.3 on the facing page).

Filling ZCT triggers the reconciliation mechanism. Examining the stack, reconcile finds R, 6, 12 and gcd and marks them (increases their reference counts). Examining the ZCT, reconcile reclaims A and 18, since they are unmarked (their count is zero), and adds them to the free-list. 12 and gcd are preserved and kept in the ZCT since they are pointed to from the stack (see Diagram 3.4 on the next page) .

The abstract machine would now link gcd and 12 to B, and pop the top three items from the stack. It would then be in a state where it can perform the next step of the recursion, evaluating gcd(12,6) (not shown).

ZCT overflow

A drawback apparent in this example is that the ZCT is reconciled when it overflows, but recursive freeing may add further entries to the ZCT each time an object is freed. There are

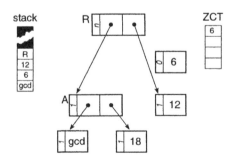

Diagram 3.2   A new cell for t=x-y is acquired and added to the ZCT.

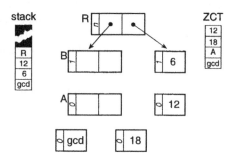

Diagram 3.3   R is updated, recursively freeing its contents.

several solutions to this dilemma. If freeing an object would cause the table to overflow, its reclamation can be aborted and the object left in the ZCT until the next reconciliation. Alternatively, if Weizenbaum's lazy freeing technique is used, any pointers contained in a freed object are not deleted until the object is reallocated. The ZCT can be reconciled when allocation would lead to overflow. Alternatively, ZCT overflow will not be an issue if it is implemented as a bitmap [Baden, 1983]. In the garbage collection context, a bitmap is an array of bits, each of which represents a word in the heap. An object is entered into or removed from the ZCT by setting or unsetting its bit. At the cost of a small proportion of the heap (for example, 1:32), overflow checks can be eliminated.

The efficiency of deferred reference counting

Deferred reference counting is very effective at reducing the cost of pointer writes. Experience of Smalltalk implementations on the Xerox Dorado in the mid-eighties suggested that it typically cut the cost of pointer manipulations by 80 percent or more at a cost of a relatively small space overhead (25 kilobytes 'on a typical personal computer') [Ungar, 1984; Baden,

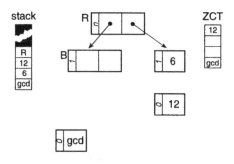

Diagram 3.4   The ZCT after reconciliation but before updating B.

1983]. Table 3.1 shows Ungar's comparisons of the costs of pointer updates, reconciliation and recursive freeing for a standard reference counting system and deferred reference counting. Ungar also states that the pauses to reconcile the ZCT were also short (30 milliseconds in every 500 milliseconds) compared with those for mark-sweep garbage collection.

Table 3.1 Immediate *vs.* deferred reference counting. Figures are percentages of total execution time [Ungar, 1984].

	Immediate	*Deferred*
Updates	15	3
Reconciliation		3
Recursive freeing	5	5
Total	20	11

The chief drawback of deferred reference counting is that, apart from the space cost of the ZCT, it reduces reference counting's advantage of immediately recycling memory as garbage objects are retained until the ZCT is reconciled.

3.3 Limited-field reference counts

Reference counting techniques require space in each cell to store the reference count. In the theoretically worst case, this field must be large enough to hold the total number of pointers contained in the heap and in the roots: it must be as large as a pointer (this is why Weizenbaum's scheme could use the reference count field to chain cells in the free-list). However, it is inconceivable that any application would cause counts to grow so large. Space can be saved by using a smaller reference count field at the cost of taking precautions to handle overflow.

Sticky reference counts

The per-cell overhead for reference counting depends inversely on the size of the cell. If a pointer-sized field is used (to avoid overflow checks), the overhead for Lisp *cons* cells is 50 percent; if a single byte is used it is 12.5 percent. Small reference count fields may overflow and hence break the reference count invariant that RC(N) is equal to the number of pointers to N for all heap cells N. Two problems arise.

First a count cannot be allowed to exceed its maximum permissible value. Second, once the reference count reaches this value, it is 'stuck': it cannot be reduced since the true count of pointers to the object may be greater than its reference count (see Algorithm 3.5 on the next page). We call this maximum value 'sticky'.

```
incrementRC(N) =
    if RC(N) < sticky
        RC(N) = RC(N) + 1

decrementRC(N) =
    if RC(N) < sticky
        RC(N) = RC(N) - 1
```

Algorithm 3.5   Incrementing and decrementing 'sticky' reference counts.

Tracing collection restores reference counts

This implies that an object cannot be reclaimed once its reference count reaches the maximum since it can never be returned to zero by reference counting alone. A backup tracing garbage collector must be used to restore true reference counts (see Algorithm 3.6). This collector starts by making an additional sweep through the heap to set all reference counts to zero (i.e. unmarked). As each pointer in the active graph is traversed, the mark routine increments the reference count of the object it visits (up to the maximum value). At the end of the marking phase, the reference count of every object in the heap will have been restored to its true value or sticky, whichever is less. The use of a backup tracing collector is not burdensome since it is likely that it will be needed anyway to collect cyclic garbage. For simplicity, we express mark recursively. In practice a more efficient technique would be used (see Chapter 4 where we discuss mark-sweep collection in more detail).

```
mark_sweep() =
    for N in Heap
        RC(N) = 0
    for R in Roots
        mark(R)
    sweep()
    if free_pool is empty
        abort "Memory exhausted"

mark(N) =
    incrementRC(N)
    if RC(N) == 1                                    —first visit
        for M in Children(N)
            mark(*M)
```

Algorithm 3.6   A backup tracing garbage collector that restores 'stuck' reference counts.

One-bit reference counts

More radically, Wise and others have suggested restricting the reference count field to a single bit [Wise and Friedman, 1977; Stoye *et al.*, 1984; Chikayama and Kimura, 1987; Wise, 1993]. The reference count bit then simply determines whether a cell is shared (sticky) or unique. Empirical studies of Lisp and other languages have shown that most cells are not shared and so can be reclaimed immediately their pointer is deleted [Clark and Green, 1977; Stoye *et al.*, 1984; Hartel, 1988]. Wise argues that reference counting should therefore concentrate its efforts on these unshared objects. The aims of *One-bit Reference Counting* are to postpone garbage collection (and its consequent pause) for as long as possible, and to reduce the space overhead to that of mark-sweep garbage collection. Reference counting also affords opportunities for optimisations, such as *copy avoidance* or *in-place updates*. If a modified copy is required of an object for which there are (about to be) no other references, the 'copy' can be performed by borrowing the pointer and side-effecting the object, rather than duplicating and deallocating the original node. The advantages of copy avoidance for programs that manipulate large arrays, for example, is obvious.

The simplest implementation is to store the unique bit in each cell [Wise and Friedman, 1977], but a better technique is to store the bit in each *pointer* [Stoye *et al.*, 1984] in the same way that run-time tags are used for type checking [Steenkiste and Hennessy, 1987]. The first pointer to a newly created object is tagged as `unique`. When a pointer is copied by `Update`, the replica pointer is tagged as `sticky`, and an extra check is made of the source pointer's reference count. If it is `unique` then it too must be tagged as `sticky` in the original field from which it was fetched (see Algorithm 3.7). Notice that reference counting cannot make `sticky` pointers `unique`: shared cells can only be reclaimed, and uniqueness can only be restored, by a tracing garbage collection. However, as we noted above, a backup tracing collector is likely to be necessary in any case to collect cycles.

The advantage of the Stoye *et al.* scheme is that a remote cell's status (uniquely referenced or shared) can be determined and modified without fetching the cell itself (for example, T in Diagram 3.5 on the facing page), and hence reduces the chance of cache misses or page faults. The cost of even a primary cache miss is likely to be of the order of five cycles; a page fault will cost many hundreds of thousands. Thus the cost of the extra instruction is a price well worth paying. We discuss the interaction between garbage collection and the cache further in Chapter 11. A potential problem is that the site of the original pointer might be difficult to discover if the pointer's value has been passed through registers or the stack.

```
Update(R,S)  =
    T = sticky(*S)
    if RC(*S) == unique
        *S = T
    delete(*R)
    *R = T
```

Algorithm 3.7   One-bit reference counting with tagged pointers.

Restoring uniqueness information

Once a count becomes shared, it is stuck — the reference counting mechanism cannot make it revert to unique. If the last pointer to a `sticky` node is deleted, the node cannot be reclaimed immediately but must wait for garbage collection. If the reference count bit is stored in the node itself, its field can be shared with a mark-sweep collector's mark-bit by equating `sticky`

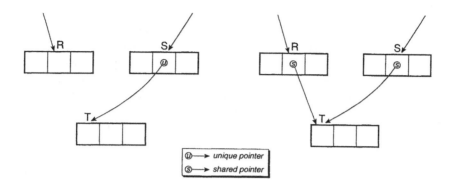

Diagram 3.5 Update(R,S).

with 'marked'. After the marking phase is complete, all surviving cells will be marked as
sticky. Unfortunately marks do not distinguish between shared and uniquely referenced
cells. Although uniqueness information has been lost, Friedman and Wise argue that there will
be plenty of opportunity for the one-bit reference counting scheme to get going again before
another garbage collection is required provided that the collector is relatively successful in
reclaiming space.

If a two-pass compacting compactor is used (see Chapter 4 where we discuss mark-compact
schemes), unique references *can* be restored (see also [Wise, 1979]). Mark-compact collectors
typically operate in a further two phases after the marking phase: live cells are compacted
toward the bottom of the heap and references to these cells are updated to reflect their new
locations. The compactor can determine whether a cell has multiple references as it corrects
these references.

Wise has also used a semi-space copying collector to restore unique tags to pointers that
have become sticky in the past but should be no longer [Wise, 1993] (see Chapter 6 for
a discussion of copying garbage collection). A suitable copying collector must maintain the
invariant that, for any cell N in Tospace, the tags of any forwarding address and of all pointers
to N are equal, and sticky if and only if there is more than one such pointer (excluding the
forwarding address). Wise's algorithm requires that each cell be large enough to hold two
pointers, source and forward, rather than one. The source pointer is set to point at the
original Tospace reference to this cell. The forward pointer is used as a forwarding address
in the usual way. It is tagged as unique when first set and returned as the result of copy,
ensuring that the new value of original Tospace pointer is also unique. If the Fromspace cell is
revisited by the collector, the forward pointer is changed to sticky. In this case the tag on
the original Tospace pointer must also be changed to sticky: this pointer can be found from
source.

The 'Ought to be Two' cache

Many adjustments to reference counts are only temporary. Consider the assignment
N = select(N), where N has a reference count of unique and select is a projection
function returning a currently unique field of N. A typical example of such a projection
function might be taking the tail of a list. The problem is that the reference count of the
cell select(N) must be raised to sticky before N is dereferenced (otherwise the cell will
be reclaimed before its field is retrieved) and so uniqueness information will be lost. Friedman
and Wise retain uniqueness by using a software cache of nodes whose real reference count is
two but whose RC is still set to unique — it 'ought to be two' [Wise and Friedman, 1977].

When a pointer to a unique node is copied, the node is inserted into the cache unless it
is already there — a hit — in which case the node is removed from the cache and marked as
shared. Cache overflow is handled by evicting an arbitrary entry from the cache (for example,
the least recently used) and setting its count to sticky. When a pointer is deleted, it is
removed from the cache (if present), i.e. its reference count reverts from 'ought to be 2'
to unique. If the cell is not in the cache but it is unique, then it is freed recursively (see
Algorithm 3.8).

```
hit(N) =
    if N in cache
        remove N from cache
        return true
    else return false

insert(N) =
    if hit(N)
        RC(N) = sticky
    else put N in cache

delete(N) =
    if not hit(N)
        if RC(N) == unique
            for M in Children(N)
                delete(*M)
            free(N)

Update(R,S) =
    if RC(S) == unique
        insert(S)
    delete(*R)
    *R = S
```

Algorithm 3.8   The 'ought to be 2' cache.

This strategy can only be successful if the cache is very fast. Friedman and Wise suggest
dedicating a small number of registers to the cache. A single register is sufficient to avoid
incrementing reference counts for the assignments of the form N = select(N) that are
common in compiled images of applicative code, for example when traversing a list. In this
case, the assignment is typically twice as expensive as it would be under standard referencing

counting. Two registers suffice for code sequences of the form $r = f(s); s = g(t); t = h(r)$, for example, the code to swap the values of r and s. However, apart from the cache's management overhead, its use increases the pressure on the compiler's register allocator. If this causes register spills that would not otherwise occur, the real overhead may be even greater.

3.4 Hardware reference counting

Despite these optimisations, the execution time of reference counting is generally accepted to be greater than that of tracing techniques. To obtain the benefits of reference counting without imposing such a tax on the mutator program, hardware support must be sought. Wise and others have designed and built self-managing heap memories based on reference counting [Wise, 1985; Wise *et al.*, 1994; Gehringer and Chang, 1993; Chang and Gehringer, 1993a; Chang and Gehringer, 1993b]. Active memory departs from the traditional von Neumann architecture that separates intelligence (the CPU) from memory. In Wise's design, all book-keeping to maintain reference counts is devolved to banks of reference counting memory (RCM), leaving the processor free to do 'useful' processing. Apart from releasing the processor from the burden of managing the heap, reference counting in the memory itself offers a major gain to multiprocessing systems: it also obviates the need for synchronisation between client programs and tracing garbage collectors, or locks on reference counts.

Special-purpose architectures do not have a history of commercial success. Development costs make them simply too expensive. An advantage of the active memory approach over more radical designs is that benefits, and hence development costs, can potentially be shared amongst different conventional architectures if the self-managing heap appears to the processor to be just another bank of memory.

Wise's design includes data memory and reference count memory, each associated with the same addresses, in each bank of reference counting memory. Each of the two memories has its own bus and ports: a data port to processors and a narrower port to other RCMs. The latter runs at twice the speed of the data port since a single data write can generate two remote reference counting operations (the increment and the decrement). Each bank of RCM maintains its own available-space lists. To obtain a new node, the processor reads from one of a number of distinguished memory locations, depending on the type of node required. A mark-sweep garbage collection mode, using a Deutsch–Schorr–Waite collector in order to operate in constant space (see Section 4.3 where we discuss mark-sweep garbage collection in more detail), is also provided.

Initial tests of the RCM system suggest that it is potentially very effective although overall performance depended on the size of the problem. Reference counting itself is performed at no cost to the mutator program, and the in-RCM mark-sweep garbage collector ran at twice the speed of a software-only stop-and-copy collector. However, the prototype sat on a NextBus as a 'device' and hence was uncached. Lack of caching cost around 40 percent of user execution time compared with using stock, cached RAM. Nevertheless, given a sufficiently large problem, code using the RCM executed in between 40 and 70 percent of the time of that using stop-and-copy collection on stock, cached hardware.

Gehringer and Chang proposed using a coprocessor as a second-level cache. The coprocessor would manage its memory by reference counting with the intention of performing all reference count manipulations in this cache. Simulations of their design show that the co-processor can remove 50 to 70 percent of objects before they age out of the cache, saving 57 to 72 percent of bus write traffic, and 53 to 63 percent of fetch traffic [Chang and Gehringer, 1993a; Chang and Gehringer, 1993b]. Garbage collection is still necessary, for instance to collect cycles, but coprocessor reference counting extends the collection interval by approximately 60 percent.

3.5   Cyclic reference counting

Possibly the most powerful argument against reference counting is its inability to reclaim cyclic data structures (an example is shown on page 25) first noted by McBeth [McBeth, 1963]. Cyclic structures are common, both at the application level and at the systems level. Cycles are typically created by programmers when they use back-pointers or they aim to express domain-specific problems in a natural manner. Cycles can also be created unintentionally, for instance the back edge in the link in a hash table chain [Boehm, 1994b]. Implementations of functional programming languages also commonly use cycles to express recursion [Turner, 1979].

Under a standard reference counting regime, programmers must either modify their style, or break cycles explicitly by deleting pointers. Unfortunately it is not always apparent which pointer should be cut. Manual intervention is both burdensome and inherently unsafe. We know of no good large-scale methodology for avoiding cycles. One alternative is to use a hybrid memory manager, in which most cells are handled by reference counting (since cells are usually unshared), but a mark-sweep collector is periodically invoked to collect cyclic garbage. However, considerable effort has been devoted to solving the problem of reclaiming cyclic data without resort to global garbage collection. Some of the algorithms that have been devised are specific to functional programming languages [Friedman and Wise, 1979; Hughes, 1987] or to certain programming idioms [Bobrow, 1980; Wise, 1985], while others are generally applicable [Christopher, 1984; Lins, 1992a]. Other proposals, often widely cited without comment, are either simply incorrect [Brownbridge, 1984] or fail to terminate in pathological cases [Salkild, 1987]. To our knowledge, none of the schemes proposed below have been adopted for use by significant systems.

Functional programming languages

Friedman and Wise observed that references to cyclic data structures are created in a well-defined manner in pure functional programming languages, and so can be handled specially [Friedman and Wise, 1979]. Since cycles can only be generated by recursive definitions, references into such circular environments can be controlled provided the following restrictions are observed:

- the circular structure is created all at once;
- any use of a proper subset of the cycle that does not include its root is copied as an independent structure rather than shared;

• cycle-closing pointers to the head of the cycle are tagged as such.

These restrictions ensure that the cycle is treated as a single entity. In particular access to the cycle may only be through a pointer to its root. The consequence is that no part of it will be created before or survive after any other part. When the last pointer to the head of the cycle is deleted, the entire cycle can be reclaimed.

Bobrow's technique

More general techniques rely on being able to distinguish pointers internal to the cycle from external references. *Internal* references point from one member of the cycle to another and need not be counted. All other pointers to the cycle are *external* references and are counted as references to the structure as a whole. For example, the cycle on page 25 contained two internal pointers, from S to T and vice-versa, and one external pointer, right(R), until it was deleted. The entire cycle can be reclaimed when, and only when, there are no external references to it.

Bobrow used this idea to collect groups of cells [Bobrow, 1980]. All cells allocated are assigned by the programmer to a *group*. Cells can also be transferred between groups if the programmer declares certain pointers to be internal. Each group is reference counted, and the group of any cell must be determinable from its address (maybe the cell contains its *group number* or a pointer to the *group reference count*). When a pointer is overwritten, the group numbers of the three cells involved in the transaction are examined. If any inter-group pointers are created or deleted, then the relevant group reference counts must be adjusted.

```
Update(R,S)  =
    T = *R
    gr = group_no(R)
    if gr ≠ group_no(S)                      —external reference
        increment_groupRC(S)
    if gr ≠ group_no(T)                      —external reference
        decrement_groupRC(T)
        if groupRC(T) == 0
            reclaim_group(T)
    *R = S
```

Algorithm 3.9   Bobrow's algorithm.

This scheme only reclaims groups as a whole. If individual members or sub-groups of an active group become disconnected, they will not be reclaimed until the entire group is deallocated. Note that individual nodes are not reference counted. Once the group's reference count is zero, the entire group can be reclaimed. If a zone of memory is allocated exclusively to the group, it could be swept to free these individuals. Alternatively, all members of the group could be linked through an additional pointer field, also used by the free-list. In this case the entire group can be returned to the free-list in a single operation.

A fundamental drawback of Bobrow's algorithm is that it can only reclaim intra-group cycles but not inter-group ones. Hughes observed that Bobrow's scheme works best if each group comprised a single *strongly connected component* (SCC) of the graph, that is, a minimal set of nodes each of which is reachable from every other node in the set [Hughes, 1983; Hughes, 1987]. In this case, every cell could be freed as soon as it became unreachable. Partitioning the graph into SCCs would be prohibitively expensive in general, but Hughes suggested that it might be feasible for a graph reducer since graph reduction does not modify the graph in arbitrary ways. Graph reduction operates by repeatedly creating new graph and then overwriting a redex node with this graph. Since allocating new nodes does not affect the rest of the graph, the new sub-graph can be split into SCCs independently (except for nodes from which the root is reachable) using Tarjan's algorithm. Overwriting the redex similarly affects the redex's group only.

Weak-pointer algorithms

Several authors have attempted to tackle the problem of reclaiming cyclic data structures by distinguishing cycle closing pointers (*weak* pointers) from other references (*strong* pointers) [Brownbridge, 1985; Salkild, 1987; Pepels *et al.*, 1988; Axford, 1990]. The basis of this approach is as follows. Each active node in the heap must be reachable from a root via a chain of strong pointers (*strongly reachable*). Strong pointers must never be allowed to form cycles. The graph whose arcs are the strong pointers is acyclic and hence amenable to standard reference counting techniques if only strong references are counted. The correctness of weak-pointer algorithms depends crucially on two invariants:

- active nodes are reachable from root via a chain of strong pointers;   (SW.1)
- strong pointers do not form cycles.   (SW.2)

The most widely cited weak-pointer algorithm is due to Brownbridge. It is less widely known that, unfortunately, his algorithm may reclaim objects prematurely in some cases (for an example, see the structure ABC in Diagram 3.6 on page 61). Salkild corrected the algorithm at the cost of introducing non-termination in certain pathological cases (for an example, see Diagram 3.7 on page 62). We shall review as briefly as possible the Brownbridge–Salkild algorithm and the work by Pepels *et al.* which corrects it, albeit at considerable cost.

Brownbridge's general purpose algorithm stores two reference counters in each cell: one for strong pointers to the cell, and the other for weak ones (see Diagram 3.6 on page 61). Since allocating new cells cannot create cycles, pointers to new cells are always strong (see Algorithm 3.10 where SRC(R) is the strong reference count of cell R and strong(newcell) makes the pointer returned strong).

```
New() =
    if free_list == empty
        abort "Memory exhausted"
    newcell = allocate()
    SRC(R) = 1
    return strong(newcell)
```

Algorithm 3.10   Brownbridge's New.

Copying pointers, on the other hand, may lead to cycles being introduced, in which case the closing link must be weak. Salkild modified Brownbridge's algorithm to make all copies of pointers weak. This allows weak pointers to occur everywhere; they no longer simply close cycles but the invariants remain valid (see Algorithm 3.11). Furthermore, this method is suitable for general pointer manipulation systems rather than just the combinator machines that were Brownbridge's interest. In Algorithm 3.11 `WRC(S)` is the weak reference count of `S` and `weaken(*R)` causes the pointer at `R` to be made weak (we explain later how this can be done efficiently).

```
Update(R,S) =
    WRC(S) = WRC(S) + 1
    delete(*R)
    *R = S
    weaken(*R)
```

Algorithm 3.11   Salkild's `Update`.

Deletion of pointers is more delicate. Weak pointers can simply be removed and the weak reference count decremented without further action (case *(i)* in Algorithm 3.12). If an object is in use then it is reachable via a chain of strong pointers by invariant (SW.1), so it must have a strong reference count of at least one. Deleting a weak pointer, or any but the last strong pointer, to an object cannot cause it to be freed. If the strong pointer being deleted is the last reference (strong or weak) to this cell, then the cell can be safely returned to the free-list (case *(ii)* in Algorithm 3.12). Any pointers from this cell should also be deleted.

```
delete(T) =
    if is_weak(T)                                   —(i)
        WRC(T) = WRC(T) - 1
    else                                            —T is strong
        SRC(T) = SRC(T) - 1
        if SRC(T) == 0 and WRC(T) == 0              —(ii)
            for U in Children(T)
                delete(*U)
            free(T)
        else if SRC(T) == 0 and WRC(T) > 0          —(iii)
            . . .
```

Algorithm 3.12   Deleting strong and weak pointers.

If, however, there remain any weak pointers to this cell, we have case *(iii)* of Algorithm 3.12: the situation in which the classic version of reference counting fails. The cell no longer has any strong pointers to it — its strong reference count is zero — but it might be part of a cycle which may be detached from the roots. Alternatively, there may be a strong pointer to another cell in the cycle which would mean that all the cells in the cycle are still reachable. To determine which case applies when the pointer from one cell to another, `T`, is deleted, a search is made of all the descendants of `T` to try to find a pointer external to any cycle containing the cell `T`, which would mean that it is still reachable from root.

First, all pointers to T are made strong. If the cell is not garbage, it is strongly reachable once more. However this action might have created strong cycles, so the data structure reachable from T is traversed (along strong pointers only) in order to identify and remove any strong cycles, as well as looking for external pointers. This description of the algorithm begs two questions:

- how can we decide if a pointer is strong or weak?
- how can we *efficiently* turn all the weak pointers to T into strong ones?

Brownbridge provided an elegant solution to this dilemma. Each pointer and each object has an associated *strength-bit*. If a pointer and the object to which it is pointing have the same strength-bit value, then the pointer is strong. If the bit-values differ, then the pointer is weak. The strength-bit is also used to determine which of the two reference counters is the SRC and which is the WRC. To strengthen all weak pointers to T in a single operation we simply invert the value of T's strength-bit.

We can now return to delete(T). If a strong pointer was the last strong reference to the cell, T, but there are other weak references (case *(iii)* in Algorithm 3.12 on the page before), delete strengthens all the weak pointers and then corrects the pointers in its sub-graph to preserve the invariants (SW.1) and (SW.2). If SRC(T) remains zero, the sub-graph is freed recursively.

```
    . . .
    if is_strong(T) and SRC(T) == 1 and WRC(T) > 0      —(iii)
        invert_strength(T)
        for U in Children(T)
            suicide(T,*U)
        if SRC(T) == 0
            for U in Sons(T)
                delete(*U)
            free(T)
```

Algorithm 3.13 delete continued.

The searching routine, suicide, takes a starting point, T, and follows strong pointers, weakening them where necessary to preserve the invariants (see Algorithm 3.14 on the facing page). Herein lies the problem. If suicide's traversal of strong pointers has brought it back to its starting point, a cycle of strong pointers has been discovered, one of which must be weakened in order to preserve the invariants. The only possible candidate is the closing link, S. If there are other strong pointers to the cell S, the pointer S does not need to be strong as well. The pointer is weakened to break any strong cycle that may have been formed. Otherwise suicide continues its traversal of strong pointers.

Unfortunately this does not take *weak* external pointers into consideration. Salkild showed that this oversight may lead to cyclic structures being discarded incorrectly as garbage, as the example below shows. Brownbridge's algorithm would have discarded the left-hand cycle ABC in Diagram 3.6 on the next page when the pointer from root to A is deleted, although ABC is still *weakly* reachable from root via D and E.

```
suicide(Start_node, S) =
    if is_strong(S)
        if S == Start_node
            weaken(S)
        else if SRC(S) > 1
            weaken(S)
        else for T in Children(S)
            suicide(Start_node, *T)
```

Algorithm 3.14   suicide searches for, and breaks, strong cycles.

Salkild proposed that if suicide should discover a cell with weak pointers but only one strong pointer (the one along which the traversal reached the cell), the cell's strength bit should be flipped and the search for external references and strong cycles be restarted from this cell. Although this version of suicide is correct in the sense that the invariants are maintained and only garbage cells are discarded, the algorithm now fails to terminate in certain cases. Consider what happens in Diagram 3.7 on the following page when the last strong pointer to A is deleted.

One way to prevent an infinite number of searches by suicide is to use a marking scheme. The solution offered by Pepels *et al.* was to use two kinds of mark: one to prevent an infinite number of searches, and the other to guarantee termination of each search. Their version of the algorithm is extremely complex. We refer the reader to [Pepels *et al.*, 1988] for details and for a proof of the algorithm.

Although correct, and now terminating thanks to Pepels *et al.*, is the algorithm efficient? If there are no cycles in the graph and deleting the last strong reference to a cell always results in the reclamation of that cell, then it is twice as expensive as the classic reference counting algorithm (due to the suicide pass). At the other extreme, it is possible to imagine pathological cases in which each incarnation of suicide invokes further instantiations of suicide at each node of the sub-graph. The complexity of their algorithm is at least

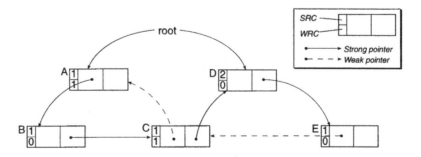

Diagram 3.6   Brownbridge's algorithm incorrectly reclaims the structure ABC when the strong pointer from root to A is deleted.

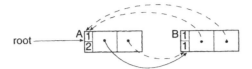

Diagram 3.7   Deleting the pointer to A throws Salkild's algorithm into a loop.

exponential in the worst case. Furthermore, the space overheads are also high: each cell requires two reference count fields, and a strength- and mark-flag (although it turns out that both types of mark can share the same bit), more than double the overhead of standard reference counting.

Partial Mark-Sweep Algorithms

The final algorithms in this chapter take a very different approach to the problem of reference counting cyclic data structures. Their general idea is to perform three *partial* traversals of the data structure, in the first place removing the contribution of pointers internal to the sub-graph being traversed from cell reference counts. At the end of the first traversal, the reference counts will only reflect external pointers to nodes in the sub-graph. The second traversal restores the counts of nodes reachable from external pointers whilst the third phase sweeps garbage into the free-list.

Christopher's algorithm

This method was originally invented by Christopher [Christopher, 1984] but has since been re-discovered by several other researchers [Vestal, 1987; Martinez *et al.*, 1990; Kennedy, 1991]. Christopher developed his algorithm to provide dynamic storage allocation with garbage collection for languages such as Fortran that do not have such facilities. The primary method of reclaiming garbage is reference counting. However, a tracing collector is called periodically to reclaim nodes in the heap that have non-zero reference counts but are not externally reachable. Because the collector only visits nodes in the heap, it does not need to be able to locate the roots of the computation (which may be impossible to discover accurately without knowledge of, or cooperation from, the compiler).

Lins's algorithm

The algorithms developed by Lins and his colleagues are also hybrid algorithms. Most cells are freed by reference counting but garbage cycles are reclaimed by a mark-sweep collector. Any cells that are uniquely referenced are candidates for reclamation by reference counting when their count drops to zero. If, on the other hand, a pointer to a shared node is deleted, the collector is called to mark-sweep the transitive closure of the deleted pointer [Martinez *et al.*, 1990]. Cyclic reference counting would be prohibitively expensive if sub-graphs were to be traced every time a shared pointer was deleted — the Martinez *et al.* algorithm is clearly impractical. Lins's lazy cyclic reference counting algorithm postpones these traversals by saving the values of deleted pointers in a *control set* [Lins, 1992a]. At some suitable point, all or part of the control set can be searched for garbage.

Lins's algorithm traps pointer writes and saves the old target of the pointer in the hope that it will *not* be preserved[2]. This highlights the difference between his reference counting with lazy mark-sweep algorithm and standard mark-sweep collection. The latter traverses only the active data structure whereas, in the best case, Lins's collector traces only cyclic garbage (although it may have to trace, unsuccessfully, live data as well).

We shall first consider Lins's lazy algorithm in detail. Christopher's scheme can be thought of as a special case of Lins in which every cell with a non-zero count is in the control set, and we return to it later. In addition to the reference count, Lins uses an extra field to keep the colour of the cell. Four colours are used: *black*, *grey*, *white* and *purple*[3]. Intuitively, active cells are painted black, and garbage and free cells white. Cells visited in the marking phase are coloured grey — they need to be visited again. Purple cells may be members of isolated cycles: they need to be traversed by the collector.

Whenever a pointer to a shared cell is deleted, the cell is painted purple and its address is placed in the control set. Colouring deleted cells purple avoids adding duplicate entries to the set and ensures that only those cells in the control set that are not subsequently discovered to be active will be traced. The control set heuristic is that, by the time that the mark-sweep can no longer be avoided, there will be further evidence as to whether cells in the control set are garbage or not. Either their last references will have been deleted, in which case they will have been returned to the free-list (and possibly reused), or their pointers will have been copied (in which case they must be still in use). In either case, the cells will not be purple.

The only difference between Lins's New and that of the standard version shown on page 20 is that he allocates new cells black, and he must decide when to collect the control set. For the moment, let us skip over this question.

There is also just one difference between Lins's Update (see Algorithm 3.15 on the next page) and the standard one. Both arguments to Lins's Update must be active and hence should be removed from the control set to prevent them being mark-swept; this is done (logically) by painting the cells black. If the control set was implemented as a hash table or a bitmap, the entry could be removed physically as well; otherwise the cost of removal is not worthwhile. If the set is full, it must first be scanned (or extended) to make room for the new reference. If the set is organised as a linked data structure in the heap, it will only become full if the heap is exhausted, in which case garbage collection is inevitable.

It is desirable to avoid multiple control set references to a single cell, although this is not always possible to do efficiently unless a hash table or bitmap is used. Not all cells in the queue will be purple. Some may have been repainted black by Update or by a previous call to the mark-sweep routine: these cells and their descendants are still in use. Other cells may have had their last reference deleted. Such cells will either be in the free-list (white) or have

---

[2] Lins's control set is reminiscent of what might be called an *anti*-remembered set (see the discussion on generational garbage collection in Chapter 7) together with a snapshot-at-the-beginning write-barrier (we discuss incremental garbage collection techniques in Chapter 8).

[3] Lins used green, red, blue and black respectively. However black, grey, white fits in better with the tricolour abstraction used in incremental garbage collection (which is discussed in Chapter 8).

been recycled by New (black). Deleting pointers to either of these kinds of active cells will duplicate their entries in the control set. The control set is used to identify potential free space. On picking a cell from it, its colour is tested (see Algorithm 3.16). If it is still purple it is still uncertain whether the last pointer to a cycle has been deleted, and a local mark-sweep must be performed.

```
delete(T) =
    RC(T) = RC(T) - 1
    if RC(T) == 0
        colour(T) = black
        for U in Children(T)
            delete(*U)
        free(T)
    else if colour(T) ≠ purple
        if control_set is full
            gc_control_set()
        colour(T) = purple
        push(T,control_set)

Update(R,S) =
    RC(S) = RC(S) + 1
    colour(R) = black            —'remove' R,S from control set
    colour(S) = black
    delete(*R)
    *R = S
```

Algorithm 3.15   Cyclic reference counting Update.

```
gc_control_set() =
    S = pop(control_set)
    if colour(S) == purple
        mark_grey(S)
        scan(S)
        collect_white(S)
    else if control_set ≠ empty
        gc_control_set()
```

Algorithm 3.16   Lins's three-phase mark sweep.

Mark_grey traces the sub-graph below its calling point and removes reference counts that are due to pointers internal to this sub-graph (see Algorithm 3.17 on the next page). Cells are painted grey to ensure termination.

Any non-zero reference counts in the grey sub-graph can only be due to external references. Scan searches for these, calling scan_black to paint the transitive referential closure of such external references black (see Algorithm 3.18 on the facing page). Cells with no external references are painted white to indicate that they may be garbage. White cells may be repainted black by a later stage of this scan.

```
mark_grey(S) =
    if colour(S) ≠ grey
        colour(S) = grey
        for T in Children(S)
            RC(*T) = RC(*T) - 1
            mark_grey(*T)
```

Algorithm 3.17   `mark_grey` removes reference counts due to internal pointers.

`Scan_black` paints the sub-graph below its calling point black and restores the reference counts of each cell visited to take into account any active pointers internal to the sub-graph that had been removed from its count by `mark_grey` (see Algorithm 3.19 on the next page).

Finally `collect_white` recovers the white cells in the sub-graph and returns them to the free-list (see Algorithm 3.20 on the following page). Although the code below implements `collect_white` by a traversal, following pointers, it could equally be done by sweeping the entire heap linearly. If the sub-graph of white cells is sufficiently large, a sweep may be faster than a recursive trace.

An example

Since the operations New and Update are largely the same as in the standard reference counting algorithm we will only demonstrate how the deletion of a pointer causing the isolation of a cycle — precisely the situation in which standard reference counting fails — leads to collection of the cycle ABC.

Suppose the pointer from root to A is deleted in Diagram 3.8 on page 67. Since A is shared, it will be painted purple and placed in the control set (not shown). Suppose further that after further allocations it becomes necessary to invoke the garbage collector. Mark_grey is called at the purple A to remove the effect of internal pointers from the graph ABCDE (see Diagram 3.9 on page 67). Notice that if a pointer to A had been copied, or one of its fields overwritten, even with a non-pointer, A would have been blackened and so `gc_control_set` would simply pop it from the control set and try the next entry.

Now scan is called starting at A to check whether components of the transitive closure of

```
scan(S) =
    if colour(S) == grey
        if RC(S) > 0                          —external references
            scan_black(S)
        else
            colour(S) = white
            for T in Children(S)
                scan(*T)
```

Algorithm 3.18   The second phase of Lins's algorithm.

```
scan_black(S) =
    colour(S) = black
    for T in Children(S)
        RC(*T) = RC(*T) + 1
        if colour(*T) ≠ black
            scan_black(*T)
```

Algorithm 3.19   scan_black restores reference counts decremented by scan_grey.

A are completely isolated from root. An external reference is found at D — RC(D) is one — provoking a call to scan_black. The graph before scan_black is shown in Diagram 3.10. Notice how the reference count of E is wrong. It is restored by scan_black which also corrects the colours of D and E (see Diagram 3.11 on page 68). Collect_white is now called from A and the whole cycle ABC is collected. The sub-graph below D was transitively connected to root through a path that did not involve the deleted pointer and thus will be preserved with correct reference counts.

Control set strategies

Lins's algorithm is lazy in the sense that the mark-sweep garbage collection is performed on demand. Different strategies can be easily incorporated to manage the control set. The simplest would be to run the collector only when the free-list is empty or when the control structure is full. Alternatively, the queue could be scanned after every so many allocations; when the size of the free-list drops below a certain size; or whenever some heuristic indicates that the heap may be excessively fragmented. The set can be treated as a LIFO stack or as a FIFO queue, implemented as a heap-allocated list, a bitmap or as a fixed size array; either the whole set or only a part of it can be processed each time. Effects of different management strategies (for a trivial program) are shown in [Lins and Vasques, 1991]. They found that, for a large enough control set, scan_black never ran. The garbage collector only dealt with garbage cycles so no unnecessary calls to the garbage collector were made.

Like generational garbage collection, Lins's method works best when side-effects are comparatively rare, for example for programs written in a functional style. Its success also rests on the assumptions that the great majority of nodes are uniquely referenced and can be reclaimed without resort to garbage collection; and that the sub-graphs traversed are sufficiently small to make the garbage collection delay small. The drawback is that Lins

```
collect_white(S) =
    if colour(S) == white
        colour(S) = black
        for T in Children(S)
            collect_white(*T)
        free(S)
```

Algorithm 3.20   collect_white sweeps white cells into the free-list.

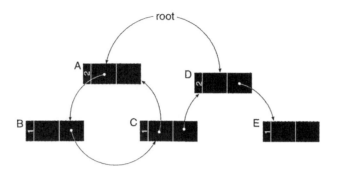

Diagram 3.8 Initially, all cells are black.

traces garbage whereas standard mark-sweep algorithms trace only active cells. Unfortunately, implementations of functional programming languages generate copious amounts of garbage: collection rates of over 80 percent of the heap are common. No thorough comparisons of cyclic reference counting against other methods have been carried out.

Christopher's algorithm revisited

Although Christopher's algorithm can be thought of as a special case of Lins's algorithm, in which the entire heap is the control set, it is nevertheless interesting in its own right. First of all, it was designed to provide automatic memory management without any support from the compiler. Secondly, since the status of entire heap is in question, Christopher uses three linear sweeps of the heap rather than three traces of the transitive closure of each deleted pointer. Linear sweeping is cheaper than tracing graph; it also has a more predictable and hence better virtual memory performance than tracing. The reduced cost of sweeping compared

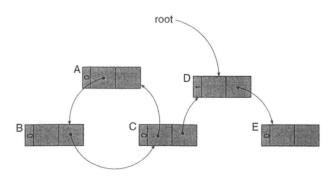

Diagram 3.9 The graph after `mark_grey`.

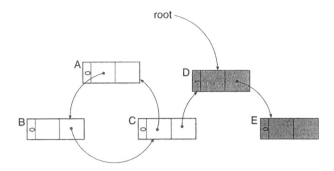

Diagram 3.10   The graph just before `scan_black` is called.

with scanning may outweigh the cost of sweeping the heap four times, depending on the data structures in question. Christopher's algorithm is also interesting in that it uses no extra space: although the count-restoration pass is recursive, the resumption stack is threaded through the objects' reference count fields.

The algorithm operates in three phases, like Lins's. Before a mark-sweep, all references due to pointers internal to the heap are deducted in a linear sweep through the heap, equivalent to Lins's `mark_grey` traversal (shown on page 65), so that only objects directly pointed at from outside the heap have non-zero reference counts. These cells and their descendants are marked in the second pass akin to Lins's `scan` (shown on page 65) by having a special value written into their reference count field. The heap is then rescanned and any object whose reference count is zero is placed on the free-list while any marked objects have their reference counts restored.

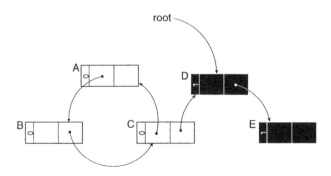

Diagram 3.11   The graph before `collect_white` sweeps white cells into the free-list.

3.6   Issues to consider

At the beginning of this chapter, we noted four deficiencies of reference counting: the delay to free garbage pointer structures recursively, the high overhead imposed on mutator operations on pointers, the space required for the reference counts, and the inability to reclaim garbage cycles. Given these shortcomings, and especially the second, why might one choose to use reference counting rather than a tracing garbage collector?

Many programmers eschew garbage collection, by which they usually mean tracing garbage collection, on the grounds that it is prohibitively expensive. Although reference counting does not need to trace data structures in the heap to determine which objects are live and which are not, in principle at least it does require that adjustments be made to cell reference counts whenever pointers to heap objects are copied, assigned to or deleted. The total execution time overhead of reference counting is generally accepted to be greater than that of tracing techniques, although compile-time optimisations may reduce this deficit. Nevertheless, these same programmers often choose to use reference counting as a storage management method of last resort for problems that are too complex to solve by explicit deallocation. Apart from lack of awareness of modern garbage collection technology, there may be four reasons for this apparently perverse choice.

Ease of implementation

In the first place, reference counters often appear to be easier to implement than tracing collectors. For example, assignments to pointers can be replaced by macros which also adjust reference counts; in object-oriented languages 'smart pointers' can be used (see Chapter 10). The ease of implementation is especially true if the programmer cannot determine all the roots of the computation — maybe the code is part of a library to be used in environments over which the programmer has no control, or maybe the programming language does not provide automatic storage management.

Control, optimisation and correctness

A second attraction of reference counting is that it can provide programmers with total control. The cost of reference counting operations need only be paid for those objects for which manual deallocation is believed to unreliable or impossible. Furthermore, reference counts can be optimised away where it is believed to be safe to do so. However, one price to be paid for easy implementation is the difficulty of guaranteeing correctness of code that uses reference counting. If a count is not incremented when it should be, storage may be freed prematurely; if it is not decremented at the right time, a space leak will occur. Not only does the close coupling of reference counting operations with 'useful' code make development more error-prone, it also make maintenance of reference counted code more difficult. Unorthodox type systems may offer reliable, but still efficient, methods of optimising reference counting.

Garbage collection delay

The third attraction of reference count is that its operations are interleaved with those of the mutator. The overheads of reference counting are distributed throughout the computation. However, the choice between techniques is not this simple. Chapters 7 and 8 describe how generational and incremental garbage collection techniques can be used to bound the length of these delays. Reference counters can also reclaim storage as soon as it becomes garbage. Immediate reuse of space offers possibilities of optimisation such as in-place update, and simplified finalisation for object-oriented languages.

Space overhead

Space for a reference count is required in each heap object's header. The relative space advantages of reference counting and mark-sweep are application dependent. In the case of a Lisp *cons* cell, a pointer-sized count would impose a 50 percent space overhead; for larger objects, the overhead would be less. This cost should be weighed in the light of reference counting's ability to operate successfully in confined heaps. On the other hand, under mark-sweep garbage collection, the interval between collections depends on the amount of space recovered. If the residency of the program is a substantial proportion of the heap, a mark-sweep collector will thrash. Mark-sweep therefore requires some headroom in the heap to operate efficiently. In practice, a reasonable overhead might be at least 20 percent for moderately large heaps. Copying collectors require double the address space of mark-sweep collectors.

We conclude by summarising the properties of the algorithms presented in this chapter. In particular, we identify the assumptions upon which they depend and the consequences of their use.

Recursive freeing

Weizenbaum's algorithm (page 44) removed the delay caused by the recursive freeing of garbage cells. Since it simply moved the responsibility for scanning garbage cells for pointers from delete to New, it is as efficient as the standard algorithm. Now delay is only incurred by New and is dependent on the size of the object at the head of the free-list. The disadvantage of Weizenbaum's method is that one of reference counting's advantages — the possibility of immediate reuse of space — is lost.

Mutator overhead

The overhead of reference counting on mutator operations can be greatly reduced by Deferred Reference Counting. No reference count manipulations are performed on the local or temporary variables. However, there are three costs to be paid. First, Deferred Reference Counting trades time for space: room must be found for the ZCT table. Secondly, although the cost to stack- and register-allocated variables is diminished, the cost of updating other global variable is increased. Finally, garbage once again is no longer detected immediately it becomes unreachable.

Space for reference counts

We noted above that the space overhead of reference counting is less than 50 percent if pointer-sized reference count fields are used. In practice, smaller fields could be used by most applications without overflow. Limiting the size of reference count fields to a few bits saves space and postpones garbage collection but the need to check for overflow increases the cost of copying and deleting pointers. Once counts are stuck, they can either be ignored (a space leak) or a backup tracing collector must be used to reset them. In this case, time has been traded for space: the assumption is that side-effects should be rare. Again, the property of immediate detection of garbage is lost.

Locality of reference

A particularly attractive option is to use one-bit reference counts placed in the pointer to a heap cell rather than in the heap cell itself. One-bit reference counts reduce the overhead as no overflow test is necessary and no arithmetic is performed on counts. Storing the uniqueness bit in pointers requires an extra instruction to test uniqueness but avoids the memory fetch which may more than offset the cost of the extra instruction. The drawback of one-bit counts is that they may easily become stuck, and can only be corrected by a collector. The assumption on which one-bit reference counting rests is that sharing is rare.

If a tracing garbage collector has to be used to restore stuck reference counts, why not just use the tracing collector? There seem to be two reasons. It is likely in any case that a tracing collector must be invoked periodically to collect garbage cycles. On the assumption that the delay imposed by the tracing collector is disruptive to the user of the program, it should be invoked as little as possible. Using limited-field reference counts as the primary reclamation mechanism can reduce the frequency with which it is necessary to call the collector.

Cyclic data structures

The most difficult problem faced by reference counting systems is how to reclaim cyclic garbage. One solution is to require the programmer to break pointer cycles explicitly when objects become garbage, but this begs the question of how garbage is to be identified and which pointer is to be deleted. The second solution was suggested above: to invoke a backup tracing collector periodically to reclaim garbage cycles. However, other solutions have been proposed to recover cyclic garbage without having to meet all the requirements demanded by tracing collectors (such as locating all roots). None of these have been implemented in any significant systems to the knowledge of the authors. If cycles can only be created in predictable circumstances [Friedman and Wise, 1979], or restrictions are placed on programming style [Bobrow, 1980; Hughes, 1987], it may be possible to treat the cycle as a whole, i.e. with a single reference count, and delete it atomically when the count drops to zero.

Alternatively, the presence or otherwise of pointers to cycles from live data can be detected either by scanning the heap [Christopher, 1984] or by traversing the sub-graph headed by nodes suspected to be garbage [Lins, 1992a]. In both cases, trial decrements are made to the reference counts of the descendants of cells encountered. Since both methods trace parts of the heap, neither can detect garbage immediately it becomes unreachable. Note that Lins's algorithm traces shared garbage rather than live data as the standard mark-sweep collector does (see page 26). Lins's algorithm therefore depends on sharing being comparatively rare, and there being few side-effects since Update is more expensive than the standard version.

3.7 Notes

Reference counting was originally developed for Lisp by George Collins [Collins, 1960]. Although generally recognised to be less efficient in terms of overall execution time than techniques based on mark-sweep or copying, it has nevertheless been used as the primary method of memory management by many systems which could not tolerate garbage collection delays, such as Smalltalk, Modula-2+ and SISAL, as well as by awk and perl (see, for example, [Goldberg and Robson, 1983; Rovner, 1985; Cann and Oldehoeft, 1988; DeTreville, 1990a]).

The first suggestion for dealing with pauses due to recursive freeing was by J. Weizenbaum [Weizenbaum, 1963]. Hugh Glaser and P. Thompson extended Weizenbaum's idea by using a *To Be Decremented* stack [Glaser and Thompson, 1987]. The TBD stack stores references to all cells that were a target of a delete instruction, rather than just those that are no longer accessible to the mutator. All decrements are left to be done by New. One advantage of this method is that all the reference count decrements for a given cell can be done at once. Glaser and Thompson suggest that the TBD stack might be implemented by a separate garbage collecting coprocessor.

One of the major drawbacks of reference counting is the overhead that updates place on the user program. These can be significantly reduced by Peter Deutsch's and Daniel Bobrow's deferred reference counting technique [Deutsch and Bobrow, 1976]. The Deutsch and Bobrow algorithm was originally designed to save space as well as the transaction time overhead by not storing reference counts in nodes and by deferring reference counting to a convenient time. All transactions were stored in sequential files and three hash tables were used. The ZCT contained cells with zero reference count, the MRT those with reference counts greater than one, and the VRT recorded those variables holding pointers into the heap. The heap is then partitioned into those cells with reference counts greater than one (MRT), those cells with reference counts equal to one (not in MRT or ZCT), live cells with reference counts equal to zero (ZCT∩VRT), and dead cells (ZCT–VRT). Object creation, pointer duplication and deletion operations manipulate these tables and periodically the VRT is recalculated and the ZCT and VRT scanned to free objects.

It may be possible to reduce the run-time cost of reference counting by compile-time optimisation. If the compiler can determine when a cell is no longer needed, it can emit instructions to reclaim the cell and thus avoid reference count manipulations or garbage collections. Reference counting within the compiler is a natural way to do this; the interested reader is referred to [Hudak, 1986; Brus *et al.*, 1987; Cann and Oldehoeft, 1988; Hederman, 1988; Baker, 1994].

Several authors have taken limited size reference counts to their logical conclusion by using just a single bit. One-bit reference counting concentrates reclamation efforts on the unshared objects that typically make up the majority of the heap [Wise and Friedman, 1977; Wise,

1993]. Will Stoye, T.J.W. Clarke and Arthur Norman showed how putting the reference count bits in pointers rather than cells could also reduce memory fetch costs [Stoye *et al.*, 1984]. A similar approach is taken by Weighted Reference Counting algorithms for distributed garbage collection where is it important to reduce communication [Bevan, 1987; Watson and Watson, 1987]. Parallel implementations of logic languages have also re-awakened interest in one-bit reference counting, for example [Chikayama and Kimura, 1987].

Several special purpose architectures have used hardware to assist memory management [Baker, 1978; Moon, 1984; Lieberman and Hewitt, 1983; Explorer, 1987, 1987; Johnson, 1991a; Johnson, 1991b]. Other researchers, notably Kelvin Nilsen and David Wise, argue that active memory units should provide garbage collection, thereby relieving the processor of this burden almost completely [Nilsen and Schmidt, 1994; Nilsen, 1994b]. Active memory units that use reference counting as the primary memory management mechanism and non-recursive mark-sweep for collecting cycles have been designed and built by Wise and his colleagues [Wise, 1985; Wise *et al.*, 1994].

The second major challenge to reference counting is the problem of reclaiming cycles, first pointed out by Harold McBeth [McBeth, 1963], although the frequency of cycles is language dependent [Hartel, 1988]. The most common, and probably the most efficient, solution to this problem is to use a hybrid reference counting and garbage collecting memory manager [Weizenbaum, 1969], if the consequent pause is acceptable. Several researchers have tackled the problem of managing cycles without global garbage collection, either in a language-dependent context or more generally. Daniel Friedman and David Wise, and John Hughes noted that cycles only occur in particular ways in pure functional languages [Friedman and Wise, 1979; Hughes, 1987]. Friedman and Wise observed that reference counting would be viable in the presence of cycles if those cycles were created and destroyed as a single unit. Daniel Bobrow suggested that all nodes should be assigned to groups by the programmer and that these groups rather than individual nodes should be reference counted [Bobrow, 1980]. In this way intra- but not inter-group cycles could be reclaimed. Hughes noted that this would be most effective if Bobrow's groups were precisely the strongly connected components (SCCs) of the graph. Maintaining this partition would be generally computationally infeasible but it might be appropriate for graph reducers.

David Brownbridge and others investigated the possibility of distinguishing cycle-closing pointers from other pointers [Brownbridge, 1985]. Jon Salkild found an error in Brownbridge's algorithm but his correction introduced termination problems [Salkild, 1987]. Independent work by Betsy Pepels, M.C.J.D. van Eekelen, and M.J. Plasmeijer [Pepels *et al.*, 1988], and by Simon Thompson and Rafael Lins [Thompson and Lins, 1988], arrived at similar algorithms which restored termination. Pepels and her colleagues also provided a proof of the correctness of their algorithm. Unfortunately these corrected algorithms are prohibitively inefficient in the general case. Tom Axford has also used a strong/weak pointer scheme to reclaim cycles in functional languages [Axford, 1990]. His method requires that each strongly connected component of the graph is reachable through exactly one external pointer. No formal proof of correctness is given.

Rather than excluding the contribution of cycle-closing pointers throughout the computation, Thomas Christopher and others sought to count the contribution of these pointers dynamically [Christopher, 1984]. Christopher's algorithm was designed to provide dynamic memory management for languages such as Fortran which do not provide such facilities. Because cyclic reference counting uses only information stored in the nodes of the graph, his algorithm can be used in 'hostile' environments where lack of root information prevents more efficient methods of managing the heap (but see [Boehm and Weiser, 1988]).

Christopher's algorithm has been rediscovered several times [Martinez *et al.*, 1990; Kennedy, 1991; Vestal, 1987]. The Martinez *et al.* algorithm was very inefficient: the collector was called every time a pointer was deleted. Its efficiency was improved by making the collection lazy: deleted references were pushed onto a control stack [Lins, 1992a]. Some limited measurements of the efficacy of his lazy algorithm are presented in [Lins and Vasques, 1991].

Although reference counting is no longer the algorithm of choice for sequential implementations, it has continued to arouse the interest of researchers working with parallel systems since reference counting does not require synchronisation between user program and garbage collection threads. Parallelism may require locks on each object's reference count, but locking facilities are usually already present (at a cost). Experience of multi-threaded systems has shown that garbage collection is extremely difficult to get right (see for instance [Dijkstra *et al.*, 1978] for an explanation of the subtleties involved). The best known parallel reference counting system is probably John DeTreville's collector for Modula-2+ [DeTreville, 1990a]. Other reference counting architectures have been proposed by [Amamiya *et al.*, 1983; Goto *et al.*, 1988; Lins, 1992b]. The Kakuta, Nakamura and Iida architecture for parallel reference counting includes a scheme for cyclic reference counting although it is unable to guarantee to treat cyclic structures properly [Kakuta *et al.*, 1986].

Reference counting is even more attractive for distributed systems since its communications are local to the objects involved in an update [Vestal, 1987; Eckart and Leblanc, 1987; Ichisuki and Yonezawa, 1990; Mancini and Shrivastava, 1991; Lester, 1992; Plainfossé and Shapiro, 1992; Birrell *et al.*, 1993]. One problem for distributed reference counting is that of ensuring that count manipulation messages arrive at their destination in the right order. If a decrement message overtakes an increment one, a node might be prematurely reclaimed. C-W. Lermen and Dieter Maurer solved this by a protocol of messages and acknowledgements [Lermen and Maurer, 1986], but more elegant techniques have since been developed, or used, to reduce the need for communication substantially [Bevan, 1987; Watson and Watson, 1987; Corporaal *et al.*, 1990; Glaser *et al.*, 1989; Foster, 1989; Goldberg, 1989; Piquer, 1991]. The question of reclaiming cycles that span processors has been addressed by [Gupta and Fuchs, 1988; Shapiro *et al.*, 1990; Lins and Jones, 1993; Jones and Lins, 1992; Lang *et al.*, 1992].

4

Mark-Sweep Garbage Collection

In Chapter 2 we considered simple recursive algorithms for reference counting, mark-sweep and copying garbage collection. In Chapter 3, we saw how some of the deficiencies of reference counting could be removed or at least ameliorated. In this chapter and Chapter 6, we examine more efficient algorithms for the two styles of tracing garbage collector and compare their relative merits.

4.1 Comparisons with reference counting

Mark-sweep garbage collection has several advantages over reference counting. For many applications, the most important of these is that no special action needs to be taken to reclaim cyclic data structures. Although techniques exist for handling cycles in a reference counting framework (see Section 3.5 of Chapter 3), these are either restricted to special cases (implementations of pure functional programming languages), rely on programmer declarations or programming idioms, or are likely to increase the cost of pointer deletion enormously. As far as we are aware, no empirical comparisons of cyclic reference counting techniques with other methods of garbage collection have been published. On the other hand, several systems that use reference counting as the primary method of storage management also use backup mark-sweep garbage collectors to reclaim cyclic data structures (e.g. Modula-2+ [DeTreville, 1990a]).

Reference counting is used primarily because it recycles memory instantly and incrementally, or because it is simple to implement and easy for programmers to control. Each object can be reclaimed as soon as the last pointer to it is deleted and user programs are not delayed significantly. Tracing collectors such as copying or mark-sweep collectors must interrupt the client program while active data structures are marked. Either the survivors will be copied to a fresh region of memory or garbage cells will be swept onto the free-list. The price paid for non-disruptive reference counting is a considerable overhead on pointer update operations. Although this overhead can be diminished substantially by more sophisticated techniques, such as deferred reference counting [Deutsch and Bobrow, 1976] (see Section 3.2 of Chapter 3), unused memory is no longer recycled immediately and small pauses may be engendered. In contrast, non-incremental, non-generational tracing collectors place no overhead on pointer operations.

The interface between the user program and a non-incremental tracing garbage collector is much simpler than that of a reference counting system. Under the latter, great care must be taken to ensure that reference count invariants are maintained. The simplicity of the interface between a tracing collector and its client program makes tracing collectors easier to maintain, and ensures that less time is spent tracing memory management errors in user programs.

Space overhead comparisons are more complex. Reference counts must be stored in each node in the managed heap. If pointer-sized counts are used, no overflow checks are necessary but the size of pair nodes (such as Lisp's prevalent *cons* node) is increased by 50 percent. Limited-size reference count fields can be used if a tracing collector is used to reclaim objects whose reference counts have 'stuck'. Mark-sweep garbage collection, by contrast, appears to require only one extra bit per node. However, this storage cost is implementation dependent. Unless a spare bit can be found for the mark-bit, a whole byte or word must be reserved for it in the node's header. The per-node space overhead of mark-sweep garbage collection may therefore be no better than that of reference counting.

If the heap residency is too large, garbage collection will become so frequent that it takes up a disproportionate part of the program's total execution time. Consequently, garbage collectors require sufficient spare headroom in the heap if they are not to thrash. For moderately large heaps, this overhead is likely to be between 20 and 50 percent. In contrast, reference counters (possibly supported by mark-sweep garbage collection) can operate in tightly constrained heaps.

Garbage collection could be made arbitrarily infrequent by increasing the size of the heap. However this is no solution. Making the heap much larger than physical memory may dilute the program's working set, dispersing currently used objects across pages of the heap and those pages across main memory and disk. The number of pages touched by the garbage collector will certainly increase, enlarging the number of page faults per collection cycle, to the extent that overall performance will be reduced rather than enhanced. The number of pages touched by the user program may also increase. We consider this issue further in Chapter 6 where we discuss copying garbage collection in more detail.

In this chapter, we consider three problems faced by mark-sweep collection. First, marking is a recursive[1] process, whether a stack is used explicitly or not. We examine how to reduce the chance of stack overflow, how to recover if that should happen, and how to mark graphs in constant space. Finally we look at techniques for reducing the cost of the sweep phase, and for improving the virtual memory behaviour of both phases.

---

[1] By recursive, we mean that its space requirements are unbounded whereas an *iterative* process uses a fixed amount of memory.

4.2   Using a marking stack

Making the recursion explicit

In Chapter 2 we described the marking procedure using recursive calls to `mark` to memorise branch-points of the data structure (see the simple mark procedure shown on page 26). These nodes could then be revisited, and the marking process restarted from each of their children. Recursive procedure call is not a practical method of marking data structures. It is neither time- nor space-efficient, and may cause the system stack to overflow. In general, whenever a sub-routine is entered, working space has to be reserved for it on the machine stack. When the sub-routine returns, this space must be discarded. Procedure call overheads cost time as well as space. The time-cost on some architectures can be high (the DEC VAX was a notorious example). Modern RISC architectures and compilers are designed to support high-level languages, and provide more efficient procedure call mechanisms, thereby reducing these costs substantially. Nevertheless, there is still a price to pay for using recursion[2].

A standard method for improving the performance of recursively described algorithms is to replace recursive calls by iterative loops and auxiliary data structures. For marking, an auxiliary stack can be used to hold pointers to nodes that are known to be live but have not yet been visited. This stack's behaviour tracks the behaviour of the system stack that executed the recursive mark program. Initially it holds just the root node (which is marked). `Mark` repeatedly pops nodes from the auxiliary stack (see Algorithm 4.1 on the following page). At each step, any unmarked children are marked, and pushed onto the stack if they in turn contain pointers. Objects that cannot contain pointers need only to be marked. The marking phase terminates when the stack is empty (for the moment, we ignore the problem of stack overflow).

This algorithm makes the space cost as well as the time cost of the marking phase explicit. The maximum depth of the marking stack depends on the size of the longest path that has to be traced through the graph. Although in the worst case this might be equal to the number of nodes in the heap, real applications (rather than contrived examples) tend to produce stacks that are comparatively shallow as a proportion of the entire heap [Standish, 1980]. Nevertheless a safe garbage collector must be able to handle abnormal situations.

Minimising the depth of the stack

A second benefit of making the recursion stack explicit is that it can be managed more easily. The first goal of a stack management policy must be to reduce the risk of the stack overflowing. If, despite precautions, it does overflow, the algorithm must be able to recover and complete the marking task. In this section we examine strategies for reducing the depth of the stack. We shall then look at methods for recovering from stack overflow. Finally we consider methods of marking in constant space, without using additional space for a mark stack.

Algorithm 4.1 on the next page marks each active node and then pushes it onto the stack if

---

[2] For example, the Glasgow Haskell compiler generates GNU C code which is then compiled to SPARC assembler [Peyton Jones, 1992]. Removing function prologues and epilogues saves about 20 percent of execution time (the size of function code sequences is typically small).

```
gc() =
    mark_heap()
    sweep()

mark_heap() =
    mark_stack = empty
    for R in Roots
        mark_bit(R) = marked
        push(R, mark_stack)
        mark()

mark() =
    while mark_stack ≠ empty
        N = pop(mark_stack)
        for M in Children(N)
            if mark_bit(*M) == unmarked
                mark_bit(*M) = marked
                if not atom(*M)
                    push(*M, mark_stack)
```

Algorithm 4.1   Marking with a resumption stack.

it was not an atom. An alternative coding might mark nodes when they are popped from the stack; in this case mark_heap would not set mark bits.

```
mark() =
    while mark_stack ≠ empty
        N = pop(mark_stack)
        if mark_bit(N) == unmarked
            mark_bit(N) = marked
            for M in Children(N)
                push(*M, mark_stack)
```

Algorithm 4.2   Alternative marking algorithm.

Do these two implementations differ? The answer is yes. The method of Algorithm 4.1 traverses each *node*, stacking branch points exactly once, whereas the alternative Algorithm 4.2 traverses each *arc* of the graph once. The number of arcs in a tree is one less than its number of nodes, but general directed graphs usually contain more arcs than nodes. Hence greater stack depths can be expected from Algorithm 4.2 than from Algorithm 4.1.

An obvious deficiency of either algorithm is that they push the last unmarked child of a node onto the stack only to pop it immediately. This can easily be avoided by following one child, having pushed the others. The branch-choosing strategy that will minimise the depth of the stack produced depends on the nature of the problem. However, empirical studies help here. Lisp lists are comprised of *cons* nodes or *nil*. Each *cons* node contains two pointer fields, the *car* which points to the head of the list and the *cdr* which points to the rest of the list. Thus the list of the three natural numbers, (1 2 3), might be represented by the structure shown in Diagram 4.1 on the next page.

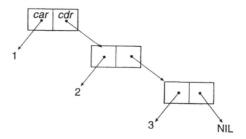

Diagram 4.1   The list (1 2 3).

Clark and Green found that, for Lisp implementations, *cdr*-fields were more than twice as likely to point to non-atomic objects as were *car*-fields [Clark and Green, 1977]. Thus shallower stacks are more likely to be obtained by stacking pointers to unmarked *cdr* nodes and following unmarked *car* pointers, rather than vice-versa.

Algorithm 4.1 on the facing page analyses the mark-bits of the children of the current node before pushing the children onto the stack. Its effectiveness depends on the likelihood of discovering nodes that are marked. The frequency of shared objects in the heap is implementation- and problem-dependent. If the structure being marked is a tree, each node will have exactly one parent, and hence no marked nodes will be discovered: the analysis will produce no benefit. On the other hand, the structure might contain shared nodes if it is a general graph or has a several roots (for example, local variables on the machine stack). Such analysis can be extended arbitrarily far, for example to grandchildren as well as children, and Kurokawa has suggested that such analysis might reduce maximum stack depth by 50 percent in a Lisp implementation [Kurokawa, 1981]. However, it is more than likely that the costs of this more complex analysis will outweigh any potential gains.

A graph may contain very large nodes. If these do not contain pointers (for example, bitmaps representing cached windows), they will not need to be stacked. But if a node is a large structure of pointers (an array, for instance), then pushing all its children is likely to cause the stack to overflow. The Boehm–Demers–Weiser mark-sweeping conservative garbage collector for C and C++ (see Chapter 9 where we discuss conservative garbage collectors) handles large objects by pushing their constituent pointers onto the stack in small groups in order to reduce the chance of overflow [Boehm and Weiser, 1988]. Their marking stack holds pairs of pointers, pointing to the start and end of each object pushed onto the stack (see Diagram 4.2 on the next page). At each iteration of the main marking loop, the object on the top of the stack is examined. If the difference between its start and its end is small (less than 128 words), it is popped from the stack and its children marked in the usual way. If the object is large, only the components of the first 128-word portion of the object are marked, and the stack entry is adjusted to point to the rest of the object.

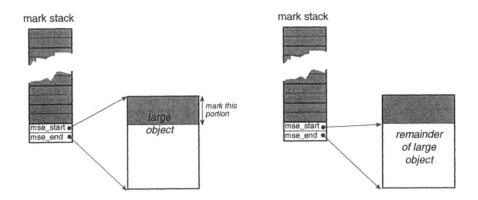

Diagram 4.2   The Boehm–Demers–Weiser collector marks large objects in portions to reduce the risk of stack overflow.

Stack overflow

The predicament of marking is that garbage collection is needed precisely because of lack of memory available to the useful part of the computation, but auxiliary stacks require additional space. Large or pathological problems may cause the garbage collector itself to run out of space. A benefit of an explicit marking stack is that overflow can be detected easily and recovery action taken. Overflow can be detected in two ways. The simpler is to use an in-line check in each push operation. A slightly more efficient method is to perform a single check by counting the number of pointers contained in the node popped from the stack at each iteration of the marking loop (this type-information may already be necessary for pushing pointers). If operating system support is available, an alternative method that requires no stack checks is to use a *guard page* [Appel and Li, 1991]. The last page of the stack region is set to be write-protected so that a memory protection fault will be triggered if mark attempts to push a stack entry onto this page. The exception can be trapped by the garbage collector and appropriate action taken.

The benefits of this approach depend on the likelihood of stack overflow and the cost of handling exceptions. The software test is likely to cost an ALU instruction and a branch for each node pushed onto the stack. Trapping a memory protection violation is expensive. The precise cost is highly machine and operating-system dependent, but Zorn found that the time to trap a write protection fault for systems based on RISC processors varied between 0.3 milliseconds for a MIPS-based DECStation 3100 to 1.8 milliseconds for a SPARC-based Solbourne Series 4 [Zorn, 1990a]. These are equivalent to tens of thousands of software overflow tests. Which method is more effective will depend on how many nodes are expected to pushed onto the stack before it overflows. This in turn depends on the size of the region allocated to the mark stack and the shape of the structures being marked. However, this approach has pitfalls which we examine on page 125 of Chapter 6.

Knuth handles overflow by treating the marking stack circularly, stacking pointers to nodes modulo h, where h is the fixed size of the stack [Knuth, 1973, Algorithm C, page 415]. This means that older branch-point information on the stack is overwritten when the stack index grows larger than h. Consequently, the stack may become empty before the marking process is complete as the live graph below a node whose pointer on the mark stack has been overwritten may not have been marked.

Knuth's solution to this problem is to scan the heap when the stack becomes empty, looking for marked nodes whose contents point to unmarked nodes. Marking is resumed from the children of these nodes in the same manner as before, until the stack is emptied once more. Eventually the heap inspection will reveal that there are no such nodes — marking is then complete. The scan need not always start from the bottom of the heap. If the forgotten node with the lowest address is remembered, the next inspection can start from either this location or just after the last address discovered by the previous inspection, whichever is the lower.

The last scan of the heap is unnecessary if the collector simply notes whether overflow has occurred or not. The Boehm–Demers–Weiser collector does exactly this [Boehm and Weiser, 1988]. While the stack is full, new entries are simply dropped. When the stack becomes completely empty but the collector knows that it had overflowed, the old stack is replaced by a new one of twice the size in order to reduce the likelihood of further overflow. The collector then searches the heap for marked objects with unmarked children, and marking continues from each of these children.

The difference between the Knuth and the Boehm–Demers–Weiser marking algorithms is that Knuth treats the stack circularly, whereas Boehm *et al.* stop pushing nodes onto a full stack. It is not clear what the effect of these different strategies will be, although one may speculate that Boehm's stack may have better cache behaviour.

Sharing of heap nodes may mean that some nodes on the mark stack may have children, all of which are marked. There is no point in keeping such branch-points in the stack — they play no useful rôle. Kurokawa suggested handling stack overflow by removing such unnecessary items from the stack [Kurokawa, 1981]. On overflow, his *Stacked Node Checking* algorithm removes nodes from the stack that have fewer than two unmarked children. If none of the node's children are unmarked, that stack slot is deemed to be empty and is squeezed out by sliding up the next useful entry. If exactly one child is unmarked, it is marked and a search for a descendent with two or more unmarked children is commenced from that point, marking each node it passes through. The stack slot is then overwritten with a pointer to that descendent, should it exist. If it does not, the stack slot is marked as empty. At the end of this process, every slot in the stack will contain a root of two or more unmarked sub-graphs. Kurokawa claims that his method is effective in practice and that the stack clearing process is cheap, as the work done by its searches must be done in any case. Against this, the algorithm is clearly not robust as it is quite possible that no additional space will be found on the stack. Its success depends on finding sufficiently many nodes that have been marked already, i.e. shared nodes, to make the cost of squeezing the stack worthwhile. However, empirical studies suggest that very few nodes are shared (at least in Lisp and functional languages [Clark and Green, 1977; Stoye *et al.*, 1984; Hartel, 1988]). If it is to be used, Kurokawa's algorithm must be supported by a safe, last-resort algorithm.

4.3   Pointer reversal

So far we have seen techniques for reducing the risk of stack overflow and algorithms for recovering from such overflow. It turns out that it is also possible to mark arbitrary graphs in linear time without using an unbounded amount of additional space. We now turn to a class of algorithms developed independently by Schorr and Waite [Schorr and Waite, 1967], and by Deutsch [Knuth, 1973, Exercise 2.3.5.8].

Any efficient marking process must record the branch-points that it has passed through. If an algorithm is to operate in constant space, this list can only be kept in the nodes of the data structure being traced. One solution, which we immediately reject as wasteful of space, is to use an additional field in each node to store a back-pointer to the previously marked node. The only alternative is to store such back-pointers in a pointer field visible to the user program.

The key to these constant space marking algorithms is the notion of *pointer-reversal*. As the marking process traverses down a sub-graph it 'reverses' the pointers that it follows: the address of the parent node is placed in one of the pointer fields of the node currently being examined. As the trace ascends the graph, the original values of all pointer fields are restored. In effect, these algorithms store the mark stack in heap nodes on the path between the root and the node currently being marked.

We shall first consider the case when all branch-nodes are binary: each non-atomic node contains exactly two pointer fields, which we shall call *left* and *right*. Later we shall extend the algorithm to cover variable-sized nodes.

The Deutsch–Schorr–Waite technique overwrites the *left* and then the *right* fields of each node visited with a back-pointer to the parent node. At the first visit, the node is marked and the *left* field is replaced with the address of the parent. The trace continues from the old value of the *left* field. At the second visit, the parent's address is moved to the *right* field and the original value of the *left* field is restored. The trace continues from the old value of the *right* field. At the third and final visit, the original value of the *right* field is restored and the process retreats to the parent node, whose address was stored in that field.

The algorithm can be concisely described by a finite state machine (see Diagram 4.3 on the facing page). The machine has three states: it is either advancing down a left sub-graph, switching to the right sub-graph, or retreating. The advance is halted by meeting either a marked node or an atom. The retreat moves back to the first node that has not had all its sub-graphs marked, and switches to advance down the next sub-graph.

At each visit to a node, the marking algorithm must be able to determine which node it should visit next. The algorithm needs to know whether a node is being visited for the first time, or whether it is being revisited after one of its sub-graphs has been marked — and if so which (if any) sub-graph should be marked next.

The node is being visited for the first time if the mark-bit of the node is not set. On the next two occasions, the mark-bit will be set but the algorithm must be able to decide which pointer field to replace, the *left* or the *right*. An additional flag-bit is required in each non-atomic node to indicate whether the parent pointer is stored in the *left* field (the flag is not set) or the *right* field (the flag is set).

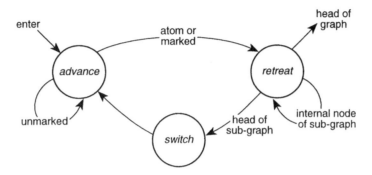

Diagram 4.3   A finite state machine for pointer-reversal marking algorithms.

The Deutsch–Schorr–Waite algorithm

Three variables are used to mark the data structure (see Algorithm 4.3 on the next page): `current` points to the current node, `previous` follows one step behind `current`, and `next` one step ahead. `Current` is initially set to the root of the graph to be marked, and `previous` to `nil`.

The algorithm can be thought of as operating in three phases. In the first stage, `mark` follows `left` pointers, marking nodes as it does so, until it reaches an atom or a marked node. At each step, the `left` field of the current node is overwritten with a pointer to the previous node (see Diagram 4.5 on page 85).

When the first phase cannot continue or discovers a marked node, `mark` sets the flag-bit of the `previous` node and attempts to restart marking from the `right` node. A flag-bit set in a node indicates that the *left* subgraph rooted at the node has been marked, and that the parent pointer has been moved from the node's `left` field to its `right` field. The original value of the `left` field, now held in `current`, is restored (see Diagram 4.6 on page 85).

On the third and final visit to this node (the flag-bit is set), the original value of the `right` field is restored from `current` and the algorithm retreats to the parent node. This address was held in the `right` field. This phase is repeated until an ancestor node is discovered whose flag-bit is not set, i.e. whose *right* subgraph is not yet known to have been marked (see Diagram 4.7 on page 86). The algorithm terminates when `previous` becomes `nil` again.

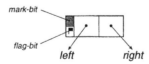

Diagram 4.4   A binary Deutsch–Schorr–Waite node.

```
mark(R) =
    done = false
    current = R
    previous = nil

    while not done
            — follow left pointers
        while current ≠ nil
        and mark_bit(current) == unmarked
            mark_bit(current) = marked
            if not atom(current)
                    next = left(current)
                    left(current) = previous
                    previous = current
                    current = next

            — retreat
        while previous ≠ nil
        and flag_bit(previous) == set
            flag_bit(previous) = unset
            next = right(previous)
            right(previous) = current
            current = previous
            previous = next

        if previous == nil
            done = true
        else
                — switch to right subgraph
            flag_bit(previous) = set
            next = left(previous)
            left(previous) = current
            current = right(previous)
            right(previous) = next
```

Algorithm 4.3   The Deutsch–Schorr–Waite pointer reversal algorithm.

Pointer-reversal for variable-sized nodes

The Deutsch–Schorr–Waite technique can be extended to mark variable-sized nodes: we outline a method due to Thorelli [Thorelli, 1972]. Each node contains a variable number of pointers plus two additional fields used only by the marking algorithm. The n-field holds the number of pointer fields that the node contains (which may be necessary in any case or encoded in the node's type). The i-field is used for marking: it must be large enough to store integers in the range zero to the largest number of pointers contained in any heap object. Initially i is set to zero for all nodes in the heap. A pseudo-root node is set up, with both i and n set to one, pointing to the root node. This node acts as a sentinel to halt the algorithm's retreat.

The algorithm operates in the same way as Deutsch–Schorr–Waite pointer reversal but

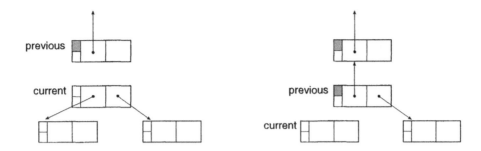

Diagram 4.5 The advance phase.

increments the i-field each time it visits a node. A node is considered marked if the value of its i-field is non-zero. The trace then continues to the ith child of this node. If that child is marked, the algorithm increments i again and proceeds to the next child in the same way. This process continues until all the children of this node have been marked, in which case i is equal to n, at which point the algorithm retreats to the parent node. Eventually, the pseudo-root will be reached and the algorithm terminates.

Appleby *et al.* describe a similar algorithm for marking implementations of Prolog based on the WAM [Appleby *et al.*, 1988; Warren, 1983]. Their heap consists of objects made up of *pointer-cells*, each of which contains a two-bit tag, two one-bit flags used for marking and a single pointer to another pointer-cell. Their scheme has the advantage for Prolog of being able to mark a part rather than the whole of an object, at the cost of using extra space for the two mark-bits associated with each pointer.

Costs of pointer-reversal

The advantage of pointer-reversal algorithms is that they only require constant space in which to operate. On the other hand, each node in the heap carries an overhead. For systems in

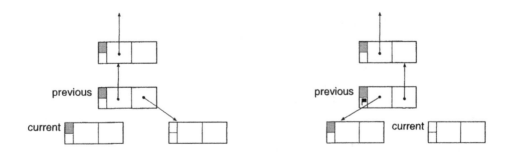

Diagram 4.6 The switch phase.

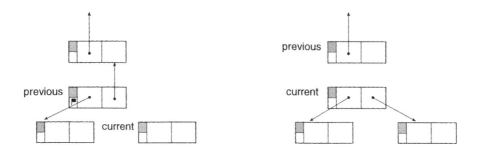

Diagram 4.7   The retreat phase.

which all non-atomic nodes contain exactly two pointers, the cost is one extra bit per node. For systems with variable-sized nodes, the size of the i-field is $\lceil \log_2 n \rceil$ bits per cell, where n is the number of pointers the node holds. It is sometimes possible to smuggle flag-bits into node header fields at no extra cost, but unfortunately not all implementations conveniently leave room. For example Lisp *cons* nodes typically comprise exactly two pointer words.

Wegbreit noted that flag-bits are required only for those nodes on the paths from roots whose tracing has been postponed. He suggested using Deutsch–Schorr–Waite traversal, but storing flag-bits in a stack rather than in the nodes themselves [Wegbreit, 1972b]. This scheme reduces the total amount of storage used in practice but risks stack overflow once more (although it uses a very much smaller stack, say 1/32 the size of the standard pointer stack). In the worst case, Wegbreit's method would use the same number of bits as the standard pointer reversal technique.

Wegbreit's compromise highlights an interesting feature of the Deutsch–Schorr–Waite algorithm. Pointer-reversal does not abolish the marking stack, but simply hides it in heap nodes. Deutsch–Schorr–Waite has long been a popular exemplar for demonstrating novel program proving techniques. The most elegant proof, in our opinion, is due to Veillon [Veillon, 1976]. He uses correctness-preserving transformations to turn the simple recursive marking algorithm into the pointer-reversal Algorithm 4.3 on page 84. His technique makes it apparent that the stack has been moved into heap nodes.

The performance of Deutsch–Schorr–Waite traversal is considerably worse than that of the pointer-stack method (Schorr and Waite suggested that it may be 50 percent slower for shallow structures). Whereas the stack algorithm visits each branch-node at least twice, Deutsch–Schorr–Waite visits each node at least $(n + 1)$ times, where n is the number of pointers the node contains. The extra visits require additional memory fetches, which is particularly undesirable in an environment where objects might lie on swapped-out pages, or might have been evicted from the cache. Furthermore, each visit is more expensive than stack-based marking. Rather than popping a node from the stack and marking and pushing its children, the Deutsch–Schorr–Waite technique must cycle four values (previous, current, next and one of the pointer fields) on each visit as well as reading and writing mark- and flag-bits. A minor optimisation is to reverse pointers by using an exclusive-or operation, $\oplus$, taking advantage of the identity $(A \oplus B) \oplus B \equiv A$ [Siklossy, 1972]. Then pointer-reversal can be accomplished by setting, for example, `left = previous ⊕ left`. The expense of pointer-reversal led Schorr and Waite to suggest that it should be used as a method of last resort, invoked only on pointer-stack overflow. Nevertheless the Deutsch–Schorr–Waite method is used as the only method of marking in several systems, notably the pure functional language Miranda (which also uses it for unwinding its execution stack) [Turner, 1985], and by Wise for hardware garbage collection (which must operate in bounded space) [Wise *et al.*, 1994].

4.4 Bitmap marking

So far we have assumed that mark-bits must be placed in the objects that they mark. Many systems require that objects be tagged with their type, often represented by a small integer in the header of the object. In this case, space for the mark-bit can often be found in the header. But this is not always the case. Other implementations may encode the type in the address of the object (for example, Lisp's Big Bag of Pages (BiBOP) method [Foderaro *et al.*, 1985]) or in pointers to that object (see [Steenkiste, 1987]), or may represent type information by a pointer to an information table shared by all objects of that type (a technique commonly used by graph reducers [Johnsson, 1987; Peyton Jones, 1992; Thomas, 1993]).

For mark-sweep garbage collection, an effective organisation is to store mark-bits in a separate bitmap table rather than wasting space for headers for small objects. A bit in the table is associated with each address in the heap that may contain the start of an object. If the table is implemented as a simple linear array of bits, the fraction of the heap that it occupies will be inversely proportional to the size of the smallest object that can be allocated in the heap. For instance, if the smallest object in a 32-bit word architecture is a binary pointer cell two words long, the size of bitmap would be just over 1.5 percent of that of the heap. The bit corresponding to an object at address p can then be accessed by using the shifted value of p as an offset into the bitmap.

```
mark_bit(p) =
    return bitmap[p>>3]
```

More sophisticated implementations may use separate bitmaps for each different kind of object (see Diagram 4.9 on page 91). In this case, access is typically via a hash table or search tree (for example, [Boehm and Weiser, 1988]). This technique also has the advantage that the heap does not need to be even nearly contiguous, and that not every location in the heap requires a mark-bit (large objects may span several pages).

Mark bitmaps have two major advantages for the virtual memory sub-system other than minimising the amount of memory needed to store mark information. If the bitmap is comparatively small, it can be held in RAM so that reading or writing mark-bits will not incur page faults (all other things being equal). No heap object is written to during the marking phase. The garbage collector will never cause a heap page to be dirtied and hence written back to the swap disk when it is dislodged from the operating system's virtual memory page frame. Page faults will only be incurred by the garbage collector when pointers need to be traced. In particular, atomic objects (and especially large numerical or screen objects) need never be touched by the collector. This is particularly important if atomic objects comprise a significant proportion of the heap. For example, in Cedar atomic objects commonly account for three-quarters of the heap[3]. Use of separate bitmap tables may equally improve the cache performance of the collector since cache lines occupied by heap objects are not dirtied (but see Chapter 11 where we discuss the interaction between the garbage collector and the cache in more detail). Bitmaps can also improve the efficiency of the garbage collector's sweep phase.

The only disadvantage of using a bitmap for marking is that mapping the address of an object in the heap to a mark-bit is more expensive than it would be if the mark were stored in the object, particularly if the bitmap or the heap is not contiguous. For example, Zorn requires approximately twelve instructions to access the bitmap [Zorn, 1989] compared with simply writing to a fixed offset from the start of an object (one instruction). For a collector with little or no paging and good cache behaviour, cheaper access to the bit might be worthwhile.

4.5 Lazy sweeping

Part of the case made against mark-sweep garbage collection is that its cost depends on the size of the heap because the sweep phase must examine the whole heap. In contrast, the cost of a copying collection depends on the size of the surviving data, which be comparatively small. This argument ignores the cost of copying objects. For small nodes, the cost of marking and the cost of copying may be similar, but copying a larger node will certainly cost more than marking it. In Section 2.4 we made such a simple comparison of the efficiencies of mark-sweep and copying collectors. However, the matter is more complex for state-of-the-art mark-sweep collectors. In this section we show that there may be no difference between the asymptotic complexities of mark-sweep and copying collectors.

Analysis must also include consideration of the algorithms' virtual memory and cache behaviour. The sweep phase scans the heap linearly from bottom to top whereas the access pattern of the marking phase is random. The benefit of such predictable access patterns is that fetching one object has the desirable side-effect of also fetching its neighbours (which will be swept next). Thus pre-fetching pages or cache lines (if they are sufficiently large) will be profitable. At the least, the sweep phase is much less likely to effect virtual memory behaviour than the traversal of the active graph.

One of the virtues of using bitmaps for marking is that it reduces the frequency of page faults and cache write misses in the mark phase (providing that the bitmap does not have to be fetched). In the sweep phase live objects do not need to be accessed at all — only their bits in the bitmap must be tested and unset — although garbage nodes may have to be linked into a free-list. If paging would otherwise be likely, this is an important gain since the cost of a single page fault is likely to be several hundred thousand cycles.

There is also evidence that many objects live and die in clusters [Hayes, 1991]. If this is so, the mark-bits of clusters of live objects can be tested and cleared in groups of 32^4 at a cost of approximately three instructions per group. Likewise, empty memory can be returned cheaply to the free-list in chunks.

Simple mark-sweep collectors interrupt the user program while they mark the graph. Although the length of these pauses can be bounded, for instance by performing a fixed

---

[3] Hans Boehm, private communication.

[4] Assuming a 32-bit word.

amount of marking at each allocation, such incremental collectors are complex and place greater overheads on the user program (we discuss incremental collection in Chapter 8). This is because changes made by the client program to the connectivity of the graph may interfere with the collector's marking traversal of the graph: the mutator must inform the collector of these changes.

Hughes's lazy sweep algorithm

The length of non-incremental garbage collection pauses can be reduced if the sweep phase is done in parallel with mutator execution. This is possible because the mutator cannot interfere with the collector's sweep phase since the mark-bits of live nodes are invisible to the user program. Although the collector may modify mutator-fields of garbage nodes to link them into the free-list, these nodes are by definition inaccessible to the mutator. The simplest way to execute the mutator and the sweeper in parallel is to do a fixed amount of sweeping at each allocation. Each invocation of allocate sweeps the heap until it finds an appropriate free node (see Algorithm 4.4) [Hughes, 1982]; an implementation of mark_heap is given on page 78.

```
allocate() =
    while sweep < Heap_top                          —continue sweep
        if mark_bit(sweep) == marked
            mark_bit(sweep) = unmarked
            sweep = sweep + size(sweep)
        else
            result = sweep
            sweep = sweep + size(sweep)
            return result
    mark_heap()                                     —heap is full
    sweep = Heap_bottom
    while sweep < Heap_top                          —try again
        if mark_bit(sweep) == marked
            mark_bit(sweep) = unmarked
            sweep = sweep + size(sweep)
        else
            result = sweep
            sweep = sweep + size(sweep)
            return result
    abort "Memory exhausted"
```

Algorithm 4.4 Lazy sweeping.

Lazy sweeping reduces garbage collection pauses by transferring the cost of the sweep phase to allocation. Hughes argues that a second benefit is that no free-list manipulations are necessary: garbage nodes are recycled to the mutator program directly rather than via a free-list buffer. If mark-bits are stored in nodes themselves rather than in a bitmap, this argument seems valid, and indeed it is the method used by Miranda, for example.

However, his case does not extend well to mark-bitmap systems. The most efficient way to sweep a bitmap is to deal with every bit in a word (or small set of words) at the same time, rather than having to reload and save bitmap indexes and bit-masks at each call to `allocate`. Nodes reclaimed by the lazy sweep must be saved somewhere, either in a free-list or in a fixed-size vector. The Boehm–Demers–Weiser conservative collector for C and C++ adopts the former approach whilst Zorn's generational mark-sweep collector for Lisp adopts the latter.

The Boehm–Demers–Weiser sweeper

Allocation is done in the Boehm–Demers–Weiser collector at two levels. A low-level allocator acquires four-kilobyte[5] *blocks* from the operating system using a standard allocator (for example, `malloc`). Each block will contain only objects of a single size in order to reduce fragmentation. We discuss the merits of this approach further in Chapter 5 when we discuss mark-compact garbage collection. A high-level allocator then assigns individual objects to these blocks. A free-list for each common object size is maintained, threaded through the blocks allocated for that size.

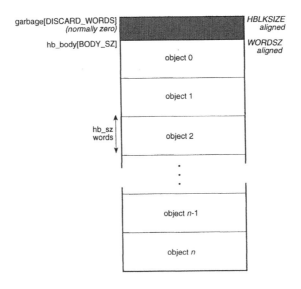

Diagram 4.8 Structure of a block, `struct hblk`, in the Boehm–Demers–Weiser conservative garbage collector, version 4.2.

Each block has a separate block header and these are held on a linked list, ordered by block address. Note that this is a different organisation from the early one described in [Boehm and Weiser, 1988]. That paper suggests placing header information at the start of each block; this configuration interacted extremely poorly with caches, and especially direct-mapped ones. The heap can be expanded at any time by requesting further blocks from the operating system

---

[5] The block size is configurable.

and typically this is done when a garbage collection has failed to recover sufficient free space. The block header holds, amongst other information, the size of the objects allocated on its block, `hb_sz`, and the mark bit-map for its block, `hb_marks`.

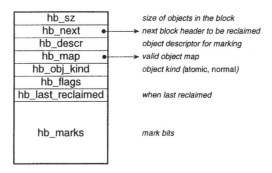

hb_sz	size of objects in the block
hb_next	→ next block header to be reclaimed
hb_descr	object descriptor for marking
hb_map	→ valid object map
hb_obj_kind	object kind (atomic, normal)
hb_flags	
hb_last_reclaimed	when last reclaimed
hb_marks	mark bits

Diagram 4.9   Structure of block headers in the Boehm–Demers–Weiser conservative garbage collector, version 4.2.

Small objects (less than half a heap block) are allocated from the free-list for that size of object. If this free-list it empty, the sweep phase is resumed in an attempt to refill it. The next unswept block is removed from a queue of reclaimable blocks for that object size and swept completely. Any unreachable objects are added to this free-list. The sweep continues with the next block until this free-list is no longer empty. By using a mark bitmap, the Boehm–Demers–Weiser sweeper can also detect cheaply that an entire block is empty and so return it to the low-level allocator. If no space is reclaimed by the sweep, the allocator invokes a garbage collection provided sufficient allocation has occurred. Otherwise the heap is expanded by obtaining new blocks from the operating system. The heap is also expanded if the collection is unsuccessful.

Zorn's lazy sweeper

Zorn takes a different approach to sweeping the bit map lazily [Zorn, 1989]. Rather than using free-lists, he allocates from a cache vector of n objects for each common object size. If the required vector is empty, the heap is swept to refill it. His algorithm both allocates and sweeps very rapidly, particularly for *cons* nodes since these are ubiquitous in Lisp: a *cons* node is allocated in five cycles on a SPARC processor when no marking or sweeping is required (see the code fragment in Algorithm 4.5 on the following page). Other objects take slightly longer since no global registers are dedicated to their use. Allocation is competitive with 'bump-a-pointer' allocation of copying collectors — Zorn's version of copying collection uses five instructions to allocate a cell regardless of object size.

Each iteration of the lazy sweep scans a single word of the bitmap, inserting free nodes into the cache vector. The loop can be unrolled to sweep each bit of the bitmap word in a single iteration to reduce loop overhead. The sequence uses four instructions if a bit is set, and seven if it is not.

— is a collection needed?
```
      subcc %g_allocated, ConsSize, %g_allocated
      bg,a noCollect
      subcc %g_freeConsIndex, 4, %g_free_ConsIndex
      call Collect
      nop
      subcc %g_freeConsIndex, 4, %g_free_ConsIndex
noCollect:
```
— need to sweep?
```
      bg,a done
      ld [%g_freeCons + %g_freeConsIndex], %result
      call lazySweep
      nop
      ld [%g_freeCons + %g_freeConsIndex], %result
done: ...
```

Algorithm 4.5 Zorn's allocation sequence for *cons* cells.

Zorn's code shows that the cost of sweeping an object can be made small. Using mark-and-lazy-sweep, the cost of sweeping the heap is accounted to the cost of allocating new cells. The overall cost of allocating a new cell with his code sequences is likely to be between ten and twelve cycles. If this is small relative to the cost of initialising the cell, the difference in instructions executed between allocation under mark-sweep and under copying collection will be minor.

Marking with a bitmap is more expensive per object marked than marking without one, if we ignore paging costs. Nevertheless its cost will be less than that of copying a moderately large object. For small objects the issue is less clear-cut and caching considerations are likely to be important. Which algorithm will be more efficient will depend on the average size of objects, the costs of initialising them, their lifetimes, the residency of the client program

```
lazySweep:
      ...
```
— %bitsLeft contains the remaining bits
```
      andcc %bitsLeft, 1, %thisBit
      bnz,a nextBit
      add %currentRef, ConsSize, %currentRef
```
— sweep the word into the cons free-list
```
      st %currentRef, [%g_freeCons + %g_freeConsIndex]
      add %g_freeConsIndex, 4, %g_free_ConsIndex
      add %currentRef, ConsSize, %currentRef
nextBit:
```
— on to the next bit
```
      srl %bitsLeft, 1,%bitsLeft
```

Algorithm 4.6 The inner loop of Zorn's lazy-sweep allocator and the paging behaviour of the program and collector combined as much as the collectors' asymptotic complexities.

4.6   Issues to consider

There are a number of reasons why implementors might choose to use mark-sweep garbage collection in preference to other methods. Tracing garbage collectors, whether mark-sweep or copying, place much lower overheads on the user program than reference counting. Even with reference counting's better locality, the overall elapsed time of a garbage collecting system will be better. Tracing collectors are also able to recover cyclic data structures. For these reasons, debate has concentrated on which of the mark-sweep and copying methods provides the better underlying technology for garbage collection.

Until comparatively recently, copying collection held the day. Its advantages of compaction, cheap allocation and good asymptotic behaviour were generally felt to give it the advantage over mark-sweep methods. It was also easier to incorporate into generational systems (which we cover in Chapter 7). However, more recent work, especially that concentrating on the behaviour of collectors in caching and virtual memory environments, has undermined this consensus. The choice of collector now depends as much on the kind of application it is to support as on the intrinsic properties of the collector itself. Unfortunately there are no easy answers.

Space and locality

Mark-sweep collectors require less address space than semi-space copying collectors. There is some evidence that they exhibit better cache and virtual memory behaviour than copying collectors [Zorn, 1989; Zorn, 1991]. We examine this further in Chapters 6 and 11 where we discuss copying garbage collection, and garbage collection and the cache in more detail. A mark-sweep collector should be designed with a view to good virtual memory and cache behaviour. If mark-bits are kept in separate bitmaps, the collector need only read heap objects in the tracing phase, and does not even have to touch live objects in the sweep phase. Furthermore, several mark-bits can be examined in a single instruction. Copying collectors not only use twice the address space, but must write forwarding addresses into live Fromspace objects and update pointers in Tospace data. Mark-sweep collectors may have to add garbage objects to a free-list or vector. Writing a pointer into a garbage object to link it into the free-list may cause a cache miss or a page fault. But this miss or fault would have occurred anyway when the object was allocated, which will be soon if reclamation is interleaved with allocation. Thus the two pointer writes and one pointer read to link the object to the free-list are both effectively cache hits.

Time complexity

Let us review the phases of a single collection cycle for both mark-sweep and copying collection. Both must perform some preparatory work: mark-sweep collectors may have to clear mark-bits, and copying collectors must flip semi-spaces. The costs of initialisation are negligible in practice. Both mark-sweep and copying collectors must trace active data structures in the heap, either to mark them or to copy them.

The cost of the trace is proportional to the number of pointers held in roots and in live objects in the heap. Although this cost is approximated by $O(R)$ for both methods, where R is volume of live data in the heap, the cost of copying large objects between semi-spaces is certainly larger than that of simply marking them (the matter is less clear cut for small objects).

The simple mark-sweep collector described in Section 2.2 (page 27) followed the marking phase with a linear sweep though the heap to free garbage cells. In Section 4.5 of this chapter, we showed that this sweep is unnecessary. Instead, the allocator can be used to search lazily for unmarked objects. Boehm notes that 'this search will terminate quickly in precisely those cases in which a copying collector is claimed to be superior, namely when most of the heap is empty' [Boehm, 1995b]. The cost of allocation for a mark-sweep collector is likely to be dominated by the cost of initialising data, rather than the cost of sweeping or of manipulating free-lists. Equally, the cost of allocation and initialisation for a copying collector is proportional to the size of the unused portion of the heap, $M - R$.

Table 4.1 Asymptotic complexities of the phases of mark-sweep and copying garbage collection. M is the size of the heap, R is the residency of the user program. Originally appeared in *Mark-sweep vs. copying collection and asymptotic complexity*, `ftp://parcftp.xerox.com/pub/garbage/complexity.ps`, Hans Boehm. ©1995 Xerox Corporation. Reprinted with permission.

Method	Mark-sweep	Copying
Initialisation	negligible	negligible
Tracing	$O(R)$	$O(R)$
Sweeping	–	–
Allocation	$O(M - R)$	$O(M - R)$

Table 4.1 summarises the complexities of these two methods of garbage collection. Although the asymptotes of the complexities of sophisticated mark-sweep and copying collectors are the same, the constants are not. Marking any but very small objects will be less expensive than copying them, regardless of locality effects. On the other hand, a copying collector's cost of allocation will be less than that of a mark-sweep collector. In the end, the choice of collector may be determined by the demographics of the heap data used by the mutator, and whether garbage collection time dominates allocation time. If allocation rates are very high (as they are for mostly functional languages), or the lifetimes of most objects are very short (as they should be in the youngest generation of a generational collector: see Chapter 7), then the argument in favour of copying collection is very strong. Otherwise, it is no longer at all clear that copying garbage collection will perform better than mark-

sweep, although it may be easier to implement a reasonably efficient copying collector than an efficient mark-sweep one.

Object mobility

Some environments may demand, or operate more easily with, a non-moving collector. For example, programs may assume that addresses of objects do not change. So-called conservative garbage collectors are designed to provide automatic heap management for languages like C or C++ without cooperation from the compiler. Without communication between the compiler and the collector it is difficult to use moving collectors since roots must be updated with the new locations of their referents; accurate root information will not be available. However, this problem is not insurmountable (for example, see [Bartlett, 1988]).

Copying collectors re-order data in the heap as they compact it into Tospace. This may be undesirable in some environments. For example, if data is maintained in allocation order, an unbounded amount of memory can be recovered in constant time when a Prolog machine backtracks [Bekkers et al., 1992]. Arbitrary re-ordering of heap data may also degrade a program's locality of reference. There is evidence that allocation order may provide a reasonably good estimate of the order of future accesses to data [Clark and Green, 1977; Hayes, 1991; Wilson, 1994]. Other work suggests that breadth-first copying may also be detrimental [Moon, 1984; Wilson, 1991]; we consider solutions to this problem in Chapter 6.

4.7 Notes

F.L. Bauer and H. Wössner provide a good survey of techniques for replacing recursion by iteration [Bauer and Wössner, 1982]. A treatment of marking algorithms can be found in [Knuth, 1973]. Further discussion of stack and queueing disciplines for marking algorithms, and proofs of their correctness, can be found in [Thorelli, 1972]. H.B. Baecker proposed that the cost of marking could be reduced by marking pages rather than cells [Baecker, 1972]. T. Kurokawa's Stacked Node Checking algorithm was designed for Lisp 1.9 [Kurokawa, 1981].

Douglas Clark and Cordell Green studied the shape of Lisp list structures [Clark and Green, 1977]. Pieter Hartel considered the data structures produced by graph reducers for lazy functional languages [Hartel, 1988]. Several authors have compared the interaction of depth-first and breadth-first traversal and virtual memory behaviour [Stamos, 1982; Blau, 1983; Stamos, 1984; Moon, 1984; Andre, 1986; Wilson, 1990]. Discussion of the cost of software-only tests and memory protection traps for garbage collection can be found in [Zorn, 1990a; Johnson, 1988].

The Schorr–Waite algorithm was designed for Maurice Wilkes's list processing language, Wisp, on the IBM 7094 [Wilkes, 1964a; Wilkes, 1964b]. It has been used for marking in a number of systems including various SNOBOL4 and Icon compilers [Hanson, 1977; Dewar and McCann, 1977; Fernandez and Hanson, 1992]. The lazy functional language Miranda [Turner, 1985], an interpreted system based on graph reduction, is completely stackless. It uses Deutsch–Schorr–Waite both for marking and for its execution stack. David Wise's reference counting memory modules use Deutsch–Schorr–Waite marking for backup garbage collection in hardware (which must operate in bounded space) [Wise *et al.*, 1994]. The Deutsch–Schorr–Waite method has also been extended to handle variable-sized nodes [Thorelli, 1972; Appleby *et al.*, 1988]. The latter can also mark parts of structures. There have been numerous proofs of correctness of the Deutsch–Schorr–Waite algorithm including [Knuth, 1973; Thorelli, 1976; Yelowitz and Duncan, 1977; Topor, 1979; Gries, 1979; Kowaltowski, 1979; Gerhart, 1979].

Other authors have proposed more limited methods for traversing data structures in constant space. Some require no additional storage overhead, but may be unable to cope with cycles or shared nodes; others require $O(n \log n)$ time rather than $O(n)$ (see for example [Lindstrom, 1973; Robson, 1973; Dwyer, 1973; Fisher, 1974; Lyon, 1988]).

Analysis of the caching behaviour of garbage algorithms has been considered by several authors, notably Benjamin Zorn and Andrew Appel [Zorn, 1989; Wilson *et al.*, 1991; Zorn, 1991; Koopman *et al.*, 1992; Wilson *et al.*, 1992; Diwan *et al.*, 1994; Appel and Shao, 1994; Gonçalves and Appel, 1995].

5

Mark-Compact Garbage Collection

In Chapter 4, we saw how mark-sweep garbage collection could be made competitive with semi-space copying collection in some circumstances. In particular, mark-sweep had better virtual memory behaviour. Its main remaining drawback is its tendency to fragment the heap if required to handle a variety of objects of different sizes. After each garbage collection cycle, the heap may contain many small 'holes'.

5.1 Fragmentation

Fragmentation may mean that it is impossible to place a large object without expanding the heap because no hole is sufficiently large to accommodate the new object, though the total amount of free space is sufficient. Conversely, a dilemma is faced when allocating small objects. Which allocation discipline should be used? Should it be First-Fit, with the risk of permanent fragmentation leading to the problem above, or is the allocator to pay the price of discovering a Best-Fit position for the new object? Or should a Buddy system be used? This problem is not unique to mark-sweep collectors; it is faced by any system that allocates objects of varying sizes but does not move them. Reference counters and systems for explicit allocation and deallocation of dynamic memory share this quandary.

In contrast, collectors that compact heap memory, including semi-space copying collectors, have particularly cheap allocation costs. The heap allocation strategy of such systems can be considered to obey a stack discipline: the area of memory believed to be in use always grows until a garbage collection takes place when, hopefully, it shrinks by a large amount. Object allocation is then simple. Provided there is sufficient room in the heap, an object may be allocated by nudging a 'next-free-space' pointer by the size of the object.

One attractive heap organisation for non-moving collectors is to maintain segregated free-lists for each different size of object. In this case the cost of allocation need not be much greater than that of a copying collector (as we saw in Chapter 4). Although this technique eases the problem of allocation and freeing fixed-size objects, it does not cure the problem of fragmentation *per se*. It is still possible that the area maintained by one free-list is full, while that maintained by another is comparatively empty.

Two-level allocation

Two-level allocators, such as that used by the Boehm–Demers–Weiser collector, can substantially alleviate this problem [Boehm and Weiser, 1988]. At the lower level, the allocator maintains a list of *blocks* of memory. If a free-list for a certain size of object is empty, a further block can be allocated to that list. At the higher level, each free-list allocates objects of a single size in the blocks it has acquired from the low-level allocator. Providing that its free-list is not empty, small objects can always be allocated cheaply. If the sweep phase of a garbage collection discovers that a block is entirely empty, it can be returned to the low-level allocator to be recycled between the different free-lists (sweeping techniques were discussed in Section 4.5). A further advantage of two-level allocation systems is that the heap need not be contiguous.

Two-level allocation does not cure the fragmentation totally. Allocation of objects larger than a single block may still be difficult since sufficient adjacent free blocks must be found to accommodate the object. One solution to this problem is to manage large objects separately by splitting them into a fixed size header and a body (for example, Kyoto Common Lisp uses this technique [Yuasa and Hagiya, 1985]). The headers can then be managed by a mark-sweep collector using a free-list for the appropriate size, whilst the bodies are allocated to a separate region of the heap. This *Large Object Area* is managed by a separate strategy, maybe one that uses compacting collection.

Two-level allocation also still allows fragmentation within the blocks managed by a single free-list. While not impeding allocation, such fragmentation may affect the spatial locality of the client program. After garbage collection, areas of free space will be interspersed with live objects. These free areas will then be filled by new objects, leaving pages of virtual memory containing objects of different ages, allocated and used by different parts of the user program. The net result is that the program's working set will be spread across more pages than is necessary, which may result in excessive paging traffic. For this reason, simple mark-sweep collectors are sometimes considered to be unsuitable for virtual memory environments. The working set argument is also relevant to other non-moving systems, such as reference counters, or to systems that move objects without regard to locality issues. An example of the latter is the 'Two-Finger' compaction scheme discussed in Section 5.3 below.

However the locality problem may not be as bad as simple analysis might suggest. Objects that are active at the same time are often created at the same time and may share similar lifetimes. If such clusters of objects do indeed live and die in groups, the objects are likely to be allocated closely, spatially as well as temporarily, and likely to be reclaimed at about the same time [Hayes, 1991; Wilson, 1994].

5.2 Styles of compaction

In this chapter we discuss methods for compacting live data structures in the heap. By *compaction* we shall mean that, at the end of a compacting phase, (the compacted region of) the heap will be divided into two contiguous areas. One area will hold all active data whilst all free words of the heap will be held in the other area. Some authors refer to this technique by the term *compactifying*, in order to distinguish it from techniques for compressing data structures. In practice, it may be desirable to use both techniques together — in this way structures can be compressed as they are relocated — although techniques such as *cdr-coding* lists have fallen out of favour with the advent of cheap memory because of the cost of accessing compressed data [Bobrow and Clark, 1979]. However, some authors have suggested recently that compression might be worth considering once more in order to reduce memory requirements and disk seeks (as processor speeds continue to increase more rapidly than disk speeds) [Baker, 1991; Wilson, 1992a; Douglis, 1993; Wilson, 1994]. We shall be careful to indicate where such a distinction needs to be made; otherwise we shall use the term compaction.

Compacting algorithms make several passes over the active data structure or the heap. The number of passes varies depending on the algorithm used and whether optimisations to combine passes are possible. In general, compacting collectors have three phases, although they may differ on whether relocation of cells is done before or after pointers are updated:

- mark the active data structure;
- compact the graph by relocating cells; and
- update the values of pointers that referred to moved cells.

Care needs to be taken with regard to the placement of relocated cells. Ideally the arrangement of cells in the heap should reflect the way in which they are accessed by the user program. Poor object orderings may lead to reduced virtual memory performance and fewer cache hits. Algorithms can be categorised into three classes according to the relative positions in which cells are left after compaction:

Arbitrary: cells are moved without regard for their original order, or whether they point to one another. Such methods may be simple to implement and fast to execute, particularly if all nodes are of a fixed size, but they generally result in poor spatial locality.

Linearising: cells which originally pointed to one another are moved into adjacent positions, as far as this is possible. Copying collectors that scavenge the graph in depth-first order (such as the Fenichel–Yochelson collector described in Section 2.3) fall into this category. Data structures can then be compressed by techniques such as *cdr*-coding if this is felt to be desirable.

Sliding: cells are slid to one end of the heap, squeezing out free cells, thereby maintaining the original order of allocation.

The latter two styles of compaction offer a number of advantages. For some systems it is particularly important that the spatial ordering of objects in the heap reflects their ordering of allocation. Implementations of Prolog, for example, can use this property when back-tracking to reclaim unbounded amounts of memory in constant time: the heap is treated as a stack. It has also been argued that a sliding strategy tends to give the best locality of reference, and that it is not worth trying to second-guess the user program [Clark and Green, 1977; Clark, 1979]. Studies by Hayes and experience with the Xerox PCR system suggest that many objects live and die in clumps [Hayes, 1991]. If this is so, and if these clumps are allocated reasonably adjacently, sliding compaction will keep them together (or, at any rate, will not worsen their spatial spread).

Other issues that should be considered when comparing compaction algorithms are whether the algorithm handles objects of different sizes; how many passes through the heap are needed to relocate objects and to update pointers; how much, if any, extra space is required by the algorithm; and whether the algorithm places any restrictions on pointers — are interior pointers permitted[1], can pointers point backwards; and how much work is done at each step.

Many different algorithms and optimisations of algorithms exist in the literature. We shall restrict ourselves to examining a representative sample of methods. Apart from semi-space copying algorithms, techniques used include:

Two-Finger algorithms: two pointers are used, one to point to the next free location, the other to the next active cell to be moved. As cells are moved, a forwarding address is left in their old location. Such methods are generally only applicable to fixed-size cells.

Forwarding address algorithms: forwarding addresses are written into an additional field within each cell before the cell is moved. These methods are suitable for collecting nodes of different sizes.

Table-based methods: a relocation map, usually called a *break table*, is constructed in the heap either before or during cell relocation. This table is consulted later to calculate new values for pointers.

Threaded methods: each cell is chained to a list of those cells that originally pointed to it. When the cell is moved, the list is traversed to readjust pointer values.

We consider four specific algorithms in detail. Edwards's *Two-Finger* compactor is fast, with complexity $O(M)$ where M is the size of the heap. Its compaction phase makes just two simple passes through the heap. It is usually used only with fixed-size objects (or a fixed range of sizes), but its major drawback is that it re-orders objects arbitrarily and hence will not improve spatial locality (and might indeed worsen it). The other algorithms we consider are all sliding compactors, and can handle objects of different sizes. The *Lisp 2* compactor also has asymptotic complexity $O(M)$, but it makes three passes through the heap and requires an extra pointer-sized field in each object. It is possible to compact the heap in just two passes with a sliding compactor and without any space overhead. The *Haddon–Waite* compactor does precisely this, albeit with a complexity of $O(M \log M)$. Alternatively, if each object contains a pointer-sized field that is guaranteed never to contain data indistinguishable from a heap pointer, *Jonkers's* compactor can compact the heap in two passes with $O(M)$ complexity.

Throughout this chapter, we treat the heap as a contiguous array, Heap, with indices in the range Heap_bottom to Heap_top. For fixed-size cell algorithms, each slot in the array is thought to be a cell; for variable-sized cell algorithms, each slot is a single word.

---

[1] A pointer is called an *interior pointer* if it points to the interior of an object rather than to its head.

5.3   The Two-Finger Algorithm

Our first example is a two-finger algorithm, due to Edwards [Saunders, 1974]. The live data structure is first marked, and the number of live cells, nlive, counted. The first pass relocates cells from the upper part of the heap (above Heap[nlive]) to the holes in the lower part of the heap, overwriting the first field of vacated slots with forwarding addresses. No extra space is needed. The second pass scans cells in the lower (compacted) part of the heap (up to Heap[nlive]), updating pointer values to reflect the new location of cells. At the end of the compaction phase, free indexes the first free slot in the heap (see Algorithm 5.1).

```
Compact_2Finger() =
    no_live_cells = mark()
    relocate()
    update_pointers(no_live_cells)
    free = no_live_cells + 1
```

Algorithm 5.1   Edwards's Two-Finger compaction algorithm.

The algorithm

Two pointers are used: free sweeps from the bottom of the heap, looking for free nodes, while live sweeps from the top of the heap looking for live cells (see Algorithm 5.2 on the next page). Cells discovered by live are then moved into the holes discovered by free, and a forwarding address is left in the first field of the old cell. Notice that the forwarding address can be written over user data; no additional space is required. Move(old,new) copies each field of Heap[old] to its new location, starting at Heap[new]. The pass terminates when the two pointers meet.

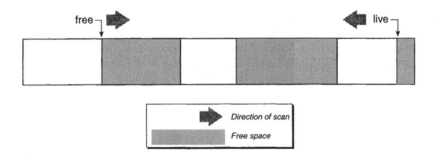

Diagram 5.1   The Two-Finger compaction algorithm.

The second pass scans the live cells, all of which are now in the bottom part of the heap (see Algorithm 5.3 on the following page). This pass updates the values of any pointer fields that refer to cells that have been evacuated, i.e. with addresses greater than nlive, by referring to the forwarding addresses left by the first pass.

```
relocate() =
    free = Heap_bottom
    live = Heap_top
    mark_bit(Heap[heap_top+1]) = unmarked
    repeat
        while marked(free)                              —find next hole
            mark_bit(Heap[free]) = unmarked
            free=free+1
        while not marked(live) and live > free
            live=live-1                                 —find previous live cell
        if live>free
            mark_bit(Heap[live]) = unmarked             —unmark it
            move(live, free)
            Heap[live] = free                           —leave forwarding address
            free=free+1
            live=live-1
    until live <= free
```

Algorithm 5.2   The first pass of the Two-Finger compaction algorithm.

Analysis of the two-finger algorithm

The two-finger algorithm is attractive despite its antiquity and simplicity. It has linear complexity and makes no more than two passes of the heap after the live graph has been marked, once scanning the entire heap to relocate objects and once scanning only the compacted portion of the heap but reading the forwarding address fields of nodes in the rest of the heap. The amount of work done as each slot in the heap is encountered is minimal. It requires no additional memory as forwarding pointers are written over the contents of relocated cells, and it permits pointers to refer to interior words of objects which other algorithms may not. Its chief drawback is that the order in which cells are relocated is arbitrary. Cells that were once adjacent may now be dispersed, although the relative order of relocated cells is unaltered. The algorithm therefore will not be suitable if the reason for compaction is to improve the spatial locality of the user program.

```
update_pointers(nlive) =
    for i = 1 to nlive
        for j in Children(Heap[i])
            if Heap[j] > nlive                  —points into relocated area
                Heap[j] = Heap[ Heap[j] ]
```

Algorithm 5.3   The second pass of the Two-Finger compaction algorithm.

Variable-sized cells

Although it is only suitable for fixed-size cells, the algorithm can easily be extended if variable-sized cells are allocated to different regions of the heap. In this case, the mark phase must calculate `no_live_cells` for each region and the cells in each region must be relocated separately. Alternatively, the algorithm could compact variable-sized data to fresh pages of the heap. Bartlett uses a variation of this compactor to trace and compact the oldest generation of his *Mostly Copying* collector for C and C++ when the heap becomes more than 85 percent full (see Section 9.3 of Chapter 9 and [Bartlett, 1989a]).

Bartlett's heap is divided into fixed-size *blocks*, and objects are allocated from the current free block by bumping a pointer. The compacting phase is designed to minimise the amount of data that is moved between blocks, trading mild fragmentation for reduced movement. It compacts individual blocks rather than the entire heap, which it scans twice. The first pass looks for blocks less than a third full. Marked objects on these blocks are moved into the current free block, leaving behind a forwarding address; fuller blocks are not compacted. Another free block is also queued up, if one is available, in case the current block should overflow. The second phase corrects pointers in the same way as the two-finger algorithm: the heap is scanned and pointers to moved objects are replaced by the appropriate forwarding addresses. If the heap remains more than three-quarters full after compaction, Bartlett expands the heap in one megabyte increments.

Although the original two-finger algorithm compacted objects into an arbitrary order, Bartlett's collector is much better behaved. Since relocated objects are moved to fresh blocks, his compactor is effectively a sliding collector. The only caveat is that objects that originally shared the same page might be moved to different pages.

5.4   The Lisp 2 Algorithm

The next algorithm has the virtues being suitable for nodes of varying sizes, and of sliding cells to preserve their order rather than rearranging objects in an arbitrary fashion (see Algorithm 5.4). The compaction phase is fast, despite making three rather than two passes over the heap, but a price has to be paid for this speed: a pointer-sized field is needed in the header of each object for storing forwarding addresses. This field is also used by the marking process — a non-`nil` value indicates that the cell is in use.

```
Compact_LISP2() =
    mark()
    compute_addresses()
    update_pointers()
    relocate()
```

Algorithm 5.4   The Lisp 2 compaction algorithm.

The first compacting pass computes the new address of each active cell and stores this in the `forwarding_address` field in the header of each object (see Algorithm 5.5 on the following page). The new address is simply the sum of the sizes of the live cells encountered so far,

free. This phase may also combine adjacent garbage nodes into a single hole to improve the
speed of subsequent passes.

```
combine(P) =
    — P is unmarked
    next = P + size(P)
    while forwarding_address(next) == nil          —not marked
        size(P) = size(P) + size (next)
        next = P + size(P)

compute_addresses() =
    free = Heap_bottom
    P = Heap_bottom
    while P ≤ Heap_top
        if forwarding_address(P) ≠ nil             —marked
            forwarding_address(P) = free
            free = free + size(P)
        else combine(P)                            —optional
        P = P + size(P)
```

Algorithm 5.5   The first phase of the Lisp 2 algorithm.

The second pass simply updates the values of pointer fields of active cells, including root
pointers, by referring to the forwarding_address field of the cell to which they refer (see
Algorithm 5.6).

```
update_pointers() =
    for R in Roots
        R = forwarding_address(R)
    P = Heap_bottom
    while P ≤ Heap_top
        if forwarding_address(P) ≠ nil
            for Q in Children(P)
                Heap[Q] = forwarding_address(Heap[Q])
        P = P + size(P)
```

Algorithm 5.6   The second phase of the Lisp 2 algorithm.

Finally the third pass clears the forwarding_address field in preparation for the next
garbage collection and moves cells to their new address (see Algorithm 5.7 on the facing
page). At the end of this phase, all active data are compacted into the lower part of the heap,
and free indexes the first free location in the heap.

Although the Lisp 2 compactor makes three passes over the heap, the amount of work done
at each iteration is small. Apart from the extra pass, the main deficiency of the algorithm is
that it requires an extra pointer-sized field that can only be shared with the mark-bit. Cohen
and Nicolau analysed time-formulae for this algorithm, the two algorithms shown below and
Morris's algorithm, a restricted form of threading algorithm (which did not fare well) [Cohen

```
relocate() =
    P = Heap_bottom
    while P ≤ Heap_top
        temp = P + size(P)
        if forwarding_address(P) ≠ nil
            free = forwarding_address(P)
            forwarding_address(P) = nil          —unmark
            move(P,free)
        P = temp
    free = free + size(free)
```

Algorithm 5.7   The third and final phase of the Lisp 2 algorithm.

and Nicolau, 1983; Morris, 1978]. They rated the Lisp 2 compactor as fastest of the algorithms they modelled. While such theoretical analyses are interesting, they ignore effects of caching and paging on the program's execution. Studies by Zorn and Grunwald suggest that models have only limited use as predictors of actual performance [Zorn and Grunwald, 1992].

5.5   Table-based methods

Edwards's two-finger compactor required no additional space, but compacted cells into an arbitrary order. The Lisp 2 collector preserved cells' relative order, but needed an additional pointer field for each object to store the relocation map. Table-based methods, however, can preserve cell ordering without any space cost. They keep account of the location of blocks of active data and the size of holes, and use this information for updating pointers [Haddon and Waite, 1967]. In principle, they incur no space overhead: there will always be sufficient room to store relocation information in the holes themselves, provided that the size of the smallest object in the heap is at least two words. However, in practice any additional space found in the heap can be used to speed up pointer readjustment.

The algorithm

After marking the active graph, table-based compactors proceed as follows (see Algorithm 5.8 on the next page). As the heap is compacted, a *break table* of relocation information is constructed in the free area. The break table specifies the locations of holes in the heap. As areas of active data are relocated towards the bottom of the heap, it may be necessary to move the break table in the opposite direction. If this movement causes the information in the table to become jumbled, then the table must be sorted before the table can be used. Finally, the compacted area of the heap is scanned and pointer fields are readjusted by referring to the break table.

```
Compact_Table() =
    nlive = mark()
    relocate()
    sort_table()
    update_pointers(nlive)
```

Algorithm 5.8   The Haddon–Waite compaction algorithm.

The break table

The break table is built as each contiguous area of active data is compacted by determining the address of the start of the area, a_i, and the total amount of free space discovered so far, s_i. The pair (a_i, s_i) is written into the free slot that can be found at the end of the break table. As active areas are discovered, they are slid down to the compacted region, and the break table is moved if necessary. An inductive argument shows that there will always be a free slot for the next table entry. The example in Diagrams 5.2 to 5.5 shows how the break table is constructed. The numbers below the heap indicate the addresses of free and active areas of the heap. The initial configuration of the heap is shown in Diagram 5.2.

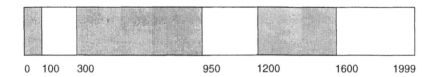

Diagram 5.2   Before compaction (shaded areas are free).

The active heap block held between locations 100 and 299 is moved to the bottom of the heap (see Diagram 5.3). Its starting address, 100, and the amount of free space found so far, also 100, is written at location 300.

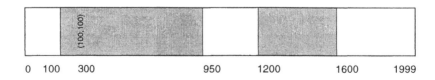

Diagram 5.3   The first area is moved and the first entry is written into the break table.

The second active block starts at location 950. It is slid to the first free location, 200, and its relocation data and the old break table is written behind the moved block (see Diagram 5.4 on the facing page). Finally the last block is slid down and the break table is moved again (see Diagram 5.5 on the next page).

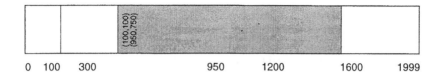

Diagram 5.4   The second area is moved and the next entry is added.

Unfortunately rolling the break table causes it to become unsorted. Table entries must be in order at the end of the relocation phase if the table is to be searched efficiently. Theoretically sorting has a cost of $n \log n$, where n is the size of the break table and, in the worst case, this may be half the size of the heap. In practice costs are likely to be much smaller. Entries added to the break table since it was last rolled will be in the correct order. If a count is kept of these 'correct' entries, then only part of the table needs to be sorted [Fitch and Norman, 1978]. Alternatively, provided that there is sufficient room, the correct position of each break table record could be stored in the record itself. In this case, a linear scan would suffice to sort the table.

Updating pointers

The final phase of the algorithm is to re-adjust pointer fields of objects in the compacted region, searching the break table for relocation information. To adjust a pointer p, the break table is searched for adjacent pairs (a, s) and (a', s') such that $a \le p < a'$. The adjusted value of p will then be $p - s$. Although this, too, is apparently an $n \log n$ operation, matters can usually be improved. If there is sufficient space in the free area after the break table, a hash table can be constructed to improve searching. The k most significant bits of the pointer can be used as a hash key to look up the start and end of the region of the break table containing a and a' (where the size of the hash table is 2^k). Fitch and Norman suggest that, wherever possible, the hash table should be roughly twice the size of the break table [Fitch and Norman, 1978].

Alternative possibilities for table-based methods include storing the table as a linked data structure in the holes in the heap and updating pointers *before* moving cells. The advantages of not having to move or sort the break table must be weighed against the efficiency with which such a linked list can be searched. Hash table methods are also applicable to this technique [Wegbreit, 1972a].

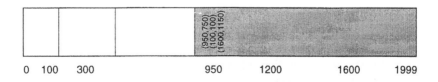

Diagram 5.5   Rolling the break table.

5.6 Threaded methods

The problem of updating is to discover all the pointers to any cell P, and to adjust them to point to the cell's new location, P′. All the methods examined so far have relied upon scanning the heap for all pointers and then looking up their new value. Fisher was the first of several researchers to solve this problem with a different technique [Fisher, 1974]. Rather than examining the pointer fields in every active cell, he arranged the heap so that all the pointers to cell P could be found from P. This technique, called *threading*, manages updates by reversibly rearranging pointers in the following fashion.

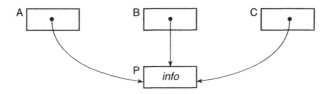

Diagram 5.6   Before threading P.

Threading pointers

If locations A, B and C point to P which has contents `info` (see Diagram 5.6), this structure can be represented, without loss of information, by constructing a list of those locations pointing to P, emanating from P itself (see Diagram 5.7). The original contents of P are stored at the end of the list. The only restriction is that the original data must always be distinguishable from pointer data.

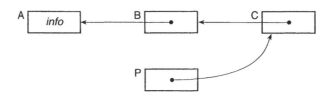

Diagram 5.7   After threading P.

Two nodes can be threaded by reversing the pointer and storing the contents of the target word in the source word. In this example, we would call `thread` on A, B and finally C (see Algorithm 5.9). Once the new location of P is known, the list can be traversed and each pointer field be replaced with the new location of P. Finally the contents of P can be reinstated.

```
thread(p) =
    if Heap[p] ≠ nil
        Heap[p], Heap[Heap[p]] = Heap[Heap[p]],p
```

Algorithm 5.9   The threading procedure.

Jonkers's compaction algorithm

We now examine the threading algorithm due to Jonkers [Jonkers, 1979]. Although Morris's threading algorithms are probably better known, Jonkers imposes fewer restrictions (see the Notes on page 114 at the end of this chapter for further details of Morris's techniques). Nevertheless, three restrictions are placed upon the heap organisation before compaction starts:

- pointers may only point to the header of a cell;
- this must be large enough to contain an address;
- headers must contain values that are distinguishable from pointers into the heap (although pointers to other areas of memory are possible).

As usual, the collector starts by marking the active data structure. Two further passes through the heap are then required (see Algorithm 5.10). The first pass handles pointers that point forward, updating each one to refer to the new location of its referent (see Algorithm 5.11 on page 111). The second pass updates pointers that point backwards and also moves objects (see Algorithm 5.12 on page 112).

```
Compact_Jonkers() =
    mark()
    update_forward_pointers()
    update_backward_pointers()
```

Algorithm 5.10   Jonkers's compaction algorithm.

The easiest way to understand this complicated algorithm is to consider what happens to an individual node.

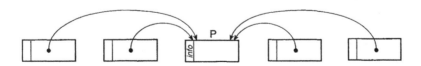

Diagram 5.8   The initial configuration, showing all objects with pointers to P.

Forward pointers

Let P be a typical cell, shown in Diagram 5.8 on the page before, and suppose that the (non-pointer) contents of its header are info. The first pass starts by threading the roots of the computation so that they can be updated if their referents are moved (see Algorithm 5.11 on the facing page). As the scan sweeps linearly through the heap it updates each cell, and threads each pointer, that it encounters. The next free space variable, free, is incremented at each step with the size of the cell being scanned. By the time that the scan reaches P, all forward pointers to P have been threaded and the contents of P have been placed at the end of the threading chain (see Diagram 5.9).

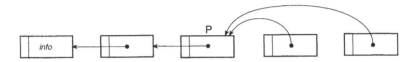

Diagram 5.9   All forward pointers to P are threaded.

When P is reached, these forward pointers can be updated with the new address of P: this is held in free, which has been calculated by cumulatively adding the sizes of all marked cells encountered so far (Diagram 5.10).

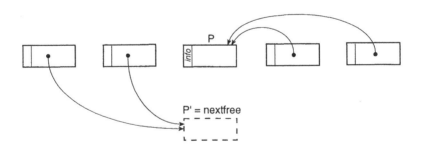

Diagram 5.10   Forward pointers to P are updated to refer to its new location.

The pass then continues, threading pointers which point back to P — remember that we are considering the effect of the algorithm on P alone. A self-reference, i.e. a pointer that refers to the cell that contains it, is treated as a back-pointer. At the end of this pass, all forward references have been updated to point to the new locations of their referents and all backward pointers have been threaded (see Diagram 5.11 on the next page).

Backward pointers

The second pass updates backward pointers and moves objects (see Algorithm 5.12 on page 112). As it reaches the live cell P, it updates back pointers to refer to P's new location,

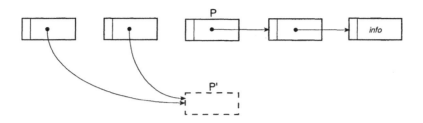

Diagram 5.11 Backwards-pointers to P are threaded.

P', by following P's thread. P' is again calculated on the fly by accumulating the sizes of cells already moved into free. Once this has been done, the contents of P are moved to their new location (see Diagram 5.12 on the next page). The speed of this pass can be improved if adjacent free areas are combined in the first pass (as in the Lisp 2 algorithm described on page 103).

Analysis of threaded algorithms

The Jonkers algorithm is suitable for abstract machine architectures in which each heap node has a pointer-sized header. It requires no extra space and makes only two passes of the heap. Its main drawback is that each iteration of each pass must do a substantial amount of work unthreading pointers, and each iteration may touch several other objects.

```
update(P,free) =
    t = Heap[P]
    while pointer(t)
        Heap[t], t = free, Heap[t]
    Heap[P] = t

update_forward_pointers() =
    for R in Roots
        thread(R)
    free = Heap_bottom
    P = Heap_bottom
    while P ≤ Heap_top
        if marked(P)
            update(P,free)
            for Q in Children(P)
                thread(Q)
            free = free + size(P)
        else combine(P)
        P = P + size(P)
```

Algorithm 5.11 Jonkers's first pass through the heap updates forward pointers.

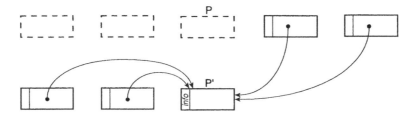

Diagram 5.12   Backward pointers are updated and P is moved.

Each object in the heap is touched three times before it is moved (if live), once by update_forward_pointers, once by update_backward_pointers and once by thread; each pointer field of live objects is touched again by update on one or other of the two passes. It is possible to improve on this by combining the marking phase with the first pass of the compaction phase. Martin has claimed that this optimisation gives a performance improvement of one third [Martin, 1982]. Even so, each live object will be accessed at least four times.

Break-table compactors, in contrast, touch each node in the heap exactly twice, once to move it and once to update its pointer fields. On the other hand they must also roll the break table through the heap, sort it and search it when updating pointers. The Cohen–Nicolau formulae suggest that while Jonkers's algorithm may be more efficient for programs with small residencies, break table methods appear increasingly attractive compared with threaded methods as heap occupancy rises.

5.7   Issues to consider

Compaction is undoubtedly expensive, but there are several reasons why it might be contemplated. The first is to reduce the cost of allocation to that of a copying collector. If

```
update_backward_pointers() =
    free = Heap_bottom
    P = Heap_bottom
    while P ≤ Heap_top
        if marked(P)
            update(P,free)
            move(P,free)
            free = free + size(P)
        P = P + size(P)
```

Algorithm 5.12   Jonkers's second pass through the heap moves cells and updates backwards pointers.

the free area of the heap is contiguous, new objects of any size can be created simply by incrementing the next free space pointer. Nevertheless, we saw in Chapter 4 how a two-level allocator with separate free-lists and mark bitmaps can reduce the cost of allocation in a mark-swept heap substantially.

Smaller address space

A semi-space copying collector might be undesirable because of the amount of address space that it uses for a program of given residency. If this is larger than the physical memory of the computer, the collector's paging behaviour will suffer in comparison with a mark-sweep or mark-compact collector whose heap can be accommodated in real memory. A smaller address space is particularly beneficial for small machines, such as personal computers, which also may not support paging. Fernandez and Hanson describe an implementation of ICON for which a compacting collector was found to offer some improvement over a copying collector [Fernandez and Hanson, 1992].

Repeated copying

Simple non-generational copying collectors copy long-lived data repeatedly from one semi-space to the other. A third advantage of mark-compact collection, observed by Fernandez and Hanson, is that such data is unlikely to be moved again once it is compacted. A better solution to this problem is to use generational methods (which we discuss in Chapter 7), although this would have required substantial changes to their run-time system.

Handling abnormal residencies

Sansom has proposed an interesting solution to the dilemma of limited address space. We observed on page 31 of Chapter 2 that the performance of a copying collector degrades rapidly as the program residency approaches half the size of the heap. However, expanding the size of the heap is not necessarily a sensible tactic (see Chapter 6 where we discuss semi-space copying methods). Sansom suggests that the trade-off point between copying and a Jonkers compacting collector occurs when the heap is about 30 percent full (though this is implementation-dependent) [Sansom, 1992; Sansom, 1991]. He employed a *dual-mode* garbage collector for an implementation of the pure functional language Haskell [Hudak *et al.*, 1992; Peyton Jones, 1992]. His collector used the occupancy of the heap as a heuristic for switching dynamically between a non-generational two-space copying collector and a mark-compact collector. Although the compacting collector was very much slower than the copying collector, he believed that it might be useful for programs whose typical residencies are well within the limits of a copying collector, but have occasional spikes.

Locality

The chief reason for choosing to perform a mark-compact collection may be to improve the spatial locality of objects in the heap and hence reduce the number of page faults incurred by the user program. For this purpose, a sliding or linearising collector is essential. It may not be necessary to compact the heap at each collection, but rather to do so occasionally when heuristics suggest that the improvement in paging may be worth the cost of the compaction phase.

The way in which memory management systems lay out data in the heap may be critical to a program's overall performance. As we saw earlier in this chapter, several studies have shown that objects should be laid out in the heap in such a way that objects that refer to each other, or are related in some other way, are placed in close proximity in order to reduce the size of the program's working set. There is considerable evidence that allocation order is a good indicator of such a relationship between objects, and a sliding compactor preserves this ordering (for example, [Clark and Green, 1977; Stamos, 1982; Blau, 1983; Moon, 1984; Andre, 1986; Wilson *et al.*, 1991]). Some systems, such as Prolog, must maintain temporal information to operate efficiently. Matching address order to creation order is an efficient way to do this. We examine locality issues further in the next chapter.

Choosing between compacting collectors

There are issues to consider other than the effect of compaction on the layout of data in the heap. The first is whether the algorithm imposes any undesirable restrictions on user data. For example, two-finger algorithms cannot handle variable-sized heap objects unless the heap is divided into regions, each of which holds objects of a single size. Threading algorithms may either demand that pointer data can be distinguished unambiguously from non-pointer data, or impose restrictions on the direction of pointers, or require that the heap can be scanned for live objects in both directions. Algorithms may also restrict the use of interior pointers.

The space and time performance of the compactors will also be important. The Lisp 2 algorithm requires a separate pointer-sized field in each object to store its forwarding address. Other algorithms either require no extra space, or can use user fields of live objects or holes in the heap to store relocation information. The execution time of each compactor is a more subtle question. The number of passes compactors make over the heap varies between two and three, but the first pass of Jonkers's algorithm may be combined with the marking phase. The amount of processing done at each iteration is also important. The two-finger and Lisp 2 algorithms perform little work at each step, but break table and threaded methods do much more. Even worse, threaded methods may access many other heap objects at each iteration at the risk of incurring more cache misses and page faults.

Table 5.1 on the facing page summarises the characteristics of the compacting collectors presented in this chapter according to their style of compaction, whether they can handle variable-sized objects, how many passes over the heap they make, their space overhead and their asymptotic time complexity.

5.8 Notes

The first compaction algorithm published was by Timothy Hart and Thomas Evans for Lisp 1.5 on a version of the Univac 490 [Hart and Evans, 1974]. It shared similarities with Edwards's two-finger collector, also for Lisp 1.5 [Saunders, 1974]. Guy Steele and Joel Bartlett have also used versions of this technique [Steele, 1975; Bartlett, 1989a]. Daniel

Table 5.1 Characteristics of compacting algorithms. M is the size of the heap.

Algorithm	Style	Cell size	Passes	Space	Time
Two-Finger	arbitrary	fixed	2	none	M
LISP 2	sliding	variable	3	1 pointer-sized field per cell	M
Table-based	sliding	variable	2	none	$M \log M$
Threaded	sliding	variable	2	headers at least pointer-sized	M

Bobrow and Daniel Murphy pointed to the poor virtual memory performance of compactors that give arbitrary cell orderings [Bobrow and Murphy, 1967]. Details of the Lisp 2 compactor can be found in the answer to Exercise 2.5.33 in [Knuth, 1973, pp. 602–3].

The first description of a table-based compactor was by B.H. Haddon and W.M. Waite [Haddon and Waite, 1967]. Techniques for storing the table as a linked list in the holes in the heap (thereby obviating the need for moving or sorting the table, but paying a higher access price) have also been suggested by B. Wegbreit who proposed using a hash table to speed searches [Wegbreit, 1972a], Bernard Lang and Wegbreit [Lang and Wegbreit, 1972], Derek Zave who proposed radix sorting the break table [Zave, 1975; Knuth, 1973], and Motoaki Terashima and Eiichi Goto [Terashima and Goto, 1978]. John Fitch and Arthur Norman suggested a number of improvements to Haddon and Waite's method [Fitch and Norman, 1978].

The first threaded methods were discovered independently by David Fisher [Fisher, 1974] and Lockwood Morris [Morris, 1978; Morris, 1979; Morris, 1982]. Similar methods can also be found in [Thorelli, 1976] who also gives a proof, and in [Hanson, 1977] for an implementation of SNOBOL4. These methods imposed restrictions on the direction of pointers, which were lifted by H.B.M. Jonkers [Jonkers, 1979]. Jonkers also required just two passes through the heap, both in the forward direction (unlike Morris who required the second pass to be in the opposite direction, which may be difficult), and eliminated the need for additional tag bits to distinguish ordinary pointers, threaded pointers and data, by assuming that the header of a cell is large enough to contain an address. On the other hand, unlike Morris's compactor, Jonkers requires pointers to point only to the head of a cell. An optimisation can be found in [Martin, 1982], and related work in [Dewar and McCann, 1977; Wise, 1979]

A comparative survey of the efficiency of compacting collectors is given in [Cohen and Nicolau, 1983]. Mary Fernandez and David Hanson describe an implementation of ICON for which a compacting collector was found to offer some improvement over a copying collector [Fernandez and Hanson, 1992]. One of the main reasons for choosing to use compaction is to improve virtual memory performance. Jacques Cohen and Laurent Trilling noted as early as 1967 that compaction could also improve marking time in virtual memory environments, even though the total time taken for garbage collection is longer [Cohen and Trilling, 1967].

H.D. Baecker suggested a method of marking virtual memory pages, and only making a page available for reuse when it is completely empty, in order to save on compaction costs while retaining a stack discipline for allocation [Baecker, 1972]. Obviously the cost to pay is in consumption of virtual memory and extra page table entries. Studies of the relationship between spatial ordering of heap objects and access patterns by the user program can be found in many places, including [Clark and Green, 1977; Clark, 1979; Stamos, 1982; Blau, 1983; Stamos, 1984; Moon, 1984; Andre, 1986; Zorn, 1989; Zorn, 1990b; Hayes, 1991; Llames, 1991; Wilson *et al.*, 1991].

6

Copying Garbage Collection

In this chapter we examine the copying method of garbage collection, introduced in Chapter 2, in more detail. Since Cheney's discovery in 1970 of an efficient iterative technique for its implementation, copying collection has proved popular with implementors. Although garbage collection technology has moved beyond simple stop-and-copy collection, this technique remains the most widely adopted basis for more sophisticated techniques, such as generational and incremental collection.

Copying collection has a number of immediate attractions compared with other forms of automatic memory management. Like any non-incremental tracing collector, it places no overhead on user program writes. The cost of copying is proportional to the volume of live data rather than to the entire heap. This makes copying particularly attractive if the surviving data is a small proportion of the total heap. Low survival rates are typical of many systems, not least implementations of functional languages: for example, Standard ML of New Jersey (SML/NJ) typically reclaims over 98 percent of the heap at each garbage collection [Appel, 1992]. For systems with very large address spaces, an eager sweep of the entire heap would produce an unacceptable delay not engendered by copying collection. It is also easier to implement a moderately efficient memory management system based on stop-and-copy collection than on any other form of tracing collection.

Copying garbage collection compacts active data structures into the bottom of the semi-space. This has three potential advantages. First, the heap is now a 'push-only' stack. Memory can be allocated linearly simply by incrementing a free space pointer by the size of the object to be allocated. Consequently space for variable-sized objects can be allocated for the same cost as other objects; complications of separate free-lists, or other fit-finding tactics, are unnecessary. Thirdly, compacting the active part of the heap onto fewer pages should reduce the size of the program's working set.

Although it divides the heap into two semi-spaces, thereby doubling the size of address space required compared with non-copying collectors, iterative copying garbage collection uses no further heap memory. Mark-bits are not required and forwarding addresses can usually be written over user data fields. The Fenichel–Yochelson collector given in Chapter 2 was recursive, and hence needed a stack whose size was only bounded by the length of the longest path through the active data structure — in principle the stack could grow as long as the number of cells in the heap. If a limited-size stack is used, stack pushes must be checked for overflow and the collector must be able to recover if it should occur. In this chapter we consider Cheney's non-recursive algorithm, which requires just a pair of pointers to copy the surviving data.

Copying garbage collection was originally considered eminently suitable for virtual memory machines since pages of the unused semi-space could be evicted to disk. Unfortunately matters are more complicated than this simple review of copying's virtues suggests. Although the asymptotic complexity of copying garbage collection is greater than that of mark-sweep collection, the constants in these formulae must not be ignored. Copying objects, and especially large objects, is likely to be more expensive than marking them. We saw in Chapter 4, when we discussed mark-sweep garbage collection, how the sweep phase could be accounted to allocation, and its cost substantially diminished by using mark bitmaps separate from the objects. The analysis above also takes an optimistic view of the interaction between the user program, the garbage collector and the memory hierarchy. The case for abandoning pages of the unused semi-space to disk ignores paging costs altogether. Copying compacts data into Tospace but this reorganises the layout of data structures in the heap. Unless care is taken with this regrouping, the spatial locality of the resulting structures may be poor. We consider these matters in more detail below. Copying collection's pattern of cyclic reuse of the heap may also interact poorly with data caches. We examine this issue in Chapter 11. We also note that moving objects behind the compiler's back may defeat certain pointer-register caching optimisations [Chase, 1987].

6.1 Cheney's copying collector

The disadvantages of recursion were covered on page 77 of Chapter 4: recursive calls cost CPU-time and the recursion stack occupies precious space. Furthermore, recursion risks stack overflow. Cheney's elegant algorithm shows that copying collection can be made iterative, using just two pointers [Cheney, 1970]. Rather than remembering branch points of the active graph in a stack, it stores them in a queue. The pointers scan and free point to each end of this queue. Instead of using additional memory for the queue, it is stored in the new semi-space of the heap, in the nodes that have been copied.

The tricolour abstraction

It is useful to introduce an abstraction at this point. Dijkstra's *On the fly* concurrent marking algorithm required the mutator to communicate with the collector by colouring objects black, grey or white [Dijkstra *et al.*, 1978]. However, this tricolour marking abstraction can usefully describe stop-and-collect as well as parallel methods. Colours are assigned to heap cells (or words) in the following manner.

Black indicates that the cell (or word) and its immediate descendants have been visited: the garbage collector has finished with black nodes and need not visit them again.

Grey nodes (or words) have been visited but their components may not have been scanned. Alternatively, in an incremental or concurrent context, they may have been subject to 'hostile' action by the mutator that has rearranged the connectivity of the graph. In either case, the collector must visit them again.

White nodes (or words) are unvisited and, at the end of the tracing phase, are garbage.

A garbage collection cycle terminates when all reachable nodes have been scanned (i.e. blackened) — there are no unscanned grey nodes left. Any nodes left white at this point are garbage and can be reclaimed. We shall use this abstraction to describe Cheney's algorithm. Note that it can also describe mark-sweep collection: nodes on the marking stack are grey, other marked nodes are black, and those that have not been marked yet are white.

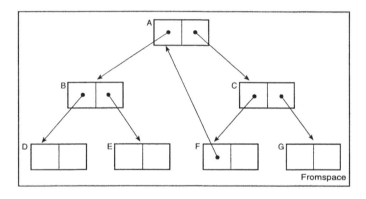

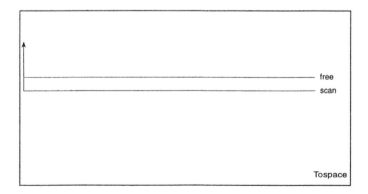

Diagram 6.1   Cheney's algorithm: at the flip.

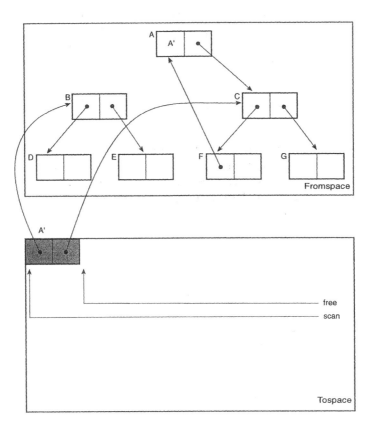

Diagram 6.2   First, the roots are copied to Tospace.

The algorithm

Cheney's collector repeatedly copies live objects to Tospace, and then scans these Tospace replicas for pointers to further nodes that have not been copied. The algorithm terminates when no such nodes can be found. In terms of the abstraction, copying a node to Tospace makes the node grey whilst scanning it for uncopied offspring colours it black. Two pointers are used to keep track of the progress of the collection. Scan marks the boundary between black nodes (those that have been completely scanned) and grey nodes (those whose component pointers have yet to be traversed by the collector). Free, as usual, indicates the next free location in Tospace (the end of the region of grey nodes). Since black nodes have, by definition, been completely scanned, any pointers they contain refer only to Tospace objects. Grey nodes have not been scanned yet and hence contain pointers to Fromspace only, although some of these Fromspace objects may have been copied to Tospace (see Diagram 6.3 on the next page).

The algorithm starts by flipping the rôles of Tospace and Fromspace, and by initialising

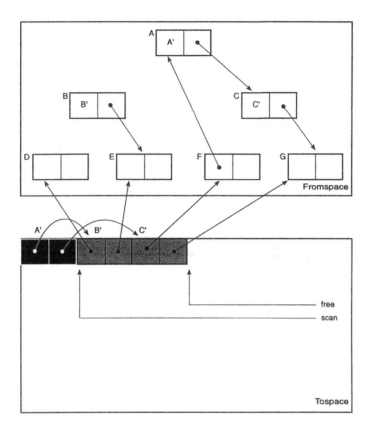

Diagram 6.3   A′ is scanned, copying B and C. 'Black' nodes have been scanned, 'grey' nodes have been copied but not scanned.

scan and free to point to the bottom of Tospace (see Algorithm 6.1 on page 123). The roots of the graph are then copied into Tospace. At each iteration of the main copying loop, the next grey cell (pointed to by scan) is scanned for pointers to objects in Fromspace that have not been copied yet. If one is found, it is evacuated to the location in Tospace pointed at by free, and a forwarding address is left behind. The forwarding address is typically, but not necessarily, written over the first field of the Fromspace object[1]. The Tospace child pointer is also updated to refer to the new grey replica rather than to the Fromspace object. Free and scan are moved along by the size of the object copied and that of the object scanned respectively. The scanned object is now black — it need not be considered again in this collection cycle. The algorithm terminates when there are no grey Tospace cells left, i.e. when scan catches up with free. There are no further nodes to consider.

[1] Systems such as Smalltalk that refer to heap cells through object tables need only revise the object table entry to refer to the Tospace object.

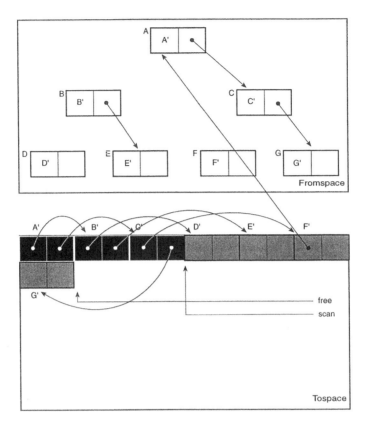

Diagram 6.4   All Fromspace nodes have now been copied.

This version of the algorithm assumes that all objects have headers, and that the components of an object can be discovered from the header. Furthermore, all heap pointers are assumed to point to the head of the object, i.e. internal pointers are not allowed. However, it is not hard to relax these conditions. If objects are segregated in the heap by type, their type and hence the location of their constituent pointers can be discovered from their address. Alternatively, if references are tagged to distinguish pointer words from non-pointer words, the algorithm can iterate through each address in Tospace, rather than object by object.

An example

Cheney's algorithm is extremely elegant and is actually simpler than the recursive version of copying. In Chapter 2 we observed that copying garbage collectors correctly copy re-entrant data structures, preserving sharing by using a forwarding address mechanism. Cheney's algorithm also uses forwarding addresses to maintain this essential property. Let us now see

```
flip()=
    Fromspace, Tospace = Tospace, Fromspace
    top_of_space = Tospace + space_size
    scan = free = Tospace

    for R in Roots
        R = copy(R)

    while scan < free
        for P in Children(scan)
            *P = copy(*P)
        scan = scan + size (scan)

copy(P) =
    if forwarded(P)
        return forwarding_address(P)
    else
        addr = free
        move(P,free)
        free = free + size(P)
        forwarding_address(P) = addr
        return addr
```

Algorithm 6.1   Cheney's algorithm.

how Cheney's algorithm copies a small graph. Initially, Tospace is empty and both scan and free point to its start (see Diagram 6.1 on page 119).

The root of the structure, A, is copied into Tospace at the location pointed to by free. The pointer fields of the Tospace replica, A′, still refer to Fromspace objects (see Diagram 6.2 on page 120). A forwarding address, A′, is written over A's first field, destroying the reference to B. However, B is still accessible from A′. The value of the root pointer (not shown) is also updated to refer to A′ rather than A. The initialisation phase is complete.

The algorithm now enters its scanning loop, examining the next grey node — pointed at by scan — and evacuating its components. First A′ is scanned and B and C are copied to Tospace at free. The pointer fields of A′ are updated to refer to the Tospace objects, B′ and C′. A′ need not be examined again, so we colour it black (see Diagram 6.3 on page 121).

The scan is repeated for each grey node in Tospace. The state of the heap after C′ has been scanned is shown in Diagram 6.4 on the facing page. The free pointer will not be moved again as all Fromspace nodes have now been copied. The grey nodes, D′, E′ and F′, are scanned for pointers, with scan is incremented at each iteration. The scan finds a pointer to A at left(F′). This pointer is updated with the forwarding address A′ found in A (see Diagram 6.5 on the next page).

Once G′ is scanned, scan points to the same location as free, at which point the algorithm terminates and the user program is resumed.

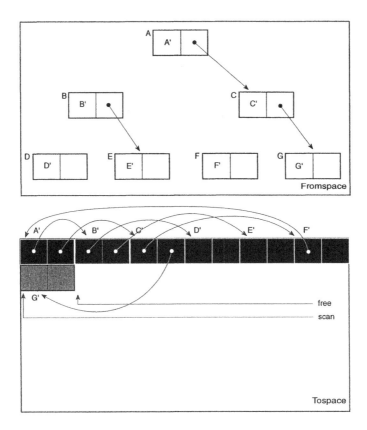

Diagram 6.5 left(F′) is updated with the forwarding address found in c.

6.2   Cheap allocation

Copying garbage collection is extremely attractive. It is comparatively simple to implement: there are no mark bitmaps to manipulate; and allocation of variable-sized objects is straightforward since the heap is compacted and free-lists are unnecessary. The CPU-cost of stop-and-copy garbage collection is generally cheap since only active nodes are visited and the cost of scavenging small objects is slight. For example, each loop of a copying collector can process a reference to a *cons* cell in just 27 SPARC instructions and fewer if the cell's referents are already copied [Zorn, 1989]. This is similar to the cost of marking a node using a bitmap.

Since the heap is compacted, allocation is both simple and cheap. All that is needed is to check that sufficient room is available in the semi-space, to increment the free space pointer and to return the address of the new cell. Zorn allocates *cons*-size cells in just five instructions (see the code fragment shown in Algorithm 6.2 on the facing page).

Heap allocation is now no more expensive than stack allocation. In Chapter 4 we saw how

— is a collection needed?

```
    subcc %g_allocated, ConsSize, %g_allocated
    bg,a noCollect
    mov %g_free, %result
    call Collect
    nop
    mov %g_free, %result
noCollect:
    add %g_free, ConsSize, %g_free
    or %result, ConsType, %result        —tag pointer with its type
```

Algorithm 6.2   Zorn's allocation sequence for *cons* cells.

software tests for mark stack overflow could be removed by placing a write-protected page at the end of the stack region: any attempt by the user program to write to this page causes an exception which is caught by the garbage collector's overflow handling code. The same technique can be applied to allocation in a compacted heap, whether managed by copying or mark-compact, since this is a push-only stack. Any attempt to allocate and initialise a node in the guard page will be trapped and the garbage collector called. Note that the allocator must attempt to initialise the new cell to trigger the trap; simply allocating space is insufficient. Processors with auto-decrement modes can now allocate *cons* cells in just two instructions if free is kept in a register [Appel, 1987] (see Algorithm 6.3); the pointer to the start of the new cell is left in the free register. The cost of a memory protection trap on a 20 MHz SPARCStation I under SUNOS 4.1 is approximately 230 microseconds, or 4,600 cycles. This is equivalent to 2,300 compare and branch instructions for a software-only overflow check.

```
    movl cdr, -(free)
    movl car, -(free)
```

Algorithm 6.3   VAX code sequence to create a new *cons* cell.

However this approach should be used with caution, as it may be unreliable in highly-pipelined architectures [Appel and Li, 1991]. On these machines there may be several outstanding faults and the heap overflow fault may not be notified to the processor until it has executed several instructions after the fault. Consequently the faulting instruction cannot be resumed after the trap handler has completed. Appel and Li note that this use of memory protection faults to detect heap overflow can be unreliable even on such comparatively simple machines as the Motorola 68020. A better way to reduce the cost of the overflow check is to combine all the heap space checks for a basic block[2] into a single check made at the start of the block.

---

[2] A code sequence that does not contain calls to procedures that may allocate an unbounded amount of memory.

6.3 Multiple-area collection

Copying garbage collection copies surviving data from one semi-space to the other. The CPU-cost of scavenging objects depends in part on their size and we have seen that for small objects this may be no more expensive than marking with a bitmap. Copying garbage collection is particularly effective at reclaiming small, ephemeral objects that live for no more than a few collection cycles — if they live and die between two consecutive garbage collections their space can be reclaimed 'for free'. On the other hand, the cost of copying large objects may be prohibitive. Some objects may be relatively permanent, loaded in at start-up or created soon after and surviving until the end of the computation. Repeatedly copying such objects from one semi-space to the other is wasteful.

Static areas

Collection effort can be reduced if large objects and long-lived objects are treated specially, by dividing the heap into a number of separately managed regions. Data that is known to be relatively permanent can be allocated to a *static area*. Although static data may need to be traced if it contains pointers to heap objects outside the static area, it should not be moved.

Large object areas

Similarly large objects may be assigned to a *large object area*, possibly, but not necessarily, by separating them into a small header and a body [Caudill and Wirfs-Brock, 1986; Ungar and Jackson, 1988]. The header would be kept in the region of the heap managed by the semi-space copying collector but the body would be kept in the large object area. This large object area is usually managed by a non-moving collector such as mark-sweep in order to avoid the cost of copying large objects, although it may be necessary to compact the area occasionally to reduce fragmentation [Lang and Dupont, 1987; Hudson and Moss, 1992].

Large objects are commonly comprised of bitmap or string data, such as cached images of occluded windows. Although these objects must be preserved, they do not need to be scanned since they do not contain pointers. If large atomic objects can be identified, either by their header or by segregating them into a separate region of the heap, both the copying time and the scanning time can be eliminated. Ungar and Jackson observed that, by reserving even a comparatively small region for large bitmap and string data, they were able to reduce pause times by a factor of up to four [Ungar and Jackson, 1988].

On the other hand, if sufficient support is available from the operating system, large objects can be copied comparatively cheaply by allocating each large object to its own pages. Instead of copying an object word by word from Fromspace into Tospace, the operating system's page table can be re-mapped to place the object's pages in Tospace rather than Fromspace [Withington, 1991].

The notion of segregating objects into different regions of the heap, each of which are managed separately, is fundamental to *generational garbage collection*. Here, objects are segregated by age on the assumption that younger objects are likely to die soon. The garbage collector can therefore concentrate its efforts on the youngest region of the heap where, it is hypothesised, its rewards will be greatest. Generational techniques have proved to be widely successful and we look at this in the next chapter.

Incremental incrementally compacting garbage collection

Dividing the heap into multiple, separately managed areas has other benefits, even if generational garbage collection is not used. One advantage of copying collection is that it compacts the heap, eliminating fragmentation. Its cost is that the address space is doubled to accommodate the second semi-space. One way to gain some of the benefits of compaction without the space cost of full copying collection nor the time penalty of mark-compact, is to compact parts of the heap incrementally.

Lang and Dupont divide the heap into $n + 1$ equally sized segments [Lang and Dupont, 1987]. At each garbage collection cycle, two of these segments are treated as a pair of semi-spaces and managed by a copying collector while the rest of heap is mark-swept. The pair of segments chosen as semi-spaces rotates through the address space at each collection, incrementally compacting the heap.

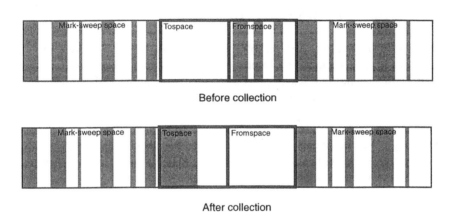

Before collection

After collection

Diagram 6.6   Incremental incrementally compacting garbage collection.

This arrangement is simplest if the semi-space segments are adjacent, say segments i and $i + 1$. Segment i is free at the start of the collection and will be the Tospace; $i + 1$ will be the Fromspace. As the collector traces the active graph, visited cells will be marked (by setting a mark-bit) unless they are in Fromspace. Objects in Fromspace are evacuated to Tospace, leaving behind forwarding addresses in the usual way. References to those objects, whether held in objects in Tospace or in mark-sweep space (all segments but i and $i + 1$), must be updated to refer to the Tospace replicas. At the end of the collection, all active data in segment $i + 1$ will have been compacted into segment i. Segment $i + 1$ can then be used as the Tospace for the next collection cycle to compact data from segment $(i + 2)$ modulo n. The fragment of Tospace that remains unused can be added to the free-list.

If a Cheney collector is used to manage the semi-spaces rather than a recursive copying collector, the state of the collection is represented by two data structures. The state of mark-sweep part of the collection is a stack of resumption points (whether an auxiliary stack or pointer-reversal is used). The state of the copying part of the collection is represented by the queue of grey cells in Tospace. The collector therefore has a choice of which transition to take next: whether to pop the marking stack or to advance the scan pointer. Lang and Dupont recommend that the mark-sweep collector always be preferred to the copying collector in order to limit the growth of the stack.

The main effect of incremental compaction is to compact small fragments into a single piece. The incremental compactor will pass through every segment of the heap in n collection cycles. It requires no extra passes unlike every mark-compact algorithm, but does have a small memory cost: the extra segment used for a semi-space. Lang and Dupont suggest that the algorithm might be improved by letting Tospace be larger than Fromspace so that data-structures that are partially held in mark-sweep space can also be compacted or allowing the size of the semi-spaces to be adapted dynamically. In any event, care must be taken to ensure that objects do not straddle Fromspace and mark-sweep space. They also suggest that it may be combined with an incremental mark-sweep collector but give few details.

6.4   Garbage collector efficiency

Appel has argued that copying garbage collection can be made arbitrarily cheap by expanding the size of the heap [Appel, 1987]. To preserve an object, the collector must first copy the object into Tospace and then scavenge its offspring. If the number of reachable cells is R then Cheney copying requires cR operations, for some constant c dependent on the cost of processing a cell and the average number of pointers in each cell. The number of cells allocated between garbage collections is $M/s - R$, where M is the size of each semi-space and the average size of each cell is s. This will also be the number of garbage cells reclaimed at each collection if the number of reachable cells remains constant. The CPU-cost of garbage collection per cell reclaimed, g, is therefore

$$g = \frac{c}{M/sR - 1}.$$

In theory, g can be made arbitrarily small by increasing M. Appel argues that, with sufficient memory, it is cheaper to garbage collect than to free a cell explicitly, even if the cost of freeing a cell is only a single instruction. He suggests that a sufficient ratio of real memory to average volume of live data to make heap allocation of three-word objects cheaper than stack allocation is 7 to 1. Thus the heap should be fourteen times larger than the set of reachable objects.

Diagram 6.7 on the facing page illustrates the effect of increasing heap size. Imagine that a program is run twice, once with semi-spaces of 350 kilobytes and then with semi-spaces of 700 kilobytes. To simplify matters, let us further suppose that the amount of active memory used is approximately constant, say 100 kilobytes, and that the program allocates 1800 kilobytes in total. To complete, the run with the smaller heap must garbage collect six times, copying $6 \times 100 = 600$ kilobytes of data. The run with the larger heap, on the other hand, needs to collect only twice, copying 200 kilobytes.

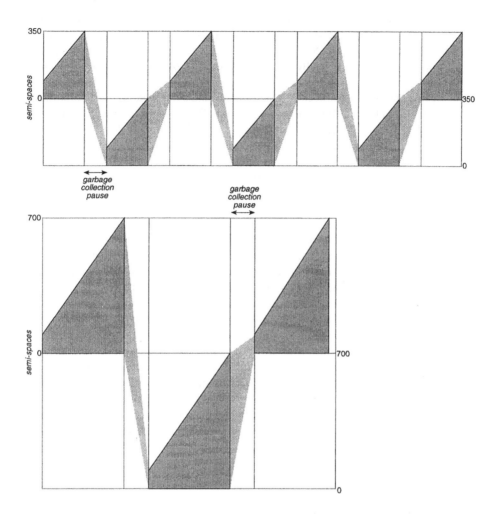

Diagram 6.7   Increasing heap size reduces garbage collection time.

6.5   Locality issues

This argument only considers CPU-costs attributable to garbage collection. In reality, virtual memory behaviour will be an important factor in the overall performance of the system unless the entire heap can be held in main memory. Cache misses will also be an important, though much less significant, factor in overall performance. Once the heap is too large, any benefits of reducing the number of collections needed will be outweighed by the cost of increased paging. Since the cost of a page fault will be hundreds of thousands, or even millions, of cycles, additional CPU effort to avoid paging is worthwhile [Hennessy and Patterson, 1996].

There are two issues of spatial locality here. First, the memory management system (the garbage collector and the allocator) will generally touch every page in Tospace in each collection cycle. Increasing the size of the heap increases the number of pages that will be touched in each collection cycle. Secondly, copying garbage collection reorganises the layout of objects in the heap. This will affect the spatial locality of heap data structures and may compromise the mutator's working set.

Sophisticated mark-sweep collection, using a stack and a mark bitmap, only modifies heap memory at allocation time, as the heap is lazily swept. During the marking phase, heap pages are not dirtied. For mark-sweep collection, paging behaviour is unlikely to be affected by a lazy sweep (as objects are linked into a free-list) as these objects will soon be reallocated anyway. Lazy sweepers that use a vector of cached free slots do not touch heap pages at all until they are reallocated. Zorn compared the paging behaviour of generational copying and generational mark-sweep collectors for SPUR Lisp and found that the virtual memory behaviour of mark-sweep was noticeably better than that of copying [Zorn, 1989]. Each garbage collector was called whenever 500 kilobytes of memory had been allocated since the last collection — this threshold was sufficiently low to give non-disruptive pauses. Although the CPU overhead of mark-sweep collection was between 1.5 and 4.7 percent higher than that of copying, copying required a real memory between 30 percent and 40 percent larger than that required by mark-sweep in order to achieve the same page fault rate.

Wilson argues that the chief cause of this impairment is the regular reuse of the two semi-spaces, rather than worsened locality within the compacted data [Wilson, 1994]. This pattern of cyclic reuse means that the next page to be allocated is likely to be the one least recently used. This pattern conflicts with virtual memory page replacement policies that typically evict the least recently used page, on the assumption that it is the least likely to be used again. If the set of pages held in real memory is insufficient to accommodate both semi-spaces simultaneously, Tospace pages will always have been evicted before they are used for allocation. The most effective way to reduce these paging costs is to ensure that both semi-spaces fit within main memory. If the heap is too large for this, then it can be divided into smaller regions which are collected separately: this is the basis of generational collection.

Operating system support

Paging can also be reduced with cooperation from the operating system. At the end of each garbage collection, data on Fromspace pages and all Tospace pages with addresses above `free` are garbage. When a fresh, unloaded Tospace page is allocated, the data on the swapped-out page will be loaded into real memory although it contains nothing but garbage. Loading this page may cause a Fromspace page to be evicted. This page is likely to be marked as dirty, either because the mutator has modified its data or because the collector had written forwarding addresses on it. In either case, the virtual memory system will copy the page's contents out to the swap disk. From the point of view of both the mutator and the collector, this disk traffic is unnecessary.

It would be better if the operating system and the dynamic memory manager cooperated so that the page frame in real memory belonging to the Fromspace page was simply re-mapped to the Tospace page without any disk operations. The Symbolics 3600 architecture closely intertwined garbage collection with the virtual memory system and did precisely this [Moon, 1984]. Wang has also suggested that a lightweight version of the AIX system call `disclaim` might be used by the collector to unmap Fromspace pages explicitly in order to save disk traffic [Wang, 1994b; AIX, version 32].

There may be several garbage-collected processes with large heaps running concurrently. Each process will want to make maximum progress by expanding its heap as much as possible without thrashing. This will lead to contention for real memory. Alonso and Appel have suggested that heap sizes might be allocated centrally [Alonso and Appel, 1990]. At each collection, each process should ask a central advisor whether it should expand or contract its heap. The advisor could then make the decision on the basis of the amount of time each process has spent on useful work and garbage collecting, and each process's minimum memory requirements.

6.6 Regrouping strategies

It is desirable that relationships between data are reflected in their layout in the heap: the more closely data are related, the more closely they should be placed in the heap. Relationships between mutator data may be structural — the nodes are part of the same data structure — or temporal — the objects are accessed by the mutator at similar times. Placing related data on the same pages reduces paging traffic since bringing one object into main memory also brings in its neighbours, and these are likely to be required by the user program soon.

Research by Hayes suggests that objects are typically created and destroyed in clusters [Hayes, 1991]. He found that over 60 percent of the longest lived objects were allocated within one kilobyte of each other, and that this correlation was even stronger if younger objects were considered. These objects also died in clusters, which strongly suggests that the initial layout of objects in the heap reflects future access patterns by the user program. Work with Lisp and Smalltalk implementations also confirms this view [Clark and Green, 1977; Clark, 1979; Blau, 1983; Andre, 1986]. The sliding compactors studied in Chapter 5 preserved the initial layout of data in the heap: garbage objects were simply squeezed out. Copying collectors, however, do not share this property. The ordering of objects in the heap may be rearranged as they are copied.

The way that live data is regrouped depends on the order that the live graph is traversed. The simplest orders are depth-first and breadth-first traversal. Depth-first traversal visits all the descendants of a node before it visits the node's siblings. Breadth-first search visits siblings before descendants. The Cheney copying collector presented earlier in this chapter copied data structures breadth-first whereas recursive algorithms, such as mark-sweep or Fenichel–Yochelson copying, traverse the graph in depth-first order. Diagrams 6.8 on the next page and 6.9 on page 133 show how a tree might be laid out on virtual memory pages in the heap by a depth-first and a breadth-first copying collector respectively.

As well as studying the locality characteristics of the garbage collector itself, researchers have investigated using the garbage collector to improve the locality of reference of the user program. There are two approaches that may be taken.

Static regrouping analyses the topology of heap data structures in order to rearrange structurally-related objects more closely. It is called static because it analyses the structure of the graph at collection time rather than considering how the mutator accesses that data.

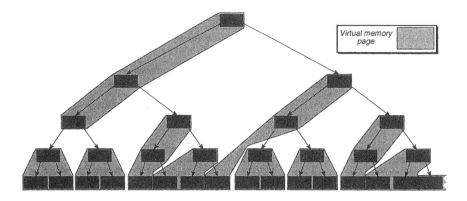

Diagram 6.8 A binary tree copied depth-first. Each shaded area represents a virtual memory page [Wilson *et al.*, 1991]. PLDI'91, ©1995 Association for Computing Machinery. Reprinted by permission.

Dynamic regrouping clusters objects according to the mutator's pattern of access to the data. This requires objects to be regrouped on the fly by an incremental copying collector: we examine how successful this strategy can be in Chapter 8 where we discuss incremental collection techniques.

Depth-first *vs.* breadth-first copying

Moon found that depth-first copying generally yields better locality than breadth-first copying for Lisp because it is more likely to place parents and offspring on the same page, particularly if data structures tend to be shallow but wide [Moon, 1984]. In Diagram 6.8 we can see that depth-first copying tends to place nodes on pages with their offspring or parents. Breadth-first copying on the other hand tends to place much more remotely related objects together — first and second cousins in this example (see Diagram 6.9 on the next page). Such grouping reduces the chance that loading an object into real memory will also load another soon-to-be-accessed object, and hence increases the probability of another page fault. In general, breadth-first copying initially copies all root nodes, then copies the second-level descendants of each node, then the third-level descendants, and so on. The reachable data structures are interleaved in Tospace, rather than grouped coherently.

Stamos and Blau compared the effect of different groupings of Smalltalk objects on paging. As well as creation order, and depth- and breadth-first order, they also grouped objects by type, by reference count and randomly [Stamos, 1982; Blau, 1983; Stamos, 1984]. Both simulations revealed that breadth-first and depth-first orderings produced fewer page faults than random ordering, but that depth-first's advantage over breadth-first was slight except for very small real memory sizes. Both orderings gave worse locality than optimal or creation ordering. Not surprisingly, larger page sizes gave rise to fewer page faults than smaller ones. The lack of differentiation between depth-first and breadth-first copying shown by these results seems to

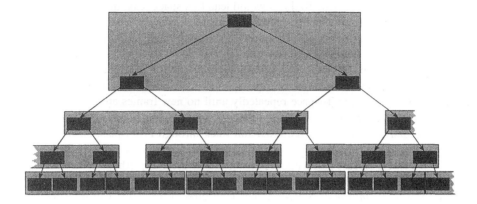

Diagram 6.9   A binary tree copied breadth-first [Wilson *et al.*, 1991]. PLDI'91, ©1995
Association for Computing Machinery. Reprinted by permission.

contradict our intuition.

Wilson *et al.* argue that the Stamos and Blau studies ignored the topology of typical
program images [Wilson *et al.*, 1991]. Rather than comprising well-proportioned trees, Lisp
and Smalltalk system images tend to contain a few extremely wide root nodes but have
relatively shallow structures. These roots are typically hash tables of all interned symbols
and methods. Hash tables group data into a pseudo-random order. For good performance (few
clashes) they are designed to spread keys across the table rather than clustering data. Not only,
Wilson *et al.* say, did the earlier studies fail to group data structures in a manner reflecting their
actual use, but they also ignored the disastrous grouping effects on locality of traversing hash
tables linearly. Page faults could be reduced if hash tables were treated specially and 'normal'
data structures were copied in an approximately depth-first fashion. A collector that does copy
data depth-first is the Fenichel–Yochelson collector but it requires additional memory to hold
the recursion stack and hence also risks stack overflow. There are two ways to circumvent this
problem.

Stackless recursive copying collection

One way to remove the stack problem from depth-first copying collection is to use Deutsch–
Schorr–Waite pointer reversal [Reingold, 1973]. However, this requires additional space for
flag-bits and is slow, since bits must be interrogated and pointers manipulated at each iteration.
Thomas and Jones describe a recursive copying garbage collector for a shared environment
closure reducer for Lazy ML (LML) that does not require extra memory nor is interpretive
[Thomas and Jones, 1994; Thomas, 1995]. The basic unit of heap allocation is a variable-
length *frame* of *closures*. Each closure contains a code pointer and an *environment* pointer to
a heap frame.

At collection time, some closures in a frame may be live but others may be garbage.
Although the frame itself must be preserved if any of its closures are live, garbage closures

must not be recursively copied. To do so would lead to a space leak, that is, garbage may be falsely preserved and hence memory made permanently unavailable for recycling[3]. When a closure is scavenged, the live slots in its environment can be determined from its code pointer since LML is statically typed (see Diagram 6.10).

A Cheney-style collector, that scans each frame just once, is inadequate since a frame might be shared between different closures, each of which uses a different set of live slots. One solution might be to rescan Tospace repeatedly until no new frames are scavenged, but this would increase the collector's complexity to $O(n^2)$. Instead Thomas and Jones implement the collection recursively, but thread the recursion stack through Fromspace closures that have already been visited. The question arises: how can a description of a set of environment slots be stored in a single closure slot without placing an interpretive overhead on the collector?

Their collector is tailored specifically for each program by the compiler. Closure code pointers point to an *information table* rather than directly to code. The information table includes the code to evaluate the closure and a pointer to the scavenger for that code sequence (see Diagram 6.10). The scavenger's code knows precisely which slots in the closure's environment are used by the evaluation code.

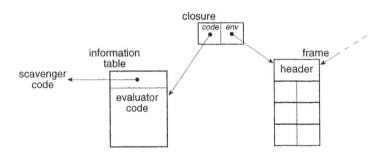

Diagram 6.10   Code-environment closures for 'stackless' recursive copying.

The state of the collector is modelled by a *continuation*, i.e. a pointer to code. To scavenge, say, slots 1, 3 and 5 of an environment frame of a closure, the collector writes a single continuation into the closure and pushes (links) the closure into the its stack of continuations. The collector then visits slot 1. When the continuation is resumed, its code will push a second continuation onto the stack (which is held in already visited Fromspace frame slots) (to scavenge slot 5) and then scavenge slot 3.

Thus Thomas and Jones implement recursive copying without using any extra space for the stack, nor suffering the costs of pointer reversal. By using continuations their collector avoids all interpretive overheads.

---

[3] This is akin to the tenured garbage and nepotism problem faced by generational garbage collection (see Chapter 7).

Approximately depth-first copying

Moon, on the other hand, modifies Cheney's algorithm to make it 'approximately depth-first' [Moon, 1984]. Rather than scavenging from the cell pointed at by scan, the scavenge is always continued from the last partially-filled page of Tospace — call this page page(free) — treating grey Tospace pages more like a stack than a queue. Scan_partial scans the page at the end of Tospace until the last allocated page of Tospace is completely scanned, i.e. it is either completely filled or no further Fromspace references are found on it (see scan_partial in Algorithm 6.4 on page 139). Although scan_partial is breadth-first it ensures that objects are placed on the same page as references to them as far as possible. If an object should be copied onto a new page, the scan restarts on that page; if a newly copied object straddles page boundaries, the scan restarts from the part of the object on the newest page, in an attempt to fill it.

Whenever scan_partial completes scanning the last Tospace page, the algorithm returns to scanning Tospace objects breadth-first in the usual way (scan_all in Algorithm 6.4 on page 139). Scan_all is almost the standard breadth-first scavenger, but its scan stops as soon as it copies an object from Fromspace into Tospace. This object is used as a seed for scan_partial. Copy is almost unchanged from Cheney's algorithm except that it must test for pointers already followed. Flip alternates between scanning pages at the end of Tospace and the standard breadth-first search.

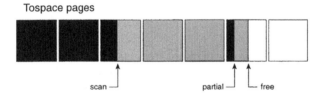

Diagram 6.11   Black and grey Tospace pages may be interleaved in Moon's algorithm.

The drawback of this scheme is that scan_all may scan addresses that have already been scavenged by scan_partial (see Diagram 6.11) — this is a special case of the problem that Thomas was trying to overcome. Moon argues that the cost of this extra scanning is small (around 30 percent of objects may be re-scanned [Wilson *et al.*, 1991]) compared with the cost of avoiding re-scanning objects. If the scavenger finds an unscanned reference to Fromspace, the collector must do work that would have been done in any case. If it does not find any Fromspace references, the object evacuation mechanism is not used and no page faults are incurred. On the Symbolics 3600, which had hardware support for tagged memory, the time to scan a 256-word page without page faults or transport traps to evacuate Fromspace objects, was approximately twice that of transporting one minimally-sized object. Moon reports that 'approximately depth-first' copying increased the elapsed time for garbage collection by around 6 percent. He does not give figures to show how effective his traversal was at reducing page-faults, but Courts measured a 15 percent improvement using a recursive, depth-first scavenger [Courts, 1988].

Hierarchical decomposition

Wilson *et al.* eliminate re-scanning in Moon's algorithm by modifying it to become a two-level version of Cheney [Wilson *et al.*, 1991]. As well as major scan and free pointers, each page of Tospace also has a minor scan and minor free pointer. Their algorithm repeatedly scans the first unscanned address in the first incompletely scanned page in Tospace. This page is pointed at by the major scan pointer; the location on this page is pointed at by the page's minor scan pointer. As in Moon's algorithm, if a reference to an uncopied Fromspace object is found, the object is evacuated to the end of Tospace to seed a new breadth-first scan limited to that page. This scan halts when either the page is full or all of the object's descendants have been visited.

Both Moon's 'approximately depth-first' algorithm and the Wilson–Lam–Moher modification result in a hierarchical decomposition of the graph (see Diagram 6.12 on page 142), with upper nodes of a tree grouped on the same page, and so on, recursively, for each of the sub-graphs below. Rather than being nearly as effective as depth-first traversal, Wilson *et al.* claim that their and Moon's traversals are actually better because any access to a node will typically also load its offspring into main memory. If a node is touched by the mutator, it is argued, it is more likely that the node's offspring or parent will be touched soon, than, say, its ancestors or descendants in the *car*-line. Hierarchical decomposition attempts to group more important nodes together, rather than grouping data structures in diagonal slices (depth-first traversal) or horizontal slices (breadth-first traversal). This, it is argued, more closely reflects patterns of access by the user program.

Hash tables

Wilson *et al.* also avoided traversing the graph from system hash tables. Instead, they modified their compiler to construct a linear list of the binding cells of global variables in the hash table in the order that these are defined. This list is only used by the garbage collector and so has little effect on the normal execution of the program. They also grouped global procedures with the variables that pointed to them[4]. By traversing this list, Wilson's collector can reach global objects in the order in which they were defined — earlier studies confirmed that definition order copying results in superior locality not only to random order (for example, hash table order) but also better than depth- or breadth-first search. Their results showed a significant reduction in the incidence of page faults, particularly for programs that were small relative to the system image. Repeated page faults in particular were reduced by up to an order of magnitude. The authors assign much of this improvement to better treatment of hash tables. They also found that their regrouping led to better static locality characteristics, with the majority of pointers pointing to other objects on the same page.

In a later study, the authors found that the optimal grouping was very dependent on the shape and type of data structure being copied [Lam *et al.*, 1992]. Although hierarchical decomposition performed well for trees, it was disappointing for other structures. The authors suggest that further improvements may be made by modifying the traversal order according to the kind of object being created. For their Scheme examples, functions should be grouped in

---

[4] Andre, too, obtained improved performance from Symbolics Lisp by moving binding cells of procedure variables out of hash tables and into compiled code objects [Andre, 1986].

calling order, association lists in depth-first order and other lists in hierarchical decomposition order. For small real memory sizes, they observed order of magnitude reductions in the number of page faults incurred compared with breadth-first search.

Although these techniques reduce the rate of page faults of copying garbage collectors, it would be better if they did not fault at all. This can only be achieved if both semi-spaces can be held in real memory: either larger real memory or smaller semi-spaces are necessary. Smaller semi-spaces will also reduce the garbage collection pause. This is the approach taken by generational garbage collectors, which we examine in Chapter 7. This style of collection segregates objects in the heap by age. The premise is that the turnover of younger objects is more rapid than that of older ones, and hence that most reclamation gains are to be made amongst the youngest generation. However, improving the virtual memory performance of garbage collection turns the spotlight onto the next level of the memory hierarchy: the cache. We turn to this matter in Chapter 11 when we discuss data caches.

6.7   Issues to consider

Copying is probably the most widely adopted method of garbage collection, either in its own right or as the basis for more sophisticated generational or incremental collectors. We discuss these in Chapters 7 and 8 respectively. In this section, we review two issues: the circumstances in which copying might be an appropriate method of garbage collection, and ways in which its efficiency might be improved.

Which method of collection?

One disadvantage of non-moving storage managers is their susceptibility to fragmentation. Wilson *et al.* provide a useful survey of allocation techniques in [Wilson *et al.*, 1995]. Although there are allocation techniques that can ameliorate this problem, it can only be eliminated by compacting collectors such as mark-compact or copying. Compaction may also bring locality advantages by reducing the working set of the program. The mark-compact collectors discussed in Chapter 5 offer two advantages over copying collectors. First, they operate in smaller address spaces: a second semi-space is not required. If the memory occupied by the two semi-spaces of a copying collector is greater than that available in real memory, paging is likely to cause extremely poor performance. Because of the LRU disciplines of linear allocation and of virtual memory systems, the next page to be allocated is the page most likely to have been evicted. Each time a new page is allocated, it will have to be swapped in. Second, mark-compact collectors preserve the allocation order of objects in the heap which may be important for some applications. For example, Prolog compilers can take advantage of the reflection of spatial and allocation ordering to reclaim unbounded amounts of memory in constant time: the heap is treated as a stack. The drawback of mark-compact collectors is the cost of the compaction phase, which requires two or three passes through the heap.

Allocation in a compacted heap is extremely cheap. If the cost of storage management is dominated by allocation rather than collection, copying garbage collectors provide good performance. For this reason, the heaps of systems with very high rates of allocation are usually managed by copying collectors. On the other hand, copying collection performs less well for certain heap configurations. The cost of copying an object depends on the object's size; for all but the smallest objects, the cost will be greater than that of simply marking it. If the heap is mainly composed of large objects, the cost of copying collection will increase. Likewise, if the heap contains a substantial proportion of long-lived objects, copying collection is not necessarily the best option.

There is no reason why a single method of collection should be adopted for all objects in the heap. Instead, a hybrid collector that manages different types of object under different collection policies may be appropriate. Many collectors adopt such a hybrid strategy by dividing the heap into a number of separately managed areas. Objects known to be relatively permanent can be kept in a static area. Although they must be scanned for pointers, they need not be marked, swept nor copied. Objects in the static area known to be atomic can be simply ignored by the collector: since they cannot contain pointers, they need not be scanned.

If the delay caused by copying large objects is prohibitive, they can be allocated to a large object area, possibly with a small header allocated in the normal, copied region of the heap. The large object area can then be managed by a non-moving collector such as mark-sweep, possibly supported by an occasional compaction phase.

Nevertheless, the copying collectors presented in this chapter are intrinsically stop/start collectors. All useful processing must be suspended until the heap is completely collected. Depending on the volume of data surviving a collection, the garbage collection delay may be disruptive to interactive or real-time programs. One solution is to scavenge the heap incrementally, interleaving garbage collection operations with the user program: we discuss this in Chapter 8. Another solution is to concentrate garbage collection efforts on that region of the heap most likely to contain garbage. Such a solution is particularly appropriate if the heap contains a mix of long- and short-lived objects. This is the basis of generational garbage collection which we discuss in the next chapter.

Performance

If copying collection is to be used, either as a stop-and-copy collector or as the basis for a generational collector, the Cheney algorithm presented on page 123 is almost always a substantial improvement over the recursive Fenichel–Yochelson collector described in Section 2.3. One exception is Thomas's closure reducer, described on page 133.

In the previous subsection, we noted techniques that can be used to avoid copying some objects. If sufficient operating support is available, where copying must be done, it can be made more efficient. If large objects are assigned to their own virtual memory pages, they can be moved to Tospace without copying by re-mapping the operating system's page table. Paging can also be reduced. At the end of a collection, all Fromspace pages and all unscanned Tospace pages contain garbage. Any effort spent either writing the contents of Fromspace pages (which will have been dirtied by forwarding addresses) out to the swap disk, or loading Tospace pages before they are allocated, will be wasted. If the collector can cooperate with the virtual memory system, this disk traffic can be avoided.

Finally, breadth-first copying collection disturbs the order of objects in the heap. It may be worth using more sophisticated traversal orders to improve the way related objects are grouped on virtual memory pages. In particular, certain data structures, such as hash tables, may benefit from special treatment rather than being traced linearly.

```
flip() =
    Fromspace, Tospace = Tospace, Fromspace
    top_of_space = Tospace + space_size
    scan, partial, free = Tospace
    for R in Roots
        R = copy(R)
    while scan < free
        scan_partial()
        scan_all()

scan_partial() =
    while partial < free
        *partial = copy(*partial)
        — scan partially-filled page at end of Tospace
        partial = max(page(free),partial + 1)

scan_all() =
    oldfree = free
    while oldfree == free                        —nothing evacuated yet
    and scan < partial
        *scan = copy(*scan)
        scan = scan + 1
    — set up scan of any partially-filled page
    if free > oldfree
        partial = max(page(free),partial)

copy(P) =
    if atomic(P)
        return P
    if tospace(P)                    —already scavenged by scan_partial
        return P
    if forwarded(P)
        return forwarding_address(P)
    else
        addr = free
        move(P,free)
        free = free + size(P)
        forwarding_address(P) = addr
        return addr
```

Algorithm 6.4   Moon's approximately depth-first algorithm.

6.8   Notes

One advantage of copying garbage collection is that its cost depends on the number of survivors at each collection, rather than the size of the heap. For many applications and languages the proportion of survivors is low [Deutsch and Bobrow, 1976; Foderaro and Fateman, 1981; Ungar, 1984; Swinehart et al., 1986; Zorn, 1989; Hudak et al., 1992; Appel, 1992; Sansom and Peyton Jones, 1993; Barrett and Zorn, 1993b].

The first semi-space copying algorithm was due to Robert Fenichel and Jerome Yochelson [Fenichel and Yochelson, 1969]. Although it was recursive, they suggested that space for the stack could be avoided by using pointer reversal [Schorr and Waite, 1967; Knuth, 1973]; this was done by E.M. Reingold [Reingold, 1973]. The best-known copying algorithm is due to C.J. Cheney [Cheney, 1970]. His elegant algorithm is iterative rather than recursive and so runs in constant space. Experiments with a recursive copying collector by Douglas Clark and Cordell Green produced a *cdr*-cell linearisation — the property that a cell that points to another will be next to each other in Tospace after collection — of over 98 percent [Clark and Green, 1977]. The incidence of off-page pointers was also low (between 2.7 and 8.4 percent).

James Miller and Guillermo Rozas measured Andrew Appel's claims for the efficiency of heap allocation compared with stack allocation [Appel, 1987; Miller and Rozas, 1994]. Although they accepted Appel's general case, they found that heap allocation of procedure activation frames required an extra two instructions per call (to save the frame pointer and move the heap pointer) — 18 percent more instructions than was needed for stack allocation. For small numbers of frames allocated, the actual overhead was less than predicted — 3 to 5 percent — but it was larger if the capacity of the secondary cache was exceeded. Heap frames were also larger than stack frames (an extra pointer is needed to link the stack), provoking paging more easily, which was disastrous.

Many systems divide the heap into separately managed regions. This idea seems to have first appeared in Peter Bishop's thesis [Bishop, 1977]. Results for regrouping garbage collected heap data reflect those for conventional systems: good locality is often achieved by following the textual ordering [Ferrari, 1990]. Studies comparing the effect on locality of different static regrouping of the graph have been carried out for Smalltalk by James Stamos and Ricki Blau, and for Lisp by David Moon, David Andre, Robert Courts, and Paul Wilson, Michael Lam and Thomas Moher [Stamos, 1982; Blau, 1983; Stamos, 1984; Moon, 1984; Andre, 1986; Courts, 1988; Wilson et al., 1991].

Jon White first suggested that regrouping should reflect actual program accesses rather than the topology of the graph [White, 1980]. This technique was incorporated in the TI Explorer [Explorer, 1987, 1987] and studied by Robert Courts and Douglas Johnson [Courts, 1988; Johnson, 1991a].

Several observers have noted that statically typed programming languages do not require run-time tags to determine types. P. Branquart and J. Lewi used tables to map locations of variables within activation records to garbage collection routines for Algol-68 [Branquart and Lewi, 1971]. The drawback of this method is that the tables must be updated every time a local variable is bound to a heap allocated structure. Appel used the return address in the activation record to determine the procedure called, and hence the type information of the variables in the activation record [Appel, 1989b]. For polymorphic procedures, the caller too may have to be examined, and so on. This quickly becomes very complicated and

Appel provides few details. Ben Goldberg also used return addresses to handle polymorphic and higher order functions [Goldberg, 1991; Goldberg and Gloger, 1992; Goldberg, 1992]. Other references can be found in [Cheong, 1992; Tolmach, 1994]. However, his method also leads to traversing the stack, possibly twice, and again the method is complex. Amer Diwan, Eliot Moss and Richard Hudson have the compiler emit tables at each point where a garbage collection might occur [Diwan *et al.*, 1992]. They too use return addresses to access the tables; their concern is to be able to collect in the presence of a highly optimising compiler. The Spineless Tagless G-machine compiler for the functional language Haskell [Peyton Jones, 1992] replaces interpretative object tags by pointers to an information table for the object's type in the same way that Stephen Thomas does [Thomas, 1993]. These tables contain a pointer to code to collect the object [Sansom, 1991; Sansom, 1992; Sansom and Peyton Jones, 1993].

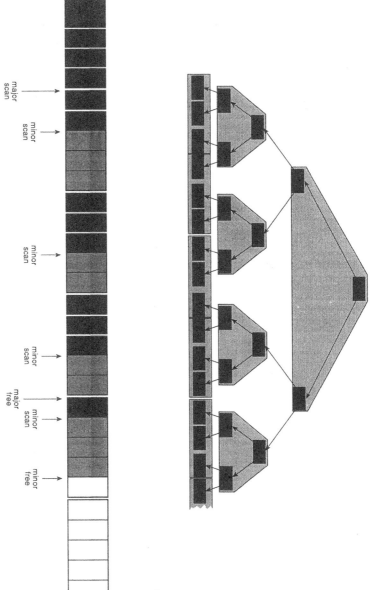

Diagram 6.12   A binary tree copied hierarchically [Wilson *et al.*, 1991]. PLDI'91, ©1995 Association for Computing Machinery. Reprinted by permission.

7

Generational Garbage Collection

7.1 The generational hypothesis

Simple tracing collectors, such as mark-scan and copying collectors, suffer from a number of drawbacks. Because all the active data must be marked or copied, delays caused by garbage collection can be obtrusive: studies from the 1970s and 1980s found that large Lisp programs were typically spending between 25 and 40 percent of their execution time in garbage collection [Steele, 1975; Foderaro and Fateman, 1981; Gabriel, 1985]. For these reasons some systems, such as the Xerox Dorado Smalltalk-80, largely designed for interactive programs, used deferred reference counting to spread the cost of garbage collection evenly throughout the program, despite its high CPU overhead and inability to collect cycles [Deutsch, 1983]. Incremental garbage collection techniques have also been used to try to spread the costs of reclaiming storage more smoothly. However, the overheads of incremental systems are high unless support from the virtual memory system or from specialised hardware is available.

Several authors have argued that the role of the garbage collector is not simply to reclaim memory, but that it should also improve the locality of the system as a whole [Fenichel and Yochelson, 1969; White, 1980]. Poorly designed garbage collectors can certainly interact badly with virtual memory and caches. Tracing requires that every active object be touched. In the case of copying collection, each page of the heap is touched every two collection cycles although only half the heap is in use by the user program at any one time. Such poor locality of reference leads to an excessive number of cache misses and page faults unless the entire heap can be held in memory, although this is somewhat ameliorated by the strongly sequential behaviour of copying collection. We saw in Chapter 4 that the number of page faults caused by mark-sweep collection can also be reduced with better marking schemes, for example by using an array of mark bits to avoid having to touch an object in order to determine if it has been marked or not.

Tracing algorithms also spend considerable time dealing unsuccessfully with relatively long-lived objects (unsuccessfully in the sense that the job of the garbage collector is to recycle storage). Straightforward collectors will either repeatedly mark and trace these objects, or repeatedly copy them from one semi-space to the other. In Chapter 6 we saw that the time spent by copying collectors in tracing and evacuating long-lived objects could be reduced by partitioning the heap into quasi-static, read-only and dynamic spaces. Although heap objects in the static area must be scanned, they are not moved. Read-only objects are guaranteed to contain pointers only to objects in the static area or into the read-only area itself. Objects in this space do not even need scanning. Unfortunately, the lifetimes of objects cannot in general be determined statically. Hanson observed that the bottom of the transient object area in his SITBOL system tended to accumulate objects that remained active throughout the program [Hanson, 1977]. His solution was to keep track of the height of this 'sediment' dynamically and to avoid collecting it unless absolutely necessary.

On the other hand, the lifetime of many objects is short. As early as 1976, Deutsch noted that "statistics show that a newly allocated datum is likely to be either 'nailed down' or abandoned within a relatively short time" [Deutsch and Bobrow, 1976]. Foderaro and Fateman found that over 98 percent of storage reclaimable at one garbage collection had been allocated and discarded since the previous garbage collection [Foderaro and Fateman, 1981]. Modern languages such as ML often allocate short-lived objects representing intermediate expressions, or even control structures (such as environment frames), on the heap. Many other researchers have gathered considerable evidence to support the *weak generational hypothesis* that "most objects die young" [Ungar, 1984]. The insight behind generational garbage collection[1] is that storage reclamation can be made more efficient and less obtrusive by concentrating effort on reclaiming those objects most likely to be garbage, i.e. young objects.

A number of benefits accrue if this can be done effectively. By collecting only a part of the heap, pause times can be diminished. If these delays can be reduced sufficiently, say to 100 microseconds or so, then garbage collection becomes feasible for interactive systems: a common measure of feasibility is "Can I garbage collect while tracking the mouse?". Furthermore, by avoiding repeatedly processing objects that remain active, the overall effort of garbage collection, measured over the entire program, may be reduced. The locality of the collector too can be improved by concentrating on just a small part of the heap. However, there is a price to pay: the system must be able to distinguish older from younger objects. In particular, the cost of storing in an old object a pointer to a young object becomes much more expensive.

The generational strategy is to segregate objects by age into two or more regions of the heap called *generations*. Different generations can then be collected at different frequencies, with the youngest generation being collected frequently and older generations much less often, or even, in the case of the oldest generation, possibly not at all. In a sense, this is the dynamic automation at run-time of the segregation into read-only, unscanned and dynamic areas that we discussed above. The number of generations used varies between implementations. Until recently, Standard ML of New Jersey (SML/NJ) used just two generations whereas Tektronix 4406 Smalltalk used seven [Appel, 1989b; Caudill and Wirfs-Brock, 1986]. Other schemes are able to vary the number of generations dynamically: for example, the University of Massachusetts Language-Independent Garbage Collector Toolkit is an example [Hudson *et al.*, 1991]. Generational garbage collection has often been used in conjunction with

---

[1] Sometimes called *ephemeral garbage collection*.

incremental collection schemes but the two are quite different, and generational garbage collection is not dependent on incremental collection [Lieberman and Hewitt, 1983; Moon, 1984]. Indeed generational garbage collection may be used as a substitute provided that *minor* collections of the youngest generation can be kept sufficiently short and that *major* multi-generation collections are hidden from the user.

Generational techniques have been demonstrated to be very successful and generational collectors are now in widespread use including all commercial Lisps, Modula-3, Standard ML of New Jersey, Glasgow Haskell, and commercial Smalltalk systems from Digitalk, Tektronix and PARCPlace Systems. For many applications today (but not all), generational garbage collection is the system of choice but whether the generational strategy is effective or not is application-dependent. The questions to ask include: Do most objects tend to die young? If young objects do not have a sufficiently high death rate, generational garbage collection does not reclaim storage efficiently. How frequent are pointer stores and in particular old–young pointer stores? What is the overhead of these stores? We address these and other issues in this chapter.

Object lifetimes

In order to be able to measure the age of an object, it is necessary to decide how to measure time. The most obvious way is to use wall-clock time. Time-based lifetime distributions do give insight into the object demographics of particular implementations but they are machine-dependent. In particular they depend on the speed of particular machines and of particular implementations. A better measure is to count bytes of heap allocated. As well as being machine-independent, this measure better reflects the demands made upon the memory management sub-system. In particular, it is closely related to the frequency of garbage collections since these are largely dependent on the amount of heap available.

However, heap allocation is not a perfect measure. Virtual memory algorithms may consider time in their page eviction policy. Objects supporting human interaction have lifetimes determined by the user's activity. Both of these considerations affect the garbage collector and argue for a measure based on wall-clock time. Some languages are also likely to have much higher rates of memory consumption. Implementations of Smalltalk and functional languages typically allocate objects in the heap that implementations of more conventional imperative languages might have stored on the stack or in registers. Not only do these implementations allocate more rapidly, but they also discard data at a higher rate as well.

Many systems today, particularly those written in modern functional, object-oriented or logic languages, make prodigious demands on memory. Allocation rates of one megabyte per second are common. SML/NJ programs, for example, may allocate a new word for every thirty instructions executed [Appel, 1989b]. Programs written in object-oriented languages also make much greater use of heap allocated data structures than those written in their predecessor procedural languages. However, there is strong evidence that the overwhelming majority of objects die very young, although a small proportion may live for a long time. In his recent garbage collection survey, Wilson finds that typically 80 to 98 percent of objects die before one further megabyte of heap storage has been allocated [Wilson, 1994]. Statistics for particular languages suggest that:

- between 50 and 90 percent of Common Lisp objects die before they are ten kilobytes old [Zorn, 1989];
- for a highly optimised Haskell compiler, the ten-kilobytes threshold sees the death of between 75 and 95 percent of the heap data. No more than 5 percent will survive beyond one megabyte [Sansom and Peyton Jones, 1993];
- only 1 percent of Cedar[2] objects survive beyond 721 kilobytes [Hayes, 1991];
- SML/NJ reclaims over 98 percent of any given generation at each collection [Appel, 1992];
- even for C programs, a large proportion of heap allocated data may be comparatively short-lived. Investigating four substantial C programs, Barrett and Zorn found that over half the heap data lived for less than ten kilobytes, and that less than 10 percent lived for longer than 32 kilobytes [Barrett and Zorn, 1993b].

Ungar and Jackson found similar results for Smalltalk-80 [Ungar, 1984] and support for the weak generational hypothesis, that most objects die young, can be found throughout the literature.

On the other hand, the *strong generational hypothesis*, that the older an object is the less likely it is to die, does not appear to hold generally. Object lifetime distributions do not fall off smoothly. Although most objects die young, some objects may last very much longer, possibly in clumps. Certainly object behaviour does not seem to fit the exponential decay model, in which the rate of decay is constant. On the contrary, the probability that an object will die is often inversely dependent on its age. Measurements with multi-generational collectors show large drops in reclamation rates from generation to generation. The distribution is also lumpy. Hayes found that more than 80 percent of objects successively deallocated differ in age by less than 1 kilobyte, and that this proportion became even larger if the criterion were relaxed to include 'nearly successively' deallocated [Hayes, 1991].

There is less agreement on whether the longevity of objects is related to their size. Although some researchers have found that large objects exhibit a tendency to live longer [Caudill and Wirfs-Brock, 1986], others have found no such correlation [Ungar and Jackson, 1988; Barrett and Zorn, 1993b]. Nevertheless it is worth treating large objects specially (see Chapter 6 where we discuss large-object areas).

7.2 Generational garbage collection

Generational garbage collection schemes divide the heap into two or more generations, segregating objects by age. Objects are first allocated in the youngest generation, but are *promoted* into older generations if they survive long enough. Accepting the weak hypothesis that most objects die young, generational schemes concentrate their effort to reclaim storage on the youngest generation since it is there that most recyclable space is to be found. Rather than occasional but lengthy pauses to collect the entire heap, the youngest generation is collected more frequently. Since the youngest generation is small, pause times will be comparatively short. Furthermore, because older objects are promoted out of younger generations, CPU cycles can be saved by not having to copy these items from one semi-space

---

[2] Cedar is a Modula-like language developed at Xerox [Swinehart *et al.*, 1986].

to another, although it is still necessary to scan some older objects for pointers into younger generations.

A simple example

Let us consider how generational garbage collection may be applied to a simple example. Diagram 7.1 shows the initial state of the heap, which is split into two generations. We suppose that all cells apart from cell s are in the younger generation, and that this generation is now full.

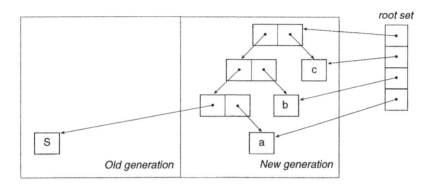

Diagram 7.1   The initial configuration.

Suppose that the mutator overwrites the first slot in the root set with a pointer to a new cell R. Suppose further that a second new cell is requested, but that this request triggers a minor collection of the younger generation (see Diagram 7.2 on the next page). The only reachable cells in the younger generation are a, b, c and R. These are moved to the older generation and the remaining cells are reclaimed.

The new cell can now be allocated, initialised to point at b and c, and right(R) is set to point at it. A further new cell is acquired and initialised to point at a and c. left(R) is updated to point at this new cell. The pointers to a, b and c are now popped from the root set. The final state of the heap is shown in Diagram 7.3 on the following page.

This example reveals five interesting properties of generational garbage collection. First, it is possible to collect the younger generation without collecting the older one. The pause-time to collect this generation is shorter than that required for a full collection. Second, young objects that survive sufficiently many minor collections — in this case just one — are promoted to the next generation. Third, the minor collection successfully reclaimed all short-lived cells in the graph. Fourth, the writes to R resulted in an *inter-generational pointer* (shaded grey in Diagram 7.3 on the next page), from the old generation to the young one. If a further minor collection was to occur now, these fields must be treated as part of the root set of the younger generation. In general, generational algorithms must record inter-generational pointers. Finally, node s is no longer reachable. Garbage in older generations, often called *tenured garbage*, cannot be reclaimed by minor collections of younger generations.

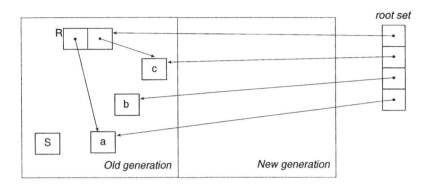

Diagram 7.2   After the minor collection of the younger generation.

In this example, we did not specify how objects in either generation were collected. We simply stated that any objects that survived sufficiently many collections were promoted to the next generation. Most generational collectors are copying collectors, although it is possible to use mark-sweep based schemes [Zorn, 1989; Demers *et al.*, 1990]. In this chapter we concentrate on generational copying collectors as these are simpler to understand.

Pause times

The generational collector exhibits several space advantages. Its pauses for garbage collection are shorter since it has less data to trace and copy at each collection, and the total volume of data moved throughout the entire program run is smaller. The graphs in Diagram 7.4 on the facing page compare the behaviour of a two-space copying collector and a generational

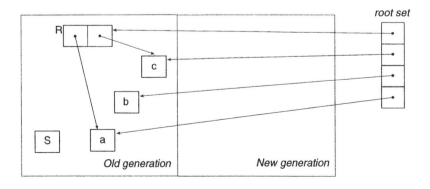

Diagram 7.3   Overwriting R creates old–young pointers.

collector[3]. For the two-space copying collector the amount of data copied is the sum of the heights of lightly shaded areas, whereas for the generational collector it is only the size (height) of the rightmost bar in the old generation. The spatial locality of the generational collector is also better since the allocation area (i.e. the new generation) is recycled at each scavenge in this example rather than being flipped from one semi-space to the other as it is by the copying collector.

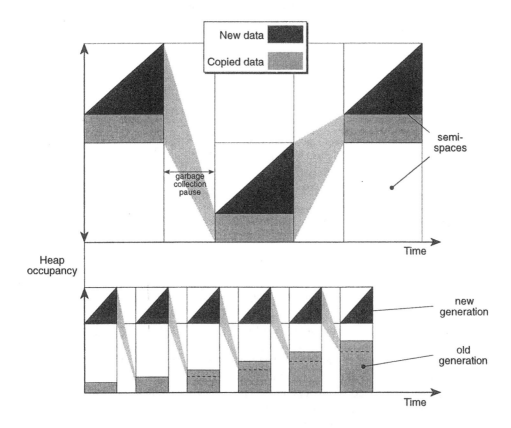

Diagram 7.4 Garbage collection pauses: a two-space copying collector (top) *vs.* a generational copying collector (bottom).

The root set for minor collections

However there is a price to pay. Garbage collection starts by tracing from a known root set. Unfortunately determining the roots of a generation is more difficult than determining the

---

[3] For the generational collector, we assume that there are just two generations, and that all live data in the young generation are promoted *en masse* to the old generation at each scavenge.

roots of the entire heap. As well as scanning registers and the stack for roots, a generational
collector must check whether any pointers to objects in one generation are stored in objects
of other generations. Any such pointers must be treated as roots of the first generation. In
the example shown in Diagram 7.5, all the shaded words are roots of the new generation.
Notice that as well as the standard root set of the computation (registers, the program stack
and pointer-valued objects in the static area) the collector must also start its trace from words
in the old generation that point into the new generation. On the other hand, it is not necessary
to continue the trace from a word in the old generation unless it contains a pointer to an object
in the new generation.

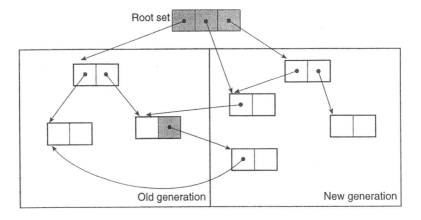

Diagram 7.5   Younger generations may have roots in older generations.

Inter-generational pointers can be created in two ways: either by storing a pointer in an
object or when an object containing pointers is promoted to an older generation. It is vital to
keep track of these inter-generational roots. The burden of this may fall on the shoulders of
the garbage collector or the mutator or both. Those created through promotion are easily
recognised by the garbage collector. For those created by assignment, a *write-barrier* is
needed to trap and record these pointers as they are written. Recording all pointer stores
would impose a substantial and unacceptable overhead on the user program. Fortunately we
can do better than this. If local variables are always considered to be part of the root set, there
is no need to record assignments to them, since they will be scanned by the garbage collector
in any case. As most stores are indeed into local variables, the cost of the write-barrier is
substantially reduced. Studies have shown that, for modern optimising compilers for Lisp or
ML for example, other pointer stores account for less than 1 percent of instructions executed
[Taylor *et al.*, 1986; Appel, 1989b; Zorn, 1989].

Furthermore, if we guarantee to collect all younger generations whenever we collect an
older generation, we only need to record old–young pointers. Old–young references are
much rarer than young–old, at least for mostly functional languages. Most pointer stores
in these languages are initialising stores (for example, Lisp's *cons*), and so can only point
backwards in time. These stores cannot generate references from older objects to younger

ones. User programs can only create old–young pointers by using assignment or assignment-like operators (for example, *rplaca* in Lisp, or redex updating in lazy functional languages), so only these operations need to be trapped by the write-barrier. Fortunately they are sufficiently rare to make generational garbage collection effective.

Only recording old–young pointers means that younger generations can be collected independently of their elders, but not vice-versa. Since cells in younger generations are likely to be mainly garbage (and so will not be traced) and also to contain references to objects in older generations that need to be traced anyway, the restriction that younger generations must be collected when older ones are is not too burdensome. Collection of the youngest generation is usually called a *minor* collection, in contrast to less frequent *major* collections of several generations. To collect an older generation independently of a younger one would mean treating the whole of the younger generation as possible roots. The possibility of treating the entire younger generation as part of the root set is only plausible because younger generations are likely to be smaller, and because scanning is generally faster than tracing and has better locality.

Performance

Some care is needed when examining claims in the literature for the performance of garbage collection algorithms. What is effective for an interpreted language may be less so for a compiled version of the same language. While the write-barrier overhead may be slight in an interpreted system, it may be much more obtrusive in an optimising compiler. For example, Ungar's generation-scavenging garbage collectors for the Berkeley Smalltalk-80 [Ungar, 1984] and SOAR [Ungar, 1986] suffered garbage collection overheads of less than 2 percent and 3 percent respectively. However, these results measured a hand-tuned assembly language garbage collector against an interpreter in the Berkeley case[4], and a non-optimising compiler for SOAR. These figures compare remarkably favourably with those for other systems. Chambers reports overheads of between 4 and 27 percent for his optimising compiler for SELF, a Smalltalk-like language [Chambers *et al.*, 1989; Chambers *et al.*, 1991]. Similarly, Appel finds a 5 percent to 10 percent garbage collection overhead for the New Jersey ML compiler (depending on the amount of memory available) [Appel, 1989b]. However, both Smalltalk and ML, but not SELF, create closures for control structures, thus reducing average object lifetimes — since these closures last only for the duration of the control structures — while increasing the allocation rate. Although high rates may increase garbage collection overheads, short object lifetimes certainly increase the effectiveness of generational collectors. More conventional procedural languages typically allocate objects at much lower rates, and those objects tend to have longer lifetimes. Insights obtained from any one system are unlikely to universally applicable.

Having set out the basic ideas, the next sections explore the details of generational garbage collection. The ideal collector should have low CPU overhead, good virtual memory and cache performance, and short pause times. Space overheads should also be minimised. Inevitably there will be trade-offs between these constraints and we compare some of the solutions that

---

[4] The Berkeley Smalltalk interpreter ran at 9,000 instructions per second and used 50 instructions to do a store.

have been proposed. For the purposes of discussion, we assume a copy-based generational collector, but many arguments apply equally to mark-sweep based collectors.

7.3 Promotion policies

Generational garbage collection has two aims. The first is to reduce the overall cost of dealing with long-lived objects and thereby allow the collector to concentrate its efforts on young objects, where the rewards are likely to be greater. The second objective is to reduce garbage collection pause times to a level where they no longer disturb interactive users. Both goals are achieved by segregating objects by age, and by collecting older generations much less frequently than younger ones.

Pause-time is largely dependent upon the amount of data that survives a collection. In general, the number of survivors in the youngest generation depends on its size: the smaller the generation, the shorter the pauses will be. However, a small generation will be filled more rapidly than a large one, thus increasing the frequency of scavenges. This poses a dilemma. Unless objects are promoted early, we cannot fulfil the aim of reducing the amount of copying that must be done in the younger generation. On the other hand, objects should not be promoted prematurely since the basis of generational garbage collection is to allow as many objects as possible to die in the young generation. If the promotion threshold is too low, objects that would have died in a younger generation will be copied into an older one, and so die in a less frequently collected generation. This will cause the older generation to fill up too soon, resulting in a major collection with a longer pause time. Worse still, garbage 'tenured' in older generations leads to 'nepotism': the young offspring of these elderly dead cells will be preserved by minor collections or will even be promoted themselves. Premature promotion also has an adverse effect on the user program's locality, since it is likely that most program accesses will be to younger objects. Moving these objects will dilute the program's working set. The cost of maintaining the write-barrier must also be considered. If it is high, it may be advantageous to lower promotion rates in order to reduce the number of inter-generational pointer stores. In short, the choice appears to be between reducing pause times by restricting the size of the youngest generation or risking more tenured garbage by increasing the rate of promotion. We now examine how far the horns of this dilemma can be blunted.

Multiple generations

If the benefits of reduced pause times and copying overhead can be obtained by dividing the heap into two generations, then it is logical to see whether further improvement can be gained by using more than two generations. Intermediate generations serve to filter objects prematurely promoted from the youngest generation, thereby increasing the chance that they will die in a generation where they can still be reclaimed fairly quickly and efficiently. These intermediate and older generations fill much more slowly than the youngest generation, and hence will need to be collected much less frequently. Multiple generations allow new objects to be promoted quickly, keeping the youngest generation fairly small and reducing the pauses incurred when scavenging it, without increasing the volume of permanent garbage. Multi-generational methods, on the other hand, have drawbacks apart from their extra complexity. Pause-times for collecting intermediate generations may still be disruptive, although they will still be shorter than that for a full collection. More pointers from objects in old generations to young ones will be created, and the size of the root set for younger generations will be increased (assuming that objects are advanced earlier than in a two-generation collector).

The survival rates for each generation are unlikely to be the same (which they would be if object lifetimes were independent of object ages). If this were so, older generations would allow objects more time to age than younger generations. Hence the volume of data promoted should decrease exponentially with each generation. Measurements of generational collectors do not exhibit this effect: rather, multi-generational collectors show a large drop in reclamation rates. The very large difference in reclamation rates between very new and slightly older objects is not reflected in subsequent generations [Hayes, 1991; DeTreville, 1990a; Shaw, 1987]. For this reason, many collectors are limited to just two or three generations.

Promotion threshold

Promotion rate also depends on the number of minor collections that an object must survive before it is advanced to the next generation. A copy count of one leads to *en masse* promotion: all objects are promoted at each collection even though some promoted objects may be very young indeed. Although this has some advantages for heap organisation, which we discuss below, it gives young objects little opportunity to die, and may lead to promotion rates as much as 50 to 100 percent higher than can be achieved with larger copy counts [Zorn, 1993].

The graph, due to [Wilson and Moher, 1989b], shown in Diagram 7.6 on the following page shows the proportion of objects in the youngest generation that survive until the second scavenge after they were allocated, plotted against their time of allocation. The graphs show, respectively, the proportions of objects (a) allocated after scavenge $n - 2$ that survive until scavenge n, (b) allocated after scavenge $n - 1$ that survive until scavenge $n + 1$, and (c) allocated after scavenge n that survive until scavenge $n + 2$. Under the weak generational hypothesis, most objects die young. Therefore, the closer to a scavenge that an object is allocated, the less opportunity it has to die, and hence the greater its chance of surviving that scavenge.

Let us consider the period between scavenge n and scavenge $n + 1$. Most objects allocated shortly after scavenge n do not survive until scavenge $n + 1$, and hence are never copied; these are the objects in the lightly shaded area marked 'never copied'. On the other hand, most objects allocated shortly before scavenge $n + 1$ do survive to be copied. All objects below curve (b) are copied at the next collection. Now suppose that objects are promoted if they survive until the second scavenge after their allocation. Some objects allocated between scavenges n and $n + 1$ will survive long enough to be promoted. These are the objects in the black area marked 'copied twice'. The objects in the area between the two curves will survive the first scavenge but do not live long enough to be promoted.

The graphs show that the number of objects that survive two scavenges is much less than the number that survive just one scavenge. A copy count of two scavenges denies promotion to very recently created objects and is highly effective, reducing survivors by a factor of two whilst increasing copying costs by less than half. On the other hand, increasing the number of scavenges beyond two is likely to reduce the number of survivors only slightly [Ungar, 1984;

Shaw, 1988; Ungar and Jackson, 1988]. Indeed Wilson argues that it is generally necessary to increase the threshold by a factor of four or more to kill off half the remaining survivors [Wilson and Moher, 1989a].

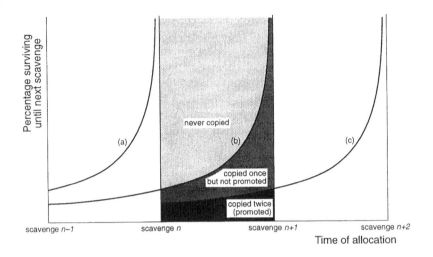

Diagram 7.6 Copying behaviour when objects are promoted with a copy count of two [Wilson and Moher, 1989b]. OOPSLA′89, ©1989 Association for Computing Machinery. Reprinted by permission.

The Standard ML of New Jersey collector

The SML/NJ collector takes a different approach to the management of promotion rates [Appel, 1989b]. Appel's concern was to provide an easy to implement yet efficient garbage collector with a fast allocation time. In order to reduce the chance that a young object will ever be copied, only two[5] generations are used, with the new generation kept as large as possible. This gives acceptable results because the New Jersey compiler expects that very few objects (typically only 2 percent in the younger generation) will survive a minor collection. After a major collection, the region of the heap not used by the old generation is divided into two equal-sized parts, the *reserve* and the *free* regions. Allocation is done from the free region until the new space hits an inaccessible page at the end of the heap[6] (see Diagram 7.7 on the next page).

At this point, the memory protection fault is trapped and a minor collection scavenges the new generation, copying survivors, *svr* in Diagrams 7.8 on the facing page and 7.9 on page 156, *en masse* to the end of the old region. The remainder of the heap is again divided in half.

---

[5] Recent versions of SML/NJ use multiple generations [Reppy, 1993].

[6] In Unix this is the program break. See Chapter 6, page 125, for a discussion on virtual memory methods for heap overflow checks.

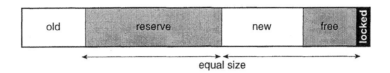

Diagram 7.7   Appel's collector: configuration of the heap between the last major collection and the next minor one.

Minor collections are about fifty times faster than major collections on average. A major collection is performed immediately following a minor collection if the older generation occupies about half the heap. This is made possible since survivors from the old area are first copied into the new area *old'*, leaving the survivors from the minor collection where they are, although objects in *svr* must still be scanned (see Diagram 7.9 on the following page). Both sets of survivors can then be block moved back to the bottom of the heap. Note that there is always sufficient room to do this provided the volume of live data is never more than half the heap size — this is the same guarantee that copying collection demands.

For good performance Appel suggests that the heap residency ratio of a program should be kept below 1:3 (the garbage collection overhead for ML is 11 percent at this level, 6 percent if the ratio is 1:7). Since the residency can be calculated readily after each major collection, the system can be asked for more memory if this ratio falls below the desired value, or if a minor collection only delivers a free region slightly larger than that requested by the mutator.

Adaptive tenuring

The interval between scavenges and the pause length can be shortened by reducing the size of the youngest generation. Conversely, the promotion rate can be reduced by increasing the size of generations, thereby giving objects longer to die. The copying overhead is reduced by scavenging less often, but increasing the size of generations increases pause lengths. Thus techniques based on fixed promotion policies can only hope to perform well on average. Worse still, tuning generational garbage collectors is complex and time consuming, even if the programmer knows the resource constraints under which the program will finally run. For example, the Allegro Common Lisp User Guide devotes 27 pages to this topic [Franz, 1992, 1992, Chapter 15].

Unfortunately object demographics are not stationary; rather objects seem to be born in

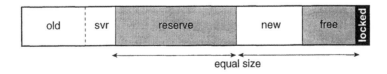

Diagram 7.8   Between minor collections.

Diagram 7.9   Immediately after a major collection, but before the old generation is compacted.

clumps which slowly diminish — in Ungar's and Jackson's phrase 'rather like a pig that has been swallowed by a python'. Baby booms of fairly long-lived objects will fill the younger generation and may cause extra tenuring. If many objects live for a relatively long time and then die, the performance of generational garbage collection will suffer. Ungar and Jackson argue that fixed-age tenuring policies are too restrictive [Ungar and Jackson, 1988; Ungar and Jackson, 1992]. If the tenuring threshold (i.e. the size of the youngest generation) is made too large, pauses will be long; but if very few objects are scavenged at each minor collection, a fixed-age policy will still promote objects even though there is no need to advance any.

One way to resolve the problem of widely varying allocation rates, and consequent thrashing of the garbage collector, is to forswear fixed-size semi-spaces. Instead of triggering a minor collection when an allocation request cannot be fulfilled, the collector is invoked when the volume of data allocated since the last garbage collection exceeds an allocation threshold. This policy presumes that the size of the semi-spaces can be varied dynamically. Zorn suggests that threshold-based collection policies are more stable than fixed-size semi-space policies if net allocation rates vary widely [Zorn, 1989].

Ungar and Jackson solve this dilemma by using a dynamic advancement mechanism, which they call *demographic feedback-mediated tenuring*, for a two-generation collector. Their mechanism has two rules:

Only tenure when it is necessary. The number of objects that survive a scavenge is used to predict the pause time of the next scavenge (since pause time is proportional to the number of objects that have to be copied). If few objects survive a scavenge, it is probably not worth advancing them, particularly if the cost of the write-barrier is high (as it is in Ungar's system).

In the example shown in Diagram 7.10 on the next page, the volume of survivor data is less than the threshold. This suggests that the garbage collection pause time will be less than the longest pause that would be acceptable. The promotion age threshold is set to infinity so that no objects will be promoted next time (see Algorithm 7.1 on the facing page).

Only tenure as many objects as necessary. If the survivor size suggests that the maximum acceptable pause time would be exceeded at the next scavenge, the age threshold is set to a value designed to advance the excess data. The survivors are scanned to produce a table recording the volume of objects of each age. The table is then scanned, in decreasing order of age, to look up the appropriate promotion threshold for the next minor collection.

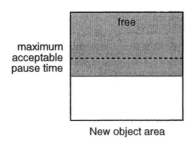

Diagram 7.10   Demographic feedback-mediated tenuring. The volume of survivor data suggests that the pause time will be acceptable.

In the example shown in Diagram 7.11 on the next page, the survivors exceed the maximum acceptable pause time threshold by 10 kilobytes. Unless the threshold is lowered, future scavenges are likely to disturb the user. The age table shows that the promotion age threshold must be set to two collections to advance at least 10 kilobytes.

Although Ungar and Jackson's collector adapts the threshold dynamically in an attempt to avoid premature promotion, it cannot do anything to reduce the amount of tenured garbage in the old generation (other than to invoke a full collection). Barrett and Zorn address this problem by modifying the Ungar–Jackson collector, abandoning the fixed distinction between the two generations [Barrett and Zorn, 1993a]. Instead a *threatening boundary* between the two generations is allowed to move in either direction. As with standard generational collectors, only objects younger than the threatening boundary are liable for reclamation at each minor collection. Since the boundary can move backwards in time, this means that the allocation time of all objects must be preserved. Furthermore, a single *remembered set*[7] (like Ungar and Jackson, Barrett and Zorn use just two generations) must record all forward pointers, not just inter-generational ones, since the boundary between the generations at future scavenges is not known. This will increase the size of the remembered set. Barrett and Zorn allow the user to choose one of two policies for setting the boundary. Since generational collectors trade reduced pause time for increased tenured garbage, the collector can be tuned

---

[7] Remembered sets are discussed in more detail on page 167.

```
excess = size(survivors) - max_pause_time
if excess ≤ 0
    threshold = ∞
else
    generate_table()
    threshold = look_up(excess)
```

Algorithm 7.1   Demographic feedback-mediated tenuring.

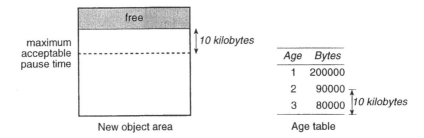

Diagram 7.11 Demographic feedback-mediated tenuring. Too much data has survived.

either to attempt to keep pause times below a given value, or to reduce the amount of tenured garbage needed. In the discussion below, time is measured in bytes.

If the length, `last_trace`, of the last collection pause at heap-time `last_t` exceeded the desired pause time, `max_trace`, the pause-time constrained collector moves the boundary between the generations using Ungar–Jackson feedback mediation (see Algorithm 7.2). Otherwise there is an opportunity to reclaim some tenured garbage. Before calling the collector, the distance between the current time, `t` bytes, and the threatening boundary, `TB` bytes, is increased by an amount proportional to the ratio of the desired pause-time to the length of the last garbage collection pause.

```
if last_trace > max_trace
    TB = Feedback_Mediation()
else
    TB = t - (last_t - TB) * max_trace/last_trace
```

Algorithm 7.2   The pause-time constrained threatening boundary.

The memory-constrained collector, on the other hand, attempts to restrict the amount of tenured garbage, `heap_size - live`. Without a full collection the collector cannot calculate the volume of live data, but it must lie between `last_trace` and the volume of surviving data, `last_survivors`. The mean of these two values, `live_est`, is used as an estimate (see Algorithm 7.3). On the reasonable assumption that the amount of garbage decreases linearly as the threatening boundary moves backwards in time, the memory-constrained collector then moves the threatening boundary back in time by the ratio of the amount of tenured garbage desired, `max_memory - live_est`, to the amount of memory currently used, `last_mem`, or to the time of the last collection, whichever was earlier.

```
live_est = (last_survivors + last_trace)/2
tmp = t * (max_memory - live_est)/last_mem
TB = min(tmp, last_t)
```

Algorithm 7.3   The memory-constrained threatening boundary.

There is evidence that both feedback mediation and dynamic threatening boundary techniques work well for many programs, giving reasonable pause times without excessive CPU overhead, provided that, in the Barrett–Zorn case, the constraints given are realisable. Later in this chapter, we examine other ways to vary promotion policy dynamically.

7.4   Generation organisation and age recording

One of the drawbacks of copying collection is the poor locality of the garbage collector, despite the advantages of compaction for quick allocation and for the working set of the user program. Although only half the available heap is in use at any one time, the collector touches every page every two collection cycles. At the level of the whole heap, generational garbage collection improves matters by arranging for minor collections to concentrate on just the youngest generation. However, the collector's locality pattern *within* a generation remains unchanged if generations continue to be arranged as a pair of semi-spaces.

One semi-space per generation

The simplest promotion policy is to advance all live data *en masse* at each scavenge. As well as removing the need to record object ages, this method has the advantage that it does not need a second semi-space in any but the oldest generation; the next generation acts as the Tospace. Even better, the youngest region can be recycled at each scavenge. If this region is kept in memory, and even better in a large cache, virtual memory and cache performance will be good. This scheme requires multiple generations to filter tenured garbage because the promotion rate is high as even very young objects are advanced. Early promotion leads to more inter-generational references and hence more write-barrier traps, imposing additional mutator overhead.

Creation space

A more subtle technique is to divide a generation into a *creation space* and an *aging space* [Ungar, 1984]. All objects are initially allocated in the creation space. The aging space holds survivors from the creation space. This space must be organised into semi-spaces since objects may be held in it for more than one scavenge: at each scavenge, survivors from both the Fromspace and the creation space are copied into the Tospace (see Diagram 7.12 on the following page). As the number of survivors of each scavenge is likely to be low, the two semi-spaces can be kept comparatively small. Ungar's original scheme, for example, used 140 kilobytes for creation space and only 28 kilobytes for each of the two aging semi-spaces. Since the creation space is emptied at each garbage collection cycle, it can be reused immediately, just as in single space per generation methods. If it can be kept permanently in physical memory, and even better in a large cache, the locality characteristics of this scheme will be good. Again, for good performance the creation space must not be swapped out.

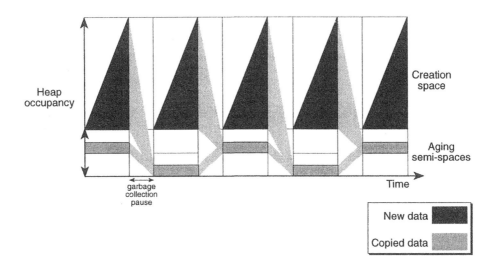

Diagram 7.12   Use of a separate creation space within the youngest generation.

Age recording

The advantage of *en masse* promotion schemes is that it is unnecessary to record each object's age as all survivors are promoted. Methods that use more precise guarantees of an object's age must either record the age of each object in its header, or segregate objects of different ages within a generation, thereby encoding the object's age in its address. For objects like Lisp *cons* cells that may comprise just two pointers, any per-object overhead to record ages will increase memory consumption significantly. Per-object age-counts also incur a time cost since these counts must be manipulated, and indeed copied, at each scavenge.

Shaw has suggested a method that avoids storing ages in each object. Each generation is subdivided into two or more spaces called *buckets* [Shaw, 1988]. The young generation is divided into a New space and an Aging space. Every n scavenges, all survivors in the new bucket are advanced to the aging bucket, and those in the aging bucket are promoted to the next generation (see Diagram 7.13 on the next page). This arrangement guarantees that any data that reach the old generation will have survived between n and $2n - 1$ scavenges. Shaw used a simple heap layout, trading precision of age warranty for simplicity of promotion.

The old generation grows upwards from the bottom of memory. Immediately above it, the new generation is arranged as a pair of semi-spaces. New space is allocated from the top of the semi-space, and the aging space occupies the bottom. Promotion only happens when a garbage collection is due to copy new generation data upwards, away from the old generation. Figure 7.14 on page 162 illustrates the configuration in which the younger generation comprises two buckets and objects are promoted when they have survived three

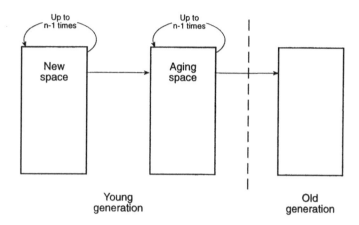

Diagram 7.13   The younger generation is divided into two buckets to record object ages.

collections. At this point, the old generation and the aging bucket are contiguous. All the data
in the aging bucket can be promoted at once by simply moving the boundary between the two
generations upwards. The new bucket now becomes the aging bucket.

This method guarantees an object's age upon advancement without demanding additional
space and time overheads. It is important to understand the difference between generations
and buckets. Although objects are segregated into generations by age, generations are
discriminated by the frequency with which they are scavenged rather than the age of their
contents. In particular, newer generations are collected more frequently than older ones. On
the other hand, the buckets of a single generation are used solely to record the ages of objects
within that generation. When the generation is collected, all its buckets are scavenged. There
is no need to identify buckets, in contrast to generations, when pointers are stored.

Shaw's scheme allows advancement age to be varied by holding objects in buckets as long
as necessary rather than copying them to the next bucket at each scavenge. This level of control
is useful if it is important to prevent premature promotion, for example if the write-barrier is
expensive, as it is in Ungar's collector (see page 159). On the other hand, his scheme does
not have such economy of memory as Ungar's. Because an object may be copied back into its
own bucket, Shaw's buckets must each contain a pair of semi-spaces.

Wilson and Moher combined the improved locality of Ungar's creation spaces with Shaw's
age recording technique in a comparatively simple system [Wilson, 1989]. Their scheme uses
three generations rather than two in order to reduce the need for Shaw's complexity of control
over advancement: objects in the intermediate generation can still be reclaimed before being
promoted to the oldest generation. Like the youngest generation, this one is comparatively
small so that pause lengths are not excessive. Each generation is divided into a creation region
and an aging region, the latter comprising two semi-spaces. As in Ungar's scheme all objects
are initially allocated in the creation region. Each generation also contains two buckets with
(part of) the creation region doubling as the first bucket. In this way, the buckets can be thought
of as sub-divisions of a single pair of semi-spaces. When a generation is scavenged, survivors

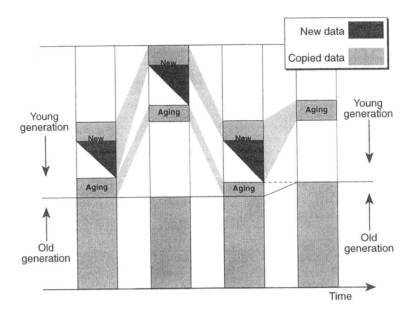

Diagram 7.14   Shaw's heap layout.

from the creation space are evacuated into the Tospace of the second bucket (see Diagram 7.15 on the next page), and the survivors from that bucket are advanced to the next generation.

With this organisation, the system has an age threshold of two scavenges. If all survivors of both buckets were to be promoted at each scavenge, the threshold would be one. However, notice that the data in the creation bucket are arranged in chronological order (unlike those in the aging space which are reordered by the scavenge). We can take advantage of this observation to adjust the age threshold dynamically to any value between one and two. All that is required is to draw a 'high water mark' across the creation region to separate the two buckets of the generation (see Diagram 7.15 on the facing page). Objects below the high water mark, i.e. older ones, are advanced to the next generation. Those younger objects above the high water mark are retained in this generation — they are copied to its aging space. Under this scheme the promotion decision is cheap, since discrimination between the two buckets is by a single pointer comparison.

This organisation offers efficient use of space, eliminates per-object age counts and yet prevents promotion of young objects. However, is anything to be gained by drawing a high water mark across the creation space? Wilson suggests that the ideal threshold may lie between one and two scavenges: certainly thresholds higher than two give only diminishing returns. The effect of choosing a threshold value of one and a half scavenges can be seen in the graph shown in Figure 7.16 on page 164 — the amount of copying is reduced but very young objects are still not promoted at the first scavenge [Wilson and Moher, 1989a]. The cost is increased space requirements. Decisions on where the threshold should be set can be made

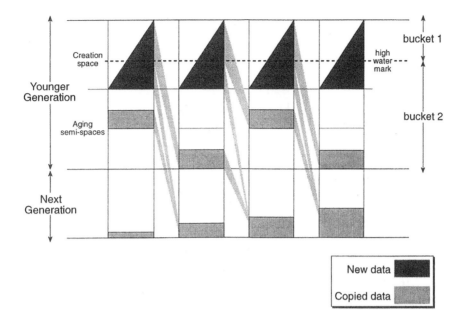

Diagram 7.15 The Wilson–Moher high water mark bucket system. The structure of the intermediate generation is not shown [Wilson and Moher, 1989b]. OOPSLA'89, ©1989 Association for Computing Machinery. Reprinted by permission.

on economic as much as technical grounds, taking note of the continuing trend of memory costs to decline.

Since the high water mark is easily changed, between scavenges or even during a single scavenge, this method provides a simple adaptive tenuring mechanism. If too much data is copied, the high water mark can simply be lowered in much the same way as in Ungar and Jackson's technique. This means that aging spaces can be kept small even for badly behaved programs. As soon as it becomes apparent that most data is going to survive a scavenge, and hence increasingly likely to survive the next one too, the threshold can be lowered to exile remaining survivors to the next generation, thereby avoiding copying them twice. The drawback is that early promotion creates more inter-generational pointers. But if the targets of these pointers are also likely to be promoted then the volume and duration of these cross-generation references may be small. The other problem of early promotion — too much tenured garbage — is not so likely to be a problem since Wilson and Moher use an intermediate generation and this intermediate generation is small, allowing it to be collected fairly rapidly.

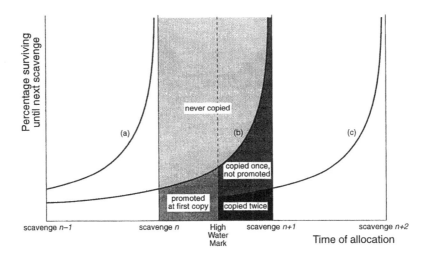

Diagram 7.16 Chance of survival *vs.* allocation time under the Wilson–Moher high water mark scheme [Wilson and Moher, 1989b]. OOPSLA'89, ©1989 Association for Computing Machinery. Reprinted by permission.

Large object areas

Generational techniques segregate heap objects by age, but this is not the only criterion by which to consider the arrangement of the heap. It is also worth considering treating large objects specially because of the cost of copying them; it is worth considering the type of objects if it is known that certain types of object do not contain pointers or are likely to be long-lived. Large object areas can make significant improvements to performance. Ungar and Jackson, for example, found that pause times could be reduced by a factor of four, saving over a megabyte of tenured garbage by dedicating 330 kilobytes to a large object area [Ungar and Jackson, 1988; Ungar and Jackson, 1992]. The typical candidates for this treatment are large strings and bitmaps (for example, images of hidden windows). 'Large' can be an absolute measure (for example, objects larger than 1024 bytes [Ungar and Jackson, 1988]) or a relative one (those that occupy more than 10 percent of Tospace [Hosking *et al.*, 1992]). The usual technique is to separate such objects into header and body parts [Caudill and Wirfs-Brock, 1986; Ungar and Jackson, 1988; Ungar and Jackson, 1992; Hosking *et al.*, 1992]. A *large object area*, managed by a free-list, is used to store the bodies while the headers are stored in the generational part of the heap. The headers are scavenged like other objects but no time is spent copying the bodies. Some algorithms may promote headers [Hudson *et al.*, 1991], whilst others never risk letting headers become tenured garbage provided that the large object area can be made sufficiently large to hold all large objects [Ungar and Jackson, 1992]. It may also be possible to retrieve an object from the large object area, if it is found to have shrunk sufficiently, by merging the header and body parts of an object.

7.5   Inter-generational pointers

Generational garbage collection reduces pause times by collecting only a region of the heap rather than its entirety. However, the only reference to an object in this region may reside in an area of the heap outside the region. It is vital that these inter-generational pointers be identified so that they can be treated as part of the root set by the scavenger. This can be done by the mutator, the garbage collector or a combination of the two.

The simplest way to find inter-generational pointers would be to scan older generations at collection time. The advantage of this method is that it can be done at no cost to the mutator, but it requires more scanning and has worse locality than a fully generational collector. However, linear scanning is faster than tracing and has better locality. Studies by Shaw and Swanson suggest that this technique can reduce overheads due to garbage collection by nearly a third compared with a completely non-generational two-space copying collector [Swanson, 1986; Shaw, 1988]. Bartlett uses a similar technique for his conservative garbage collector [Bartlett, 1989a]. The collector conservatively marks immediately reachable objects (i.e. global variables, references held in registers and on the stack), and then these objects are searched for inter-generational pointers. In this section, we consider more precise methods of recording inter-generational pointers.

The write-barrier

Pointers into a generation generally arise in two ways, either through pointer stores or through promotion of objects that contain pointers[8]. The latter are easily detected by the scavenger. If scanning older generations is ruled out, then pointer stores must be trapped and recorded. Barriers can be implemented in several ways, by either hardware or software, or with operating system support. Software barriers can be provided by having the compiler emit a few instructions before each pointer read or write. Hardware techniques do not require additional instructions, and so are especially advantageous in the presence of uncooperative compilers. Although hardware methods give the least mutator overhead, they may require special purpose hardware or modifications to the virtual memory system not generally available.

If software techniques are used, the implementor must consider three factors: how the cost to the mutator can be minimised, the space overhead of recording pointer store and how efficiently old–young pointers can be identified at scavenge time. If the barrier is sufficiently simple it can be compiled inline. However, pointer accesses may be very common, particularly in functional and object-oriented languages. Zorn found that the static frequencies of pointer loads and stores in SPUR Lisp were 13 to 15 percent and 4 percent respectively [Zorn, 1990a]. Inlining barriers may cause the size of the code generated to explode. If code expansion is sufficiently small (less than 30 percent) it may have negligible effect on performance provided that the processor's instruction cache is sufficiently large [Steenkiste, 1989].

An alternative is to use the operating system's virtual memory protection mechanisms,

---

[8] Inter-generational pointers also arise in system-specific circumstances. For example, a generational system for Prolog using the WAM might start a new generation whenever a new choice point is set. Old–young pointers have to be recorded by Prolog's unification algorithm since they must be reset on backtracking [Appleby *et al.*, 1988].

either to trap access to protected pages, or to use the page modification dirty bits as a map of the locations of cells that might have had pointer fields updated. The advantage of using virtual memory is that it is portable, requiring no changes to the compiler. However, Zorn's measurements suggest that its performance may be substantially inferior to software methods, although different architectures and operating systems vary considerably [Zorn, 1990a].

Fortunately it is not necessary to trap all stores. The proportion of stores that have to be trapped can be reduced by compile-time analysis. Stores to registers or to the stack need not be trapped if these locations are part of the root set of every garbage collection. Many stores, for example that of Lisp's *cons* operator, are initialising stores. As such, they cannot point forward in time so need not be trapped. Fortunately these two cases form the great majority of pointer stores. Zorn estimated that only 5 to 10 percent of all memory references were non-initialising pointer stores, and that two-thirds of these were writes to objects in the youngest generation [Zorn, 1990a]. Not all languages can readily recognise initialising stores, however. Many imperative languages separate the *allocation* of a heap object (for example, x=malloc(...); in C) from its *initialisation* (for example, x->p=...;). Even though only 1 percent of instructions generated by Lisp or ML compilers may be non-initialising pointer stores, optimising the write barrier is critical for overall performance. For example, if the write-barrier were to add 10 instructions to each of these stores, overall performance would be diminished by ten percent. We now consider methods of trapping and recording inter-generational pointers.

Entry tables

The first generational collector, by Lieberman and Hewitt, arranged for pointers from older generations only to point indirectly to objects in younger generations [Lieberman and Hewitt, 1983]. Each generation had an *entry table* of references from older generations associated with it (see Diagram 7.17). Whenever a pointer to a younger generation object was to be stored in an older generation object, a new entry was added to the younger generation's entry table, pointing to the young object, and the old object was modified to point to this entry. If the old object already contained a reference to an item in an entry table, that entry was removed.

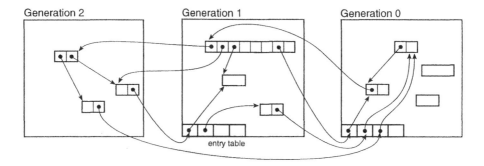

Diagram 7.17   Lieberman–Hewitt entry tables.

The advantage of this scheme is that when a younger generation is collected, it is only necessary to scavenge its entry table rather than to search every older generation. The TI Explorer garbage collector modified this scheme by maintaining a separate table for each pair of generations [Johnson, 1991a; Explorer, 1987, 1987, Section 10]. For a multi-generational collector this simplifies scanning further as only entries relevant to the generation being collected are be examined by the garbage collector.

However, indirection schemes suffer from a number of disadvantages. Entry tables may contain duplicate references to a single object, making the cost of scanning tables proportional to the number of store operations rather than simply to the number of inter-generational pointers. Trapping pointer stores and following indirections in the Lieberman and Hewitt collector would have been prohibitively expensive if the MIT Lisp Machine's specialised hardware and microcode had not made these operations invisible to the user program [Greenblatt, 1984]. Most modern generational garbage collection schemes therefore allow pointers to be used freely, referring directly to their targets. Rather than representing old–young pointers by indirections and recording the value of the pointer, these schemes record the location of the pointer.

Remembered sets

Ungar's *Generation Scavenging Collector* recorded objects that contained pointers to younger generations [Ungar, 1984]. The write-barrier, implemented in software, intercepted stores to check (a) whether a pointer was being stored, and (b) whether a reference to a young generation object was being stored into an old object. If so, the address of the old object that was to contain the pointer was added to a *remembered set* (see Diagram 7.18 on the next page). This contrasts with Lieberman and Hewitt entry tables which record pointed-to objects. To avoid duplicates in the remembered set, each object had a bit in its header indicating whether the object was already a member of the remembered set.

Scanning costs at collection time were therefore dependent on the volume of remembered set objects, rather than on the number of pointer stores. Nevertheless, the cost of store checking was high, although it was easily accommodated within interpreted Smalltalk. Worse still, if an old object were stored into several times between collections, these checks would be repeated. If the object were large, it would have to be scanned in its entirety at collection time, as the remembered set recorded the location of the object stored into rather than the location of the pointer — scanning large objects has been observed to thrash Tektronix Smalltalk [Wilson, 1994].

Collection-time scanning costs could be removed if the address of the slot within an object were remembered rather than the address of the object itself. Slot recording causes two other problems, both of which increase the size of the remembered set. Firstly, it would be impossible to avoid duplicate entries in the remembered set unless there is room to store a remembered-bit in each inter-generational pointer. Secondly, the remembered set would have to include multiple entries for a large object that had had different slots modified. We will now examine various approaches that have been used to reduce write barrier costs while also limiting the space and collection overheads that must be incurred.

Appel uses a simple and fast implementation of remembered sets [Appel, 1989b]. After every assignment into a record, instructions are emitted by the compiler to add the stored-

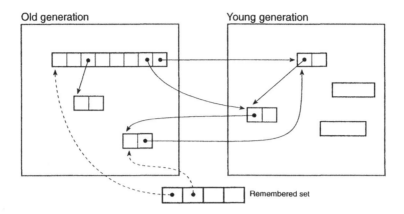

Diagram 7.18   Ungar's remembered set.

into record to an assignment list. This list need not necessarily be stored as a linked list: a contiguous vector of addresses could be used. If the vector were to overflow, either more space could be allocated for the list, not necessarily adjacent to the rest of the list, or the garbage collector could be invoked. The write-barrier is fast and unconditional: no tests that the stored value is indeed an inter-generational pointer, nor that the assignment list does not already contain the stored-into record, are used. Instead, the garbage collector filters the list, scavenging only those objects that meet these criteria. The collection-time cost of Appel's method therefore depends again on the number of pointer stores rather than on the number of objects stored into. The costs of the write-barrier and the collection-time tests were each about four instructions on a VAX. As the dynamic frequency of pointer stores for SML/NJ is less than 1 percent, the overheads caused by garbage collection as a whole are between 5 and 30 percent. This technique benefits from two features of SML/NJ. As a strict, mostly functional language, pointer stores other than initialising ones are comparatively rare. Secondly, the size of the remembered set is further reduced by the policy of *en masse* promotion at each minor collection: after each minor collection all the entries in the list can be discarded. With more generations or a different promotion policy, the list would have to be pruned and retained for use by future collections. Without these considerations, a more complex mechanism would undoubtedly be required.

Sequential Store Buffers

Hudson and Diwan maintain the remembered set for Modula-3 and Smalltalk in a way that similarly minimises the processing cost of a store, yet removes duplicate entries from the remembered sets [Hudson and Diwan, 1990; Hosking *et al.*, 1992]. A fixed-size *Sequential Store Buffer* (SSB) is again filled with addresses that might contain pointers to younger generations. The write-barrier unconditionally adds these addresses to the end of the SSB, and a 'no access' guard page is used to trap overflow. If the pointer to the next free slot in the buffer is kept in a register, adding a word to the SSB can be done in just two additional instructions, one to store the word and the other to increment the pointer (see the code fragment in Algorithm 7.4).

```
st   %ptr, [%obj]          —store ptr into obj
st   %obj, [%ssb]          —add obj to SSB
add  %ssb, 4, %ssb
```

Algorithm 7.4   The write-barrier for a sequential store buffer.

The remembered sets themselves are built as circular hash tables using linear hashing, with $2^i + k$ entries. Items to be entered are hashed to obtain i bits to index the table. If that location already contains another item, the next k slots are examined (but not circularly). If an empty slot still cannot be found, a circular search of the table is made. Hash tables are kept relatively sparse by growing them whenever an item cannot be placed in its natural slot or the next k slots, and more than 60 percent of the table is full. Hudson and Diwan set k to 2, and incremented i by one each time that it was necessary to grow the table (i.e. the table size was doubled).

If the SSB overflows, values in the SSB are moved to the remembered set of the youngest generation. Notice that hashing prevents duplicate entries from being introduced from the SSB; other uninteresting values are filtered out in a tight loop. At collection-time, entries in the SSB are similarly distributed into the appropriate remembered sets. Any values placed in the remembered set of the youngest generation when the SSB overflowed are moved to the remembered sets of the generations to which they belong. The SSB system has the advantage of a fast write trap and precision of recording, but it must still expend effort ensuring that duplicate addresses are not added to the remembered sets.

Page marking with hardware support

The CPU cost of trapping pointer stores can be reduced to nothing with specialised hardware. The Symbolics 3600 made extensive use of hardware to support both incremental and generational garbage collection. Each word stored was examined for references by the same hardware that implemented the read-barrier trap for its Baker-style incremental garbage collector (see Chapter 8 where we discuss incremental garbage collection). Any references found were stored in one of two tables (see below), but rather than recording addresses of objects, the entries referred to small virtual memory pages. This medium-level of granularity solves the problem of scanning very large objects although it increases costs if small objects are sparsely written to, as the entire page must still be scanned. At collection-time, the scavenger searched those pages recorded in the tables linearly to find references. Three features of the 3600 architecture made this technique feasible. Firstly, the Symbolics hardware write-barrier ignored any word that was not a pointer to generational data. Secondly, its tagged architecture removed the need to consider object boundaries while searching the page: pointer words could always be distinguished from non-pointer words. Finally, the pages were small — only 256 words — so a page could be scanned rapidly (in about 85 microseconds, for the 1.2 mips 3600 system, if no references were found).

Whenever a reference to generational memory (either forward or backward) was stored in any page, the write-barrier hardware set a bit in the *Garbage Collector Page Table* (GCPT) of the corresponding page-frame of physical memory. This method also had the advantage of preventing duplicates — however many times the bit is set, the page will only be searched once. Swapped-out pages were handled differently. Although swapped-in pages can be searched rapidly for pointers to the generation being collected, the cost of swapping a page in from disk, only to search it unsuccessfully, is too high. Details of swapped-out pages were held in the *Ephemeral Space Reference Table* (ESRT), a B*-tree maintained by software in non-pageable memory. The ESRT contained a bit-mask for each page, with one bit for each generation referenced by that page. When a page was evicted, its GCPT bit was cleared and the page was scanned for references, updating its ESRT table if necessary. If the page had not been written at all, its ESRT entry need not be changed. If the page had no ESRT entry, it only need be scanned if its GCPT bit was set. Otherwise the ESRT had to be updated regardless of the GCPT bit, since it was possible that data written to it might have overwritten pointers to generational objects.

Garbage collection was initiated by filling the youngest generation. All generations that were sufficiently full were flipped and a single pass was made through the GCPT, scavenging each page whose bit is set. A similar pass was made through the ESRT to complete the scavenging of the entire root set, only swapping pages in to search them if the ESRT bit for the generation being collected was set. Scavenging then continued in the normal way (although the scavenger used the 'approximately depth-first' search technique described on page 139, rather than breadth-first search, to improve locality). An advantage of this mechanism is that the Symbolics garbage collector could collect generations independently of each other, since the hardware recorded any pointer into any generation, regardless of its direction. Most other generational garbage collectors must collect all younger generations when they collect an older one.

Page marking with virtual memory support

Ephemeral Garbage Collection relied on the 3600's specialised hardware for performance. Although this is not available on stock machines, virtual memory machinery may be. Virtual memory systems use hardware to maintain a set of *dirty bits*, one for each page-frame in memory, that determine whether a page needs to be written back to disk when it is evicted. It might seem that these bits could be used as the GCPT to determine whether any pointers have been stored on a page; as far as the garbage collection system is concerned, this costs nothing. However, the situation is slightly more complex than this. A copying collector only needs to scan those pages that were written during or since the last garbage collection. We shall call this period the garbage collection interval. Shaw uses three dirty bits per resident page to keep account of modified pages [Shaw, 1988]. The `Dirty` bit, maintained by hardware, is used to track modifications made to pages since the start of the current interval. However, the virtual memory system needs to know about the state of resident pages before the interval began as well as during it — the `Old_Dirty` bit is used for this. Thus all virtual memory reads of dirtiness information must read the disjunction, `Dirty ∨ Old_Dirty`. The `Dirty_on_Disc` bit is used for pages that have been swapped out. This system requires that the virtual memory mechanism provides two new system calls. One is a request to clear all dirty bits for the pages of the process making the call. The other returns a map indicating which pages of the process have been written in the last interval. At collection time the garbage collector uses this map to search dirty pages for inter-generational references, having first cleared all this process's dirty bits.

However there are two problems with this approach. The virtual memory mechanism must be intercepted in order to determine which page needs scanning before it is swapped out. This may not always be possible, and is certainly operating system specific (although Shaw claimed this was very easy to do: only seventeen statements in the operating system kernel needed to be changed in addition to providing the new system calls). As an alternative to modifying the operating system kernel, pages can be write-protected by a system call. Any resulting write-faults will be trapped, and the trap handler can set a dirty bit for the page, before unprotecting it so that no further faults on this page will occur until after the next garbage collection. This technique has been used on the Xerox Portable Common Runtime system [Boehm *et al.*, 1991]. Clearly it replaces a free mechanism with one of some cost: on a SPARCStation 2, catching the Unix signal and executing the system call to unprotect the page takes about half a millisecond. However, the trap is taken at most once per page in every garbage collection cycle, rather than on every access. Boehm suggests that the virtual memory barrier can perform better than the software barrier provided that allocation rates are very low and read/write rates are moderate[9]. Reliance on virtual memory protection mechanisms makes this method unsuitable for applications with hard real-time demands.

A second problem with virtual memory based methods is that they provide a coarse write-barrier. Pages in modern systems tend to be much larger than those in the Symbolics 3600, and the virtual memory dirty bits record any modification to the page, not simply generational pointer stores. Both of these factors increase the costs of scanning a page for inter-generational references, particularly if writes are sparse.

Card marking

An ideal solution would be one that has the cheapness of a write-barrier and the economy of pointer recording of the Ephemeral Garbage Collector, but is portable and available on stock hardware. Sobalvarro proposed two methods of implementing Moon's collector for Lucid Common Lisp [Sobalvarro, 1988]. *Word marking* divides the address space into large pieces called *segments* of, say, 64 kilobytes. A *Modification Bit Table* (MBT) is associated with each segment to save space; segments which do not require pointer recording, such as those in the youngest generation, unscanned segments, and those that only contain non-pointer data, share a single MBT. Sobalvarro's MBTs occupied some 3 percent of allocated storage. When a location is modified, the bit in the MBT corresponding to that word is set unconditionally. Checking for pointers to generational data is deferred to collection time. Since the location of these modified words is recorded exactly, it is not necessary to scan segments to find them. To save the collector having to examine the MBT for each segment that might have been modified, a second-level data structure, the *segment modification cache*, is used. A byte of this cache is set non-zero whenever an entry is made in its corresponding MBT.

The cost of this write-barrier was not cheap: it used ten instructions, an address register

---

[9] Hans Boehm, personal communication.

and two data registers on the Motorola MC68020. A routine of this size cannot be used inline without significantly increasing the size of the program image. It is also important to restrict the number of registers needed: excessive use of these precious resources by an inline write-barrier will have a deleterious effect on the register allocation of the surrounding code.

A compromise between marking virtual memory pages and marking words, suggested by Sobalvarro, is to divide the heap into small regions called cards. *Card marking* offers several advantages provided that the cards are of the 'right' size. As they are smaller than pages, the amount of collection-time scanning is reduced. On the other hand, the amount of space a card table occupies is less than that used for word marking. Card marking is also portable and independent of the virtual memory system (although cards should not span virtual memory pages). It is also flexible since card sizes can be picked to optimise locality of reference, and to avoid allowing single stores to cause thousands of locations to be scanned at collection-time. As with word marking, a bit is set unconditionally in a card table whenever a word in the card is modified. The *Opportunistic Garbage Collector* uses a smaller card size (32 four-byte words) than either Moon's pages or Sobalvarro's segments [Wilson and Moher, 1989a; Wilson and Moher, 1989b]. Wilson and Moher argue that this size is closer to the average size of objects in Lisp or Smalltalk (excluding *cons* cells which are unlikely to be modified). By making the size of a card similar to the size of the object likely to be guilty of dirtying it, there is less room left on the card for innocent bystanders. Thus fewer objects should need scanning at collection time.

Bit manipulations usually require several instructions on modern RISC processors. This is why Sobalvarro marked bytes in the segment modification table. Using bytes rather than bits speeds up the write-barrier, reducing it to just three SPARC instructions in addition to the actual store (see the code fragment in Algorithm 7.5) [Chambers, 1992].

```
st    %ptr, [%obj + offset]          —store ptr into obj's field

add   %obj, offset, %temp            —calculate address of updated word
srl   %temp, k, %temp                —divide by card size, 2^k
clrb  [%byte_map + %temp]            —clear byte in byte_map
```

Algorithm 7.5 Chambers's write-barrier. k is $\log_2$ (card size).

The memory overhead is fairly small: with a 128-byte card, a byte map is still less than 1 percent of the heap. The cost of the barrier can be reduced still further if the accuracy of card marking is reduced. Hölzle has suggested a method of reducing the cost of the write-barrier to just two SPARC instructions in most cases, at a slight increase in scanning costs, by relaxing the accuracy with which cards are marked (see the code fragment in Algorithm 7.6 on the facing page) [Hölzle, 1993]. If byte i marked in the card table means that any card in the range $i \ldots i + l$ may contain a pointer, the byte marked may be up to l bytes from the correct one. Provided that the offset of the updated word is less than $l * 2^k$ bytes (i.e. less than l cards) from the beginning of the object, the byte corresponding to the object's address can be marked instead. A leeway of one ($l = 1$) is likely to be sufficient to cover most stores except those into array elements: these must be marked exactly in the usual way. With a 128-byte card, any field of a 32-word object can be handled.

Ambiguity only arises when the last object on a card extends into the next card. Although

```
st     %ptr, [%obj + offset]              —store ptr into obj's field

srl    %obj, k, %temp                     —calculate approximate byte index
clrb   [%byte_map + %temp]                —clear byte in byte_map
```

Algorithm 7.6 Hölzle's write-barrier.

the object's address has been marked, a pointer could have been stored in any of the cards that the object straddles. This means that the garbage collector must scan the whole of the last object on a card even if only part of it belongs to the dirty card. Hölzle's figures for the SELF system on a SPARCStation 2 suggest a total garbage collection overhead of between 5 and 10 percent. In all cases, the cost of scanning cards is a fraction of the costs of store checking or scavenging.

Card marking collectors must scan dirty cards for inter-generational pointers at collection time. If none are found, the dirty bit (or byte) is cleared in the card table. The cost of scanning is proportional to the number and size of cards marked rather than the number of stores performed since duplicates never arise. Dirtiness information can also be used by the garbage collector to segregate objects on written-to cards from clean ones. By gathering dirty cards onto the same virtual memory pages, the number of pages holding cards to be scanned, and likely to be scanned again at the next scavenge, can be reduced [Wilson and Moher, 1989a].

The small size of cards presents a problem when scanning them. The tagged architecture of the 3600 allowed it to discriminate between pointer words and other data, but this facility is not available on stock hardware. Nevertheless, card marking requires that it is possible to scan a card accurately for pointers, even if the card does not start with the beginning of an object. The Opportunistic Garbage Collector uses a *crossing map* similar to that of the incremental collector described in [Appel *et al.*, 1988] (see Chapter 8). This bit- (or byte-) map, which is the same size as the card table, indicates those cards that cannot be scanned from the beginning. Cards are only scannable if they begin with the header of an object, or in the midst of an object whose subsequent data fields are tagged. If a card is unscannable, the garbage collector must skip back through the crossing map until it finds a scannable one. Page faults caused by skipping back to an earlier card from which to start the scan are undesirable. If 32-word cards are used, a 4-kilobyte page will hold 32 cards. This gives, on average, a choice of 15 cards on which to start the scan without risking a page fault. Larger card sizes would increase this risk, but smaller sizes would increase the size of the card table.

The chance of a card being scannable is also increased if large unscannable objects are stored separately in a large object area. Headerless, unscannable objects, such as floating point numbers (often represented by a tagged pointer to a one or two word value in the heap), also cause problems. These can be handled specially if all headerless objects are required to be entirely scannable or entirely unscannable. Unscannable headerless objects can then be allocated in 'containers', pseudo-objects in the heap which have a header indicating that they contain unscannable data. When a container becomes full, a fresh one is acquired from the storage manager, and new headerless unscannable objects are allocated from within the new container.

Remembered sets or cards?

For general purpose hardware, two systems look the most promising: *remembered sets with sequential store buffers* and *card marking*. Although the write-barrier costs are about the same — two instructions — in both systems, card marking provides a more predictable write-barrier overhead since the SSB may overflow. Remembered sets offer precision of pointer recording, but allow duplicates in the sequential store buffer. Processing effort at collection time is proportional to the number of stores performed between scavenges rather than the volume of data modified; this and the size of the SSB might be large. On the other hand, cards that contain inter-generational pointers remain dirty and hence have to be searched again even if they are not modified again. Hosking and Hudson took the best of both systems to provide a hybrid card marking/remembered set garbage collector for a high-performance Smalltalk interpreter [Hosking and Hudson, 1993]. The write-barrier uses card marking, but older–younger pointers are summarised to the appropriate remembered set at collection time. The remembered set is then used as the basis of the scavenge and the cards are cleaned. The write-barrier is predictable since the card table cannot overflow; no duplicates are recorded. At the cost of storing a remembered set for each generation as well as the card table, card scanning time is reduced as only those cards dirtied since the last collection need to be scanned. It would also be feasible for such a hybrid system to switch to pure card marking if the remembered sets grew excessively large. Hosking and Hudson found the hybrid scheme offered a significant improvement over pure remembered sets, with the optimal card size found to be one kilobyte. They also found that, even using sympathetic assumptions, virtual memory techniques were unlikely to be competitive, though there are other reasons (such as uncooperative compilers) that may mandate its use.

7.6 Non-copying generational garbage collection

So far we have assumed that generational garbage collectors are based on copying garbage collection. Although copy-based collectors are conceptually simpler, it is quite possible to build mark-sweep based generational collectors. Zorn examined the trade-offs between promotion threshold size, garbage collection overhead and pause length for generational garbage collection based on both stop-and-copy and mark-sweep, and concluded that his mark-and-deferred-sweep generational collector performed significantly better, for a range of substantial Allegro Common Lisp programs running on a Sun 4/280, than his copying collectors [Zorn, 1993].

Zorn's system used four generations, each of which contained a mark bitmap (see page 92), a fixed-size-object region and a variable-sized-object region. The fixed-size-object region was divided into a number of areas, each of which contained objects of a single size. These regions used mark-and-deferred-sweep garbage collection, with *en masse* promotion by copying after three collections. The variable-sized-object region contained objects that did not fit in any of the fixed-size-object areas, and was collected with a two-space copying collector. Zorn found that, although the total CPU overhead of the mark-sweep collector was slightly greater than that of the copying collector, it required 30 to 40 percent less real memory to achieve the same page-fault rate.

Mark-sweep collection also often showed a lower cache-miss rate, although this depended on promotion policy and cache size. The compacting effect of copying collection gave no advantage provided that the new space resided entirely in memory. The drawback of the mark-sweep collector was that *en masse* promotion led to much higher promotion rates; collection-count promotion would be possible if a few bits per object were reserved to record object ages (maybe in a table to the side of the heap like the mark bitmap). Increasing thresholds above one megabyte, however, led to noticeable pauses whilst thresholds less than 250 kilobytes caused increased overhead and poor locality as objects were moved out of the creation area prematurely. Zorn's results are in keeping with those of Demers *et al.* for a conservative, mark-and-deferred-sweep, generational collector for Ibuki Common Lisp on the Xerox PCR [Demers *et al.*, 1990]. Although the CPU overhead was much greater than for a non-generational collector, an order of magnitude fewer pages were touched by the generational collector.

There is no reason why all generations should be collected in the same way. In particular the oldest generations may have to be treated differently to younger ones. If a copying collector is used throughout, the oldest generation must be organised into semi-spaces since there is no older generation into which scavenge survivors can be promoted. If the cost of two semi-spaces is too high, then the oldest generation must be handled with a non-copying collector, or maybe not collected at all. If mark-sweep is used, it may occasionally be worth compacting the generation as well, especially if this can be done without paging. Ungar and Jackson built a twin-track garbage collector for PARCPlace Smalltalk-80, Release 4 [Ungar and Jackson, 1991]. In this system, most objects are reclaimed by a generational copying collector, for its efficiency and its non-disruptiveness. Compaction, which gives fast allocation for high bandwidth objects, is provided at no cost. Tenured objects, on the other hand, can be dealt with at a more leisurely rate: the key requirement is that older generations should never become so full that a major collection is needed. An incremental mark-sweep collector is used to reclaim tenured garbage. Although a first-fit (or best-fit) allocator for old objects is slower than simply incrementing a free pointer, its performance is still acceptable since objects become old at a much lower bandwidth than new ones are allocated.

7.7   Scheduling garbage collections

One of the aims of generational garbage collection is to reduce pause times. As well as concentrating on those objects most likely to be garbage, it may also be worth considering when to schedule garbage collection. Two possible strategies are either to *hide* collections at points where the user is least likely to notice pauses, or to trigger *efficient* collections when there is likely to be most garbage to collect. One way of hiding pauses in long lived systems is to arrange that major collections happen overnight, or when the machine is idle. Alternatively garbage collections can be performed at points in the program where the pauses are least likely to be disruptive. Two candidates for this are during compute-bound periods and when the user is presented with an opportunity to interact but does not do so [Wilson and Moher, 1989b; Wilson, 1990]. If garbage collection phases are attached to the end of much larger compute-bound phases, they may not exacerbate those pauses excessively. Furthermore, by garbage collecting then, much more disturbing interruptions during interactive phases may be avoided.

There may also be points at which a program expects the user to interact, but they do not do so. If the user does not interact for a few minutes then it is probably safe to initiate a short collection. If user inactivity continues, it may be an opportune moment for a more major collection. Wilson advocates incorporating these heuristics into interactive programs by attaching code to user interaction routines. Whenever a significant pause is detected, the system can decide whether to garbage collect and if so, how many generations to scavenge. The Emacs text editor system uses a variant of this strategy: if sufficient idle time has passed, the file is auto-saved and a garbage collection is performed if sufficient allocation has been done since the last collection.

Garbage collection will be made more efficient if it is run at times when the volume of live data is low. The ends of compute-bound periods or user interaction points may also of themselves be good times to collect, since they are often dispatching points between major computations. It is quite likely that the volume of live data is low at these times. Other opportune moments include at the local minima of stack height [Lieberman and Hewitt, 1983], or when the number of page-faults becomes excessive. In the latter case, the goals of the collection are to compact data to improve locality of reference [Wilson *et al.*, 1991]. The garbage collector itself may also be able to detect likely opportunities. If the number of objects reclaimed during the last scavenge of a younger generation was high, it may be worth scavenging its older neighbour as well [Hudson and Diwan, 1990].

Detecting true local minima of the stack height is problematic. One approximate solution is to trigger a collection whenever the stack height drops below a certain point. Wilson suggests that one method may be to place a bogus return address in the stack [Wilson, 1991]. If this is used as a return address, control can be passed to a routine that determines whether it is worth calling the collector. This decision may be based on the amount of memory currently available, and the height of the stack. Wilson reports that the success of this strategy is application dependent. Where it is successful, it tends primarily to decrease the amount of data copied at the first scavenge but the proportion of data that survives two scavenges increases slightly.

Key objects

Hayes observed that the deaths of objects allocated at nearly the same time are closely correlated [Hayes, 1991]. He observed the behaviour of the 1 percent of objects with the longest lifetimes and found that more than 60 percent of these words came from a spread of ± 1 kilobyte. If young objects were included, the correlation was unsurprisingly much stronger. These object demographics arise from typical styles of programming. There are usually only a few static pointers into large data structures: an example would be the root of a tree. Other pointers into the structure are created dynamically as it is used by the program. When the program has finished with the tree, it will only be reachable by its root. When this pointer is deleted, the entire tree is garbage.

Hayes suggests using these *key* objects as indicators for garbage collections. When the death of a cluster of objects can no longer be predicted from their age, the cluster should be promoted out of the time-based generational scheme altogether: no effort should be made to collect it (see Diagrams 7.19 and 7.20). One key object, for example the root of a tree

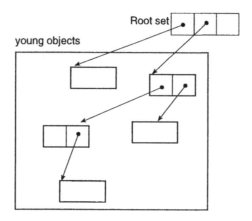

Diagram 7.19   Key objects: before promotion.

or the head of a list, should be retained within the generational scheme. The reachability of this key object is then used to suggest when to collect the cluster. Reclaiming a key object is interpreted as a hint that it might be worth trying to reclaim the keyed cluster associated with it. Collecting older generations along with all young generations in a large heap without disruption is problematic. Avoiding collecting objects unless there is a good reason to think that the attempt might be successful is a sound strategy, if it can be implemented.

Mature object spaces

The difficulty with this scheme is how key objects are to be identified. One method is a manual one, with the programmer offering hints on which objects are thought to be good predictors. Alternatively, if a cluster was accessible from the stack, these direct references could serve as keys. An added bonus is that this technique would also indicate that the stack had shrunk without explicitly monitoring it. Hudson and Moss describe a further mechanism, inspired by key object opportunism, that collects clusters of objects by detecting when the cluster is unreachable [Hudson and Moss, 1992]. Like Hayes, they promote very old objects out of the time-based generational scheme altogether and into a *mature object space* in order to avoid disruptive collections. Their design is similar to the distributed algorithm described in [Shapiro *et al.*, 1990]. The mature object space is divided into *areas*, each of which has a remembered set. These are collected one at a time, in a round-robin fashion, thus placing an upper bound on the length of any collection. An area is reclaimed in its entirety when its remembered set is empty, i.e. when there are no references to objects in the area from outside the area.

A difficulty arises if a cluster of linked objects is too large to fit in a single area, since areas are bounded in size (unlike the areas described in [Bishop, 1977]). Hudson and Moss use a train analogy to describe their solution to this problem, with *carriages* representing areas, and *trains* representing groups of carriages holding linked structures. At each collection, a single

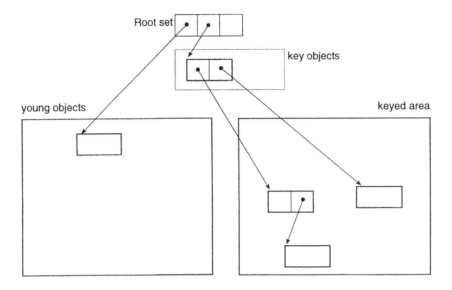

Diagram 7.20   Key objects promoted out of the generational scheme.

carriage is chosen for collection: call it the *From-carriage*. If there are no references to the From-carriage's train from outside that train, the entire train can be reclaimed. Otherwise, collection proceeds in four phases.

First, any object that is referenced from outside the mature object space is moved into a fresh train. Suppose that the top-left carriage in Diagram 7.21 on the next page is the From-carriage. The only external reference is to object A; A is copied to a new train (see Diagram 7.22 on page 180). These objects are then scanned in the usual copying collector way, and any descendants also in the From-carriage (for example, B in the diagrams) are moved to this new train. Promoted objects are also moved into trains in this phase. At this point, references to objects in the From-carriage are held only in mature-space objects.

In the third phase, From-carriage objects referenced from other trains in the mature object space (for example, P) are moved to those trains. Those referenced from other carriages in the From-train (for example, X) are moved to the last carriage in this train. This leaves the From-carriage containing only unreachable objects (for example, the group of three objects shown in the lower left-hand corner of the From-carriage), so the entire carriage is recycled. Once an entire structure is held in a single train, it can be reclaimed if there are no external references to it (for example, in the collection cycle that follows the state shown in Diagram 7.22 on page 180, the train holding Y and X can be reclaimed in its entirety). This system has a number of attractive features. It is incremental since the number of bytes moved at each collection is bounded. Objects are clustered and compacted as they are copied into cars. The system is efficient in that it does not rely on special hardware or virtual memory mechanisms.

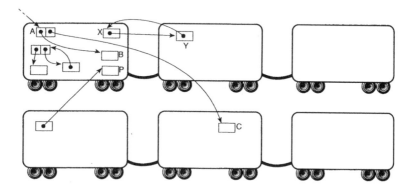

Diagram 7.21   The mature object space before the From-carriage is collected. Only details of interesting carriages are shown.

7.8   Issues to consider

Generational garbage collection has proved to be highly successful in a wide range of applications. It can reduce pause times for minor collections to a level where it is worth considering instead of incremental techniques for some applications. By concentrating allocation and collection effort on a smaller region of the heap, paging and cache behaviour of both the mutator and the collector can often be improved. Finally, by delaying collection of long-lived objects, generational techniques can reduce the overall cost of garbage collection. Programming styles which allocate large numbers of short-lived objects, and in which non-initialising pointer writes are comparatively rare, benefit particularly from this approach. However, generational garbage collection is not a universal panacea and certain circumstances may not satisfy the weak generational hypothesis.

The goal of short pause times is defeated by large root sets. These may be caused by any combination of very large programs, an unusually large number of global variables pointing into the heap, or highly recursive calls leading to very deep stacks. One solution to the problem of large stacks is to apply the write-barrier to local variables as well, although this would considerably increase the cost of the barrier.

Alternatively, if objects are promoted to the next generation *en masse* at every minor collection, it is not necessary for the collector to scan every stack frame. In this case, the only activation records that can contain old–young pointers are those created since the last allocation. All that is necessary is that the collector mark the top frame of the stack. At the next minor collection only frames above this one need to be scanned for pointers into the young generation. The only difficulty with this approach is that the 'high water mark' frame might be popped between collections. Appel and Shao suggest that the frame be marked by replacing its return address with the return address of a 'mark-shifting' procedure [Appel and Shao, 1994]. When the frame is popped, control will pass to this procedure, which will mark the next-lower frame in the same way before jumping to the real return address. Appel and Shao estimate the cost of handling high water marks at between 10 and 100 instructions.

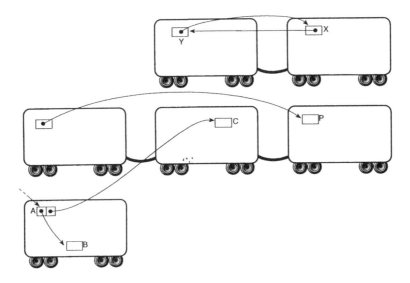

Diagram 7.22   The mature object space after the From-carriage is reclaimed.

The residency of older generations is also an important factor. If object lifetimes are not sufficiently short, minor collections will reclaim too few objects, leading to increased promotion and hence more frequent major collections. Moreover, frequent references to older generations will spoil the spatial locality of the mutator if only the youngest generation can be held permanently in real memory or the cache. This will lead to poorer paging behaviour and/or will increase the ratio of cache misses. High heap occupancy rates are not uncommon[10].

Frequent pointer writes into older generations will also increase the overall cost of the write-barrier. Wilson notes that large arrays of heap allocated data, such as floating point numbers, are particularly troublesome in this respect. Such arrays commonly have long lifetimes, and hence will be promoted to an old generation. Each iteration of the program may update many (or even all) of the slots in the array, and each of these writes must be trapped by the write-barrier. Furthermore, the target of each write will be added to the root set of the next minor collection.

7.9   Notes

Ideas for separating the heap into separately collectible areas can be found in many early papers. D.T. Ross's AED system divided storage into separately managed *zones* [Ross, 1967]. AED was not garbage collected and no mechanism was provided to handle inter-zonal pointers. D.B. Lomet described a similar approach [Lomet, 1975]. H.D. Baecker suggested dividing the Algol-68 heap into different regions [Baecker, 1970; Baecker, 1972; Baecker,

---

[10] Hans Boehm, Joel Bartlett, personal communication.

1975]. Each region maintained a table of objects resident in that region. The MIT Lisp machine had *areas* with *exit vectors*, regenerated at each collection [Knight, 1974; Greenblatt, 1984]. At collection time, only those areas modified since the last collection were collected. Peter Bishop's thesis contains a number of interesting ideas, including separately collected areas of the heap [Bishop, 1977]. Areas could also be linked, or *cabled*, to each other, either automatically or under programmer control, so that an area would be collected if any areas cabled to it were.

The first paper published on generational garbage collection was by Henry Lieberman and Carl Hewitt [Lieberman and Hewitt, 1983]. However, this collector intertwined generational garbage collection with incremental collection, as did David Moon's *Ephemeral Collector* [Moon, 1984]. These techniques were successful because both the MIT Lisp Machine and the Symbolics 3600 made extensive use of special hardware to support garbage collection [Greenblatt, 1984; Moon, 1985]. A more accessible early paper is [Ungar, 1984], but the best brief survey is [Wilson, 1994]. Julian Davies provides mathematical support for the lifetime model [Davies, 1984].

Multiple generations have been used in several implementations, most notably for Tektronix 4406 Smalltalk-80 which used seven generations [Caudill and Wirfs-Brock, 1986], TI Explorer II Lisp (effectively five generations) [Courts, 1988; Johnson, 1991a], and Paul Wilson's Opportunistic Garbage Collector (small young and intermediate generations and a larger old one) [Wilson and Moher, 1989b; Wilson *et al.*, 1991]. The SPUR processor provided hardware support for four generations although SPUR Lisp used only three of them [Zorn, 1989]. Other implementors have allowed a variable number of generations, for example Symbolics 3600 Lisp (which also allowed the user to specify the capacity of each generation) [Moon, 1984], and the University of Massachusetts Garbage Collector Toolkit [Hudson *et al.*, 1991; Hosking *et al.*, 1992].

Bucket brigade systems have been used by [Shaw, 1988; Wilson and Moher, 1989a; Hudson *et al.*, 1991]. Robert Shaw advocated a heap organisation similar to Andrew Appel's [Shaw, 1988; Appel, 1989b], in which the old generation is allowed to grow into the new region. He also suggests using software to mark pages if the virtual memory system is unavailable.

Write barriers are maintained either by software alone or with hardware support. Lieberman and Hewitt used entry tables, supported by the MIT Lisp Machine's hardware; Ungar used software-only remembered sets. The Symbolics machines write barrier and page marking were possible because of the close integration of hardware, operating system and garbage collector. Word and card marking were suggested by Patrick Sobalvarro in his Bachelor's thesis [Sobalvarro, 1988]. Combinations of these techniques with sequential store buffers have been suggested by Amer Diwan, Tony Hosking, Rick Hudson, Eliot Moss and Darko Stefanović [Hudson and Diwan, 1990; Hosking *et al.*, 1992; Hosking and Hudson, 1993].

8

Incremental and Concurrent Garbage Collection

For interactive or real-time applications, the chief question facing the designer of an automatic memory management system is how to reduce the length of garbage collection pauses. We saw in Chapter 7 that generational garbage collection can often be an effective strategy for reducing garbage collection latency. Generational garbage collectors concentrate storage reclamation efforts on the region of the heap in which memory is most likely to be recovered. If this region is comparatively small, and if the survival rate of objects is sufficiently low, generational techniques will be successful in limiting pause times. If an application or an implementation does not exhibit the right object demographics, generational collection cannot provide a solution. Frequent major collections of larger regions of the heap will defeat the generational strategy. Incremental, and especially real-time, garbage collection has a different priority to that of generational garbage collection. It demands guarantees for the worst-case performance whereas generational collection attempts to improve the expected pause time at the expense of the worst case.

In order to avoid the pauses incurred by stop-and-collect reclamation, many researchers have turned to incremental garbage collection techniques. The simplest of these is reference counting, which is naturally incremental for all operations except the deletion of the last pointer to an object, but we saw in Chapter 3 that such recursive freeing can be avoided. The drawbacks of reference counting are its computational expense (even with sophisticated techniques such as deferred reference counting), its close coupling to the user program (hindering program development), and its inability to reclaim cyclic data structures without using hybrid techniques. In this chapter, we examine parallel garbage collection techniques based on tracing. For the main part we shall concentrate on sequential architectures, but we shall also describe concurrent collectors, using threads or multiple processors. Concurrent garbage collection started almost two decades ago as an academic exercise. With today's technology the cost of adding extra processors to a machine is small. Most new large mainframes are multiprocessors already and shared memory multiprocessors are becoming widespread. Some of the algorithms in this chapter were originally designed for multi-processors but are easily adapted for serial machines. Serial execution also simplifies implementation since the problem of maintaining a coherent view of data structures between different processes can be relaxed somewhat. In particular, locks are not required and certain subtleties of fine-grained concurrency do not arise. Synchronisation is still expensive, but less so than for truly concurrent systems. Likewise it is very much easier to track the state of the running processes.

Sequential garbage collection can be made incremental by interleaving collection with the user program's activity. Care must be taken to ensure that the collector makes sufficient progress to prevent the user program from running out of memory before the collection cycle is complete. One way to do this is to tune the rate of collection to the rate of consumption of memory — the idea is that a small amount of marking or copying can be done at each allocation. To do so without the client program running out of memory before the collection cycle has terminated, incremental collectors need additional headroom in the heap in comparison with their non-incremental counterparts.

If the collector traces k words at each allocation, and there are R active words at the start of a cycle, these words will have been marked after R/k calls to the allocator. At the end of the tracing cycle the heap will contain at most $R + R/k$ active cells. If all cells allocated during a collection cycle are allowed to survive until the next cycle (and do not need to be traced), the storage required to guarantee that the user program is not starved is $R(1 + 1/k)$ words[1] — this value is doubled for a semi-space copying collector. The value of k should not be set too large, however. Although allocation time increases linearly with k, changes have much less effect on the amount of storage required. Alternatively, for a heap (or semi-space) of size M and a program with maximum residency $R < M$, it is sufficient to set k to be larger than $R/(M - R)$ to guarantee sufficient progress.

Many incremental algorithms are described by their authors as *real-time*. Hard real-time systems demand that results be computed on time: a late result is as useless as an incorrectly calculated one. Such systems require worst-case guarantees rather than average-case ones, and these may have to be in the order of a millisecond. Indeed, many hard real-time systems demand guaranteed space bounds, and even eschew the use of virtual memory. Memory management is not the only problem faced by real-time systems.

Other advances in hardware design such as super-scalar, pipelined architectures have also made performance less deterministic. Soft real-time systems prefer results to be delivered on time, but accept that a late result is better than no result at all. It is clear that many so-called real-time garbage collectors cannot meet realistic worst-case deadlines for many hard real-time applications. At best, they offer average-case pause times that are bounded by small constants. This is often adequate for interactive applications but is not hard real-time. We shall avoid calling such incremental algorithms 'real-time'.

---

[1] If new cells must also be traced, the maximum storage requirement becomes $R(1 + \frac{1}{k-1})$ words.

8.1   Synchronisation

Parallel garbage collection systems can be viewed as comprising two (or more) processes running asynchronously but sharing the same workspace. This view is useful whether the garbage collector is implemented as a separate process or thread, or has a fixed interleaving within a single sequential process. Asynchronous execution of the mutator and collector introduces a consistency problem. Consider an example in which there are two cells, A and B, both of which are in use at all times. Suppose furthermore that C is initially connected to A as shown in the figure at the top of Diagram 8.1, and that the following code sequence is executed:

```
Update(right(B), right(A))
right(A) = nil                          —Step (i)
Update(right(A), right(B))
right(B) = nil                          —Step (ii)
```

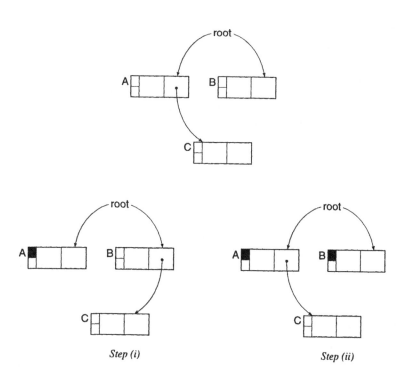

Step (i)   Step (ii)

Diagram 8.1   Mutator activity may interfere with the collector's marking traversal.

If the collector visits A at step *(i)*, shown in the left-hand figure of Diagram 8.1, and then B at step *(ii)*, shown in the right-hand figure, it may conclude wrongly that C is garbage. Synchronisation is needed between mutator and collector to indicate that the connectivity of the data structure has altered.

In his survey paper, Wilson suggests viewing this as a coherence problem [Wilson, 1994]. An incremental mark-sweep collector poses a multiple-readers, single-writer coherence problem since both the mutator and the collector read pointer fields but only the mutator can modify them. Incremental copying collectors provide an example of a multiple-readers, multiple-writers problem since the collector also writes pointer fields when it moves objects. It is also necessary to ensure that the mutator's view of the world is consistent, i.e. that it does not attempt to access objects through obsolete references. Fortunately it is not necessary for the mutator and the collector to share an identical view of the computation graph. The consistency requirement can be relaxed to allow the collector to work with a conservative approximation of the graph of active objects. While the collector must treat any reachable object as active, the semantics of garbage collection are preserved even if the collector treats some objects that are unreachable as if they were still visible to the mutator. Typically such *floating garbage* consists of objects that became unreachable in the last garbage collection cycle; these will usually be reclaimed in the next cycle. Relaxing the consistency between the collector's and the mutator's view of the world is not unique to incremental garbage collection. It is also fundamental to generational garbage collection, where tenured garbage is allowed to accumulate at least temporarily in older generations.

As consistency requirements are relaxed, the collector's view of the reachability graph becomes more conservative, and more floating garbage accumulates. Floating garbage fragments the heap, increases the effective residency of the program and puts more pressure on the garbage collector. The degree of conservatism is one parameter by which we can judge incremental algorithms. Incremental collection should also delay computation only briefly at each step, so the bounds on these pauses provide a second measure. Incremental collectors may also contain uninterruptible sections, for example to process the root set or to check for termination of a garbage collection cycle. If these pauses are too great, the incremental nature of the algorithm is again compromised.

Tricolour marking

In Chapter 6 we introduced a tricolour abstraction to describe copying collection. This abstraction was originally introduced by Dijkstra to describe incremental garbage collection. We restate the abstraction here, but cast in the light of incremental collection. Nodes in the heap are painted one of three colours.

Black indicates that a node and its immediate descendants have been visited: the garbage collector has finished with black nodes and need not visit them again.

Grey indicates that the node must be visited by the collector. Either grey nodes have been visited by the collector but their constituent pointers have not been scanned, or their connectivity to the rest of the graph has been altered by the mutator behind the collector's back. In either case, the collector must visit them again.

White nodes are unvisited and, at the end of the tracing phase, are garbage.

A garbage collection cycle terminates when all reachable nodes are black. This implies that no grey nodes remain in the heap. Some unreachable nodes may also be black but these cannot be reclaimed in this cycle. Any nodes left white at this point are garbage and can be reclaimed.

Cheney stop-and-copy collectors provide a particularly clear illustration of the tricolour abstraction. Black nodes are those nodes in Tospace whose address is less than scan. Nodes between scan and free are grey, and unvisited Fromspace nodes are white. The collector sweeps a wave-front of grey objects across the heap, separating black objects from unreached white ones. Notice that there are no pointers from black objects to white ones: this guarantees that no active nodes will be overlooked by the collector.

Diagram 8.1 on page 185 showed how the mutator might interfere with the collector's marking traversal by altering the connectivity of the graph. Black means that the collector has finished with the node and should not need to revisit it. The problem was that the mutator was able to install a pointer to a white object C into the black A. In this example, node A was blackened at step *(i)*. Since right(A) was the only reference to C, C would never be reached by the collector and hence would be falsely reclaimed. Other mutator actions are not problematic. Any grey or active white cells that are modified will be visited by the collector at some point in the future, and creating black–black or black–grey pointers does not alter the collector's view of the reachability of the graph.

8.2   Barrier methods

There are two ways to prevent the mutator from disrupting garbage collection by writing white pointers into black objects. The first method is to ensure that the mutator never sees a white object. Whenever it attempts to access a white object, the object is immediately visited by the collector. To ensure that this happens, white objects must be protected by a *read-barrier*.

The second method is to record where the mutator writes black to white pointers so that the collector can visit or revisit the nodes in question. Objects are protected by a *write-barrier*. In order to falsely reclaim a live object, a white object must become invisible to the collector but still be reachable by the mutator. This means that at some point during the marking phase both of the following preconditions must hold.

- A pointer to the white object is written into a black object.   (Cond.1)

Furthermore this must be the only reference to the white object:

- The original reference to the white object is destroyed.   (Cond.2)

If either of these conditions does not hold, the object will be retained and no special action is required. If (Cond.1) does not hold, the graph will not contain any black–white pointers during the collector's traversal. In this case, there must be a path to each reachable white node from a (black) root that passes through a grey node. The collector's traversal will eventually reach the white node from the grey one. On the other hand, if a pointer to a reachable white node is installed in a black node, the white node will still be reached by the collector through the original reference to it if (Cond.2) does not hold, i.e. unless this pointer is destroyed. Write-barrier methods solve the mutator–collector communication problem by tackling one or the other of these two conditions for failure. Wilson classifies write-barrier methods as either *snapshot-at-the-beginning* or *incremental-update*, depending on whether they prevent the loss of the original reference or catch changes to the connectivity of the graph [Wilson, 1992b]. We explain these techniques in more detail below.

We discussed techniques for implementing write-barriers in Chapter 7 in the context of trapping inter-generational pointer stores. The read-barrier can similarly be implemented in hardware, by having the compiler emit a few instructions before each pointer read, or with support from the operating system. The cost of the barrier is diminished to a negligible amount if the barrier is provided in hardware. Symbolics, Explorer and SPUR architectures all provided hardware support in the past, but modern general purpose machines do not do so [Moon, 1985; Explorer, 1987, 1987; Taylor et al., 1986].

Software read-barriers are generally considered to be too expensive. Zorn's measurements suggest that pointer loads may account for 13 to 15 percent of all instructions [Zorn, 1990a]. Inlining read-barriers may cause the size of the code generated to explode. A read-barrier of three instructions would increase the size of the code by more than 40 percent and may also have a deleterious effect on the performance of the processor's instruction buffer [Steenkiste, 1989]. A read-barrier of seven instructions would double the size of the code. Read-barriers may also be implemented with support from the operating system's memory protection mechanisms to trap access to protected pages. We examine this approach further when we discuss the Appel–Ellis–Li collector on in Section 8.6.

The total overhead of an incremental or concurrent algorithm is determined by the conservatism of the barrier used and how it affects the collector's view of the reachability of the graph (all other things being equal — which in practice they will not be). The time and space costs of the barrier depend on its selectivity (whether it is applied conditionally or unconditionally) and frequency, and how it is implemented (colour bits or a mark stack). Pause time depends on how much work is done by the barrier (whether a single node is coloured or an entire page of references is scanned). It also depends on how a collection cycle is initiated and terminated — for some algorithms these are the more significant factors.

8.3 Mark-Sweep collectors

The mutator does not need to be protected from the activity of a non-moving collector as the collector makes no changes to cell fields that are visible to the mutator. The expense of read-barriers means that they are rarely, if ever, used with non-moving collectors[2]. Many of the best-known non-moving algorithms for parallel garbage collection were designed for multi-processor architectures but they nevertheless share many of the concerns raised by sequential incremental collection. The algorithms we shall consider are Steele's Multi-processing, Compactifying algorithm [Steele, 1975]; the On the Fly collector by Dijkstra and his colleagues [Dijkstra et al., 1976; Dijkstra et al., 1978]; Kung and Song's improved four-colour version [Kung and Song, 1977]; and Yuasa's sequential algorithm [Yuasa, 1990]. These algorithms use incremental-update write-barriers except for Yuasa who uses a snapshot-at-the-beginning barrier. For each algorithm, we compare the operation of its write-barrier, its treatment of new cells, and the cost of the initialisation and termination of each garbage collection cycle.

---

[2] The only example of which we are aware is Baker's Treadmill (see Section 8.8 on page 218), and even here a write-barrier could be used.

The write-barrier

The rôle of the write-barrier is to prevent mutations of the graph interfering with the collector's traversal. We shall use the fragment of graph in Diagram 8.2 as a running example. The mutator has overwritten the pointer left(A) with a pointer to C. We do not specify whether there are other references to B but clearly there must be another reference to C, maybe held temporarily in a register. In any event, the garbage collection algorithm must ensure that B and C are eventually marked if they are live at the end of the marking phase.

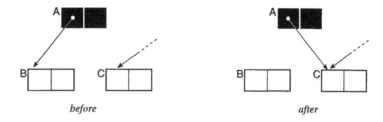

Diagram 8.2   Mutator updates A to point at C rather than B. B and C must eventually be marked if they are still live.

Snapshot-at-the-beginning algorithms prevent the loss of the original reference to a white object. Whenever a pointer is overwritten, the original reference (B in this case) is shaded grey. In effect, a copy-on-write virtual copy of the active data structure is taken at the beginning of each garbage collection cycle. Incremental-update algorithms on the other hand record potentially disruptive pointer writes. Either A or C would be shaded grey depending on the algorithm. Whatever the barrier, every grey cell must be visited and blackened by the collector before the marking phase can terminate. The tricolour abstraction can be implemented either with two colour-bits associated with each cell, or with a mark bit and a stack; marked cells are considered black unless they are in the mark stack in which case they are grey. Although auxiliary data structures for marking increase the space required by the collector, they reduce the time taken to mark active cells.

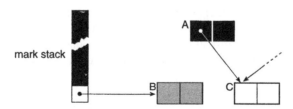

mark stack

Diagram 8.3   Yuasa's snapshot write-barrier.

One of the best known snapshot-at-the-beginning algorithms is Yuasa's algorithm (see Algorithm 8.1 on the following page). His write-barrier traps pointer updates (but not

```
shade(P) =
    if not marked(P)
        mark_bit(P) = marked
        gcpush(P,mark_stack)

Update(A, C) =
    if phase == mark_phase
        shade(*A)
    *A = C
```

Algorithm 8.1   Yuasa's snapshot write-barrier.

initialising writes) during the marking phase and shades the old white pointer grey by setting the cell's mark bit and pushing a reference to the old cell B onto a marking stack.

```
transfer(k2) =                      —move k2 items from save_stack to mark stack
    i = 0
    while i<k2 and save_stack ≠ empty
        p = pop(save_stack)
        if pointer(p)
            gcpush(p,mark_stack)
        i = i+1

sweep(k3) =                                              —sweep k3 items
    i = 0
    while i<k3 and sweeper ≤ Heap_top
        if mark_bit(sweeper) == unmarked
            free(sweeper)
            increment free_count
        else mark_bit(sweeper) = unmarked
        increment sweeper
        i = i+1
```

Algorithm 8.2   Auxiliary procedures for Yuasa's algorithm.

This method preserves B whether or not it is garbage. Snapshot-at-the-beginning algorithms are very conservative. No objects that become garbage in one garbage collection cycle can be reclaimed in that cycle: they must all wait until the next. Consequently, new objects acquired during a marking phase are effectively allocated black even though the chance of a young object dying within a single cycle is high.

Snapshot algorithms do not preserve the 'No black–white pointers' invariant. Suppose that A had already been marked and popped from the marking stack before the update. After the update, left(A) is a black–white pointer. The rôle of grey cells in snapshot algorithms is subtle. Call a path of pointers that starts with a grey object, but then passes through white objects only, a *white path*. The guarantee offered by a snapshot write-barrier is that there will be at least one white path (possibly of length one) leading to each reachable white object. (The conservatism of snapshot algorithms means that there may also be white paths to dead white

```
        mark(k1) =                                       —traverse k1 cells
            i = 0
            while i<k1 and mark_stack ≠ empty
                P = pop(mark_stack)
                for Q in Children(P)
                    if not marked(*Q)
                        mark_bit(*Q) = marked
                        gcpush(*Q,mark_stack)
                i = i+1

    New() =
        if phase == mark_phase
            if mark_stack ≠ empty
                mark(k1)
            if mark_stack == empty and save_stack == empty
                phase = sweep_phase
            else transfer(k2)
        else if phase == sweep_phase
            sweep(k3)
            if sweeper > Heap_top
                phase = idling
        else if free_count < threshold
            phase = mark_phase
            sweeper = Heap_bottom
            for R in Roots
                gcpush(R,mark_stack)
            block_copy(system_stack, save_stack)

        if free_count == 0
            abort "Heap exhausted"

        temp = allocate()
        decrement free_count
        mark_bit(temp) = temp≥sweeper          —Marked if not yet swept
        return temp
```

Algorithm 8.3   Yuasa's allocator.

cells.) A grey object in a snapshot algorithm does not simply represent the local part of the collector's wave-front. It may also represent pointers elsewhere in the graph that cross the grey wave-front otherwise undetected. This non-local property can pose problems for optimising the collector, particularly in environments with multiple concurrent collectors [Wilson and Johnstone, 1993].

Incremental-update methods are less conservative than snapshot algorithms, all other matters being equal. They incrementally record changes made by the mutator to the shape of the graph, rather than making a single, static estimate of the reachability graph at the start of a collection cycle. Incremental-update barriers prevent the first condition for failure, (Cond.1), from arising by trapping any attempt by the mutator to install a pointer to a white node into a black one, and then shading one of the two nodes involved grey. No special action has to be taken when a pointer is deleted. Either of the nodes may be coloured grey, depending on the write-barrier. In our example, if the black A is coloured grey, the collector wave-front is pushed back. If the white C is shaded, the wave-front is advanced. The latter is clearly a more conservative colouring strategy than the former policy since it preserves C regardless of whether the pointer is subsequently deleted. In either case, any white cells that become garbage during the marking phase can be reclaimed by the sweep phase of the same cycle.

Dijkstra adopts the most conservative of the incremental-update colouring strategies: white cells are shaded grey when a reference is created, regardless of the colour of the parent cell[3] (see Algorithm 8.4). Dijkstra's algorithm uses explicit colour bits in each cell for marking rather than using a mark bit and a resumption stack. Notice that the target cannot be painted black straight away as this would violate the 'No black–white pointers' invariant if C had white sons.

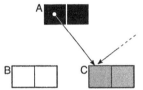

Diagram 8.4   Dijkstra's write-barrier.

```
shade(P) =
    if white(P)
        colour(P) = grey
Update (A,C) =
    *A = C
    shade(C)    ·
```

Algorithm 8.4   Dijkstra's write-barrier.

Dijkstra's algorithm permits fine-grained parallelism. For the mutator, it suffices that each line of the Update operation in Algorithm 8.4 be an atomic action. Woodger and Stenning discovered that the order of instructions in Update can introduce a subtle bug into a fine-grained implementation. Although the order appears counter-intuitive, as it may temporarily break the invariant (Cond.1) by writing a pointer to a white C into a black A, it is correct. Suppose that the order was reversed so that nodes are shaded before they are linked. Suppose further that the mutator shades a node C and then suspends activity. The garbage collector now completes its cycle, and then starts the next, reaching A which it colours black (at this point A has no descendants). The mutator now awakens and completes the update, writing a pointer

---

[3] In a parallel implementation, each statement of Update is an atomic action.

from black A to white C! Colour information has been lost and the live C will be reclaimed in the next sweep phase. The correctness of the fine-grained solution can only be ensured if updates write the pointer before shading the target cell.

Dijkstra's algorithm causes both the marker and the mutator to drive the grey wave-front forward: it is easy to see that the progress of marking is guaranteed. However, C will be preserved even if the new pointer left(A) is deleted before the marker reaches C.In contrast, Steele's algorithm reverts the black site A of the update to grey rather than shading the new white C (see Algorithm 8.5).

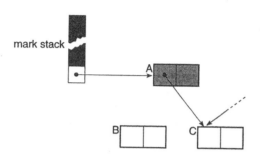

Diagram 8.5 Steele's write-barrier.

```
shade(P) =
    mark_bit(P) = unmarked
    gcpush(P)

Update(A,C) =
    LOCK gcstate
        *A = C
        if phase == marking_phase
            if marked(A) and unmarked(C)        —black A, white C
                shade(A)
```

Algorithm 8.5 Steele's write-barrier. In a parallel implementation, the mutator must be prevented from switching garbage collection phases until Update has completed.

The effect is to retreat the grey wave-front rather than advance it, making Steele's algorithm less conservative than Dijkstra's. Steele's algorithm is also more selective, at the cost of extra tests, only shading a black parent of a white son. Although Steele's technique may cost an extra visit to A, it will reduce the amount of floating garbage left at the end of the collection cycle. Like Yuasa, Steele uses a mark bit and a stack for grey references. For clarity, we omit details of synchronising access to the mark stack (see Algorithm 8.6 on the following page).

```
push(X,stack) =                          —push X onto program stack
    LOCK stack
        stack_index = stack_index + 1
        stack[index] = X
        if phase == mark_phase
        and marked(stack) and not marked(X)
            gcpush(X,mark_stack)

Create(n) =                              —create new cell with n fields
    LOCK gcstate
        temp = allocate()
        LOCK temp
            if phase == sweep_phase
                newmark = sweeper≤temp
            else newmark = true

            for i = 1 to n
                p = pop()
                temp[i] = p
                if phase == mark_phase
                    newmark = newmark and mark_bit(p)

        mark_bit(temp) = newmark
        push(temp,stack)
```

Algorithm 8.6   Allocation in Steele's concurrent algorithm.

New cells

The conservatism of an algorithm is also affected by its policy towards new cells. If the mortality rate of new cells is sufficiently high, many will die before they are reached by the marker. New dead cells that were allocated white can be reclaimed in the same collection cycle, but cells allocated black or grey will survive the collection cycle whether they are still visible to the mutator or not. The cost of allocating white is that any newborn cells that do survive must be traversed.

Dijkstra and Yuasa are more conservative in this respect than Steele or Kung and Song. Dijkstra's chief concern was the correctness of his algorithm rather than its efficiency. To simplify its proof, the mutator's instruction set contained only the Update operation (see Algorithm 8.4 on page 192): the free-list is considered to be reachable and New is a combination of Update operations. This simplicity means that the free-list has to be marked as well as the active data structure. As a consequence, Dijkstra allocates all new objects grey or black, depending on whether the head of the free list has been blackened yet or not. In either case, a dead new cell cannot be reclaimed until the next collection cycle. Yuasa is somewhat less conservative of new cells than Dijkstra (see Algorithm 8.3 on page 191). Although the snapshot means that no cell active at any point during the marking phase can be reclaimed until the next collection cycle, any cells that die outside the marking phase will be reclaimed in the next cycle. These cells are allocated white or will become white after they have been swept. Dijkstra, on the other hand, does not distinguish between phases.

```
mark() =
    phase = mark_phase
    for R in Roots
        gcpush(R,mark_stack)
        mark1()

    for S in system_stack
        LOCK S, system_stack
            gcpush(S,mark_stack)
        mark1()

    LOCK gcstate
        finished = mark_stack==empty
    while not finished
        mark1()
        LOCK gcstate
            finished = mark_stack==empty

mark1() =
    while mark_stack ≠ empty
        X = gcpop(mark_stack)
        if unmarked(X)
            LOCK X
                for Y in Children(X)
                    gcpush(*Y,mark_stack)
                colour(X) = black
```

Algorithm 8.7 Steele's concurrent marker.

The Steele (see Algorithms 8.5 and 8.6) and Kung and Song (see Algorithm 8.9 on page 199) algorithms are incremental-update and therefore inherently less conservative than snapshot-at-the-beginning algorithms. Both are concerned with efficiency rather than ease of verification, and therefore consider the colour of new cells in more detail than Dijkstra. Kung and Song allocate new cells grey during the marking phase and white otherwise. Similarly, Steele allocates white outside the marking phase but applies a heuristic to initialising writes during the mark phase (see Algorithm 8.6 on the facing page). Create(n) allocates a new cell and initialises its n fields with values taken from the program stack. The address of the new cell is then passed back to the mutator through its stack. When a new cell is created and initialised during the marking phase, the mark-bits of its components are examined. If these are all set, the new cell is allocated black, but not pushed onto the stack, on the assumption that the marking phase is near completion and that the cell will probably not be discarded before then. On the other hand, if any of its referents are white, then the cell is shaded grey if the program stack has been marked and white otherwise. Since the stack is marked last, and scanned from bottom (least volatile) to top (most volatile), most cells will be allocated white.

Initialisation and termination

A garbage collection cycle is initiated in a sequential algorithm when a request for more memory cannot be satisfied, rather than following immediately after the previous cycle as might happen in a multi-processor architecture. A serial incremental memory management system interleaves the mutator with the collector, suspending the mutator while the collector runs. To prevent mutator starvation during garbage collection, a new collection cycle is initiated whenever the amount of free memory falls below a certain threshold — Yuasa suggests that an incremental system typically needs heap space headroom of around 22 percent to be safe. The simplest way to initiate garbage collection would be to snapshot the state of the computation by pushing pointer values held in registers, global variables and the program stack onto the marking stack. However, the root set of the user program may be large. As well as global data, it may include a stack or many threads, each with their own state. The pause to initiate a garbage collection cycle would compromise the mutator's response time if it must be suspended while the collector processes an unbounded root set.

Neither Dijkstra nor Kung and Song pay any attention to how the user stack should be treated. Dijkstra ducks the issue, by stating "shade all the roots". Kung and Song simply insert roots one at a time into the collector end of a double-ended marking queue at the start of each collection cycle. Both are concurrent algorithms so mutator activity is allowed to continue unrestricted. A simple sequential implementation would shade all the roots grey in a single atomic operation, with the mutator suspended.

Yuasa ameliorates the problem by copying the entire program stack, including non-pointers, to a `saved_stack` with a fast block-copying operator such as Unix's `memcpy`, rather than selectively pushing pointers onto the mark stack (see Algorithm 8.3 on page 191). Only registers and global variables (of which it is assumed there are few) are pushed directly onto the mark stack at the start of the marking phase. Large arrays may be handled similarly or divided into a header and a body. Headers would be kept in a region of the heap managed by incremental mark-sweep while their bodies would be kept in a separated region divided into semi-spaces and compacted by copying. This arrangement also reduces fragmentation. Entries from the `saved_stack` are subsequently transferred to the marking stack $k2$ at a time whenever it becomes empty (in order to minimise the depth attained by the stack). The mark phase terminates when both the mark and save stacks are empty.

Yuasa describes his algorithm as real-time. The only justification for this is that the time complexity of the allocator is bounded by three constants. During the marking phase, up to $k1$ cells on the marking stack are processed and up to $k2$ entries may be moved from the saved stack to the mark stack, at each allocation. The sweep phase similarly sweeps up to $k3$ cells at each allocation. Each allocation step in Yuasa's algorithm is therefore bounded by $k1$, $k2$ and $k3$, provided that the user stack can be block-copied to `saved_stack` within this bound. It is far from clear that this will be true in general although it may be for his implementation of Lisp [Yuasa and Hagiya, 1985]. No empirical evidence is provided.

Yuasa also argues that there could not be a small upper bound on allocation time if the allocator were to sweep the heap lazily at each allocation (see Chapter 4 where we discuss sweeping techniques). Instead he uses a linked list of free cells. The free-list is not empty during garbage collection — if it were, the mutator would starve. To distinguish cells on the free-list from white (unmarked) cells in the heap, a fourth colour, *off-white*, is used. Off-white is indicated by writing a distinguished pointer in a spare field of each free cell.

Steele too takes care to specify how the program stack should be handled (see Algorithm 8.7 on page 195). First objects reachable from the roots are marked — each root is pushed and traced one at a time. Entries on the stack are left until last since the stack is highly volatile. Again entries are pushed and traced one at a time. Unfortunately further items may have been pushed onto the program stack or the marking stack. The mutator must push new entries onto the marking stack if it pushes them onto the program stack after that stack has been marked (see push in Algorithm 8.7 on page 195). Cells allocated by Create may also be pushed onto the marking stack by the mutator (see Algorithm 8.6 on page 194). In a concurrent system, the collector locks the mark stack while it examines it. If the stack is empty the mark phase is complete; otherwise the collector releases the lock and continues marking.

Termination is more expensive in Dijkstra's algorithm. As usual, the mark phase is complete when there are no grey cells left in the heap. Dijkstra determines this by scanning the heap for grey cells, restarting marking from any grey cell that it encounters. The marking phase only terminates if it has completed a full tour of the heap without meeting any grey cells. The complexity of Dijkstra's algorithm is thus theoretically quadratic rather than proportional to the size of the active data structure. Unfortunately it is only too easy to find realistic examples with quadratic complexity.

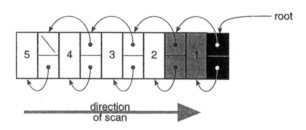

Diagram 8.6   Marking the list [1,2,3,4,5] with Dijkstra's algorithm.

Suppose a linked list is constructed in a functional style in an empty heap. The list will be laid out in the heap in reverse order: the last element will be allocated at the lowest address and the head of the list at the highest address (see Diagram 8.6). The marker will blacken the head *cons* cell and grey its children. It will not reach these grey cells again in order to continue the traversal of the list until it has completed nearly a full tour of the heap. This process will be repeated with every element in the spine of the list.

Marking could be improved by any of the techniques described in Chapter 4, provided that they could be interleaved with mutator activity. A notable exception is the Deutsch–Schorr–Waite pointer-reversal method, described on page 82, which would render objects inaccessible to the mutator during the trace. Lamport, and Queinnec *et al.* show that marking and sweeping can be performed in parallel [Lamport, 1976; Queinnec *et al.*, 1989]. Cells in Queinnec's algorithm are given two colour fields. At any point in the execution of the program, the sweep phase of collection cycle n can be run concurrently with the marking phase of cycle $n + 1$ if each phase uses different colour fields. Thus odd-numbered collections may use the first colour field, and even-numbered ones the second. There is one subtlety, however. Dijkstra's algorithm marks the free-list as well as live data. Marking must preserve the 'no black–white pointers' invariant. When sweep phase n frees a cell whose colour field for that cycle is white, it must shade the cell's other colour field in order to preserve this invariant.

Lamport also pipelines marking and sweeping phases and moreover permits multiple garbage collectors. Unlike Queinnec, markers and sweepers share a single colour field. This is possible because the sweepers only free already identified garbage and the markers do not mark garbage (garbage is not to be confused with cells on free-lists). However, a problem arises here: all cells must be white before a marking phase starts, but a sweeper would free any white cells in the heap, appending them to a free-list. To overcome this problem, Lamport repaints white cells to some new colour, say purple, and black cells to white (or grey) before starting another pair of mark/scan phases. This colour change is done in a single instruction by an ingenious reinterpretation of colour values by incrementing the value of a *base* colour modulo 3: interested readers should consult [Lamport, 1976] for more details.

Kung and Song improved Dijkstra's algorithm by using an auxiliary data structure for marking and by not marking the free-list (see Algorithm 8.9 on the facing page). Instead, like Yuasa, Kung and Song paint free cells a fourth colour, *off-white*, in the sweep phase. To reduce the need for critical sections in a concurrent implementation, they used an output restricted deque rather than a stack for marking, with the mutator appending cells at one end while the collector uses the other end. In terms of the tricolour abstraction, grey cells are those in the queue regardless of their actual colour. Kung and Song also blacken some cells that are conceptually grey to improve performance (see Algorithm 8.8).

```
New() =
    temp = allocate()
    if phase == mark_phase
        colour(R) = black
    return temp

shade(P) =
    if white(P) or off-white(P)
        colour(P) = grey
        gcpush(P, Mutator-end of queue)

Update(A,C)=
    *A = C
    if phase == mark_phase
        shade(C)
```

Algorithm 8.8   Kung and Song mutator code.

Virtual memory techniques

Software write-barriers impose an overhead on all pointer updates performed by the mutator. On many systems, the overhead on the mutator can be removed with assistance from the virtual memory.

The Boehm–Demers–Shenker collector marks objects incrementally, but relies on operating system dirty bits for synchronisation [Boehm *et al.*, 1991] (see Chapter 9 where

```
mark() =
    phase = mark_phase
    while queue ≠ empty
        N = node at GC-end of queue
        colour(N) = black
        gcpop(queue)
        for M in Children(N)
            if not black(*M)
                colour(*M) = black
                gcpush(*M, GC-end of queue)
    phase = sweep_phase
```

Algorithm 8.9   The Kung and Song marker.

we discuss algorithms for so-called conservative garbage collection). In order to terminate, the marking phase suspends all mutator threads and examines virtual memory dirty bits to discover which objects have been modified since the mark phase started. Marking recommences from roots and any marked objects on dirty pages — these are the grey objects — and the dirty bits are cleared. When the mark stack is empty, the collector again attempts to terminate. The set of dirty bits plays the same rôle as the mutation log does for Replicating Garbage Collection (page 214 in this chapter).

Since this barrier relies only on dirty bits, it often involves no traps. It does involve some extra overhead in the paging code, but this is minimal and is not executed unless the program pages. The main overhead introduced is the page scanning by the garbage collector: the granularity of the dirty-bit barrier is very coarse. The Boehm–Demers–Shenker collector fails the hard real-time test on two counts. Firstly, it must suspend mutator threads when it attempts to terminate, and secondly, the cost of examining dirty bits and scanning pages may be too expensive. Nevertheless, for less demanding applications in the Cedar environment, Boehm reports that virtual memory support for incremental collection significantly improves pause times [Boehm, 1995c]. A further advantage of this scheme is that it does not require compiler modifications to implement the write-barrier and so can be used to support different languages.

The virtual memory system can also be used to support a snapshot-at-the-beginning write-barrier by incrementally create the snapshot with copy-on-write pages. This technique has also been used by Furusou *et al.* for a concurrent conservative collector designed to support object-oriented languages [Furusou *et al.*, 1991]. The advantage of the virtual memory copy-on-write-barrier is that it has probably the best pause-time characteristics of the virtual memory synchronised algorithms. Furusou *et al.* use the Mach operating system's copy-on-write mechanism to take a virtual copy of the heap before entering the mark phase. Mutator threads are only suspended while the virtual memory tables are prepared for copy-on-write. The effect of the virtual snapshot is that the garbage collector marks the old image of the heap (using Yuasa's algorithm 8.3 on page 191), while the mutator threads run in the current image. The sweep phase then reclaims garbage in the current image based on mark information held in the old image. No further synchronisation between mutator and collector threads is necessary.

The chief disadvantage of this approach is that it is hard to avoid actually copying objects, since control is only obtained at the initial write to a page. Greying all objects referenced from the page is clearly unnecessarily conservative. Furusou *et al.* also found that their memory manager gave very poor performance, with rates of allocation of the order of thousands of objects per second rather than the millions that object-oriented concurrent languages require. They ascribe this poor performance to a bottleneck in allocation: all mutator threads make requests for memory to a single collector thread. They propose to remedy this by assigning memory to mutators in page-sized chunks. While a mutator is allocating from a chunk, the entire chunk is considered to be alive: these chunks are traced but not marked. Once the chunk has been filled, its management is taken over by the memory manager which marks and sweeps the chunk at collection time. Since objects cannot be allocated into partially used chunks after they have been placed in the care of the memory manager, this approach runs the risk of severe internal fragmentation.

8.4   Concurrent Reference Counting

Reference counting is well-suited to incremental garbage collection, as it naturally interleaves mutator and collector operations. As we noted earlier, its chief drawbacks are its inability to reclaim cyclic structures, its computational expense and its close coupling to the user program. However, reference counting is a less attractive proposition for concurrent environments. Updating a reference count must be an atomic action in order to avoid race conditions between threads that might lead to the premature reclamation of shared objects. Atomicity requires locks on all objects that might be shared between threads, and hence increases greatly the already large cost of pointer assignment.

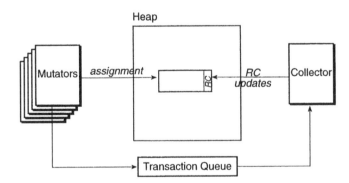

Diagram 8.7   The Modula-2+ concurrent reference counting architecture.

Several researchers have suggested improving the performance of mutators by passing the cost of reference count manipulations to a garbage collector running in a separate thread. The best known implementations of concurrent reference counting are the Cedar and Modula-2+ collectors [Rovner, 1985; DeTreville, 1990a]. In Modula-2+ system, the mutators and the collector communicate through a *transaction queue* (see Diagram 8.7). Mutators do not manipulate reference counts but log all assignments in a block of the transaction queue (see Algorithm 8.10). When the current block is full (typically, after 16,384 assignments), the mutator notifies the collector and gets a fresh empty block. Note that a lock is necessary to prevent simultaneous assignments to the same shared variable, as this would risk logging out-of-date values. The collector updates reference counts in heap objects from the information held in the transaction queue block, and frees objects whose reference count has dropped to zero.

```
Update(A, C) =
    LOCK mutex
        insert(A, C, tq)                    —insert in transaction queue
        if tq is full
            notify_collector(tq)            —send block to collector
            tq = get_next_block()
        *A = C
```

Algorithm 8.10 Mutator code for shared reference assignment.

The cost of updates can be reduced by distinguishing assignments to local variables, i.e. those held in the stack or the registers of a thread, from those assignments to global variables and heap data. The Modula-2+ collector only reference-counts shared pointer-valued variables (*cf.* deferred reference counting in Chapter 3). Unfortunately this complicates the collector since the reference counting invariant is no longer maintained. Instead, the reference count held in an object is only a lower bound on the number of references to that object held by local and shared variables.

Whether the true value of a reference count is zero or not can only be determined by examining the local variables of each mutator thread. In fact, the Modula-2+ collector needs only a weaker condition: whether a given pointer value appears in any thread's state. The collector's code is shown in Algorithm 8.11 on the following page. When the current transaction queue block has been filled (or after about 40 kilobytes of storage have been allocated), the mutator sends the block to the collector. The block holds details of shared reference assignments up to some time t_0.

The collector interrupts threads one at a time to scan their state. To avoid scanning a thread in the middle of an assignment, the collector must hold the mutex in order to stop the thread. Any word in the thread's state that might be a reference to a word in the heap is collected for later use. Call the time by which all thread states have been scanned t_1. The reference counts of the pairs of variables held in the transaction block are adjusted, and any variable whose reference count drops to zero is placed in a *Zero-Count List* (ZCL) before the block is returned to a pool of free blocks.

An object's shared reference count can only rise from zero if its local count is non-zero at that time. Conversely an object's local reference count can only rise from zero if its shared count is non-zero. Thus if an object had a zero shared reference count at t_0, and did not appear in any thread state between t_0 and t_1 and does not appear as the right-hand side of a transaction queue record between t_0 and t_1, then both its shared and its local reference counts were zero at t_1. It can be safely freed.

Finally, the ZCL must be processed. There are three possibilities for an object in the ZCL.

```
collector() =
    loop forever
        tq = wait_next_block()
        foreach thread th
            LOCK mutex
                suspend(th)
                scan_thread(th)
                restart(th)
        adjust_counts(tq)
        free_block(tq)
        adjust_shared_counts()
        process_ZCL()
```

Algorithm 8.11 Collector code for shared reference assignment.

If its shared reference count is no longer zero, it is removed from the ZCL. It it was found in a thread's state, it is left in the ZCL: it may be freed in a future collection. Otherwise the object is removed from the list and recursively freed.

The Modula-2+ collector showed a number of shortcomings. Apart from the inability to reclaim cyclic structures, the cost of assignment to shared pointer variables is high, taking ten instructions rather than the single instruction required for local assignments. DeTreville observed that this overhead sometimes led programmers to avoid using reference variables where they would otherwise be preferred. These concerns, and concerns over fragmentation, working set size, locality and a tendency for the collector to fall behind the mutator, led DeTreville to experiment with other concurrent collectors.

The collectors examined included a concurrent mark-sweep based on Dijkstra's algorithm with binary-buddy allocation, mark-sweep with the Appel–Ellis–Li pagewise read-barrier, and a mostly copying collector, again with the pagewise read-barrier (see Section 9.3 on page 241 where we discuss conservative copying collectors). However, all these collectors proved unsatisfactory. As none of the experimental collectors were generational, and Modula-2+ programs typically used very large heaps, all thrashed the Firefly workstations. The collectors were also vulnerable to programming idioms that disguised pointers from the collector, and the mostly copying collector failed under programmer assumptions of object immobility. The cost of initialisation and of trap handling in the virtual memory synchronised collectors was also considered too high.

Finally DeTreville resorted to a combined reference counting and mark-sweep collector. Both collectors ran in their own threads, but the reference counter had precedence over the tracing collector, and could suspend it while reference counting operations were performed. The mark-sweep collector did not reclaim storage: it simply broke cycles by nulling pointers. The cost of assignment was reduced to four instructions with the use of per-thread transaction queues, although this placed the onus on the programmer not to perform concurrent assignments to the same variable. Processing of transaction blocks also became more complex as entries were no longer read in chronological order of assignment.

8.5 Baker's Algorithm

At the beginning of this chapter, we remarked that copying collectors present a more complex, multiple-reader, multiple-writer coherency problem than non-moving collectors. One solution is to use a read-barrier to trap mutator accesses. If the trapped object is in Fromspace, it is copied to Tospace and the address of the copy is returned to the mutator. In this way the mutator can only see Tospace objects: the grey wave-front is made to advance just ahead of the mutator's nose. Since the mutator can never see a white object, it can never install a reference to a white object into a black one and hence disrupt the collector's traversal (Cond.1). Two related questions arise. The first issue to resolve is whether to allow the mutator to see grey nodes as well as black ones. The second issue is how much work should be done by the read-barrier. For example, the least work that can be done is to evacuate a Fromspace object into Tospace. In terms of the tricolour abstraction, the read-barrier colours a white object grey and returns the address of the grey copy to the mutator. Alternatively, a *black-only* barrier could copy and scan the object (and possibly blacken other grey objects as well) before returning the address of the black copy. We shall examine two families of collector, one of which takes the former approach and the other the latter.

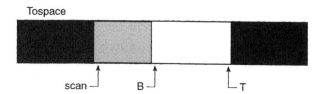

Diagram 8.8 Baker's Tospace layout. scan is the next cell to be scanned. The next cell to be evacuated will be copied at B and the next new cell will be allocated at T.

The best-known incremental copying garbage collection algorithm is due to Baker [Baker, 1978]. This algorithm is so well known that standard copying collectors have sometimes been erroneously referred to as Baker collectors. Baker modified Cheney's algorithm [Cheney, 1970] (see Chapter 6, page 118) to allow the mutator to progress during a garbage collection cycle. To do so, the Tospace region of the heap is arranged so that the scavenger can compact surviving data into its bottom end at B while allocation is made from its top end at T (see Diagram 8.8). All new objects are thus allocated black. This arrangement has the advantage that the collector does not need to scan new cells since the read-barrier ensures they cannot have been initialised with references into Fromspace. The drawback of this approach is that it also means that no new cell can be reclaimed until the cycle after its death. Consequently Baker's read-barrier is more conservative than incremental-update write-barriers but less so than snapshot algorithms.

```
New(n) =
    if B ≥ T - n                                      —Flip phase
        if scan < B
            abort "Haven't finished scavenging"
        flip()
        for root R
            R = copy(R)
    repeat k times while scan < B                     —scavenge a bit
        for P in Children(scan)
            *P = copy(*P)
        scan = scan + size(scan)
    if B == T
        abort "Heap full"
    T = T - n
    return T

read(T) =
    T′ = copy(T)
    return T′
```

Algorithm 8.12   Baker's incremental copying algorithm.

The algorithm

As usual for a copying collector, Baker's collector starts by flipping Fromspace and Tospace. A stop-and-copy collector would flip when the B and T pointers met (see Diagram 8.12), but this is not the only policy that might be adopted. Flipping when the pointers meet, provided that the collector has finished scavenging grey cells, minimises copying by allowing objects as much time as possible to die, but maximises the amount of heap allocated and hence the number of page faults incurred. Flipping as soon as a collection is complete, on the other hand, compacts data as much as possible by using fewer pages and hence reduces the chance of page faults.

As well as switching the roles of the semi-spaces, flip also checks that the new Tospace is sufficiently large, expanding it if necessary. The difference between Baker's and Cheney's allocator and collector is that collection is tuned to allocation in Baker's algorithm, with up to k cells scanned at each allocation to ensure that the mutator does not starve. If variable-sized cells are allocated, kn words should be traced when an object of n words is allocated (see the discussion in the first section of this chapter). Copy is unchanged from Cheney's algorithm in Chapter 6.

The illusion that collection is complete is maintained by a read-barrier. The read-barrier affects only read-access to objects read in (Algorithm 8.12) so only pointer load operations need to be modified to copy cells or follow forwarding addresses; write operations are unaffected. This arrangement has the advantage of allowing white objects (i.e. Fromspace objects that have not been copied) to die and their space to be reclaimed within a single collection cycle. Baker's read-barrier is a fine-grained barrier, evacuating only a single object at a time. It only denies the mutator access to white cells — the mutator is permitted to read pointers to grey objects. Later we shall encounter read-barriers that copy more objects when a pointer read is trapped and that only allow the mutator to see black objects.

Bounds on the latency of Baker's algorithm

This simple implementation of Baker's algorithm fails to provide real-time bounds in several respects. First of all, the root set is scavenged atomically at flip time. It will not be possible to maintain a small upper bound on New if the size of the root set is large, for instance if it includes a program stack. Baker tackles this by modifying New to scavenge a fixed number, k', of stack cells at each allocation as well. At each flip, k' is recomputed in order to keep the ratio k'/k equal to the ratio of stack locations to heap cells. Incremental scavenging of the stack also complicates routines that access it. Firstly, stack pops may need to adjust the value of the collector's stack scanning pointer. Secondly, the read-barrier must be applied to values picked up from the stack as well as those obtained from the heap. No special action is needed for stack pushes, on the other hand, since the read-barrier ensures that the object to be pushed will be in Tospace. Baker suggests scanning the stack from top to bottom, but Brooks (and Steele) argue that less volatile stack locations should be scavenged before more volatile ones [Brooks, 1984]. This tactic reduces the chance that a pop might destroy the only reference to an object that has just been copied — not only would the collector's efforts have been wasted but it would have moved garbage into Tospace.

The second problem facing Baker is that the cost of evacuating an object depends on its size. His solution is to copy large objects lazily. This requires that large objects contain an additional link word in their header that will hold the forwarding address in the Fromspace object and a backward link to the original in the Tospace copy (see Diagram 8.9 on the next page). When the object is evacuated, space is reserved for the large object in Tospace and the forwarding and backward addresses are set. The rest of the Tospace copy can be filled incrementally, with the backward pointer set to nil on completion. The cost of this scheme, apart from the extra header word, is that write-access to a field of the object requires the field's address to be compared with scan. If the address is greater than scan then the old object is used via the backward link; otherwise the new copy is used.

Limitations of Baker's algorithm

Baker's collector is closely coupled to the mutator. This is extremely expensive on stock hardware. Collectors that use pure Baker schemes have therefore relied on hardware support to maintain the read-barrier. Wholey and Fahlman suggest that, without hardware support, the cost of a microcoded Baker read-barrier is around 30 percent [Wholey and Fahlman, 1984], although calculations by Zorn suggest that the cost might be much lower for a well-designed software read-barrier [Zorn, 1990a]. Garbage collection pauses may also be unpredictable and tightly clustered, causing jerky interactive response.

The time to access an object depends on whether it is in Tospace or Fromspace. For example, the cost of walking a tree depends on whether it has been traversed before in the current collection cycle. In this respect, the performance of a read-barrier is likely to be less predictable than that of a write-barrier, since good real-time response requires not only small bounds on pause times but also that the mutator obtains sufficient access to the processor. In

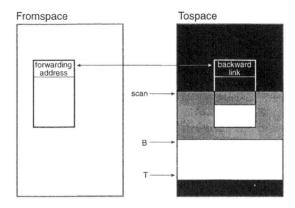

Diagram 8.9   Large objects can be scanned lazily by using a backward link.

other words, the proportion of any period of time for which the collector runs must also be bounded. Most variations on Baker's algorithm have sought either to reduce the cost of the barrier or to make the length of pauses more predictable.

Variations on Baker

Brooks reduces the cost of the read-barrier by removing the conditional test and branch that determines whether an object needs to be forwarded [Brooks, 1984]. Instead all objects are referred to via an indirection field in their header. If a cell has not been copied, its indirection will refer to the Fromspace original (for example, B in Diagram 8.10 on the facing page). If it has been copied, the indirection refers to the Tospace copy (for example, A in Diagram 8.10 on the next page). Consequently the mutator can see both Fromspace and Tospace objects, unlike Baker's scheme. To prevent the installation of black–white pointers, destructive operations such as Update are required to forward their second argument before installing it.

Although cast in the light of Baker, this is actually an incremental-update write-barrier rather than a read-barrier. Its cost is that Brooks's objects require additional space for the forwarding pointer since a mutator field cannot be overwritten (otherwise it would be impossible to distinguish forwarding addresses from other pointers to objects in Tospace). For Lisp *cons* cells this represents a 50 percent space overhead. There is also a time penalty since access to objects is indirect, but this is partially offset by the lower frequency of the write-barrier compared to a read-barrier. The North and Reppy concurrent garbage collector also uses Brooks-style indirections but keeps them in a separate forwarding pointer space [North and Reppy, 1987]. This gives lower space overheads since both old and new versions of an object share the same forwarding pointer. The drawback is that the forwarding pointer space also needs garbage collecting.

A non-interpretive write-barrier for incremental copying collection has also been used for the Spineless Tagless G-machine, an abstract machine for lazy functional languages [Peyton Jones, 1992]. Each closure in the STG-machine is associated, through an *information*

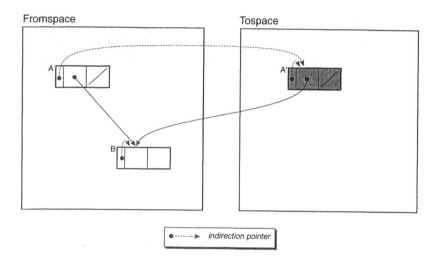

Fromspace

Tospace

indirection pointer

Diagram 8.10 Brooks's forwarding pointers.

table of entry points, to fixed code sequences that evaluate (enter) or collect the closure (this is similar to the technique Thomas used, see Section 6.6). The While and Field collector for the STG-machine modifies the evaluation entry point in the information table of a grey closure [While and Field, 1992]. The evaluation code pointer is changed to point to code that will cause the closure to scan itself when it is next entered, scavenging its components, before entering its real evaluation code. When the scan is complete, the evaluation entry in the information table is reset to its original value. The collector code in the information table similarly restores the evaluation entry point for the case when the closure is scavenged before it is entered by the mutator.

The second drawback of Baker's collector is that it conservatively allocates new objects black, allowing young garbage to survive to the next collection cycle. Dawson attempts to reduce the amount of this floating garbage by allocating in Fromspace rather than Tospace whenever possible, i.e. allocating white rather than black [Dawson, 1992] (see Diagram 8.11 on the following page). The next garbage collection cycle is initiated as soon as the previous one has finished rather than postponing the flip until Tospace is full. Like Brooks, Dawson's barrier is a write-barrier.

Baker's algorithm has also been used, rather uneasily, as the basis for multi-processor garbage collection, for example in Concert MultiLisp [Halstead, 1984]. This architecture uses a common memory addressable by all processors, but each processor is responsible for the management of its own Fromspace and Tospace regions. Apart from doubts about the scalability of such an architecture, garbage collection of this configuration requires substantial synchronisation. First, no processor can discard its region of Fromspace until all other processors have completed scanning their region of Tospace, since a grey Tospace object may hold a reference into their Fromspace. Secondly, evacuation of a Fromspace object into Tospace requires synchronisation both to move the object and to write the forwarding address,

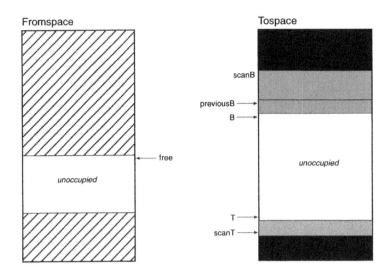

Diagram 8.11   Heap layout for Dawson's collector.

and also to update the grey pointer (since other mutators may try to read it). Halstead's solution is to include a lock bit in each pointer (for the update) and in each object (for the move).

Dynamic regrouping

In Section 6.6 of Chapter 6 we examined garbage collector strategies for improving the mutator's locality of reference, an idea first suggested by White [White, 1980]. These strategies employed different collector traversal orders to *statically* regroup objects in the heap. This reorganisation was called static because it was informed only by the topology of the active data at the moment of collection. Incremental collectors offer the opportunity, in addition, to reorganise the data *dynamically*, based on the actual pattern of access to the heap by the mutator.

First we consider a static regrouping strategy used by Baker and Dawson to improve the spatial locality of lists (see Diagram 8.11). Cells evacuated asynchronously by the read-barrier are copied to T at the top of Tospace. Cells copied by the scavenger are moved to B at the bottom of the heap to avoid interspersing them with objects copied by the write-barrier. PreviousB is always either equal to B or points to the last *cons* cell whose *cdr* has not been copied. Wherever possible the collector prefers to continue linearising (from the bottom) rather than scanning from the top. Whenever it can, the scanner copies the *cdr* of previousB to B. If previousB does not have an uncopied *cdr*, the scanner picks a new seed from which to restart linearising. The new seed will be found, in order of preference, at scanB, in a register or at scanT. Although this algorithm does not provide fully depth-first traversal, it does trace *cdr*-chains contiguously.

Courts's *Temporal Garbage Collector* for the Texas Instruments Explorer workstation regrouped objects dynamically [Courts, 1988; Explorer, 1987, 1987]. Courts observed that the amount of data touched in a typical session was small, say 4 megabytes out of 30, and that it would therefore be worth trying to place this data as close together as possible. He employed combinations of two strategies. The simplest strategy was to have the user run a training session to exercise the most frequently used system functions. Major collections of the heap are scheduled during this session but the scavenger is inhibited. Objects are only evacuated to Tospace by the read-barrier during this session. At the end of the training session, Tospace will contain all the objects touched by the mutator, in the order that they were accessed by the mutator, and only those objects. These are made static so that they will not be moved in future. A full normal collection is executed to remove all garbage and the trained image is saved to disk for future use. Depending on the amount of real memory available, Courts found that band training reduced paging time by between 30 and 50 percent.

This *band training* has two limitations: it does not dynamically regroup objects created after a boot, and it does not reflect changes in activity patterns. Courts's second strategy was to prepend a mini-training session to the front of each collection. At each collection, an older generation is flipped if it has exceeded a size threshold. If no older generation is sufficiently large, the youngest generation is flipped. The scavenger is inhibited during this collection until an allocation threshold is passed. This gives a chance for most of the data currently being used by the mutator to be copied by the read-barrier. Eventually the scavenger is allowed to run to completion.

This *adaptive training* strategy was even more successful, reducing paging time by 65 to 75 percent compared to standard generational garbage collection. Combining both strategies reduced paging time by 75 to 80 percent. This improvement was confirmed, albeit not so dramatically, by Johnson and Llames who combined it with the static regrouping strategy described in Chapter 6 [Johnson, 1991a; Llames, 1991].

8.6 The Appel–Ellis–Li collector

Without hardware support Baker's algorithm cannot provide adequate performance. The algorithm is also inherently serial: the mutator stops whenever the collector does some work. Appel, Ellis and Li produced an incremental collector that is generally portable and supports concurrency without fine-grain object locking [Appel *et al.*, 1988]. Furthermore their collector does not require any modification to the compiler. It is based on Baker copying, but uses a pagewise *black-only* read-barrier supported by the operating system's memory protection hardware. The Appel–Ellis–Li read-barrier imposes a stricter constraint on the mutator than does Baker's: not only is the mutator not allowed to see white objects, but it is only allowed to see black ones (see Diagram 8.12 on the following page). Consequently the Appel–Ellis–Li read-barrier is more conservative than Baker's since the mutator cannot delete any pointer stored in a grey object without springing the page trap. The handler will then blacken the grey object and grey its sons.

At the start of each garbage collection cycle, objects referenced from the root set are copied into Tospace and the virtual memory protection of the Tospace pages they occupy is set to 'no access'. Many operating systems today provide user level access to the memory protection mechanism (for example, many versions of Unix provide an `mprotect` system call) so this technique is generally feasible. Whenever the mutator attempts to access an object on a grey

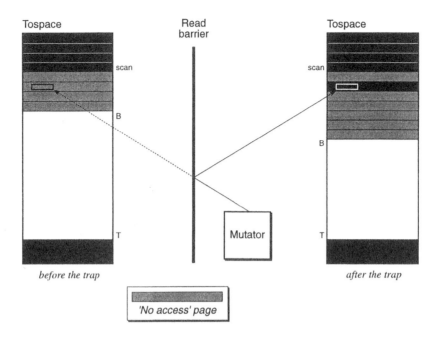

Diagram 8.12   The Appel–Ellis–Li 'black-only' read-barrier. Mutator access to grey
                 Tospace objects is trapped by the read-barrier.

(protected) page, the page-access trap is triggered and the fault is caught by the collector
(see Diagram 8.12). In a sequential implementation, the collector removes the protection
from the page that caused the fault and then scans all the objects on that page, evacuating
their Fromspace sons into Tospace pages which are then protected (see Algorithm 8.13 on
the facing page). Finally the collector restarts the mutator. To the mutator, the page appears
to have contained only Tospace pointers all along. It can never fetch white pointers into its
registers and so can never break the 'No black–white pointers' invariant.

   The garbage collector also scavenges grey pages in the background between handling page
faults. In a sequential implementation, scanning is done by the allocator, just as in Baker's
algorithm. In a concurrent implementation a separate background thread can be used to scan
Tospace pages. Like the read-barrier, the scanner scavenges complete pages at a time. As soon
as all Tospace pages have been scanned, the `scanner_thread` blocks until `flip` signals that
more pages are waiting to be scanned. `Flip` must ensure that scavenging is completed (there
are no more grey pages) before swapping semi-spaces and copying roots. In a concurrent
implementation it must also halt all mutator threads before the flip. Finally `flip` must restart
mutator threads and the scanner thread.

   The trap thread and the scanner thread must be able to access protected Tospace pages
without incurring access violation faults, if they are to operate concurrently with the mutator.
Most architectures provide two modes of execution, kernel mode and user mode, with trusted

```
            scanPage(page) =
                if unprotected(page)
                    return
                for object on page
                    scan(object)
                unprotect(page)

        trap_thread() =
            forever
                thread, page = WaitForTrappedThread()
                LOCK lock
                    scanPage(page)
                ResumeThread(thread)

        scanner_thread() =
            forever
                LOCK lock
                    while B ≤ scan
                        wait()
                    scanPage(scanned)
                    scan = min(B, scan+PageSize)

    New(n) =
        LOCK lock
            unused = T - B
            if unused < n or unused < threshold
                flip()
            T = T - n
            return T
```

Algorithm 8.13   The multi-threaded Appel–Ellis–Li collector.

components of the operating system running in kernel mode and other programs running in user mode. User mode protections do not apply to processes running in kernel mode. If the collector threads are run in kernel mode and only the user mode protection of a page is changed, the collector can read and write pages not accessible to the user program.

Improvements

The collector as presented so far suffers from a number of inefficiencies. The global lock is a bottleneck in the concurrent system as both the allocator and the collector contend for it. One solution is to use a two-stage allocator which grabs the lock to allocate a chunk of memory. Allocation can be made from within this chunk without holding the lock.

The flip latency can also be high if there are a large number of roots, for example if the user program contains many threads or a large stack — the authors note that many Modula-2+ programs contain hundreds of threads. Large stacks can be handled in the same way as Tospace pages by setting their pages to be inaccessible. They will then be scanned incrementally as they are referenced by the mutator. Appel, Ellis and Li suggest that the registers of each thread also do not need to be scanned at the flip if `flip` changes the program counter of each thread to the address of a subroutine that causes each thread to scan its own registers when it is next run before jumping back to the original value of its program counter (*cf.* the While and Field collector described on page 207).

Large objects

The algorithm presented above suggests that objects larger than a virtual memory page cannot be allocated. If the trap handler were only to scan a single page on each occasion, it would not be possible to handle objects that crossed pages. The Appel–Ellis–Li collector manages objects that span more than one page with a *crossing map* array[4]. `Crossing[p]` is set to be true whenever an object crosses the boundary between pages `p-1` and `p`. Whenever the collector catches a trap for page `p`, it must skip back to the first page `n` less than `p` that starts with a new object, i.e. the first page for which `crossing[n]` is false. The collector then scans all pages from `n` until it finds a page `m` greater than `p` for which `crossing[m]` is false again.

To reduce the cost of scanning multiple pages, the allocator prefers to avoid allocating objects across pages wherever possible. The latency caused by copying large arrays can also be avoided by using back-pointers in the same way as Baker did. On a page trap the collector can consult the crossing map to find the back-pointer and then copy and scan only those elements on the faulted page. Unlike Baker this does not impose any additional overhead on array indexing operations other than the usual cost of the read-barrier.

The time to scan a page in the Appel–Ellis–Li algorithm includes the time to copy each object referenced from that page. If the machine's page size is P bytes and each pointer occupies 4 bytes, then a page could refer to $P/4$ uncopied objects in the worst case. For typical page sizes of 4096 bytes, scanning a page could require copying up to 1024 objects, each of which may vary in size from a few bytes to a megabyte or more. Eager copying of this many objects, each of which may be very small or very large, can lead to unpredictable pauses. Johnson extends the Baker–Steele idea of lazy copying to reduce latency yet further by only copying objects when they are scanned [Johnson, 1992]. Consequently the time to scan a page depends on the number of headers on a page rather than on the total size of the objects referenced. Figures produced by Johnson suggest that lazy copying can be increasingly effective as the size of objects increases, although its overall cost is greater than that of the eager version.

Generations

Sharma and Soffa describe a way of introducing generations to the Appel–Ellis–Li algorithm [Sharma and Soffa, 1991]. Their algorithm uses a page-marked remembered set and spawns separate processes to scan the remembered set and each generation being collected. To avoid deadlock, a complex system of three lock types are used in each generation. Results were obtained through simulation with a configuration of very small pages (128 bytes), three generations of equal size, and promotion on a copy-count of three. A generation might be involved in a collection if it was more than two-thirds full, and must be if it was more than

---

[4] See also the discussion of card marking in Section 7.5 of Chapter 7.

three-quarters full. Their simulations showed that, when compared against the Appel–Ellis–Li collector, the parallel generational collector performed better for programs with larger amounts of longer-lived cells. For these programs, the parallel generational collector copied up to 67 percent less data, and elapsed times were reduced by up to 12 percent; corresponding reductions in mutator overhead were also observed.

Performance

It is difficult to compare the performance of the Appel–Ellis–Li collector since its efficiency depends crucially on the efficiency of the operating system's virtual memory protection mechanisms. Experiments by the authors on the DEC Firefly multi-processor, which has a relatively slow page trap, suggest that the sequential version was a third slower overall than stop-and-copy. On the other hand, the concurrent version showed that over 60 percent of the collector's execution could be overlapped with the mutator, giving an improvement in performance of around a third. Zorn's studies suggest that barriers that rely on the virtual memory protection mechanism can never be competitive with those implemented in software or with special purpose hardware [Zorn, 1990a]. His measurements suggest that the true cost of a protection fault may be close to 10,000 cycles. One reason for this is that protection faults are usually assumed to be irretrievable errors that can only lead to premature termination of the program. Consequently, optimisation of these traps has never been considered important by operating system designers.

However, the influence of the memory protection trap on overall performance depends on how often it is sprung. A memory protection fault can be raised at most once per page per garbage collection cycle. The cost of a software barrier, on the other hand, is paid on every access. Thus for very low allocation rates, and even moderate read/write rates, the memory protection barrier may offer better performance than the software barrier. Lisp, Scheme and ML programs do not exhibit such behaviour. It is also unlikely from C allocation benchmarks. It is clear that Appel–Ellis–Li is not a real-time collector. No system that relies on virtual memory mechanisms can provide the guarantees that hard real-time systems require. The chief benefits of the Appel–Ellis–Li collector are its portability and its applicability to multi-threaded systems.

8.7   Replication Copying Collectors

Generational garbage collectors may be an acceptable substitute for incremental collectors if the pause for their minor collection is sufficiently short and if major collections are sufficiently infrequent and scheduled for points where their disruption will be least noticeable to the user. Nevertheless, Nettles and O'Toole report that, despite its brief minor collection pause, two to five second major collection delays in SML/NJ are aggravatingly familiar [Nettles and O'Toole, 1993]. We now consider three families of incremental or concurrent collector for ML that aim to reduce garbage collection pause times in general, and the cost of synchronisation in particular.

Nettles's replicating collectors

Nettles, O'Toole and others have recently proposed a family of incremental copying collectors
that do not rely on expensive read-barriers [Nettles *et al.*, 1992]. Instead the mutator is allowed
to access the original Fromspace objects. When copying is complete, the collector replaces the
mutator's roots with pointers to their Tospace replicas, discards Fromspace and the garbage
collection cycle is finished. This requires that copying be non-destructive, which is most
simply done by storing the forwarding address in an extra word invisible to the mutator
rather than overwriting one of the object's fields. An alternative technique is to overwrite
the object's header word with the forwarding address, but require the mutator to check for a
forwarding pointer whenever it needs the header (see Diagram 8.13). This improves space-
efficiency considerably in SML/NJ where most objects are only three words long. The only
operations that incur a time penalty for the indirection are polymorphic equality and certain
other type-specific operations [Nettles and O'Toole, 1993].

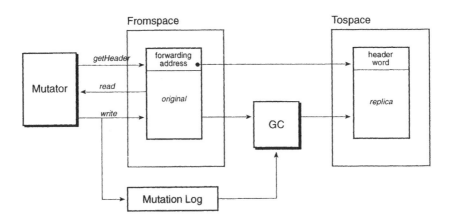

Diagram 8.13   Replicating garbage collection.

   As we have seen, the mutator may modify the original object in Fromspace after it has
been replicated. To preserve correctness, the collector must ensure that the same modification
is made to the Tospace replica before the mutator switches to using Tospace objects. All
modifications must therefore be recorded by the mutator in a *mutation log* which can be used
subsequently by the collector to ensure that the replicas are consistent. Whenever the collector
modifies a replica that has already been scanned, it must also re-scan the object to ensure that
any new child of the object is also copied. Collection is complete when there are no unscanned
objects left in Tospace and the mutation log is exhausted.

   We observed earlier that reducing consistency requirements can allow the mutator to
proceed with less disruption. Replicating collection takes advantage of this by allowing
replicated objects to be in an inconsistent state provided that these inconsistencies are
recorded in the mutation log. The log can be maintained with a write-barrier rather than
the more expensive read-barrier of the Baker and Appel–Ellis–Li algorithms. The cost of

replication depends on the application in question and the language being used. For functional languages, in which destructive writes are rare, the cost appears to be low enough to give good performance. Replicating garbage collection is also well suited to generational techniques as the same write-barrier can be used to record inter-generational pointers and mutations. The generational remembered set can be used as the mutation log provided it logs *all* mutations including non-pointer updates.

The Nettles and O'Toole collector is based on Appel's generational collector for SML/NJ [Appel, 1989b]. This collector already provides much of the support needed for replicating garbage collection. For example, it records all pointer writes unconditionally without generation tests by copying the address of the overwritten object into a store-list. Replicating garbage collection requires the barrier to be modified to record all writes. The simplest implementation uses replicating garbage collection for major collections only. After each minor collection, the collector also performs a limited amount of work on the older generation. If the minor collection exceeded a copy limit then the incremental collector simply processes the store-list mutation log, which is then discarded. Otherwise the collector does some scavenging as well.

The results obtained by Nettles and O'Toole suggest good performance for ML programs. The cost of reapplying mutations for the simple programs that they tested was less than 3 percent of total collection costs. The overall slowdown compared with stop-and-copy collection was always less than 20 percent and was typically less than 10 percent if the incremental technique was restricted to major collections (rather than being used for minor collections as well).

A further advantage of their replication garbage collector is that, since it requires little low-level synchronisation, it is well-suited for concurrent execution in a separate thread. O'Toole and Nettles report results for their collector running on a Silicon Graphics 4D/340 with four MIPS R3000 processors clocked at 33 MHz [O'Toole and Nettles, 1993]. Pause times were satisfactory with most pauses lasting around five milliseconds. The concurrent replication collector was successful compared with the standard SML/NJ collector in reducing elapsed time for major collections but not for minor collections, which increased.

The Huelsbergen and Larus collector

Huelsbergen and Larus take a similar approach to their concurrent collector for ML [Huelsbergen and Larus, 1993]. Languages like ML distinguish mutable data from immutable data, and Huelsbergen and Larus use this opportunity to reduce the cost of accessing immutable data, which are assumed to be overwhelmingly predominant — this is a reasonable assumption for functional languages like ML. The mutator is allowed access to either Fromspace or Tospace copies of immutable data without impediment, but may only use the Tospace versions of mutable objects. A separate forwarding pointer is used for each object to provide non-destructive copying. If a mutable object has been copied, the mutator follows the forwarding pointer to use the Tospace replica. If a Fromspace object is copied while the mutator is attempting to access it, the read or write is repeated in the copy. This check requires an extra access to mutable data items but Huelsbergen and Larus claim good performance: pause times for their test programs were never more than 20 milliseconds on a Sequent Symmetry. However, overall elapsed times were significantly greater than those obtained with

Appel's generational collector [Appel, 1989b] although the Huelsbergen and Larus collector could probably be improved if it were also to use a generational strategy.

The Doligez–Leroy–Gonthier collectors

A drawback of all the write-barrier schemes discussed earlier is that they place an overhead on all mutator operations. Doligez and Leroy required a collector for Concurrent Caml Light — an implementation of ML with threads — that could cope with the prodigious memory demands of ML, permitted multiple mutator threads, and yet limited synchronisation overhead [Doligez and Leroy, 1993; Doligez and Gonthier, 1994]. To handle Caml's demands for memory, a generational copying collector was believed to be necessary. But moving collectors were considered to make too heavy synchronisation demands, since pointers to relocated objects must be updated.

ML encourages a functional style of programming: most objects are immutable and the compiler distinguishes those that are not. The Doligez–Leroy takes advantage of this by allocating mutable and immutable objects to different regions of the heap. The heap is divided into two generations. Mutable objects and those referenced by global variables may only be stored in the old generation. This generation is called the *major heap* and is shared by all mutator threads (see Diagram 8.14 on the facing page). In addition, each thread contains a stack and a *minor heap*: the minor heaps comprise the young generation. Words in a thread stack may hold references into the stack's own minor heap or into the shared major heap; words in a minor heap may also point to that minor heap or to the major heap. On the other hand, references to data stored within a thread may not be held by another thread, by a global variable, nor by an object in the shared heap.

Within a single thread, minor collections use copying garbage collection (see Section 7.3) with all survivors promoted *en masse* to the shared heap. Copying garbage collection stops only the thread involved, and requires no synchronisation with either other threads or the shared heap since neither the old generation nor any other thread may hold references to this thread's data. A dedicated thread collects the shared heap concurrently with the mutator threads (and minor collections). The concurrent collector cannot move objects in the old generation since mutator threads might hold references to them, so it uses mark-sweep collection based upon Dijkstra's algorithm. The free-list is coloured a fourth colour to improve the efficiency of marking, but unlike Kung and Song, Doligez and Gonthier reject use of a deque as it would lead to too much synchronisation between their multiple mutators.

There are no pointers from the old generation to young generation objects. If an attempt is made to update a mutable object (held in the shared heap) with a reference to an object still held in the young generation, then that young object and all its descendants are copied into the shared heap. This leaves two copies of the 'young' object: one in the young generation and a replica in the old generation. Since objects allocated in the young generation are immutable, consistency problems do not arise. The copying operation leaves a forwarding address behind in the header word of the young generation replica to assist the next minor collection.

Doligez–Leroy copying collection places no overhead on mutator operations that involve only data held within a thread. Updates to mutable objects will be arbitrarily expensive if they require data to be copied, but require no synchronisation with other threads other than to reserve sufficient space in the shared generation. The more complex situation for

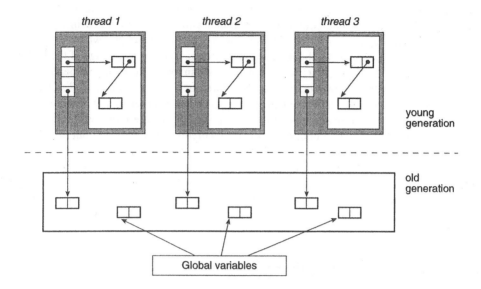

Diagram 8.14   The Doligez–Leroy architecture.

the concurrent collector is addressed by Doligez and Gonthier [Doligez and Gonthier, 1994]. Their aim is to minimise the amount of synchronisation required between threads. In particular, they avoid the cost of the write-barrier for local variables: an update to a thread register or a stack word shades neither the old nor the new value of the root. To achieve this, major garbage collection cycles must be initiated through a complex protocol.

Mutators and collectors are each synchronised by *phase* variables. Threads can only modify their own phase variable, but mutators are required to cooperate with the collector by reading its phase periodically. Initially, all threads are in the state $Asynch$. The collector starts by advancing to the phase $Synch_1$. This warns the mutators that the collector is about to initiate a new collection cycle. After all the mutators have moved to $Synch_1$, the collector advances to $Synch_2$. At this point, each mutator must ensure that any pending action, such as an update, completes before the mutator too advances to $Synch_2$. The collector need not be idle while it waits for all mutators to advance from $Asynch$ to $Synch_2$: it can trace objects in the shared generation from the global variables. Once all threads are at $Synch_2$, the collector advances to $Asynch$ to signal to the mutator threads that they should shade their local roots before advancing to $Asynch$ as well.

During the two $Synch$ phases, the mutators adopt a very conservative write-barrier: an update shades both the old and the new targets of the heap cell field being modified. This double shading is necessary if mutator threads are to avoid incurring the overhead of the write-barrier when they push or pop references to heap cells onto their stacks or into their registers. Outside these two phases, Dijkstra's write-barrier is used to shade the new reference.

Doligez and Leroy report good performance from an earlier version of their collector running on a fourteen-processor Encore Multimax, under the Mach operating system.

Although Caml Light is only a bytecode interpreter, and runs four to eight times slower than the SML/NJ native-code compiler, most minor collections completed in less than 10 milliseconds. The major collection load was below 5 percent per mutator, which suggests that their architecture might scale to about 20 mutator threads. The key advantage of the Doligez–Leroy–Gonthier collector is that minor collections can be performed independently and without synchronisation. However, their architecture does have a number of disadvantages. First, mutable data must be allocated in the shared heap whether or not it is shared: this is more expensive than allocation in a minor heap since locks are required on the free-list. Allocation of memory in large chunks to threads can reduce this overhead but not eliminate it entirely. Second, assignment of a pointer from an old object to a young object requires that the transitive referential closure of the young object be copied into the shared heap: the cost of an update cannot be bounded. Finally, pauses for minor collections can only be kept within an acceptable range by bounding the size of the minor heaps. For Caml Light, the minor heaps are only 32 kilobytes.

8.8   Baker's Treadmill collector

Heap memory in a garbage collected world falls into four sets: scanned objects, visited but unscanned objects, objects not yet visited and free space. The semi-space heap arrangement of copying garbage collectors can be considered simply to be a method of implementing these sets. However, it is not the only way in which they can be represented. Baker's Treadmill offers a new organisation of these sets in a non-moving collector that retains some of the advantages and simplicity of copying collection [Baker, 1992]. Non-moving collectors offer several advantages, especially for incremental collection. They are better suited to uncooperative environments (see Chapter 9 where we discuss conservative garbage collection), consistency requirements can be relaxed since the mutator does not need to be protected from changes made by the collector, and they do not move objects (asynchronous movement may be particularly detrimental to compiler optimisation [Chase, 1987; Chase, 1988]).

Baker organises all objects into a cyclic doubly-linked list called the *treadmill* (see Diagram 8.15 on the next page). Within the list, each colour segment is arranged contiguously: a fourth colour, *off-white*, is used for the free-list. The four segments are delimited by four pointers free, B, T and scan, just as in his incremental copying collector (see page 203). Allocation is done by simply advancing the free pointer clockwise around the treadmill. Marking is equally simple. After a grey cell has been scanned, the scan pointer is moved anti-clockwise to paint the cell black. No manipulation of colour bits is necessary.

If a scanned pointer refers to a black or grey cell, no action is taken, but if the cell is white then the cell must be unsnapped from the white segment of the treadmill and snapped into the grey segment. Snapping is a constant-time operation and offers the algorithm the potential to meet real-time bounds. This is the only point at which colours need to be discriminated so only one colour bit needs to be stored in each cell: whether or not the cell is white. Notice that this mechanism offers a choice of traversal strategies as the white cell can be added to either end of the grey segment. If it is snapped in at the T pointer, traversal is breadth-first, like a traditional copying collector. However, several authors have observed that depth-first copying

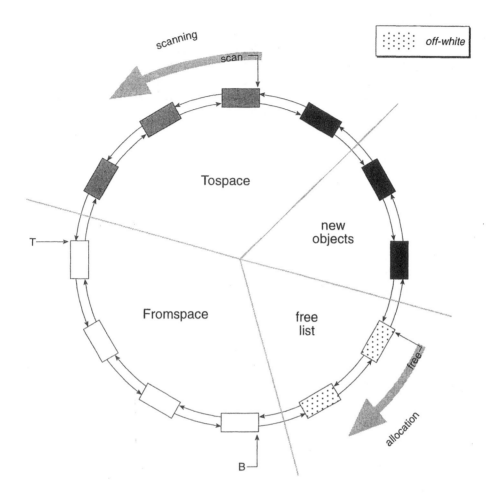

Diagram 8.15   Baker's Treadmill.

often causes fewer faults in virtual memory and/or caching environments (see Section 6.6 of Chapter 6 where we discussed traversal orders for copying collectors). Snapping the white cell into the grey segment at the scan pointer gives a depth-first traversal without need for any auxiliary stack (although it can be argued that a stack is used and, worse, occupies space permanently — it is the links of the treadmill).

A garbage collection cycle is complete when there are no grey cells left, i.e. when the scan pointer meets the T pointer. When the free pointer meets the B pointer, it is time to flip. At this point there are only two colours, black and white. The black segment is reinterpreted as white, the white segment as off-white, and the T and B pointers are exchanged. Thus the treadmill advances its segments — hence the name.

The treadmill is expensive of space compared with other non-moving collectors because of its links, although this is offset to a small extent as no further space is needed for a marking stack. On the other hand, memory utilisation is no worse than copying collection since semi-spaces are not used: the cost of the links is no more than that of the Tospace replicas of *cons* cells and it is cheaper for larger objects. Allocation is more expensive than simply bumping a pointer but is cheaper than manipulating a linked list or lazily scanning a bit map. Similarly, resnapping an object into the grey segment is probably more expensive than copying a list cell but less expensive for large objects. On the other hand, the time to reclaim white cells is constant: garbage cells do not have to be touched.

The main problem faced by the Treadmill is how to handle heterogeneous objects. Baker suggests several techniques that can be used to reduce the costs of manipulating objects of different sizes (see, for example, [Brent, 1989; White, 1990; Baker *et al.*, 1985]). Wilson and Johnstone solve this problem for their real-time garbage collector by rounding object sizes up to the nearest power of two and using separate treadmills for each class size [Wilson and Johnstone, 1993]. Using multiple free-lists means that they will not all become empty simultaneously, so reclaimed cells must be explicitly recoloured, but this can be done lazily. It also becomes necessary to distinguish white cells from off-white ones.

Baker's paper assumes that synchronisation between the mutator and the collector in the Treadmill is through a read-barrier. However, there is no reason why this should be so, as the Treadmill abstracts away from details of synchronisation. The reason for the read-barrier in Baker's incremental copying collector was to protect the mutator from changes made by the collector, but the Treadmill does not move data. On the contrary, there are good reasons why a write-barrier might be preferred: it offers better performance, is well integrated with generational garbage collection, and may offer easier optimisation paths. For these reasons treadmills based on incremental-update write-barriers have been used by Wilson and Johnstone[5] for a collector for C++ [Wilson and Johnstone, 1993], and based on a snapshot-at-the-beginning barrier for Kaleida's ScriptX collector [Hennessey, 1993]. At the time of writing, the performance of these collectors is disappointing (for example, only somewhat better than deferred reference counting). However, this may be because the barriers are implemented with smart pointers rather than any inefficiency inherent to the treadmill algorithm.

8.9   Hardware support for real-time garbage collection

No software-only garbage collection algorithm has yet demonstrated convincing hard real-time performance. Read-barrier techniques have been shown to be expensive and also to lead to unpredictable performance. Virtual memory techniques show even greater variance in the time to perform read or write operations, as each operation may spring a page trap. Nilsen suggests that the best measured latency response may be 500 microseconds [Nilsen, 1993; Engelstad and Vandendorpe, 1991]. The most promising software-only collectors are probably the Nettles and O'Toole replicating collector and Baker's Treadmill. The former has shown measured worst-case times of 50 microseconds per atomic action but it is likely to

---

[5] Wilson's collector can be configured to use either a Dijkstra or a Steele write-barrier [Wilson, 1995].

perform less effectively in environments in which writes are more frequent than they are in SML [Nettles and O'Toole, 1993]. Implementations of the Treadmill have yet to demonstrate satisfactory performance.

For these reasons Nilsen and Schmidt argue that garbage collectors for hard real-time systems must have hardware support. General purpose computers, other than supercomputers, that rely on specialised architectures do not have a history of commercial success. To reduce the economic problems of building competitive special-purpose architectures, Nilsen and Schmidt isolate the garbage collection hardware in a special memory module that interfaces to the central processor unit through a traditional memory bus: logically it looks like a bank of traditional expansion memory (see Diagram 8.16). The hope is that this will allow the technology investment to be shared between different processor architectures, thereby allowing economies of scale to be made.

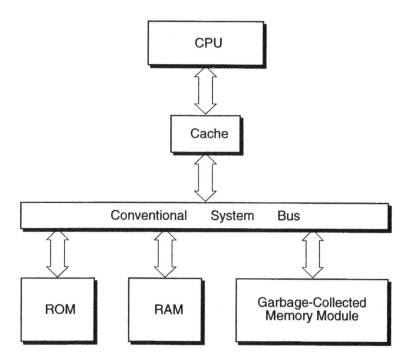

Diagram 8.16 Nilsen's hardware architecture [Nilsen and Schmidt, 1992a]. Reproduced with permission.

Their collector is based on Baker's incremental copying collector, with back-pointers for lazy copying. The read-barrier is maintained by the memory module in parallel with other memory and communication activities. If an object being read by the CPU needs to be copied to Tospace, the module stalls the processor until it is ready. Simulations suggest that the worst case delay would be approximately one microsecond.

8.10   Issues to consider

The purpose of incremental or concurrent garbage collectors is to reduce garbage collection pause times. For a collector that is incremental but not concurrent, this means trading an increase in elapsed time for a reduction in disruption to the user while garbage is collected. Concurrent collectors may be able to reduce elapsed times as well, provided that they can collect garbage concurrently with the mutator and at no cost to the collector (for example, there is no substantial contention either for processor time or for the memory bus), and that the benefit of concurrent collection outweighs the cost of the inevitable synchronisation between the mutator and the collector.

Three strategies of garbage collection can be used successfully to reduce pause times. Generational garbage collection (discussed in Chapter 7) cuts pause times (and often elapsed times as well) by concentrating collection efforts on a small region of the heap. Provided this region is small enough, pauses for garbage collection can be reduced sufficiently to be unnoticeable for many purposes. However, if too many objects live too long, the rate of promotion from younger generations to older ones will become too high and those generations will have to be collected as well. Generational garbage collection is not effective if the frequency of major collections becomes large enough to be disruptive. This behaviour is not uncommon, and generational garbage collection should not be seen as a universal panacea.

The alternative is to garbage collect in parallel with the execution of the mutator program. Parallelism need not imply true concurrency: instead the actions of the collector can be performed in small steps interleaved with mutator actions. Such incremental garbage collectors often require no special hardware, nor the use of any locks. However, parallel garbage collectors, whether incremental or truly concurrent, do require synchronisation with the mutator program. Such synchronisation does have a cost. The simplest and best known form of incremental garbage collection is reference counting. Although reference counting is naturally incremental and simple to implement, it places a heavy overhead on pointer reads and writes.

The costs of synchronisation can be reduced by relaxing the coherency of the collector's view of the heap, i.e. by allowing some garbage to live longer than it might otherwise. In general, coherence must be maintained by a barrier between the mutator and the heap. This barrier may be either a read-barrier, trapping reads, or a write-barrier, trapping writes. The choice of barrier will depend on the relative frequency of reads and writes, how often the barrier is invoked (for example, whether it is invoked on every read or just once per page per collection cycle), and on the amount of work that the barrier has to do. Write-barriers are usually used in conjunction with mark-sweep collectors: their rôle is to notify the marker of a new location whence it should continue marking. The cost of write-barriers is less than that of read-barriers. Read-barriers are used in conjunction with copying collectors. They intercept mutator reads to copy objects into Tospace. There is a trade-off between the frequency with which a read-barrier traps mutator actions, and the amount of work that it must do. Baker's collector traps every read to Fromspace, and evacuates the target of the read to Tospace. The cost and the frequency of trapping reads is such that Baker's barrier is often considered to require hardware support. Read-barriers that rely on support from the operating system trap mutator access just once per Tospace page. However, they do much more work at each step than Baker's barrier since they evacuate every object in Fromspace for which a reference is held in the Tospace page.

The cost of the barrier is not the only criterion by which to judge incremental and concurrent collectors. Any such collector is likely to defer collection of some garbage until the next cycle. The advantage of deferring collection of some garbage is that each collection will terminate faster; the drawback is that more room may be required in the heap. Collectors differ in their degree of conservatism, i.e. of how much floating garbage they leave. The most conservative collectors use snapshot-at-the-beginning barriers to preserve every object that was live when the collection cycle started. Incremental update barriers are less conservative, but also differ amongst themselves as to whether they move the marking wavefront forward or backward as each mutator write is trapped. Conservatism is also affected by the treatment of new cells: the cheapest but most conservative allocation strategy is to ensure that any cell allocated in this cycle will be preserved until the next.

Collector and mutator also need to be synchronised at the start and the end of each cycle. At the start of a cycle, the mutator may need to be suspended so that the collector can be sure that it has visited all objects that are referents of roots. At the end of a cycle, the mutator may need to be suspended while the collector checks that it is safe to terminate.

Many incremental or concurrent algorithms are described as real-time. However, *caveat emptor*. Different interpretations are put on these words. For the hard real-time community, it must be possible to prove that atomic actions of an algorithm complete within a guaranteed time, and these bounds must be small. Clearly a collector that relied on support from the operating system's page protection mechanism could not meet this criterion. For others, real-time simply means that atomic actions can be completed within some reasonable period that would not be noticed by the user. Almost all the algorithms covered in this chapter fall into the latter, rather than the former, category. The one exception is Nilsen's hardware garbage-collected memory modules.

8.11 Notes

Donald Knuth credits Marvin Minsky for first suggesting parallelism as a way to avoid suspension of operations (Exercise 2.3.5–12, p. 422 in [Knuth, 1973]). Parallelism need not imply concurrency. Garbage collection could occur, for example, during keyboard input, as long as it could be suspended on short notice to continue list processing on the input and later be resumed without losing all the previously expended effort.

The first published architecture for on-the-fly garbage collection was Guy Steele's Multiprocessing Compactifying Garbage Collection algorithm published in [Steele, 1975] (see also [Steele, 1976]). Although widely referenced, Steele's algorithm never became as popular as Dijkstra's. The reason for that is, in our opinion, the thorough presentation and considerable level of detail taken by Steele. His paper included descriptions of compaction, parameter passing mechanisms and synchronisation (with hardware supported locks), as well as of mutator–collector garbage collection. The mass of detail presented by Steele contributed to make understanding his ideas difficult.

Independently, Edsgar Dijkstra proposed a similar scheme in some unpublished notes [Dijkstra, 1975], later published in [Dijkstra *et al.*, 1976]. Dijkstra and his colleagues tackled this problem 'as one of the more challenging — and hopefully instructive — problems' in parallel programming. Their architecture attracted considerable interest in the computer science community. It is more subtle than may be immediately apparent. In particular, fine-grained concurrent implementations have many traps for the unwary.

For example, it might seem counter-intuitive to allocate a cell or copy a pointer before shading the target. Certainly it temporarily breaks the 'no black–white pointers' invariant. However, Mike Woodger and N. Stenning showed that reversing the order of these operations would cause a bug to appear in a fine-grained concurrent implementation. In describing his proof of the algorithm David Gries reported that he had 'seen five purported solutions to this problem, either in print or ready to be submitted for publication' [Gries, 1977]. A correct version of the algorithm appeared in [Dijkstra et al., 1978]. S. Ramesh and S.L. Mehndiratta formalised the proof of termination and absence of live-lock [Ramesh and Mehndiratta, 1983] by using Susan Owicki's and Leslie Lamport's proof procedure [Owicki and Lamport, 1982]. Other proofs can be found in [Francez, 1978; Müller, 1976]. Mordechai Ben-Ari considered the on-the-fly collector to be one of the most difficult concurrent programs ever studied. He presented several parallel mark-scan algorithms based on Dijkstra's algorithm but with much simpler proofs of correctness than those presented by Kung and Song, Gries, and Dijkstra et al. [Ben-Ari, 1982; Ben-Ari, 1984]. Ben-Ari's algorithms used only two colours but required an extra pass by the marker to check that the number of black cells had not changed. Gries also credits Stenning for an unpublished version of the on-the-fly algorithm which also used only two colours. An indication of the complexity of these programs is that Ben-Ari believed incorrectly that his version was immune to the Woodger scenario [van de Snepscheut, 1987; Pixley, 1988; Russinoff, 1994]. [Doligez and Gonthier, 1994] provide yet another proof of correctness, this time based on Leslie Lamport's Temporal Logic of Actions [Lamport, 1991].

H.T. Kung and S.W. Song developed a more efficient version of Dijkstra's algorithm. They used four colours to avoid having to trace the free-list, and a marking queue to reduce the cost of marking [Kung and Song, 1977]. Lamport generalised the architecture for using multiple processes [Lamport, 1976] and Christian Queinnec et al. showed how the sweep phase could execute concurrently with the marking phase [Queinnec et al., 1989]. Dijkstra's algorithm has been used more recently for reclaiming global data in an implementation of ML using multiple threads [Doligez and Leroy, 1993]. It was also implemented in hardware and software in the Intel iAPX-432 microprocessor and iMAX operating system [Pollack et al., 1982].

The first snapshot-at-the-beginning garbage collection algorithm using virtual memory to create the snapshot with copy-on-write pages was for a concurrent collector [Abraham and Patel, 1987]. Taichi Yuasa also used a snapshot write-barrier for his collector for a sequential implementation of Kyoto Common Lisp [Yuasa, 1990]. Malcolm Wallace and Colin Runciman combined Yuasa's algorithm with Queinnec's to provide a collector for a lazy functional language with sufficiently low pause times to manage a real-time application [Wallace and Runciman, 1993].

The first implementation of concurrent reference counting was built by Paul Rovner for the Xerox PARC Cedar implementation [Rovner, 1985]. The initial collector by Rovner and Butler Lampson for DEC Systems Research Center Modula-2+ was based on their experience with the Cedar system. John DeTreville describes the Modula-2+ collector, and experiments to improve it, in detail in [DeTreville, 1990a]. Other very similar architectures have been proposed by K. Kakuta, H. Nakamura and S. Iida [Kakuta et al., 1986] and Rafael Lins [Lins, 1991]; Lins's collector can reclaim cyclic data structures and he has also extended his scheme to a multiple mutator, multiple collector architecture [Lins, 1992b]. Neither architecture has been implemented.

Henry Baker showed how a read-barrier could be used to provide a serial incremental copying collector [Baker, 1978]. Collectors based at least partly on his algorithm were used in several Lisp machines that could provide hardware support for the read-barrier, such as the MIT Lisp machine [Bawden *et al.*, 1977], the Symbolics 3600 [Moon, 1984], and the Texas Explorer [Explorer, 1987, 1987] and for collectors such as Henry Lieberman's and Carl Hewitt's original generational garbage collector [Lieberman and Hewitt, 1983]. Collectors cast in the light of Baker, but which actually use incremental-update write-barriers, have also been proposed by [Brooks, 1984; Dawson, 1992; While and Field, 1992]. Baker's algorithm has also been used for multi-processors. Robert Halstead's Multilisp used fine-grain locking, with lock bits on each pointer to handle updating and in each object for `copy` [Halstead, 1984]. S.C. North and John Reppy modified Brook's collector to share forwarding pointers between Fromspace and Tospace objects for their concurrent, functional Pegasus Meta-Language [North and Reppy, 1987]. Kelvin Nilsen and William Schmidt describe hardware implementations of Baker's algorithm in a series of papers [Nilsen and Schmidt, 1990a; Nilsen and Schmidt, 1990b; Nilsen and Schmidt, 1992a; Nilsen and Schmidt, 1992b; Nilsen, 1994a; Nilsen and Schmidt, 1994; Nilsen, 1994b; Nilsen, 1995; Nilsen and Gao, 1995].

Andrew Appel, John Ellis and Kai Li used virtual memory protection mechanisms to provide a pagewise black-only read-barrier [Appel *et al.*, 1988]. Their barrier has two advantages: it supports both sequential and concurrent garbage collection, and the collector can be implemented without modification to the compiler. The Appel–Ellis–Li collector has been used as the basis for several concurrent generational collectors, most notably Modula-3 [Detlefs, 1990; Yip, 1991; Sharma and Soffa, 1991; Detlefs, 1992]. Ralph Johnson showed how lazy copying techniques could also be applied to the Appel–Ellis–Li collector [Johnson, 1992]. Ravi Sharma and Mary Lou Soffa, and Niklas Röjemo used the Appel–Ellis–Li algorithm as the basis for parallel generational collectors [Sharma and Soffa, 1991; Röjemo, 1992]. Röjemo observed a reduction in garbage collection time of almost 20 percent in the $< \nu, G >$-machine, a parallel graph reducer for shared memory architectures.

However, John DeTreville found virtual memory techniques inadequate for multi-process garbage collection [DeTreville, 1990a; DeTreville, 1990b]. Virtual memory techniques can also be used to provide write-barriers for non-moving incremental collection [Boehm *et al.*, 1991].

Baker reviewed the organisation of his incremental copying collector to create a non-moving collector, the Treadmill [Baker, 1992]. As well as Baker's Lisp system built in Ada, the Treadmill has also been used for real-time garbage collection for C++ [Wilson and Johnstone, 1993], and for the Objects in C system in which Kaleida's ScriptX multi-media scripting language is implemented [Hennessey, 1993].

Baker's incremental copying algorithm ensures that the mutator sees only objects in Tospace, evacuating them from Fromspace if necessary. This can cause unpredictable delays, for example if traversing a list required each element to be copied. Replicating garbage collection offers incremental copying without unpredictable pauses [Nettles *et al.*, 1992; Nettles and O'Toole, 1993]. The mutator uses Fromspace objects but a write-barrier records any modifications made to copied objects. The modifications must then be re-applied to the Tospace replicas by the collector. Scott Nettles, James O'Toole *et al.* based their collector on Appel's generational collector for SML/NJ [Appel, 1989b]. The collector has been extended to provide concurrent collection [O'Toole and Nettles, 1993] and collection of persistent heaps [Nettles *et al.*, 1993; O'Toole and Nettles, 1993].

Phil Wadler, and Tim Hickey and Jacques Cohen analysed the performance of Dijkstra-style algorithms. Wadler showed that, for time-sharing rather than multi-processor systems, such algorithms require a greater percentage of processor time than classical sequential collection does [Wadler, 1976]. Hickey and Cohen showed that a multi-processor mutator–collector system could offer no more than a 50 percent performance improvement on the sequential one [Hickey and Cohen, 1984].

Finally, analysis of the effectiveness of different implementations of read and write-barriers can be found in [Zorn, 1990a]. Zorn argues that carefully crafted software barriers can achieve adequate performance but that virtual memory techniques are unlikely to prove competitive.

9

Garbage Collection for C

Automatic memory management has been associated with declarative and string processing languages since the early days of those implementations. The complexities of the data structures created, and the extent of their lifetimes, means that such objects cannot be allocated statically or under a stack discipline: garbage collection is essential. Many, but not all, object-oriented and object-based languages also provide automatic memory management — of these, Smalltalk, Eiffel, Modula-3 and Java are probably the best known. The philosophy of encapsulation of objects seems to many programmers to demand garbage collection. The renewed interest in automatic storage reclamation outside its traditional home in declarative programming has led researchers to examine whether garbage collection can be a viable technique for imperative languages like C and its object-oriented descendants such as C++. A witness to this renewed interest is the volume of debate on garbage collection in several Usenet news groups. A second reason for this interest is the growing use of C as a target language for other compilers. Examples of this approach include Scheme [Bartlett, 1989b]; Modula-3 [Cardelli *et al.*, 1988]; ML [Chailloux, 1992; Cridlig, 1992]; Common Lisp [Schelter and Ballantyne, 1988]; and Haskell [Peyton Jones, 1992].

Languages like C present a considerable challenge to the garbage collector implementer. To be successful and accepted in this environment, the garbage collector must meet demanding criteria. Any system must ensure that programs pay for garbage collection only if and when they use it. Even with an efficient automatic management system, many C programs would probably never use it and, of those programs that might take advantage of it, the amount of time spent handling dynamic memory is likely to be small, as the memory allocation pattern of a typical C program is very different from that of a program written in a language traditionally associated with garbage collection.

Coexistence with the underlying operating system and existing program libraries is essential for any practical system. It would be quite unreasonable to expect libraries to be rewritten, or even recompiled, just to support garbage collection. This means that the garbage collector must support standard data representations. Distinguishing pointer from non-pointer words by adding bits to the word, common in many Lisp implementations, must be precluded.

'Boxing' data with a header word is equally unacceptable. As well as being non-standard, such conventions are likely to slow down operations on integers. The same arguments apply even more strongly to floating point data.

An automatic memory management system for C must, at least in the first place, cooperate with conventional compilers as it is unlikely that vendors would be prepared to modify their compilers to maintain invariants required by garbage collection. Any automatic memory management system must be prepared to operate without any cooperation from the compiler or its run-time system, at least until the benefits of garbage collection receive wider acceptance. In particular the garbage collector will have little or no information on:

- where roots are to be found;
- stack frame layout or register conventions;
- which words are pointers and which are not.

Equally the compiler will have no understanding of the garbage collector's activities. It is important that the garbage collector does not change the value of any word unless it can be sure that it is safe to do so. This means that, in general, objects cannot be freely moved, thereby ruling out standard copying or moving collectors (though we shall see later how this restriction can be eased). Optimising compilers can also produce particular difficulties for garbage collection as current language standards make no requirement that notions of reachability of accessible data structures, required by garbage collection, are preserved.

9.1   A taxonomy of ambiguous roots collection

The garbage collectors examined so far in this book have been *type accurate*; that is, the garbage collector can determine unambiguously the layout of any object in registers, the stack, the heap or any other memory area. At the very least, the collector can distinguish pointer from non-pointer data. Such systems usually rely on intimate knowledge of and cooperation with the compiler. The alternative is for programmers to provide their own domain-specific automatic memory managers. For example, reference counting could be used to manage the heap but this would be slow, replacing register to register operations with several memory loads and stores and a conditional branch.

So-called *conservative* collectors receive no help at all from the compiler, but must assume that every word is a potential pointer unless it can be proved otherwise. Conversely, conservative collectors must also assume that potential pointers may not be pointers after all. This risk of misidentification means that the collector may not alter the value of any user program data. Even if the collector were able to guarantee that a word was a pointer, it still could not move the referent object in case there were other references to it that could not be unambiguously recognised as pointers.

In between these two extremes lie collectors that are partially accurate and partially conservative. Again, these collectors receive no assistance from the compiler and in particular have no knowledge of the stack layout or of register conventions. On the other hand, these collectors do assume knowledge of the format of collectible data structures in the heap. This requires the programmer (or the compiler using C as a target language) to observe certain conventions for heap allocated data. The user may be asked to tag data, to provide pointer identification routines, or to place data of different types in different areas of the heap.

The term conservative is somewhat of a misnomer since even type accurate collectors may identify only a conservative estimate of the garbage present in the heap. Collectors preserve any data that is reachable from the root set by following pointers. However, some of this apparently live data may not be used by the program again. There are two common reasons for this. First of all, registers or the stack may contain obsolete references simply because it is more efficient not to execute additional code to destroy them. Secondly, the run-time representation of environments (identifier bindings), for example stack frames, may retain references after the point at which they are last used. Consider the definition of f in the code fragment shown in Algorithm 9.1, where the expressions E_i and E contain no references to a. An implementation may retain a reference to a in f's environment until the computation of the if-statement is complete. A compiler may produce the stack layout shown in Diagram 9.1, for example.

```
let
    f = let
            a = ...
        in
            if ... a ... then E₁ else E₂
    in E
```

Algorithm 9.1   f's environment may retain a until execution of the conditional statement is complete.

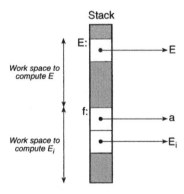

Diagram 9.1   Evaluation of f for Algorithm 9.1.

It is clear from the program text that a will not be used again after the conditional expression of the if-statement is evaluated, but the garbage collector cannot determine this. A is reachable from the current activation record and so it will be preserved (unnecessarily) by any garbage collection that takes place during the evaluation of either E_i.

Some collectors take more care to avoid tracing from locations that are either obsolete or no longer used by the program text. The SML/NJ compiler emits a *register mask* at each safe point in the program at which a garbage collection might take place. These masks specify exactly which registers contain pointers, thus preventing the collector retaining data reachable from previously used, dead registers [Appel, 1992, page 149]. Thomas's LML compiler avoids the interpretive overhead of masks by tailoring the collector for each program. The garbage collector for his closure reducer then knows precisely which slots in each closure are used by each function (see page 133 of Chapter 6).

The most appropriate name for the style of garbage collection described in this chapter is *ambiguous roots collection*. However, since the term conservative is widely used, we shall adopt it to describe collectors that operate in uncooperative environments devoid of assistance from compilers. In this chapter, we concentrate on two such collectors. The first is the conservative collector developed largely by Boehm, Demers and Weiser at Xerox PARC, and widely used both at PARC and elsewhere. This is a non-moving collector based on mark and deferred sweep, suitable for use with C and C++. Since its inception it has undergone considerable development and now supports incremental and generational collection. The collector is mature and runs under various flavours of Unix, OS/2, Macintosh, Windows95, WindowsNT, win32s and other operating systems (but not directly under MS-DOS), and on a wide range of hardware. The second collector is the Mostly Copying Garbage Collector developed by Bartlett at Digital's Western Research Laboratory. While not as developed as the Boehm–Demers–Weiser collector, it can also be used with C and C++, and is the basis for several other collectors including the SRC Modula-3 system. As well as examining how these collectors operate, we also review studies comparing the efficiency of conservative garbage collection with that of different implementations of explicit memory management routines.

9.2   Conservative garbage collection

The Boehm–Demers–Weiser collector is a fully conservative collector that places no reliance on cooperation from the compiler [Boehm and Weiser, 1988; Boehm, 1993]. It does not require the compiler to emit tables [Appel, 1989a; Goldberg, 1991; Thomas, 1993], nor to tag data, nor does it use run-time data structures to record the locations of pointers [Edelson, 1990]. Values held in data structures used by the user program and its run-time system, including registers and stack frames, may be scanned for potential pointers but are never altered. These requirements constrain the collector to be a non-moving one, thus the collector is based on mark-sweep. As well as 'stop and mark', the collector can be used in an incremental/generational mode, and is it intended to be safe for use with threads. It can also be used as a *leak detector* for C programs that manage the heap explicitly. In this case, freed data is marked but not deallocated. The collector notices any unreachable objects that have not been freed, and the tool indicates the site of allocation of these leaked objects.

The collector is efficient, usually imposing only a small penalty in overall execution time compared with explicit memory management, and may even provide a gain depending on the style of programming used. The interface to the garbage collected heap is through GC_malloc and GC_realloc replacements for the corresponding C routines; objects can also be explicitly freed by GC_free if performance is critical. Further hooks to improve performance are also available to client programs. The collector is based on mark-and-deferred-sweep, with separate bitmaps for marking (see Chapter 4), and uses segregated free-lists for different sized objects. The marking phase marks from roots in registers, on the stack and in static areas, of which there may be more than one. The marker uses a resumption stack and can restart with a larger one if it should overflow.

Allocation

A program using the garbage collector can be thought of as using two logically distinct heaps, one maintained by the garbage collector and its allocator, the other maintained by explicit calls to the standard `malloc`/`free` routines. Programmers can use both heaps side by side without fear of interference, with the proviso that the standard heap is not subject to garbage collection and objects within it are deemed not to contain any pointers into the collected heap. Pointers from the collected heap to the standard heap are also usually not followed. This means that the collector can be used alongside code from standard libraries without problems. For convenience, whenever we refer to the heap we shall mean the collected heap unless specified otherwise.

The collector uses the two-level allocator described in Section 4.5 of Chapter 4. The heap is made up of *blocks*. On most but not all Unix platforms, these blocks are usually four kilobytes and each starts on a four-kilobyte boundary. Smaller block sizes generally result in less space overhead for small applications, but incur added time overhead. Adjacent empty blocks may be merged, depending on the setting of a compiler flag. Each block contains objects of a single size (though possibly of different types), and separate free-lists are maintained for each common object size. Blocks are obtained from the operating system by the standard allocator (for example, `malloc`). Each block has a separate block header held on a linked list, ordered by block address. The heap can be expanded at any time by requesting further blocks and typically this is done when a garbage collection has failed to recover sufficient free space.

Large and small objects are handled differently. Objects larger than half a block are allocated to their own chunk of blocks. The allocator examines blocks on the heap-block free-list using essentially a first-fit strategy, though some care is taken to avoid splitting large blocks unnecessarily. If no free chunk of sufficient size is available, the allocator either invokes the garbage collector or expands the heap, depending on the amount of allocation done.

Small objects are allocated by popping the first member of the free-list for that size of object — each free-list is a linked list of slots in heap blocks. If this free-list is empty, the sweep phase is resumed in an attempt to refill it. The first block is removed from the queue of reclaimable blocks for that object size, swept and any unreachable objects are added to this free-list. This process continues until this free-list is no longer empty. If no space is reclaimed by the sweep, the allocator invokes a garbage collection provided sufficient allocation has occurred. If the collection is also unsuccessful, the heap can be expanded by obtaining a new block from the lower-level allocator.

Root and pointer finding

Conservative garbage collectors immediately face two particular difficulties. The first problem is to identify the root set of the computation, and the second is to determine whether a given

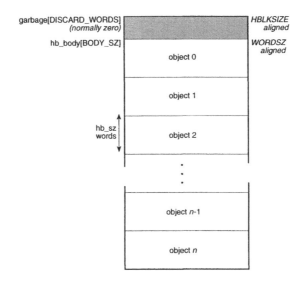

Diagram 9.2   Block structure, Boehm–Demers–Weiser collector, version 4.2.

word is a pointer. Roots can be found in registers, in the stack and in static areas. The problem is to find these areas and it is here that machine-specific dependencies lie.

Marking from registers requires assembly code, but the structure of this code is not difficult. For many architectures it consists of pushing the content of a register onto the stack and then calling a C routine to mark from the top of the stack. This is repeated for each register that might contain a pointer value. On other architectures all the registers can be flushed onto the stack. One way to do this is to use `setjmp` and then mark from the `jmp_buf` in which the registers have been saved; it may be necessary to clear this buffer before the registers are saved to remove misleading entries.

The next problem is to discover the bottom of the stack, and to determine in which direction it grows. This can be done either by using explicit knowledge of the run-time system or by using heuristics, such as taking the address of a local variable at the start of `main`. The top of the stack can be found in a similar manner. Finally, the extent of static areas must be determined. The Boehm–Demers–Weiser collector is able to handle dynamic link libraries on some systems, in which case the libraries must be re-registered at each collection (since they might change). Again this is highly system-specific.

Conservative garbage collection operates without cooperation from the compiler. It has no knowledge of heap or stack layout, and does not expect pointers to be tagged. The collector must therefore treat any word that it encounters as a potential pointer unless it can prove otherwise. The key to success is an ability to determine the validity of a potential pointer accurately and cheaply. The collector must err on the side of caution: failure to recognise a valid pointer as such might cause the referent data to be recycled as garbage. On the other hand, if the collector is too conservative, it risks retaining too much garbage which could eventually cause the program to fail by running out of space.

The collector assumes by default that every accessible object is reachable through an accessible pointer to the beginning of the object. *Interior pointers* — pointers to the interiors of objects — are considered invalid by the collector (in its simplest configuration[1]). This does not mean that such pointers are prohibited, but that if an object is reachable through an interior pointer, then it should also be reachable by a pointer to its base. For most traditional C programs this is a reasonable restraint: memory obtained dynamically by malloc can only be released if the pointer returned is passed to free. However, it is possible that this value is not retained between these two points in the execution of the program, but is derived later. Such behaviour is incompatible with the collector. Later we shall examine extensions to the algorithm that allow unrestricted use of interior pointers, albeit at some additional cost.

The collector takes considerable care to avoid misidentification. An object is only marked if the pointer passes each of three tests. On a SPARC, for example, these tests generate an extra 30 instructions or so.

1. Does a potential pointer p refer to the heap?
   The potential pointer is compared with the highest and lowest plausible addresses of the garbage collected heap.
2. Has the heap block that supposedly contains this object been allocated?
   The address of the header associated with the block that supposedly contains this object can be obtained from p by indirecting through a two-level tree, GC_top_index and bottom_index shown in Diagram 9.3 on the following page. Headers contain pointer to maps of allocated blocks, GC_obj_map.
3. Is the offset of the supposed object from the start of its (first) block a multiple of the object size for that block?
   There is essentially one obj_map for each object size. If the entry in GC_obj_map for this size of object that corresponds to this block and this object is valid, then the pointer is deemed to be a true reference.

If the pointer passes these tests, the corresponding bit in the block header is set, and the object is pushed onto a mark stack. This stack is managed by the techniques described in Section 4.2 of Chapter 4. Briefly to recap, the marker attempts to avoid mark stack overflow by pushing large objects in smaller (128-word) portions. If the stack should become full, overflowing entries are marked but not pushed. When the overflowed stack has emptied, marking is recommenced using a larger stack from marked objects with unmarked children. Finally, at the end of the mark phase, all mark bits corresponding to objects on the free-list are cleared, in case they have been set accidentally due to an undetected false reference.

Interior pointers

Interior pointers are problematic if a large object is only accessible through interior pointers. Since small objects do not span four-kilobyte heap blocks, deriving the address of the block header by masking out the least significant bits of an interior pointer will result in the same value as if the pointer had referred to the start of the block. To deal with large objects, the marker must find the start of the chunk. The index in the bottom_index array in this case will be a small positive integer indicating the minimum displacement to the start of the object

---

[1] The default configuration of recent versions of the collector accepts interior pointers as valid.

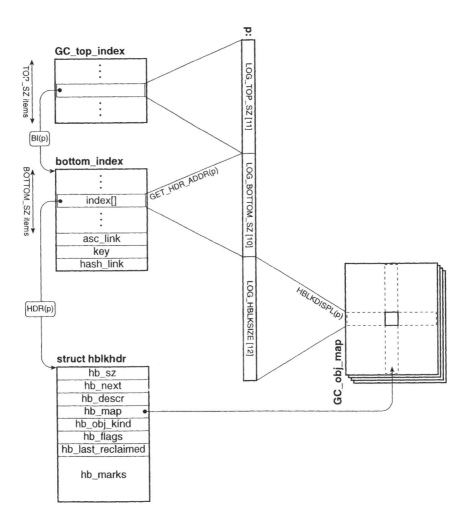

Diagram 9.3   The two-level search tree, the block header and an object map derived from a pointer p (Boehm–Demers–Weiser collector, version 4.2).

from the pointed-to address, rather than a pointer to a header block. The marker repeatedly skips back to that block and examines its `bottom_index` until it discovers the start of the chunk or discovers that the pointer was invalid. The header of this initial block holds the size of the (single) object allocated in the chunk. If the offset of the 'object' allegedly discovered is greater than this, the pointer must be invalid.

Use of interior pointers should be safe with portable, strictly ANSI-conforming C programs [ANSI-C, 1989]. However, their use greatly increases the chance of misidentification and empirical evidence suggests that it is harder to allocate space for large objects that is not 'pointed' to by integers (see the discussion of 'black listing' on page 238). Documentation with the collector recommends that programmers should either try to avoid using the interior pointers option, or, if that is not easily done, try to avoid using very large individual objects.

Problems of conservative garbage collection

Conservative garbage collectors face a number of difficulties not experienced by type accurate collectors. The most important of these is the risk of misidentifying data as heap pointers, thereby unnecessarily retaining memory that could otherwise be recycled — a *space leak*. There are several possible causes of misidentification, and the Boehm–Demers–Weiser collector uses a number of techniques to reduce the risk of such 'collisions'. The chance of misidentification is increased both by programming practice and by architecture design. Configuring the collector to accept interior pointers increases the proportion of addresses that the collector will accept as valid, and hence increases the chance that a non-pointer word may be identified as pointer. However, in practice there is little evidence of leaks in most applications despite the collector having been widely used since its release in 1988 [Boehm, 1993; Schelter and Ballantyne, 1988].

Nevertheless some circumstances have proved to be inimical to conservative garbage collection. Wentworth used an early version of the collector for experiments with interpreters for Lisp and the lazy functional language KRC [Turner, 1981]. Conservative garbage collection worked well for Lisp, giving leaks of less than 8 percent, with the amount of leakage tending to remain constant, thus declining as a proportion of larger heaps [Wentworth, 1990]. On the other hand, KRC defeated the collector to the extent that it thrashed and computation aborted. To understand why two 'functional' languages should behave so differently, consider the shape of the data that each abstract machine manipulates. Wentworth found that Lisp garbage tended to be made up of short disjoint structures. Any misidentification is thus likely to lead to the retention of only a single garbage structure; disjointness of the graph causes the size of any single leak to remain bounded.

Simple graph reducers like KRC, on the other hand, tend to manipulate a single complex data structure. At any instant, the current state of the computation can be thought of as those items that have already been constructed plus a recipe for generating the rest of the value of the computation. The system is driven by the need to print. As evaluation proceeds, the recipe is expanded and overwritten by a further partial result and a new recipe. In general, once results have been printed, say the first part of a list of numbers, they should be discarded. However, should a misidentified 'pointer' refer to some point in the list, it will gain access to all data generated from then on. Such data will not be recyclable after it becomes inaccessible to the print engine. Consequently the volume of reachable garbage will increase as the computation proceeds unless the false reference is destroyed. Diagram 9.4 on the next page shows a simple example of this scenario.

This problem may apply to any algorithm that involves a dense address space containing large, strongly connected structures. For example, Edelson reported similar problems for a large CAD application using a version of the Boehm–Demers–Weiser collector that did not provide black listing [Edelson, 1992a]. One pragmatic view is that programmers should code defensively, and avoid using data structures that are likely to become unbounded through a single false reference. Representations of linked lists that store links in objects themselves, rather than in *cons*-like cells, are particularly likely to suffer from this fault: if a false reference

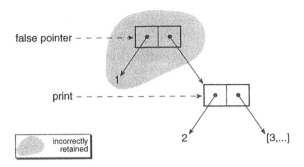

Diagram 9.4 `tail [1,2,...].`

retains a single list item, all elements that follow in the list also become reachable. The data structures used in Edelson's example were typically two-dimensional versions of the leaky list structure shown in Diagram 9.5, but also included some cycles [Boehm, 1993]. The more defensive programming strategy shown in Diagram 9.6 on the next page also applies to systems that use generational garbage collectors, although in this case the problem is one of tenured garbage rather than conservatism.

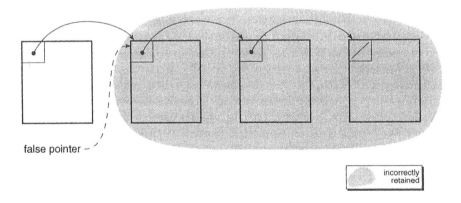

Diagram 9.5   Space leaks in a monolithic list are unbounded.

Misidentification

Many words that may be mistaken for pointers are actually integers. Fortunately small integers are never valid heap addresses on most systems. However, if pointers are not required to be properly aligned, the collector must consider all possible alignments. Two adjacent small integers (for example, 9 and 10) could then be mistaken for a pointer (for example, 0x90000)

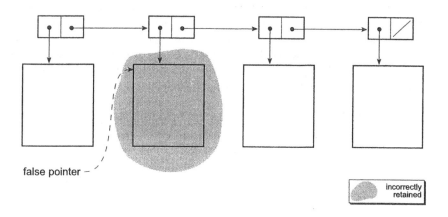

false pointer

incorrectly retained

Diagram 9.6   Space leaks in a *cons*-list are limited to the target of the false reference.

by falsely concatenating the low order half of one integer with the high order half of the next (see Diagram 9.7).

false reference

Diagram 9.7   Adjacent small integers may be mistaken for a pointer.

Since many integers are very small, the prevalence of such false references can be reduced by not allocating at addresses with a large number of trailing zeroes. Nevertheless, the combination of unaligned pointers and a requirement to recognise interior pointers can lead to an unreasonable number of false references. This tends to be less of a problem on newer architectures that penalise unaligned accesses as compilers ensure that objects are properly aligned.

Uninitialised data occupying memory that might still contain valid pointer values are also troublesome. Boehm reports that certain classes of data, such as large compressed bitmaps, introduce false references with an excessively high probability [Boehm, 1993]. His collector distinguishes two kinds of object: *atomic* data, allocated by GC_malloc_atomic, which is guaranteed by the programmer not to contain pointer data; and *normal* data (the default). Since atomic objects cannot contain references to other heap allocated objects by definition, they do not need to be scanned for pointers. This saves time and above all reduces the chances of misidentification. A further optimisation is that the allocator need not clear the space reserved for atomic objects since there is no chance of falsely discovering a reference. The space for normal data, however, must always be cleared by the allocator to remove any false references.

Architectures that encourage large procedure frames are also prone to introduce false references, especially if large parts of the frame are not properly initialised: this is typical of register window architectures. A 'random' value in a new register window may migrate to the stack, appearing to be a pointer, especially if the source of this value was a valid reference in a previous use of the window. Boehm suggests that this may be a significant effect, especially for small benchmark programs [Boehm, 1993; Cridlig, 1992]. His collector attempts to ameliorate this tendency by clearing a few stack frames before garbage collection takes place.

The collector avoids allocating at addresses that are likely to collide with invalid 'pointers' [Boehm, 1993]. It *black lists* references that appear to point to the vicinity of the heap but fail the validity tests, and the allocator ensures that black listed heap blocks are not used for allocation. In addition the allocator will not allocate an object to an address that would cause the object to overlap a black listed block. Furthermore, in order to reduce the chance of false references from variables that cannot refer to heap data, the collector is called *before* any allocation is made in the garbage collected heap. At this point there can be no references to the heap, and so all false references from statically allocated constant data, for example, can be eliminated.

Although black listing decommissions sections of memory in the heap, rendering them unavailable for recycling, it is more benign than a space leak. Unlike leaks due to false references, black listing affects only that block of memory: the leak does not spread to retain other data falsely. The cost of black listing is fairly cheap, incurring an additional overhead of less than 10 percent. Work by Shao suggests that the black listing collector does not suffer excessively from over-retention, at least for the styles of programming examined. For most of Zorn's test programs, the difference between the maximum malloc/free allocated space and the maximum reachable space found by the collector was small. Empirically, often the most significant source of leakage was not due to pointer misidentification but to dead pointers on the stack [Boehm, 1995a]. Note also that explicit memory managers can suffer from severe fragmentation under certain allocation patterns. On the other hand, Boehm reports that black listing can make it difficult to allocate objects larger than 100 kilobytes without spanning black listed addresses if interior pointers are allowed.

Efficiency

Two studies have compared the efficiency of the Boehm–Demers–Weiser collector with explicit memory management [Zorn, 1992; Detlefs *et al.*, 1994]. The approach of these studies has been to take several C or C++ programs and measure their performance when their allocator/deallocator is replaced with either the Boehm–Demers–Weiser collector or another implementation of malloc/free. The authors were concerned that synthetic behaviour patterns do not produce accurate estimators of the performance of particular algorithms [Zorn and Grunwald, 1992], so substantial real Unix programs were used, of which the best known are *perl*, a report extraction and printing language; *xfig*, an interactive drawing program; the GNU *GhostScript* PostScript interpreter; and GNU's *make* and *gawk* utilities.

The malloc/free combinations tested included those supplied with the DEC Ultrix and the SUNOS 4.1 operating systems, and the GNU C++ library libg++ as well as the Boehm–Demers–Weiser collector (versions 1.6 and 2.6 for the two studies respectively). The design and implementation of explicit allocators is not straightforward. Designs must compromise between speed of allocation and the degree of fragmentation tolerated. Freeing old objects also has a cost. Simply counting the number of instructions executed by malloc and free is not sufficient: an apparently fast implementation that is profligate of memory may incur additional page faults or cache misses that will impair its performance.

This is revealed very clearly by the performance figures quoted in both surveys. Allocators descended from the Berkeley 4.2BSD malloc/free implementation, such as the Ultrix allocator, typically used fewer instructions per object allocated than other allocators. Other explicit algorithms were less prone to fragmentation; the SUNOS allocator performed particularly well in this regard. However, when total execution time was measured, hybrid algorithms like the libg++ allocator were competitive with the Ultrix allocator, even though they executed more instructions. The reason for this disparity was that the Ultrix allocator spent more time in the operating system but Detlefs *et al.* note that the cause was not additional page faults, as one might expect. Unfortunately they were unable to determine the cause of this additional system overhead.

The surveys reveal sharp differences in behaviour patterns amongst the explicit memory managers. In the earlier survey, Zorn suggested that some applications programmers were well aware of the shortcomings of implementations of some manufacturer-supplied malloc/free combinations and had used their own domain-specific allocators instead. Unfortunately his evidence showed that, although the custom allocators were an improvement over a given standard allocator, even better results could have been had from using a different standard allocator, or even the garbage collecting allocator in some cases. This suggests that programmers' intuition may not always be a reliable guide.

Many claims have been made for garbage collection's performance compared with explicit memory management. Nevertheless, in the tests the Boehm–Demers–Weiser performed sufficiently well to be considered as a realistic alternative to explicit memory management. It had an average total execution time overhead of around 20 percent above the best of the explicit allocators, although actual times varied considerably depending on the application program running. At the time of writing, the conservative garbage collector is able to mark about three megabytes of data per second on a SPARCStation 2. Its performance compared best when the collector was used with programs that primarily allocate and deallocate very small objects. However, for some programs the garbage collector did perform significantly worse than any of the explicit routines, with an overall execution time overhead of up to 57 percent. Moreover, all garbage collectors, other than those based on immediate reference counting, require some head room if they are to avoid collecting too frequently. The Detlefs *et al.* results showed that, in certain circumstances, the conservative collector might use more than three times as much space as the best of the explicit algorithms. However, such large space overheads were generally encountered only for very small heaps, and are largely attributable to the fixed costs of the garbage collector's internal data structures. Furthermore, Boehm and Weiser have suggested that their collector might coexist poorly with cache management algorithms because of the requirement that heap blocks are aligned on four-kilobyte boundaries; this may cause different blocks to be mapped to the same cache lines. This speculation was confirmed by Zorn's survey which found that the conservative garbage collector did indeed significantly reduce the locality of reference of the programs tested.

These results need to be treated with some caution. All the allocators tested, including the conservative garbage collector, are elderly or obsolete. The Boehm–Demers–Weiser collector, for example, is at version 4.3 at the time of writing, but the surveys used versions 1.6 and 2.6: significant improvements have been made to the collector in the interim. The allocators, including the conservative collector, were also used 'out of the box' and no attempt was made to optimise their performance. The garbage collector can benefit from distinguishing objects that need to be scanned from those that do not: this was not done. Neither did the surveys take programming style into account; instead calls to malloc were simply replaced by GC_malloc and calls to free were removed. Consequently the programs supported by garbage collection were still required to maintain the invariants required by malloc/free managers. Programs written in the knowledge that a conservative collector would provide the memory management would undoubtedly be written in different ways. For example, it would no longer be necessary to copy data to avoid the risk of prematurely freeing it, and pointers to obsolete data might be explicitly destroyed to reduce the risk of retaining excessive memory. Hand-crafted reference counting would certainly not be employed.

At best, such surveys provide an upper bound on the cost of garbage collection compared with explicit memory management. Even so, the garbage collector fared comparatively well although, like any tracing garbage collector, it required substantially more space in order to avoid over-frequent collections. As experience of garbage collected systems has shown that their use can lead to reduced development time chasing memory management bugs, at the very least they are worth considering as an alternative to explicit memory management.

Incremental/generational garbage collection

The basic garbage collector described above is a stop and mark collector, but this may be too intrusive for interactive programs that use large heaps. For these configurations, the Boehm–Demers–Weiser collector is also capable of collecting incrementally/generationally provided that sufficient operating support is available. The scheme is generational in the sense that it makes use of knowledge of which pages have recently been modified. It is incremental in that each call to GC_malloc causes a small amount of marking to be done. The sweep phase is interleaved with the user program in all the collector's modes of operation (see the lazy sweeping techniques described in Section 4.5 of Chapter 4). For incremental marking or generational collection, knowledge of recently modified pages must be made available to the garbage collector either by the operating system or by the programmer. Some operating systems, such as Sun's Solaris 2, allow dirty information to be read (from the /proc file system in this case). Under other systems it may be possible to write-protect the heap and catch the resulting faults to determine which pages have been written since the last garbage collection. Unfortunately neither of these arrangements is entirely satisfactory and they are certainly not portable. Using /proc involves reading the dirty bits for the entire address space and may be slow. Write-protecting the heap is a sledge-hammer approach — the cost of catching a fault is not insignificant and care must be taken not to allow system calls to attempt to write to a protected page and hence fail.

Incremental marking is performed in small steps interleaved with the execution of the user program. Each call to the allocator in this mode causes a small amount of tracing to be done — the system attempts to touch just a few pages of memory at each allocation. Notice that there is no explicit communication between the mutator and the marker, unlike traditional schemes such as Dijkstra's (see Chapter 8 where we discussed incremental techniques). As marking is done in parallel with the mutator, it is likely that, by the end of this partial marking phase, the mutator will have changed the connectivity of the graph. One solution would be to stop the world and trace from the roots and from all marked objects with unmarked descendants. In the absence of any help from the virtual memory system, this must be done but it largely defeats the purpose of incremental collection.

With knowledge of which pages have been written since the last garbage collection cycle, the collector can do better than this. At the start of the cycle, a set of virtual dirty bits corresponding to heap pages is cleared. These bits are updated to reflect mutator writes by reading virtual memory dirty bits. When the incremental partial trace has exhausted the mark stack, the world is stopped. Using Dijkstra's terminology, marked objects on clean pages are black, marked objects on dirty pages are grey and unmarked objects are white; marking is complete when no grey objects are left. The mark phase is now run to completion from all grey objects, i.e. from the roots and all marked objects that lie on dirty pages. At the end of this phase only garbage objects will remain unmarked, although some objects may have become unreachable after they were marked: these will be collected in the next garbage collection cycle. Experiments with the incremental/generational version of the collector show encouraging results. Pause times were significantly reduced, at least on average, albeit sometimes at a cost of greater total execution times [Boehm *et al.*, 1991; Detlefs *et al.*, 1994].

9.3 Mostly Copying collection

The Boehm–Demers–Weiser system is fully conservative: it runs without any cooperation from the compiler. Because it cannot be certain that any value is a pointer, it cannot risk modifying program data and therefore it is constrained to use a non-moving collector. Bartlett was able to take a more liberal approach to a garbage collector originally designed to support high-level languages that used C as an intermediate language (such as his Scheme-to-C compiler [Bartlett, 1989b]). While his *Mostly Copying Garbage Collector* still assumes no knowledge of register, stack or static area layouts, it does assume that all pointers in heap-allocated data can be found accurately [Bartlett, 1988]. The collector is effectively a hybrid conservative and copying collector. Objects that might be referred to from the stack, registers or the static area are treated conservatively and are not moved; objects only accessible from other heap-allocated objects are copied. It is also possible to register other objects as roots. This gives the Mostly Copying collector three potential advantages: allocation is faster, finding pointers in heap objects is simpler, and garbage collection is more accurate.

Heap layout

In the classical copying algorithm, the heap is a contiguous area of memory divided into two semi-spaces, Fromspace and Tospace, and an object's space can be determined by comparing its address with that of the boundary between the two spaces. In Bartlett's algorithm, however, the heap is divided into a number of equal sized *blocks*[2]. The blocks comprising each semi-space are not adjacent but may appear anywhere in the heap. To identify its space, each

---

[2] Bartlett uses the term *pages* but this risks confusion with virtual memory pages.

block contains a *space identifier* (a small integer). This organisation offers two methods of 'copying' an object to Tospace. Either the object can be moved to a block in Tospace, or the space identifier of the object's block can be set to Tospace (in a manner reminiscent of changing virtual address maps to 'copy' large objects [Withington, 1991]). Since semi-spaces are no longer contiguous, unscanned blocks in Tospace must be held on an auxiliary list (see Diagram 9.9 on the next page).

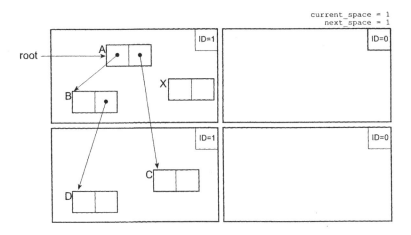

Diagram 9.8 The heap layout for Bartlett's Mostly Copying collector. The heap is composed of blocks; Fromspace blocks are those whose space identifier is equal to `current_space`.

Allocation

Allocation is a two-level process. Within a block, allocation is done in the normal way for any compacting collector by incrementing a free space pointer; the block's count of free slots is also incremented. Objects smaller than a block are stored on the current free block if they fit. If there is insufficient room in the current block, the heap is searched for a new free block. A block is deemed to be free if its space identifier is equal neither to `current_space` nor `next_space`: during normal allocation these have the same value (see Diagram 9.8). When a block is allocated, its space identifier is set to `next_space` and the count of allocated blocks is decremented. Larger objects are allocated over as many blocks as necessary.

Garbage collection

Garbage collection is initiated when the heap is half full, i.e. when half of the available blocks have been allocated. The value of `next_space` is incremented modulo n where n is large enough to ensure that all free blocks are eventually recycled. First, the roots of the computation are scanned conservatively for potential pointers into the heap. The collector checks whether each root points into the heap area and, if so, whether the space-identifier of the block to which

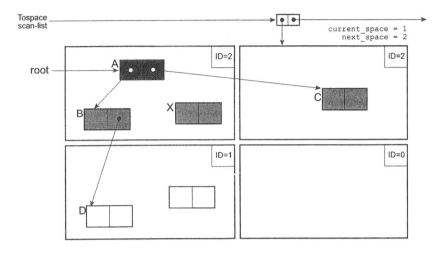

Diagram 9.9   Mostly Copying garbage collection.

it points is set to `current_space`. If the value held in a root could be a pointer into the heap, the block into which it points is added to Tospace by changing the value of the block's space identifier to `next_space`. The block is also appended to the Tospace list for scanning (see Diagram 9.9). At the end of this phase, all objects directly accessible from the root set have been 'copied' into the Tospace. A drawback is that other objects in those blocks have also been retained (for example, object X in Diagram 9.9).

The next phase moves accessible objects from Fromspace to fresh blocks in Tospace in essentially the same manner as a standard stop-and-copy collector. All objects in all blocks in Tospace are scanned, and each reachable Fromspace object is moved into a block in Tospace leaving behind a forwarding address. The only difference is that the space test is done by examining the space identifier of the page on which the object resides rather than comparing the address of the object with that of Tospace. Once tracing is complete, `current_space` is changed to `next_space` and garbage collection is complete.

Pointer finding in the heap can be done in either of two ways. The first method is to use the Lisp 'BiBOP' method to store an identifier in each block that indicates the type of object contained in that block. Its advantage is that it allows a very compact representation of commonly used types, most notably *cons* cells (for Bartlett's implementation of Scheme), but it complicates allocation as there are now multiple current blocks, one for each type. The second method is to tag each object with a header giving its type. Bartlett's Scheme compiler uses both options: blocks containing list cells are given the type identifier PAIR; other blocks are typed as EXTENDED to indicate that the objects in the block are tagged; or as CONTINUED to indicate a continuation block for a large object. EXTENDED objects are arranged so that the object header contains a count of the pointers into the heap contained in the object as well as the size of the object itself. The heap pointers must be placed at the start of the object (see Diagram 9.10 on page 245).

```
gc() =
    next_space = (current_space+1) mod 077777
    Tospace_queue = empty
    for R in Roots
        promote_(block(R))
    while Tospace_queue ≠ empty
        blk = pop(Tospace_queue)
        for obj in blk
            for S in Children(obj)
                S = copy(S)
    current_space = next_space

promote(block) =
    if Heap_bottom ≤ block ≤ Heap_top
    and space(block) == current_space
        space(block) = next_space
        allocatedblocks = allocatedblocks +1
        push(block, Tospace_queue)

copy(p) =
    if space(p) == next_space or p == nil
        return p
    if forwarded(p)
        return forwarding_address(p)
    np = move(p, free)
    free = free + size(p)
    forwarding_address(p) = np
    return np
```

Algorithm 9.2   Bartlett's Mostly Copying collector.

Generational garbage collection

Bartlett's collector can also be made generational, using block space identifiers to encode an approximation of the age of the objects they contain [Bartlett, 1989a]. The collector uses two generations: blocks in the new generation are given even numbered space identifiers and those in the old generation odd numbered ones (this technique could be extended to handle multiple generations by employing a more complex space identifier encoding). Minor collections occur when 50 percent of the space free after the last collection is filled. Objects in the young generation reachable from the root set or the remembered set are promoted *en masse* to the old generation. The remembered set is maintained by the operating system's memory protection mechanism, using the mprotect system call, to trap writes to heap blocks. Blocks containing objects referenced directly by the root set are promoted by incrementing their space identifier (to an odd number) in the same way as the non-generational algorithm 'copied' such blocks to Tospace. Accessible objects on other blocks are copied in the usual way.

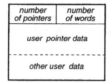

Diagram 9.10   Object format for mostly copying collection.

Following a minor collection, the amount of memory occupied by the old generation is examined. If this fraction is greater than 85 percent of the heap, a major collection is initiated using mark and compact. If the heap remains more than 75 percent full after this collection, the heap can be expanded in megabyte increments. A major collection starts by marking all accessible objects in the old generation. Bartlett's compactor, described in Section 5.3, is designed to minimise the amount of data that is moved. It compacts individual blocks rather than the entire heap, and scans the old generation twice. In the first pass, the old generation is scanned, looking for blocks less than a third full. Marked objects on these blocks are scavenged, leaving behind a forwarding address; objects on fuller blocks are not evacuated. Scavenged objects are copied to the current free block, but another free block is also queued up (if one is available) in case the current block should overflow. The final phase corrects pointers: the old generation is scanned again and pointers to moved objects are replaced by the appropriate forwarding addresses.

Ambiguous data structures

The collector described above assumes that ambiguous data is found only in registers, the stack and the static area, and that the format of all heap data is known. Unfortunately this may not be the case. Unsure references can arise in two ways for Bartlett's collector. General C programs may use undiscriminated unions in the heap

```
union {
    int     n;
    thing *ptr;
} x;
```

In this case, x is an unsure reference; it may be an int, or it may be a pointer to a thing. At run-time, there is no way that the collector can determine whether the union holds an integer or a pointer. Scheme, for which Bartlett's collector was originally designed, uses *continuations* — data structures holding the contents of its registers and the stack (pointer) — to preserve the program's state so that it can be resumed later. Continuations are first-class objects that can be freely passed as arguments or stored in the heap. As a continuation might contain references to heap objects, it must be traced like any other heap object; as it contains state information (by definition in an unknown format), it is essential that it be treated conservatively as a part of the root set. Bartlett's solution is to make four passes over the heap rather than one:

1. The root set is scanned for pointers and the blocks containing the referents are promoted. However, rather than changing the block's space identifier at this stage, a bit in the block header is set to indicate that the block has been promoted.

2. The second phase copies objects on promoted blocks to fresh ones in Tospace and then continues to copy from these objects in the usual way but with two important differences. First, it does *not* update pointers, and second, it must handle any continuations discovered in the heap. The blocks on which the (conservative estimates of the) referents of these continuations lie are promoted by setting their promotion bit.

3. The third phase corrects the values of Tospace pointers to blocks in Fromspace that were not promoted, using the forwarding addresses stored in the objects.

4. Finally the contents of promoted pages are restored. This is done by copying each object on a promoted page back, again using the forwarding address.

Handling continuations increases the complexity of the garbage collector significantly. Bartlett suggests that it is probably twice as expensive as the more straightforward method.

The efficiency of Mostly Copying

There have been no thorough studies of the efficiency of Bartlett's collectors and, of the evidence available, much is presented informally [Bartlett, 1988; Bartlett, 1989a; Yip, 1991; Detlefs, 1993]. Mostly Copying incurs a small space overhead to store space identifiers, type information (and possibly promotion bits), and to link the blocks of a space. For 512-byte blocks this would be an extra 2 percent; tagging data increases this overhead. Adding generations to the compiler adds a performance penalty for maintaining the remembered set, but this appears to be more than compensated for by reduction in time spent on garbage collection, at least for larger programs. An improvement in running time for Bartlett's Scheme-to-C compiler of 20 percent was noted. Interactive programs have also exhibited an order of magnitude reduction in pause times [Bartlett, 1989b].

A study of the comparative performance of the Boehm–Demers–Weiser Conservative Collector and the Mostly Copying Collector would be interesting, although as usual performance would be heavily dependent on implementation detail. One may speculate that Mostly Copying might perform better in an environment with a high allocation rate of short-lived objects. However, it is not clear that first generation survival rates of typical C or C++ programs are sufficiently low, nor allocation rates sufficiently high, to benefit from fast allocation. For systems with a greater proportion of longer lived objects, Mostly Copying collection for the first generation combined with mark-compact collection of the second generation can be effective. It has been used to improve the performance of a CAD system significantly by preventing paging. The benefit of the tracing compacting phase was well worth its cost[3]. On the other hand, DeTreville reported a less favourable experience with a non-generational, concurrent collector for Modula-2+, based on Mostly Copying, in an environment with very large heaps (measured in tens of megabytes) [DeTreville, 1990a]. Firefly workstations were easily provoked into thrashing and in the end DeTreville resorted to combining a deferred reference counting scheme with a mark-sweep collector. These differing

[3] Joel Bartlett, personal communication.

results again reveal the importance of choosing a garbage collection strategy that is in tune
with the behaviour patterns of the user program.

9.4   The optimising compiler devil

We have assumed so far that, given any C program, the conservative algorithm provides a safe
garbage collector. Unfortunately this is not so. Programming practices that disguise pointers
cannot be used with a conservative collector. The most common type of unsafe practice
involves arithmetic on pointers; examples include adding tag bits and reversing pointers with
exclusive-or operations. Obviously any assumption of the immobility of objects (for example,
hashing on addresses) may cause a program to fail in the presence of a moving collector. Other
examples that hide the pointer from the garbage collector will also defeat it. Fortunately most
of these possibilities are precluded by portable ANSI-compliant C programs [ANSI-C, 1989].

However, it is not difficult to contrive examples of legitimate code and valid compiler
optimisations that may render objects invisible to a conservative collector. Strength reduction,
for example, can destroy all direct references to an object. Given an array x of size SIZE, the
code fragment:

```
for(i=0; i<SIZE; i++)
    ...x[i]...;
...x...;
```

might be transformed into:

```
xend = x + SIZE;
for(; x < xend; x++)
    ...*x...;
x -= SIZE;
...x...;
```

if there is pressure on registers. Inside the loop the only references to the array are through
interior pointers, and on exit x points one beyond the end of the array. If this is not regarded as
a valid reference, any allocation may cause the array's space to be recycled. A similar example,
suggested by Boehm and Chase [Boehm and Chase, 1992], can destroy even interior pointers.
Given two vectors x and y of size SIZE:

```
sum = 0;
for(i=0; i<SIZE; i++)
    sum += x[i] + y[i];
```

might be transformed into

```
sum = 0;
diff = y - x;                    —y's register can be reused now
xend = x + SIZE;                    — so can x's
for(; x < xend; x++)
    sum += (*x) + (*(x+diff));
x -= SIZE;
y = x + diff;
```

This optimisation saves at least an increment in the loop and, on some machines, the
x + diff operation may also be free. However, within the loop, the start of neither vector is
reachable, nor is there even an interior pointer to the y vector. If there are other references to
these structures, which there typically are, no harm will be done by this optimisation. But this
is not guaranteed to be the case.

```
struct l_thing {
    char    thing[35000];
    struct l_thing *next;
}

struct l_thing *
tail(struct l_thing *x)
{
    return(x->next);
}
```

Algorithm 9.3   The tail function.

Boehm and Chase point out that other architecture-specific optimisations may conflict with
garbage collection. For example, a compiler targeting the IBM RISC System/6000 (that allows
addressing with a signed 16-bit displacement) translates the function tail, that returns the
tail of a list, shown in Algorithm 9.3 into the following code:

```
AIU    r3=r3,1
L      r3=SHADOW(r3,-30536)
BA     lr
```

This code adds one to the upper half of the register r3 in the first instruction, and then
compensates for this overshoot in the next instruction. Between these instructions the only
reference to the l_thing x is x+65536 stored in r3.

Simple solutions to these problems, such as disabling optimisation or declaring all pointers
to be volatile in order to force them to be stored in memory, would be expensive, especially
on modern RISC technology, and hence unacceptable to users. Edelson requires all heap
allocated data objects to be registered with the garbage collector explicitly but this would
also be too expensive for many applications [Edelson, 1992a].

Boehm and Chase, and Ellis and Detlefs have proposed rules for code-generator safety
that do not compromise efficiency [Boehm and Chase, 1992; Ellis and Detlefs, 1993]. The
conservative garbage collector's strategy is defeated if the compiler destroys all base pointers
to a live object only to resurrect a pointer to it later. This may be done by recomputing
the pointer by arithmetic or logical operations from some other value derived from the base
pointer. Boehm and Chase define a *global root set* and a *local root set* at any particular point
of execution of a C function. For a function f, the local root set comprises its in-scope auto
and register variables. It is also necessary to treat all previously computed values of direct
sub-expressions of incompletely evaluated expressions as local roots. For example the value
returned by malloc in the expression malloc(n) + 4 would be a local root. Global roots
are defined to be all the static and extern variables declared, all local roots of all call sites

in the call chain to the current execution point, and any values stored in other areas scanned by the collector. A valid base pointer is defined liberally to be a pointer to any position inside an object, or one past the end of it; the Boehm–Demers–Weiser conservative collector is able to handle such interior pointers. The advantage of this definition over the more strict one, that includes only values returned by the allocator, is that it allows any C program that is strictly ANSI-conforming to be used with the garbage collector. With these definitions, a conservative garbage collector will be safe provided that every accessible object allocated in the garbage collected heap is accessible through a chain of base pointers from the global root set. Incremental/generational collectors also require that all changes to variables that may cause them to hold a reference to a heap-allocated object are visible[4]. This criterion requires that the compiler never recompute the value of a base pointer from a derived value: base pointers must be explicitly stored.

Boehm and Chase suggest an implementation of their safety rules using macros to decorate expressions in the source code that are potentially dangerous. The macros are designed to make it very difficult for the compiler to discard live base pointers prematurely. While providing a solution to the code-generator problem for many compilers, their mechanism is not entirely satisfactory. A pre-compiler has to be used that adds a considerable amount of clutter to the code, and the macros depend on the undefined behaviour of `volatile` declarations. Finally a pass must be made over the assembly code generated to remove artifacts only introduced to force the code-generator to behave safely with respect to garbage collection. While admittedly these constructions are designed to be invisible to the programmer, they may increase register pressure or interfere with instruction scheduling.

The Ellis–Detlefs proposal is more radical than the Boehm–Chase one in the sense that it requires modifications to the C++ compiler. However, it is more satisfactory as it neither alters source code nor relies on the undefined behaviour of `volatile` declarations. They suggest that operations on pointers be annotated with the names of the base pointers from which the pointers involved are derived [Ellis and Detlefs, 1993]. The compiler must treat these annotations as uses of the base pointers, thus extending their live ranges, and these new ranges must be respected by all phases of code generation including register allocation, peephole optimisation, and so on.

Garbage collector safety can certainly be achieved. The question is whether this can be done in a way that will satisfy programmers, does not interfere with code readability and maintenance nor compromises efficiency, but at the same time is acceptable to compiler vendors, who are not unreasonably reluctant to modify their products without a compelling reason. A case that convinces all interested parties has yet to be made.

9.5 Issues to consider

Garbage collection has long been established as a tool that is recognised as essential for a wide range of programming styles including functional, logic and object-oriented paradigms. The Boehm–Demers–Weiser conservative collector has demonstrated that garbage collection is effective for traditional imperative languages like C as well. Bartlett's Mostly Copying

---

[4] This is intended to ensure that write-barriers are not circumvented, for example, by `memcpy`.

collector also shows promise for environments in which copying is the preferred strategy (for example, those with high allocation rates of very short-lived objects) although his collector is not as mature as Boehm–Demers–Weiser, particularly as far as coexistence with existing libraries is concerned.

Many C and C++ programmers remain deeply suspicious of releasing control of memory management to a garbage collector. It is certainly true that current garbage collection technology is not yet suitable for problems with hard real-time constraints on stock hardware or for safety-critical applications. However, conservative garbage collection is a satisfactory alternative for a wide range of applications. Errors caused by pointer misidentification or introduced by aggressive optimisers are unlikely to be an issue — the chance of generating garbage-collection unsafe code is probably no worse than that of generating other kinds of incorrectly optimised code [Boehm, 1994a]. Development time released from chasing memory management bugs could almost certainly be better spent improving performance in other areas. Garbage collection is a realistic alternative today to explicit memory management for most applications.

Several programmers have expressed concern that conservative garbage collection restricts C or C++ programming style. We believe this to be unjustified. The only restriction concerns casting pointers to integers and back again, since this may hide the pointer from the collector. If the only reference to an object is hidden in this way and a garbage collection occurs, then the object would be recycled. However, this construction is only valid for ANSI C if the implementation has an integer type sufficiently large to hold the pointer. Theoretically, programs that rely on such conversions will not be generally portable.

Comparisons with explicit memory managers have shown that garbage collecting allocators are competitive, even when the code under test was not written for garbage collection. New code designed to be supported by garbage collection would certainly fall inside this upper bound. There is no reason why the garbage collector should run in isolation, completely hidden from the programmer. It seems sensible to provide hooks that allow the programmer to indicate which objects are to be collected but do not need to be traced, and to give hints of appropriate times to collect. Explicit calls to the deallocator might usefully be interpreted as a suggestion that the amount of free memory has increased. The Boehm–Demers–Weiser garbage collector provides these facilities and others.

Finally Hayes argues that garbage collection must be conservative in open multi-language systems [Hayes, 1990]. As different languages use different type systems so locating pointers becomes a language-dependent issue unless it is done conservatively. Once located, pointers may have different layouts (maybe a small value has been added to tag a pointer), and there may be ambiguity as to which object the pointer refers (it may have stepped off the end of the array). Hayes argues that garbage collectors should be sufficiently 'broad minded' not to dictate to their compiler back-end clients but should allow the client to communicate their special knowledge to the collector. The burden of memory management should be delegated to a conservative garbage collector in the same way that I/O has been factored out into shared operating systems for many years.

9.6 Notes

The first implementation of a garbage collector for C appears to have been by Doug McIlroy of AT&T for 8th edition Unix. However, as far as we are aware, no report on this collector is available. The most widely used conservative garbage collector is that due to Hans Boehm, Alan Demers and Mark Weiser [Boehm and Weiser, 1988; Boehm, 1993]. It is available from `http://reality.sgi.com/employees/boehm_mti/gc.html`. The collector is suitable for both C and C++ code — the C++ interface was written by Jesse Hull and John Ellis. Discussion of generational and concurrent enhancements to the collector can be found in [Demers *et al.*, 1990; Boehm *et al.*, 1991; Boehm, 1991a; Boehm and Shao, 1993].

An implementation of a conservative collector for a EuLisp to ASM/C compiler can be found in [Kriegel, 1993], Vincent Russo describes a collector for an object-oriented operating system kernel [Russo, 1991], and other references to related work can be found in [Chailloux, 1992; Cridlig, 1992]. Geodesic market the commercial *Great Circle* conservative garbage collector for C and C++; their Web site can be found at `http://www.geodesic.com`.

Mostly Copying collectors based on Joel Bartlett's work have been used by researchers, mostly associated with DEC, including David Detlefs and May Yip [Bartlett, 1988; Bartlett, 1989a; Bartlett, 1990; Detlefs, 1990; Detlefs, 1991a; Detlefs, 1991b; Yip, 1991]. The collector is available from DEC at `ftp://gatekeeper.dec.com/pub/DEC/CCgc/`. The incremental, generational compiler for SRC Modula-3 also uses Mostly Copying [Cardelli *et al.*, 1992].

The efficiency of ambiguous roots collectors is considered by John DeTreville, Ben Zorn, David Detlefs and Al Dosser in [DeTreville, 1990a; Zorn, 1992; Zorn, 1993; Detlefs *et al.*, 1993; Detlefs, 1993; Detlefs *et al.*, 1994]. Problems experienced with the conservative garbage collector are reported by E.P. Wentworth and Daniel Edelson in [Wentworth, 1990; Edelson, 1993a; Boehm, 1993]. Code-generator safety matters and proposals are discussed by Hans Boehm, David Chase, Amer Diwan, John Ellis and David Detlefs in [Boehm, 1991b; Diwan, 1991; Boehm and Chase, 1992; Ellis and Detlefs, 1993].

10

Garbage Collection for C++

It is often said that the greatest strength of C++ is its C inheritance and that its greatest weakness is its C inheritance. This legacy is particularly predominant in the language's approach to memory management. Object class declarations may define *constructor* and *destructor* methods. The constructor method is called when an object is instantiated, typically to allocate storage and to initialise the object's data members. It may have other side-effects, for example acquiring resources such as window handles or opening files. The object's destructor is called when the program terminates if the object is static; when it goes out of scope if it is an automatic object; or when `delete` is called on an object in the heap. Destructors are used to perform any clean-up or *finalisation* actions that may be necessary, and to deallocate the object's storage. Typical finalisation actions invoked by the destructor might be to close any open files, or return window resources to the window manager.

Garbage collection is not a part of the C++ language [Ellis and Stroustrup, 1990]. Indeed it is a highly controversial issue and many C++ programmers strongly oppose the inclusion of garbage collection as part of the language standard. Nevertheless, many developers have found it either convenient or essential to include their own automatic storage reclamation mechanisms in their applications. Techniques for garbage collection are explained in several C++ textbooks (for example, [Stroustrup, 1991; Coplien, 1992]). Often these storage managers are based on reference counting: well-known examples include the *Adobe Photoshop* image manipulation system and the *InterViews* graphical user interface toolkit.

There are two grounds that are usually offered for opposing the inclusion of garbage collection in the language standard: efficiency and complexity. Many C++ programmers, especially those from a C background, are reluctant to release control of memory management to a collector. The use of garbage collection is not perceived to be necessary — particularly when storage debugging tools are available — and garbage collection is thought to demand an unacceptably high run-time penalty. It is also widely believed that it would be too complex to introduce garbage collection in a way that would not compromise existing code, nor overly constrain programming style. The underlying philosophy of C++ is that programs should only pay for the facilities that they use. The corollary is that programmers do not wish to pay for a garbage collector perceived to be unnecessary. In this chapter we shall examine whether these beliefs are justified — we believe they are not — and examine garbage collection systems that have been proposed for C++. One thing is clear, however: garbage collection for C++ faces hurdles that are both technical and political.

10.1   Garbage collection for object-oriented languages

Garbage collection is an integral feature of many object-oriented languages. Smalltalk [Goldberg and Robson, 1983], Eiffel [Meyer, 1988] and object-oriented flavours of Lisp incorporated garbage collection from the outset. Indeed, Meyer places automatic memory management in third place in a list of 'seven steps to object-based happiness'. Only systems that reach the last step are, in Meyer's opinion, worthy of the name 'object-oriented'.

There is considerable evidence that garbage collection is an effective software engineering tool: its use relieves the programmer from the burden of discovering memory management errors by ensuring that they cannot arise. Studies such as [Rovner, 1985] suggest that a considerable proportion of development time may be spent on bugs of this kind. That object-oriented programming languages typically allocate a greater proportion of program data structures on the heap than their conventional counterparts, and that the data structures they generate and the problems they are used to tackle are often more complex, can only increase the intricacy of explicit storage management. Sun's Java project illustrates the need for garbage collection in object-oriented languages. This project originally chose C++ as the implementation language, but the difficulties encountered with C++ grew over time to the point where the engineers felt that problems could only be overcome by designing a new language, Java. One important feature lacked by C++ but included in Java is a garbage collector.

Today there are useful tools available to assist with checking correct usage of heap memory: examples include CenterLine [CenterLine, 1992] and Purify [Purify, 1992]. The very existence of tools of this kind reveals the importance of correct memory management and the difficulty of getting it right. However, such tools are only practically useful as debugging aids, since they impose a considerable run-time overhead on programs (the CenterLine interpreter by a factor of fifty, the Purify link-time library by a factor of two to four [Ellis, 1993]). Furthermore, tools do nothing to simplify the interfaces of complicated systems, nor do they enhance the reusability of software components. Considerable effort must still be devoted to correcting the implementation or, even worse, the design after a leak or a dangling reference is discovered.

Object-oriented programs consist of sets of abstractions encapsulated in classes. Classes communicate with each other through well-defined public interfaces. Object-oriented methods make two claims to improving the development time and maintainability of code. Firstly it is argued that real world systems comprise a number of interacting objects, each with their own internal state and able to respond to certain external stimuli. Object-oriented design can provide closer models of these systems. Secondly, software engineering is about the management of complexity. Object-oriented programming separates specification from implementation and provides a structured method for reusing code, thereby producing programs that are easier to develop, maintain and extend.

Reliable code should be understandable. At the level of the module, this means that a programmer should be able to understand its behaviour from the module itself. It should not be necessary to understand the entire program before being able to develop a single module. In the worst case, it should only be necessary to examine a few neighbouring modules. This is clearly essential for large-scale projects involving teams of developers. Encapsulation restricts the effects of changes to a class to that class. The rest of the program should not become incorrect because of a change to a single class. This property permits extensible programs with easier maintenance. Classes that are extensible in this way may be composed more easily with other classes: the class is reusable in different contexts. One goal is to be able to combine software components in the same way as hardware components [McIlroy, 1976]. This requires that class interfaces should be simple and well-defined. Meyer offers five principles including (i) 'every module should communicate with as few others as possible', and (ii) 'if any two modules communicate at all, they should exchange as little information as possible' [Meyer, 1988].

We do not argue that garbage collection is mandatory for every application. However, applications with sufficient complexity of ownership demand additional care in the memory management of those objects. Nagle suggested that the problem of memory management in complex systems may only be solvable without garbage collection if programs are designed with correct memory management as their prime goal [Nagle, 1995]. While global dynamic memory management may be efficient and appropriate for monolithic systems built from hierarchical designs and stepwise refinement, this approach to design seems at odds with the philosophy of object-orientation. It conflicts with the principles of minimal communication and clutters interfaces. If objects are to be reused in different contexts, the new context must understand these rules of engagement, but this reduces the freedom of composition of objects. Garbage collection, on the other hand, uncouples the problem of memory management from class interfaces, rather than dispersing it throughout the code. This is why it has been a fundamental component of many object-oriented languages. However, it does raise its own issues in the object-oriented context in general, and for C++ in particular.

One is the question of reusability. Developers may provide their own garbage collection mechanisms through libraries but this leads to a class by class implementation, and raises the question of how components managed by different collectors are to be composed. In particular, how should cyclic garbage that includes data managed by more than one of these classes be handled? A general garbage collector, provided as part of the language, would be a more robust solution. Secondly, C++ was designed to be run-time efficient. One of its guiding principles is that code should not pay the costs of facilities that it does not use. In particular, code that does not use garbage collection should not be penalised by the presence of a module that does. The reverse should also hold: the efficiency of memory management of a garbage collected module should not be compromised by incorporating it into a larger program, providing that the complexities of the data structures used do not change. This has implications for conservative garbage collection techniques.

Thirdly, objects are often required to perform clean-up actions before they are destroyed. The most common finalisation action is to return storage to the run-time system. In a garbage collected world this is not necessary but other less common but still invaluable clean-up actions remain necessary, for example closing open files. How will these clean-up actions be executed if finalisation is only invoked by the garbage collector? Will clean-up no longer be synchronous with the client program? Does this matter?

10.2   Requirements for a C++ garbage collector

The most thorough proposal for the inclusion of garbage collection into C++ is the Ellis–Detlefs proposal [Ellis and Detlefs, 1993]. As well as specifying a language interface to the collector, it also offers a safe subset of C++ that ensures correct usage of the collector. Although restrictive, this subset is *optional*: it is designed for use in those parts of a program in which the programmer wishes to get automatic protection from storage bugs. Ellis and Detlefs recognise the reality of the C++ world: changes to include garbage collection must be evolutionary rather than revolutionary. They identify five constraints:

- Neither programmers nor compiler vendors will accept too many, or too major, changes to the language.

Programmers will not welcome changes that affect their methodology or their coding style unless they can see immediate and tangible benefits. Vendors will not wish to change either their compilers or the representation of objects unless they see a clear demand from their customers. It is also worth remarking that the ANSI standards committee receives a great number of proposals to improve C++.

- Any garbage collected code must coexist with components that do not use garbage collection.

Even though it is a comparatively young language, C++ has a legacy problem. Much code has already been written without garbage collection, some of it in 'foreign' languages such as C. It would be quite unrealistic to expect these libraries to be rewritten or even to be recompiled. In many cases, programmers do not have access to library source code and without access there is no way to verify that the library follows the rules for garbage collector safety. Even with access, the effort involved in checking their safety would be prohibitive.

A corollary of this is that automatically and explicitly managed heaps should coexist. Ellis and Detlefs also point out that making all objects garbage collected would change the semantics of destructors if this caused finalisation to be asynchronous to the user program.

- The rules for safe garbage collector operation must be defined.

Violating safe-use rules, for example by deleting an object prematurely, can lead to hard to trace errors even in comparatively simple languages like C; the complexity of C++ has been compared unfavourably with that of Ada. Although garbage collection reduces the incidence of such errors, code that accidentally violates garbage collection invariants can be even harder to debug. Garbage collectors determine the accessibility of objects by pointer reachability but, as we saw in Chapter 9 where we discussed conservative garbage collection, preserving pointer reachability of active objects may constrain either coding practice or code generation or both. Source code may disguise pointers (the canonical example is implementing pointer reversal by XOR-ing pointers), and aggressive optimisers may not guarantee that there remains an object code pointer to each object reachable from source-level pointers.

- Garbage collected programs should be portable.

The results of a program must be the same on any correct C++ implementation.

• Garbage collection will not be widely accepted unless it is efficient.

The main fear of many programmers who do not use garbage collection is that it would slow their programs down considerably. However, Ellis and Detlefs argue that programmers will sacrifice some run-time speed or memory overhead in order to eliminate storage bugs and to reduce development time (or to let the effort be spent elsewhere). One might wish to add other desirable properties:

• The programmer should not be required to provide information other than specifying which objects should be subject to garbage collection. In particular no information about the format of collected objects, such as pointer finding methods, nor about which variables are roots, should have to be supplied. Provision of such detail is error prone and such errors can be hard to trace.
• In the absence of garbage collector safe code-generators, the collector should have a strategy for coping with aggressive optimisers.
• Finalisation should be supported.

We now examine a number of strategies for garbage collection, and implementations of garbage collectors, that have been proposed for C++ in the light of these constraints before returning to the specific proposals made by Ellis and Detlefs. Finally, we examine the interaction between finalisation and garbage collection.

10.3 In the compiler or in a library?

At the implementation level, proposals for garbage collection require either changes to compilers or the provision of a garbage collection library. Both techniques have their advantages and disadvantages. Modifying the compiler would provide opportunities to enhance both the efficiency and the safety of garbage collection. The compiler can generate code that the programmer would otherwise have to write, improving convenience and at the same time reducing the chance of errors. Type information could be used to assist accurate and efficient garbage collection, and any advantages gained from compiler changes would benefit all code, including that which an application does not generate directly. Fixing the code generator to respect garbage collection safety rules would also benefit several collection algorithms. On the other hand, compiler changes would increase the complexity of these already complex pieces of software. On a pragmatic level, changes to compilers would not be welcome to compiler vendors. If the garbage collector was implemented in a library, its interface with applications would occur through the existing language. Use of a library would also make dissemination of the collector easier and, hopefully, widespread use of reasonably efficient collectors would increase the chance of garbage collection being accepted as an essential part of the language.

10.4   Conservative garbage collection

Chapter 9 examined the Boehm–Demers–Weiser conservative collector for C and C++ in some detail [Boehm and Weiser, 1988; Boehm, 1993]. This collector fits well with the constraints identified by Ellis and Detlefs. It requires no changes to the language, and makes only one restriction on coding style; that is, that a pointer should not be converted to an integer in a way that might disguise the pointer from the collector. This practice is not portable in general, but it is legal and useful. A good example is a hash table indexed by pointers, although this particular construction is safe because a hash key would not be used to reconstruct the pointer. However, safe use of this conversion cannot be checked automatically.

Unfortunately this constraint may compromise the collector's coexistence with existing code which is not required to obey the collector's safe-use rules. The collector is equally vulnerable to aggressive optimisers that may temporarily destroy references to active objects. Completely safe operation can only be guaranteed even for portable, strictly conforming programs by enforcing safety in the code-generator. The collector also provides some support for finalisation; we discuss this later. Nevertheless, the Boehm–Demers–Weiser collector is usually efficient and competitive with manual memory management, although some programming styles were problematic for early versions of it (see Chapter 9).

10.5   Mostly Copying collection

The Mostly Copying family of collectors developed by Bartlett and others (described in Chapter 9) are also suitable for use with C++ [Bartlett, 1989a]. Bartlett's collector uses two generations, with *en masse* promotion at each minor collection, and the remembered set is maintained by catching SEGV faults from the operating system's memory protection hardware (the cost of this approach was discussed in Chapter 8). A trace-and-compact collector can be used for major collections.

The C++ version of the collector differs from the version presented earlier in the way that it locates pointers. The original collector required that object headers stored a count of the number of pointers to heap objects that the object contained, and that these objects were stored at the start of the object. This organisation is restrictive and has a number of disadvantages. In particular, such grouping precludes aggregates that contain structures, or matching program structures to those in a file or in device registers. It also interferes with fast field-lookup for inheritance. The C++ version of the collector replaces the pointer count with a user-defined callback method that locates pointers.

A class is recognised to be allocated in the garbage collected heap by a GCCLASS statement in its declaration. As a simple example, a declaration of a tree of int is shown in Algorithm 10.1 on the facing page.

The GCCLASS macro defines new and delete methods for the class. An object of class Tree is allocated in the normal way, for example:

```
node = new Tree(1);
```

The first instantiation of an object in this class registers a callback Tree::GCPointers with the garbage collector. Delete becomes a null operation. The callback, Tree::GCPointers,

```
class Tree {
    public:
        Tree* left;
        Tree* right;
        int   data;
        Tree(int x);
        GCCLASS(Tree);
        ...
};
```

Algorithm 10.1 A tree of `int` class managed by Mostly Copying collection.

is defined with the macro GCPOINTERS:

```
GCPOINTERS(Tree) {
    gcpointer(left);
    gcpointer(right);
}
```

The callback is used by the garbage collector to call `gcpointer` for each pointer to the garbage collected heap that the object contains. User-defined pointer locating methods eliminate the *unsure reference* problem for discriminated unions since the programmer can write GCPointers to use the discriminant tag field to find pointers.

Fiterman points out another nice example of how user-defined marking routines can provide more accurate collection than other type-accurate methods [Fiterman, 1995]. Let us reconsider the problem of the stack implemented as an array posed on page 12 of Chapter 1. To recap, the abstract and the concrete representations of the stack differ. In particular, it is important that no element of the array above the top of the stack be traced. To avoid excess retention, a type accurate collector would require elements of the array beyond the stack to be cleared, but even so the collector would still visit each element of the array. A user-defined pointer-locating method can be written that is aware of the stack behaviour of the array and visits only elements in the live area.

The major disadvantage of user-defined mark routines is that they can lead to errors. Bartlett specifies rules that must be followed to invoke pointer location methods correctly, but observes that some users have found it difficult to define correct marking routines[1]. The collector also does not support multiply-defined virtual base classes, since it cannot know about hidden pointers constructed by the compiler. One solution to these problems might be to abandon user-defined pointer location methods and to use conservative heuristics in the heap as well as for roots, and indeed users can choose to run Bartlett's collector in such a mode.

Generating pointer finding methods automatically

An alternative is to generate pointer finding methods automatically. Detlefs has implemented a collector that extends Bartlett in this precisely this way[2] [Detlefs, 1991a]. Detlefs used

---

[1] Joel Bartlett, personal communication.

[2] Detlefs's collector is also concurrent but we do not consider this here.

a modified version of the cfront[3] pre-compiler to insert an *object descriptor* into each heap object header. The pre-compiler replaces each call to new by a call to the garbage collector's storage allocator, GcHeap::alloc, which expects an object descriptor as its second argument. Calls to delete and other destructors are removed. There are three forms that a descriptor might take:

Bitmap: a single word in which a 1 corresponds to a word in the object containing a pointer. Bitmap descriptors cannot be used for objects with unsure references — words that might or might not contain a heap pointer — and pointers must only occur in the first bitmap-size words (for example, 32 words assuming a one-word bitmap and a 32-bit architecture).

Indirect: a pointer to a byte array that encodes sure and unsure references, and non-pointer values. Arrays can be represented compactly by indicating repeats.

Fast indirect: Indirect descriptors may be slow to interpret so a faster form of representation using an array of integers is usually employed. The first integer is a repetition count for the rest of the descriptor. Subsequent values indicate the number of non-pointer items to be skipped to reach the next pointer, with unsure references represented by negative values. The array is terminated by zero.

The example in Algorithm 10.2 illustrates how these descriptors are used.

```
struct X {
    int     i;
    char*   str;
    float*  fp;
    int     j
}
struct Y {
    X       vector[3];
    union {
        int     n;
        char*   s;
    }
}
```

Algorithm 10.2   Unsure references.

Structure X can be represented by the bitmap descriptor 0x6 — only the bits corresponding to str and fp are set. A bitmap cannot be used for structure Y as it contains an unsure reference, but it can be described by an indirect descriptor:

    [REPT 3, SKIP 1, SURE 2, SKIP 1, RPT_END, UNSURE 1, DESC_END]

or a fast indirect descriptor:

                         [1, 2, 1, 3, 1, 3, 1, -2, 0]

[3] AT&T C++, version 1.2.1.

Interior pointers are handled in the same way as in Bartlett's algorithm, that is, through an allocation bitmap with the bit set that corresponds to the first word of each allocated object.

Detlefs's collector has not been thoroughly tested on a wide range of large-scale C++ programs, but initial results are encouraging. Garbage collection overheads for his test programs ranged from 2 percent to 29 percent, depending on parameters such as the amount of retained storage and the distribution of object lifetimes, as might be expected. However, extensive use of unsure unions has been found to lead to the retention of excessively large amounts of storage. It may be possible to remedy these leaks with more sophisticated handling of potential pointers, such as Boehm's black listing technique [Boehm, 1993].

Bartlett's and Detlefs's collectors share many properties of the Boehm–Demers–Weiser collector. They require no language changes; although Detlefs's collector requires the use of a pre-processor to create object descriptors, it does not make any change to the syntax of the language. Neither collector provides automatic safety checking, and both are vulnerable to aggressive optimisers. They appear to be competitive with explicit allocation. On the other hand, the semantics of objects is changed by the removal of destructors and calls to `delete`, with mostly copying collectors currently providing no support for finalisation at all. They are more restrictive than fully conservative collectors and coexist less easily with non-collected code; it is generally not safe to pass objects in the collected heap to uncollected libraries as the address of an object cannot be assumed to be immutable. One solution to this problem is to copy collected objects into non-collected *escape lists* before passing them to the library. However, this returns the programmer to the problem that garbage collection is supposed to cure: it may be difficult to know when to remove objects from escape lists, and leaks and dangling references may arise. Bartlett's collector is also vulnerable to errors and omissions in pointer locating methods.

10.6   Smart pointers

Several researchers have investigated the use of *smart pointers* to implement garbage collection, and this technique appears to be widely practised (for example, [Coplien, 1992, Counted pointers] or [Madany *et al.*, 1992, *ObjectStars*]). Template classes or pre-processors may also be used to ease implementation [Edelson, 1992b; Detlefs, 1992]. Smart pointers typically overload the indirection operators `->` and `*`, either to provide reference counting or to notify the collector of roots. Otherwise they 'imitate' the behaviour of the raw pointers directly supported by the compiler. Unfortunately smart pointers and raw pointers have different semantics. Edelson highlights the limitations of this approach [Edelson, 1992c].

Conversions without a smart pointer hierarchy

Consider the simple class hierarchy shown in Diagram 10.1 on the following page. Classes B and C are derived from A, and D is derived from C. Imagine that smart pointer classes Pa, Pb, Pc and Pd are defined, corresponding to each client class. Suppose in the first instance that there is no inheritance relationship defined between these smart pointer classes.

Standard conversions of raw pointers provide implicit conversions from derived classes to

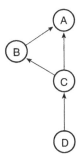

Diagram 10.1   Client class inheritance hierarchy.

both direct and indirect base classes, including both D* to C* and D* to A*. Programmers must emulate these raw conversions with smart pointer conversions. They can choose to provide conversions from every smart pointer class either (a) to all the smart pointer types that correspond to its referent's base types, or (b) only to the types that correspond to its referent's direct base types. If only direct conversions are provided, there is no conversion from Pd to Pa since user-defined conversions cannot be chained together, unlike raw conversions. If all conversions are provided, an ambiguity arises since no user-defined conversion is preferred over another. Suppose a function f is declared for an argument of class Pa or for Pc:

```
void f(Pa pa);
void f(Pc pc);
```

Which conversion should be invoked if f is invoked with an argument of class Pd? To reflect the preference of raw pointers for the direct conversion, an explicit cast f(Pc pd) must be used. The alternative of banning such widening conversions for C++ would be completely impractical.

Multiple inheritance

An alternative is to define a parallel smart pointer class hierarchy but this raises the question of how to deal with the raw pointer data in each class. If each smart pointer class in the hierarchy defines a pointer member then any assignment to a smart pointer must update all the component base pointers of the class. Although this emulates the standard conversions and supports multiple inheritance, it is inefficient. If, for efficiency, a smart pointer class is to contain just a single pointer member, then an abstract virtual base class must be defined to hold the pointer (see Diagram 10.2 on the next page).

This organisation reflects the conversion rules of raw pointers, both direct and indirect, and is efficient. Unfortunately it does not work with multiple inheritance (or some implementations of single inheritance), since one of the sub-objects, A of B, must have a non-zero offset from the start of the derived object, C. The C* to B* raw pointer conversion redirects the pointer to the start of the B sub-object by adding an offset. The corresponding smart pointer conversion uses the Derived& to Base& rule; this rule simply reinterprets the

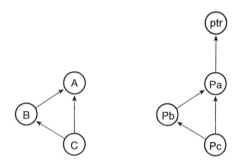

Diagram 10.2   Smart pointer and client class inheritance hierarchies.

value of the smart pointer to C in the virtual base class as a pointer to B. These smart pointers cannot be converted to base class pointers if the sub-object has a non-zero offset.

Incorrect conversions

Both the last two schemes allow an incorrect, implicit conversion. The conversion `Derived**` to `Base**` is prohibited in C++ because it allows incorrect comparison or assignment of objects of unrelated classes that share a common base class. With a smart pointer hierarchy, the smart pointer classes are related and the conversion is between `Derived*` and `Base*`, and hence permitted by the compiler, only to fail at run-time.

Some pointers cannot be smartened

Many C++ data types and expressions implicitly use raw pointers that cannot be smartened. The implicit `this` pointer cannot be redeclared as smart; and reference variables are represented by machine addresses.

Const and volatile pointers

Smart pointers do not reflect raw pointer conversions to `const` or `volatile` transparently. Raw pointers can be used in declarations in two ways:

`const T* ptr;`	—*The referent* `*ptr` *is const*
`T* const ptr;`	—*The pointer* `ptr` *is const*

but smart pointers can only be used to declare pointers of the second kind: smart immutable pointers `const PtrT ptr`. Attempts to circumvent this problem with templates, defining `Ptr<T>` and `Ptr<const T>`, will not succeed as the template simply declares two distinct types — there is no implicit conversion between them. Edelson suggests implementing `const` pointer conversions by making the smart `T*` class derive from the smart `const T*` class (see Algorithm 10.3 on the following page).

```
class CPtrT {                                              —replaces const T*
    protected:
        union { T*          ptr;
                const T* cptr;
        };
        ...
};

class PtrT : public CPtrT { ... };                        —replaces T*
```

Algorithm 10.3   A smart `const` pointer class.

Smart pointer leaks

Finally smart pointers may leak raw pointers to other components of a program, for example through `this` pointers. Unconstrained use of such leaked raw pointers leads to two types of error. If the leaked pointer becomes the only reference to an object, the garbage collector will recycle it regardless, leaving a dangling pointer. Even if the object is preserved, the raw pointer will have the wrong value after a copying garbage collection.

Kennedy pointed out a related problem [Kennedy, 1991], using as an example the statement

```
O2 = O1->makeCopy()->transform();
```

O1 and O2 are smart pointer variables, and `makeCopy` and `transform` copy and transform the object that they are given before returning a smart pointer to it. The compiler will create a temporary smart pointer object to hold the result of `makeCopy`. The result of the next `->` operator returns a *raw* pointer which is passed to `transform`. Since the smart pointer to the copy of O1 is no longer used, the compiler can destroy it, but unfortunately it was the only smart reference to the copy, which the garbage collector can now reclaim! `Transform` has nothing to transform. However this problem is resolved by requiring that temporary objects shall only be destroyed as the last step in evaluating a 'full-expression', i.e. an expression that is not part of any other expression [ANSI-C++, 1995].

Kennedy avoids this error by using *accessors* in his OATH system. Accessors lie somewhere between pointers and references, but rather than overloading `->`, they use '.' to access objects, thereby side-stepping this problem. The accessors form a parallel type hierarchy, duplicating all the externally accessible functions of their client types, in which each accessor contains a pointer to a client object as its only data member. Unfortunately they share with smart pointers most of the other problems of multiple inheritance — OATH uses only single inheritance — and incorrect type conversion.

In summary, smart pointers have a number of theoretical disadvantages. They cannot transparently replace raw pointers, there are a number of safety concerns which cannot be checked automatically, they coexist uneasily with existing libraries, and they are vulnerable to aggressive optimisation. Ginter makes some suggestions to improve the feasibility of smart pointers but these require changes to the language [Ginter, 1991]. Nevertheless, there have been many suggestions for their use and we consider some of these below.

Smart pointers and reference counting

Smart pointers are used for garbage collection in one of two ways. The most common technique is to use them for reference counting, having the overloaded indirection operators manipulate reference counts in the client objects. For example, the AIX C++ and OS/2 CSET2 library provide an `IRefCounted` class. Pure reference counting systems suffer from the well-known disadvantage that they cannot reclaim cycles. However, there is debate over whether this actually matters in practice. Many authors point out the prevalence of circular structures while others point to equally substantial examples of programs that contain no cyclic data. Examples of apparently cyclic references, such as trees whose nodes each keep a back pointer to the root, can be made acyclic as far as memory management is concerned by ignoring some pointers (these are often called *weak* pointers). However, picking the pointer to weaken may not be straightforward. Designing systems that can only cope with acyclic data (albeit modulo weak pointers) necessarily leads to a module-by-module approach to automatic storage reclamation.

The second technique uses smart pointers to inform the garbage collector of the locations of roots in the heap. Such maps are usually used either to indicate which locations on the stack or in the static area may contain roots, or to provide indirect access to objects in the heap. The advantage of the first method is that it does not add a level of indirection to the activities of the user program. Its disadvantage is that it may not always be possible to identify the addresses of these roots.

A simple reference counting pointer

A simple implementation of reference counted pointers might provide a new class to handle memory management (see Diagram 10.3 on the next page) [Coplien, 1992]. This avoids changing the representation of the client class. All counted references to the client are made indirectly through the wrapper `CountedPtrRep` which holds a reference count and a pointer to the client object. The counted pointer constructor either creates, initialises and attaches a new `CountedPtrRep` for a client object, or increments the reference count in an existing `CountedPtrRep`. The destructor decrements the reference count as expected, deleting the `CountedPtrRep` and in turn the client object if the count is zero. The assignment operator is also overloaded to handle reference counts correctly. It is also possible to supply a cast to provide more efficient, but unmanaged, access to the client object. This raw pointer and any other pointers derived from it must only be used where it can be guaranteed that the original smart pointer is preserved. This is not checked and such usage is dangerous. Safer access to the client is through duplication of its public methods.

Apart from the deficiencies of smart pointers described above, this implementation has other shortcomings. The client class is known outside the smart pointer representation: this could lead to incorrect usage. This problem could be removed by making the client a private member of the wrapper. The drawback of this is that changes to the client would require recompilation of the counted class. Reference counting is also expensive in any circumstances but counted pointers add further indirection. The cost of allocation and deletion of counted pointers is also greater. A more efficient way to handle reference counts is to use Deferred Reference Counting which we discussed in Chapter 3 [Deutsch and Bobrow, 1976].

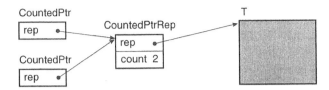

Diagram 10.3   A counted pointer representation of class T.

Smart pointers for flexible garbage collection

Detlefs investigated the use of smart pointer class templates to provide flexible support for garbage collection [Detlefs, 1992]. The chief benefits of his system are that it does not require the programmer to supply any information about the format of garbage collected objects, and that it supports finalisation. His scheme is also flexible in that it does not prescribe any particular garbage collection algorithm. He implemented and measured a conservative deferred reference counting garbage collector but his method should be applicable to other partially type-accurate algorithms.

Detlefs's smart pointer hierarchy is rooted in a class PtrAny (analogous to void* for raw pointers). The equality operator is defined in this class so that smart pointers may be compared with a single NIL value rather than a separate one for each client type. The smart pointer class for a client class T is defined by a template that (at least) overloads copy, assignment and indirection operators. The idea is that all variables of type T* are replaced by ones of type Ptr<T>. Pointer arithmetic is deliberately not defined.

Detlefs encloses garbage collected classes in wrapper classes that contain all information necessary for garbage collection, such as reference counts, mark bits or virtual marking functions (see Diagram 10.4). The new operator is overloaded in Wrapper<T> to provide a garbage collector specific storage allocator. All objects in the heap are instances of class Wrapper as far as the garbage collector is concerned, although different collectors will require different implementations of the WrapperBase class. Wrapper<T> may also implement some virtual functions of WrapperBase in T-specific manner. Both classes have empty virtual destructors in order to allow the collector to destroy wrappers and their client objects: delete WrapperBase* will invoke the destructors for the Wrapper<T> and hence for T (if it has one).

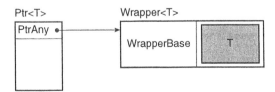

Diagram 10.4   Detlefs's Ptr and Wrapper classes.

Each `Wrapper<T>` also contains a static *reference containing map* used by the garbage collector to locate heap pointers. These maps are automatically generated by the smart pointer constructor. Implementation of the maps requires adding private members to `PtrAny` so that it can operate either in an initialising state or in its normal state. In its initialising state, the constructor causes the offset between the address of the `PtrAny` and the start of its container class to be calculated and stored in the map. In its normal state, the pointer is simply initialised to `NIL`. Each `Ptr` created during the construction of an object determines its offset within the object and records this value in the map. Interested readers should consult [Detlefs, 1992] for further details.

There are a number of disadvantages to Detlefs's framework. Some program constructions are awkward, in addition to the general problems of smart pointers raised by Edelson. A further smart pointer class template has to be used for dynamically-sized arrays, circular definitions require some trickery, and there are restrictions on the kind of class that can be used to instantiate a smart pointer class.

The garbage collection algorithm implemented and measured by Detlefs was a version of deferred reference counting. The members and methods required for this algorithm are contained in the `WrapperBase` class. Deferred reference counting overcomes the problem identified by Kennedy because it does not reclaim objects with zero reference count until it has checked that they are no longer pointed to from the stack or registers. Detlefs's algorithm scans the stack and registers conservatively in order to recognise these raw pointers to collected objects. This algorithm also has shortcomings, however. Firstly, two smart pointer class templates must be used rather than one, in order to handle non-counted stack variable types[4]. This scheme is safe if the latter type is used exclusively for `automatic` variables, but there is no checking that usage is correct. Secondly, the performance of the deferred reference counting algorithm was poor, at least on the programs he measured. It remains to be seen whether performance would be improved if another collector were to be used.

Smart pointers for tracing garbage collection

Edelson uses smart pointers to implement a garbage collector based on mark-sweep [Edelson, 1992a; Edelson, 1993a]. As an aside we note that earlier versions of Edelson's collector were based on copying [Edelson, 1990; Edelson and Pohl, 1990]. However, there is a fundamental flaw to this approach, as he discovered. Copying collectors require that *every* pointer to an object be identified and modified. This is in contrast to mark-sweep collectors which only require that at least one pointer be identified. In order to modify all references, the collector must take the address of `this` pointers, but this is illegal in C++. Mostly copying collectors are not affected by this restriction since they scan the stack rather than require the addresses of roots on the stack to be registered, but type-accurate copying collectors cannot be written. A copying collector must be either partially conservative or implemented in the compiler.

Edelson's mark-sweep collector uses smart pointers to insert or delete the address of each root in a table of root cells (see Diagram 10.5 on the next page). Access to the objects referenced by these roots from the program is indirect through the root table. A separate

---

[4] Wilson similarly distinguishes smart pointers that live on the stack from other smart pointers in his hard real-time garbage collector [Wilson and Johnstone, 1993].

root table and marking function is associated with each type, so that the appropriate marking method can be determined by compile-time overloading. The mark phase examines each cell in the root tables, marking its referent object and its descendants. Objects that are members of a class hierarchy require an additional call to a virtual function in order to be properly marked according to their dynamic type.

Since not all roots have lifetimes that are LIFO with respect to other roots, the root tables cannot be organised as stacks. Instead, the root table comprises a list of arrays of root cells through which a free-cell list is threaded. Each cell is a single word containing either a direct pointer to a client object or the link to the next cell in the free-list. To avoid conditional branches when allocating cells, the last page of the root table is read-protected: when the fault occurs a new array is acquired and linked into the table. Unfortunately this means that although root tables can grow, they can never shrink. This could cause fragmentation problems as pathological situations can be imagined in which the root table for one type grows very large before becoming largely empty, and then the table for another type grows large. None of the unused space occupied by the first table would be available to the second unless one of its sub-arrays were empty. Similar internal fragmentation can also be exhibited by conventional allocators that use segregated free-lists [Wilson *et al.*, 1995].

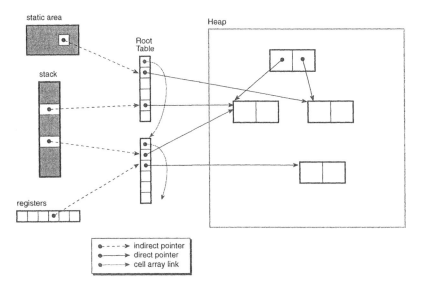

Diagram 10.5   Edelson's root table for accurate mark-sweep garbage collection [Edelson, 1993a]. Reproduced with permission.

For each collected class, two smart pointer classes must be constructed, one for pointers to mutable objects and one for pointers to `const`s. Conversions from derived to base types must also be defined. A pre-compiler, rather than templates, is used to assist coding of smart pointers since the latter cannot provide the necessary type conversions [Edelson, 1992b]. Each smart pointer contains a direct and an indirect pointer. The constructor obtains a new cell from

the root table which is returned by the pointer's destructor. The indirection operators * and ->
are overloaded to use the direct pointers to the object, but assignment is overloaded to modify
the contents of the root cell rather than the indirect pointer. This adds an extra indirection
compared with using raw pointers, but again some optimisation may be possible if a `Thing*`
can be used rather than a `Root<Thing>`. This is safe provided that at least one root to an
accessible object is preserved, but safety cannot be checked automatically.

Like Detlefs's, Edelson's results for the performance of his collector are poor. For the small
application that he tested, his collector had an execution time of around 170 percent of that
of manual reclamation. In contrast the Boehm–Demers–Weiser collector ran in less time than
the manual system.

10.7   Changes to C++ to support garbage collection

The shortcomings of smart pointers and other issues of efficient, type-accurate garbage
collection have led some authors to propose changes to the C++ language. Ginter suggested
providing better support for smart pointers [Ginter, 1991]. His proposals would include
allowing operations on primitive data types (particularly pointers) to be overloaded in order
to allow smart pointers to derived types to be assigned to smart pointers to base types; adding
new `traced` and `untraced` keywords; and modifying pointer representations to include more
information for the garbage collector.

Samples also proposed adding new type specifiers, `traced` and `untraced`, to declare
whether an object is to be allocated in the garbage collected or the standard heap and to
identify pointers that may point into the interior of objects [Samples, 1992]. His proposal also
required changes to the representations of objects. His scheme has the advantages that objects
may be freely allocated on either heap with the compiler catching errors whereby a collected
class contains an uncollected object, shown in the example in Algorithm 10.4 (due to Ginter
[Ginter, 1991]).

```
class member* untraced X;
untraced class member {
    public:
        void f(void) {X = this;}
};
traced class base {
    class member Y;
};
class base* traced Z;
Z = new(class base);
(Z->Y).f();
```

Algorithm 10.4   Ginter's example.

In this example, the call to `f` results in a reference to the untraced sub-object `Y` of the traced
`Z` being held in the untraced `X`. This untraced pointer might become the only reference into

z at which point the object can be reclaimed. Samples' compiler would require `member` to be declared as an `embedded` class and would spot as an error an assignment of an embedded pointer to an uncollected pointer. This proposal would require changes to C++ compilers and their type checkers.

10.8   The Ellis–Detlefs proposal

Ellis and Detlefs believe that garbage collection should be introduced into the language slowly and incrementally, but that it must be introduced today. Its introduction should be compatible as far as possible with current compilers and class libraries. Insisting that all objects be allocated in the collected heap, including those allocated by existing libraries, would not be feasible. Coexistence also precludes extensions to the type system such as indicating those pointers that refer to collected objects. Heap specifiers, on the other hand, do not affect the C++ type-checking rules.

With this in mind, they propose that a collected heap should coexist with the standard heap managed by `malloc`/`new`. A single change to the language is proposed to add a new heap specifier `gc` indicating the heap in which an object is to be allocated. Objects in each heap may contain pointers to objects in the other heap, and expressions of type 'pointer to `gc` `T`' may be used wherever an expression of type 'pointer to `T`' can. Ellis and Detlefs argue that experience with systems programming languages such as Cedar and Modula-2+ indicate the utility of such an approach.

As well as the new storage specifier, Ellis and Detlefs also provide an *optional* garbage-collector safe subset of C++, although the garbage collector can be used with code written outside this set if the programmer is prepared to take the responsibility that their code is safe. Code is guaranteed to be safe if it does not execute constructs labelled by the C++ Annotated Reference Manual as 'undefined' or 'implementation-dependent', nor casts an integer to a pointer unless the integer resulted from casting a non-collected pointer and the referent of the pointer is still allocated at the time the integer is cast back to a pointer. A safe-set compiler should disallow these constructs and also generate run-time checks for other constructs. The safe set is undeniably restrictive. However, the Ellis–Detlefs proposal provides a library of safe alternatives to replace some dangerous constructs prohibited by the safe subset. The interested reader should consult Section 7 of the proposals for details.

Ellis and Detlefs argue that any practical garbage collector must exhibit the following properties. It must have low pause times (less than 0.1 second) if it is to be useful for interactive applications; it must be competitive with current implications of `malloc`/`new`; and it must support multi-threading and multi-processing. Furthermore for C++, the garbage collector must support interior pointers, cross-heap pointers and untagged unions and must operate in multi-lingual environments. They do not specify a garbage collection algorithm but they note that both the Boehm–Demers–Weiser and the Bartlett families of collectors meet many of their concerns. Both collectors have generational or incremental modes, relying on support from the operating system. Neither collector requires changes to the language — indeed they even support the garbage collection of C — and both support the other desirable properties identified by Ellis and Detlefs. Finally, recent studies suggest that conservative collectors are competitive with explicit deallocation [Zorn, 1992; Detlefs *et al.*, 1994].

10.9 Finalisation

There is considerable experience of object clean-up in object-oriented or object-based languages that are supported by garbage collection (for example, Lisp, Cedar, Smalltalk, CLU and Modulas 2+ and 3). Garbage collector finalisation has been used for a range of activities including managing caches of objects, and releasing resources provided by servers or other programs. Hayes provides a survey of finalisation facilities in several languages [Hayes, 1992]. The first issue that arises is that devolving finalisation to the garbage collector may change the semantics of objects as clean-up is no longer performed synchronously with the client program. Indeed, the finaliser of a garbage object may not be called until program termination if that object has been promoted to a stable generation by a generational collector. Pointer misidentification may likewise prevent finalisation by conservative garbage collectors.

C++, on the other hand, calls the destructor for an object when the program terminates if it is a static object; as soon as it goes out of scope if it is an automatic object; or when `delete` is called on an object in the heap. However, the reader should beware that the point at which destructors are called for compiler-generated temporary objects is not defined. For most objects in garbage collected languages, finalisation is not an issue since it simply deallocates storage: this rôle is taken over by the garbage collector. However, there is a small but indispensable set of classes for which non-trivial finalisation is important and concern has been raised over how and whether it should be handled by the garbage collector. It is appropriate to ask how promptly a resource should be recovered after it has become unreachable. Clearly standard reference counting collectors are prompt, but other collectors may delay finalisation indefinitely. Such delays are not acceptable in situations where timeliness is important or where exclusive access to scarce resources is retained by the finalisable object. Ellis and Detlefs suggest that programmers should regard object clean-up as a mechanism for improving resource usage, rather than relying on it for correct behaviour of their programs. Perversely, finalisation timing may be less problematic in multi-threaded environments since synchronising concurrent access is already recognised to be a general issue.

Other questions are raised by garbage collector induced finalisation. Finalisation may resurrect objects, making them available to the user program once more. If the object is subsequently reclaimed by the garbage collector, should it be finalised again? The order of finalisation is also critical. Finalisation should usually be done in topological order — this is guaranteed in Cedar, for example. If an object A contains a reference to an object B then A must be finalised before B in case the finalisation of A requires B. The garbage collector is well placed to choose the finalisation order since it understands the connectivity of these objects. However, the handling of cycles then becomes an issue. One solution is to redesign objects to separate their finalisable parts from their other components. In the example shown in Diagram 10.6 on the next page, the finalisable resources of A might be extracted into a new object A′. Now only A′ and B are finalisable and there is no cycle of finalisable objects. B can be finalised, A reclaimed and then A′ finalised.

When C++ destructors are called and whether the garbage collector should support finalisation are separate issues. One view to take may be to accept that garbage collection should not prevent clean-up actions being invoked explicitly (à la C++ `delete`), but that it does provide the guarantee that an object's finaliser will not be called before it becomes inaccessible to the program.

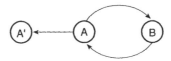

Diagram 10.6   Extracting the finalisable resource of A into A′ breaks the finalisation cycle.

Support for finalisation

The garbage collectors discussed earlier in this chapter support finalisation to greater and lesser degrees. Bartlett's and Detlefs's Mostly Copying collectors remove all instances of delete and so do not support finalisation at all. The Boehm–Demers–Weiser collector allows an object that requires finalisation to be explicitly registered with the collector by GC_register_finalizer. The motivation for remembering which objects need finalising, rather than scanning the heap for them, is that few objects are likely to require clean-up in a garbage collected world. Objects that refer to each other are finalised in stages. If finalisable objects A and B are inaccessible, and A points to B, then only A will be finalised by the current collection. If finalisation does not create any new pointers to B, then B will be finalised after the next collection. This means that any finalisable object that is reachable from itself will not be finalised (or collected).

Cycles involving finalisable objects should be avoided, or should be broken by calling GC_register_disappearing_link(&p), where p is a pointer that is not followed by finalisation code, and should not be considered in determining finalisation order. The link will be cleared when the object to which it refers is discovered to be to be unreachable. This is done before any finalisation code is invoked, and before any decisions about finalisation order are made. Ellis suggests that the need to 'disappear' links is extremely rare: in the Cedar programming environment, it was used in just one situation [Ellis, 1995]. Clearly finalisation is handled by the Boehm–Demers–Weiser collector at a very low level.

Hudson describes a method for clean-up in Modula-3 that associates finalisation with objects rather than with code (such as Modula-3's TRY FINALLY construct) [Hudson *et al.*, 1991]. As before, objects that require finalisation are registered with the garbage collector when they are created and appended to the youngest generation's set of finalisable objects, *has-finaliser*. The order in which these objects should be finalised is the reverse of their creation order and Hudson takes advantage of this by preserving the creation order in the *has-finaliser* set. He notes that this arrangement is well suited to the functional style of programming encouraged by Modula-3's NEW operator.

After a generation is scavenged, its *has-finaliser* set is scanned in this order, and any survivor is appended to the *has-finaliser* set of the region to which the object was moved. If a finalisable object did not survive the scavenge, it is added to the *please-finalise* set of Tospace. The dead object must be preserved for finalisation since it may be resurrected, so it and its descendants are also moved to Tospace. Finally the finalisation thread pops entries from the current space's *please-finalise* set in reverse creation order and executes their finalisers. Although finalisation can resurrect objects, they are never re-registered for finalisation.

10.10 Issues to consider

Many strategies for the garbage collection of C++ have been proposed. We conclude this chapter by reviewing the more commonly used techniques in the light of the virtues defined by Ellis and Detlefs. In particular, we compare any changes they require to the language standard, the strength of their guarantee of safety including any restrictions they may impose on coding style, how easily collect code coexists with non-collected code and aggressive optimisers, and their support for finalisation.

The Boehm–Demers–Weiser collector is competitive with conventional allocators and is widely used for both C and C++. It requires no changes to be made to the language, and no restrictions are placed on coding style for portable, strictly conforming programs. The only caveat is that pointers should not be disguised from the collector. The collector operates as a library so this safety consideration cannot be checked. Pointer visibility is a requirement of all code that is used with the collector — this compromises its coexistence with existing libraries. The collector is also vulnerable to aggressive optimisers that may temporarily destroy pointers to live data. The collector has limited support for finalisation.

Bartlett's Mostly Copying collector similarly neither demands language changes, nor imposes restrictions on coding style. It is sufficiently efficient to be used as the underlying technology of the incremental, generational collector for Modula-3. Programmers must write their own pointer finding methods for heap objects and cannot rely on objects having fixed addresses. Detlefs's version of Mostly Copying removes the possibility of incorrect pointer finding methods either by using a pre-compiler or by modifying the compiler to generate methods automatically. Object movement may compromise coexistence with existing libraries. Again, safety is not checked automatically, and it is vulnerable to aggressive optimisers. No support is provided for finalisation.

Many implementations of garbage collection have been built with smart pointers. Again, no language changes are required. However, smart pointers do not replace raw pointers transparently, and some changes to programming style are required. Libraries cannot be expected to use smart pointers so conversions to raw pointers will be required. Furthermore, even without such conversions, smart pointers that overload * and -> may leak raw pointers. Safety cannot be checked and many implementations of smart pointers are vulnerable to aggressive optimisers. One exception is Detlefs's Smart Pointer Templates technique, but this involves complex and subtle programming. The overheads of smartness also lead to poor performance, particularly if they are used for reference counting. More positively, finalisation is supported.

Type accurate garbage collection for C++ is fraught with difficulties. Smart pointers appear superficially to offer a solution but may mislead programmers into believing that they have the same semantics as raw pointers. All implementations using smart pointers have shown poor performance, whether for reference counting or for registering roots with the collector. Pointer finding is problematic, requiring the programmer to write methods for each class and thereby risking errors, unless a pre-processor is used. Detlefs's templates avoid this but at the cost of considerable coding complexity. Pre-processor techniques do not handle unsure references as well as existing conservative garbage collectors. Smart pointers and copying collectors are incompatible with existing class libraries and even conservative collection takes the risk that the library may not respect its rules. All the collectors proposed that do not require compiler changes are vulnerable to aggressive optimisers in one way or another.

The Boehm–Demers–Weiser appears to be the most promising collector for C++. It makes few demands on programming style, and is safe if it is used with Ellis's and Detlefs's safe subset. Its chief flaw is its vulnerability to hostile code generators. Some concern has also been expressed over excess retention of storage by earlier versions of the collector [Wentworth, 1990; Edelson, 1993a]. Other shortcomings include only limited support for finalisation and the fact that the cost of collecting a module is dependent on the context in which it is used.

It seems unlikely that garbage collection will be incorporated into C++ in the near future. Although Ellis and Detlefs originally intended to put their proposal formally to the standards committee, they withheld it when it became clear that the committee was intent on finishing the standard quickly and that their proposal would probably not be accepted. Their current intention is to encourage compiler suppliers to incorporate their proposals with a conservative collector. We hope that they are successful.

10.11   Notes

Details of the conservative garbage collector by Hans Boehm, Alan Demers and Mark Weiser can be found in [Boehm and Weiser, 1988; Boehm et al., 1991; Boehm, 1993; Demers et al., 1990]. The ·compiler is discussed in detail in Chapter 9. It is available from `http://reality.sgi.com/employees/boehm_mti/gc.html`. Other conservative collectors for C++ are marketed by Codewright's Toolworks [Codewright's Toolworks, 1993] and Geodesic Systems, `http://www.geodesic.com`. Joel Bartlett's Mostly Copying compiler, also discussed in detail in Chapter 9, is available from DEC in `ftp://gatekeeper.dec.com/pub/DEC/CCgc` [Bartlett, 1989a; Bartlett, 1989b]. Extensions to the collector can be found in [Detlefs, 1990; Detlefs, 1991a; Detlefs, 1991b; Yip, 1991]. Guiseppe Attardi, Tito Flagella and Pietro Iglio describe a collector based on Mostly Copying in [Attardi et al., 1995]; it is avaailable from `ftp://ftp.di.unipi.it/pub/project/posso/cmm`.

Paulo Ferreira takes a similar but even more complicated approach in his multi-generational garbage collection library [Ferreira, 1991]. The declaration of each garbage collected class includes a macro which must take the names of the base classes as arguments. Additional rules are provided to improve performance by avoiding reliance on conservative stack scanning. Constructors and destructors use macros to register or de-register the object and member functions deal similarly with local pointers that might point to garbage collected objects. Each class provides a pointer locating method similar to `GCPointers`. Generational collection is supported by replacing pointer assignments by yet another macro. Use of these macros clutters code considerably; anything that hinders code readability must be deprecated. It is also easy to fail to abide strictly by the rules (for example, omitting a root registering macro for a local variable).

Daniel Edelson describes attempts to build a copying collector by using smart pointers to register roots with the collector [Edelson, 1990; Edelson and Pohl, 1990; Edelson and Pohl, 1991]. Inability to take the address of `this` pointers led Edelson to reject copying collection in favour of mark-sweep [Edelson, 1992a; Edelson, 1992b; Edelson, 1993a]. Smart pointers are used again, this time to indirect access to roots through global root tables. [Edelson, 1993b] uses a modified version of the Boehm–Demers–Weiser collector. David Detlefs describes another smart pointer collector, but based on conservative deferred reference counting, in [Detlefs, 1992]. Other implementations based on reference counting are described in [Maeder, 1992; Madany *et al.*, 1992].

The problems of smart pointers are discussed thoroughly in [Ginter, 1991; Kennedy, 1991; Edelson, 1992c]. Andrew Ginter also makes suggestions for changes to C++ to facilitate garbage collection. Other proposed extensions to C++ to support garbage collection *inter alia* can be found in [Seliger, 1990; Samples, 1992]. The most thorough proposal to include garbage collection into the language came from John Ellis and David Detlefs [Ellis and Detlefs, 1993].

Surveys of systems that offer finalisation in the collection interface can be found in [Hayes, 1992; Hudson, 1991]. Other work on garbage collection for C++ can be found in Master's theses by [Wang, 1989; Ganesan, 1994; Guggilla, 1994; Satishkumar, 1994].

11

Cache-Conscious Garbage Collection

11.1 Modern processor architectures

The memory sub-system of modern computers comprises a hierachy of components, from disk drives to on-chip registers. As the disparity in performance of parts of the memory sub-system has increased, so too has the complexity of this hierarchy. Even the most modest personal computers now often contain on-chip instruction buffers and data caches, secondary or board-level caches, memory buses, main memory, I/O channels, disk drives and CD-ROMs or other high-capacity secondary storage devices.

The improvement in processor speeds has been truly dramatic. In 1976, an ICL 2960 mainframe, often serving thirty or more time-sharing users, ran at about 0.6 million instructions per second. At the time of writing, twenty years later, desk-top personal computers based on Motorola PowerPC or Intel Pentium processors are clocked at over 120 MHz, an improvement in processor speed of two orders of magnitude; high-end workstations based on Digital's Alpha chip may run at up to 266 MHz.

However, the increase in performance has not been uniform. While processor speeds have improved a hundred-fold, disk latencies have remained largely unchanged. This is why some extra processor effort to avoid page faults is so worthwhile. Equally, the performance of DRAM memory chips has not kept pace with that of CPUs. Main memory can no longer supply data or instructions to the CPU fast enough: in Baker's words, modern processor chips are 'I/O-bound' [Baker, 1991].

DRAM memory chips have an access time of 70–120 ns. Although faster memory chips are available, it is not economic to populate all of main memory in this way. Instead the average latency of memory access can be reduced by inserting a small *cache* of fast SRAM memory between the CPU and main memory. SRAM memory typically has an access time of 8–35 ns. If the CPU accesses a memory block that is held in this cache — a cache *hit* — the datum is immediately available. If not — a cache *miss* — the processor may have to be stalled for several clock cycles — the miss *penalty* — until the block is retrieved from main memory.

In earlier chapters, we saw how poorly designed collectors can interact badly with virtual memory. Equally, the performance of programs that interact poorly with the cache can be many times worse than that of those programs that 'fit' well with the cache.

The effect of cache misses on CPU time

The performance of a program can be significantly enhanced if its *miss rate* — the ratio of cache misses to instructions executed — is low. Baker argues that the management of on-chip memory space and off-chip communications has become the major problem in gaining fast execution times on modern processor architectures. Grunwald *et al.* report that increased cache misses can increase execution time by up to 25 percent in range of large allocation-intensive C programs [Grunwald *et al.*, 1993]. More dramatically, Lam *et al.* used *blocking* to improve the performance of a processor from 0.9 mflops to 4 mflops when multiplying large matrices. Blocking operates on sub-matrices, rather than whole rows or columns, in order to minimise the cache miss rate [Lam and others, 1991].

The importance of good cache behaviour to overall execution times is increasingly important. The cost of a cache miss has grown as the speeds of modern processors and the complexity of their designs have increased. The cost of a cache-miss is architecture-dependent; it also varies between read misses and write misses, and whether only the primary (level one) on-chip cache is missed or the secondary (level two) cache is missed as well. Hennessy and Patterson provide a clear example of the interaction between processor design, and cache and overall CPU performance [Hennessy and Patterson, 1996]. The CPU time spent executing a program can be divided between the time spent doing useful processing and the time spent waiting for the memory system. Thus,

$$CPUtime = IC * (CPI + miss/instruction * misspenalty) * cycletime$$

where IC is the instruction count, i.e. the number of instructions executed, CPI is the average number of cycles per instruction, and the miss rates and penalties for reads and writes have been combined. The cache miss penalty on the DEC Alpha AXP, a modern RISC processor, is 50 cycles and the CPI is 2. Suppose further that the miss rate is 2 percent, and that there is an average of 1.33 memory references per instruction.

$$
\begin{aligned}
CPUtime &= IC * (2 + 1.33 * 0.02 * 50) * cycletime \\
&= IC * 3.33 * cycletime
\end{aligned}
$$

In other words, the effect of cache misses has increased the effective CPI from 2.0 to 3.33, an increase of two-thirds. Note that without a cache, the effective CPI would be 68.5! Contrast this with the smaller effect of cache misses on older CISC designs, such as the VAX 11/780. Here we suppose that the cache miss penalty is lower, 6 cycles, but that the average CPI is much higher, at 8.5 cycles per instruction. Assume that the miss rate is the same, but that there is an average of 3.0 memory references per instruction.

$$
\begin{aligned}
CPUtime &= IC * (8.5 + 3.0 * 0.11 * 6) * cycletime \\
&= IC * 10.5 * cycletime
\end{aligned}
$$

The effective CPI has risen from 8.5 to 10.5, an increase of 24 percent. The cost of cache misses to the overall performance is therefore much greater for the modern RISC processor than it is for the older CISC processor. The deleterious effect of cache misses on performance has increased as pipelining techniques have reduced raw CPI and as processor cycle times have been cut. Moreover, the trend is for the cost of retrieving data from main memory to increase. Jouppi predicts that the cost of a cache miss may rise to 100 cycles, while Mogul and Borg suggest that the cost of missing the second-level miss in next-generation systems may be as much as 200 cycles [Jouppi, 1990; Mogul and Borg, 1991]. If these predictions are borne out, the need for programs to have good cache behaviour will be even more important in the future than it is now.

Wilson argues that normal sized main memories are designed to capture the normal components of locality of the mutator but beyond that page faults caused by allocation dominate [Wilson *et al.*, 1992]. The solution is to fit the region of the heap that is most frequently used into the fastest layer available in the memory hierarchy. Thus, real memory should be preferred to the swap disk and the cache should be preferred to real memory. One successful method of partitioning the heap is by generations (see Chapter 7 on page 143). The allocation zone is concentrated into a region of the heap populated by the youngest data. The weak generational hypothesis predicts that frequent collections of the young generations will reclaim sufficient memory to make major collections of the entire heap necessary only occasionally. If the size of the youngest generation is matched to the size of available real memory, page faults will be reduced. In this chapter we shall examine how, and indeed whether, garbage collection algorithms can be tailored to give acceptable cache performance. We shall also investigate whether certain data cache configurations are better matched to garbage collected programs than others.

11.2 Cache architectures

Before we consider the interaction between the cache and dynamic memory management, let us review modern cache configurations. Caches may be used to store both data and instructions. However, most current workstations have separate or *split* instruction and data caches (for example, Digital's DECStations and Hewlett-Packard's PA 9000 series) but some machines have *unified* caches, containing both instructions and data (notably those based on Sun's SPARC processors). Modern machines may feature both primary (level one) and secondary (level two) caches. Primary caches are placed on the CPU chip, but the secondary cache is usually packaged in a separate chip. An exception is Intel's forthcoming P6 processor which packages the secondary cache with the CPU, although on a separate wafer. For the purposes of our discussion, caches may be classified according to size, how blocks are placed in the cache, and what happens on a write.

Cache size

The size of the cache varies between implementations. The on-chip cache of the PowerPC 603 chip used in the Macintosh 5200 range is only 8 kilobytes but Unix workstations commonly have 64-kilobyte caches. Data caches on the Hewlett-Packard's HP 9000/700 range may be as large as 2 megabytes but are typically 256 kilobytes. Common cache configurations are summarised in Table 11.1 on the next page.

Placement policy

Caches are divided into a number of *blocks* or *lines* (see Diagram 11.1). At its simplest, any memory reference to an address not held in a block in the cache causes that block to be fetched from main memory. Each address in main memory is mapped into a cache block. The mapping is usually obtained by ignoring the low- and high-order bits of the address: the low-order bits identify the word or byte in the block rather than the block itself, and the high-order bits are insufficiently random to be an effective hash key. Note that this is a many-to-one mapping: different blocks in main memory will map to the same line in the cache. The high-order bits are compared with the cache block's *tag* to ensure that it does indeed store the contents of the memory block referenced. Each line in the cache also has a *valid bit* that indicates whether the tag is valid or meaningless (for example, if the line is empty).

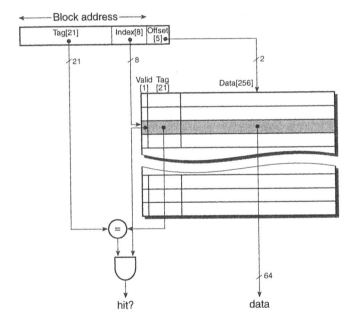

Diagram 11.1   The DEC Alpha AXP 21064 data cache. The 8-kilobyte cache is direct-mapped with 32-byte blocks. The tag field is 21 bits and the index 5. Two bits of the address are used to select the 64-bit word from the data field of the block [Hennessy and Patterson, 1996]. Reproduced by permission of Morgan Kaufman.

Table 11.1 Common cache organisations. Figures are given for primary/secondary caches.

Architecture/System	Split cache?	Write policy	Write-miss policy	Write-buffer depth	Sub-block placement?	Associativity	Block size (words)	Cache size (kilobytes)
DEC DS3100	yes	through	alloc	4	no	1	4	64
DEC DS5000/200	yes	through	alloc	6	4	1	16	64
MIPS R4400	yes	back		1		1	16 or 32	16
MIPS R5000	yes	either		4		2	32	32
DEC DS3000/500	yes		no-alloc/alloc	4	4	1	32	8/512
DEC Alpha 21164	yes/no	through/back	no-alloc	6	no/yes	1/3	32/64	8/96
HP 9000	yes	back	alloc	none	no	1	32	64–2k
SPARCStation 2	no	through	no-alloc	4	no	1	32	64
UltraSPARC	yes	through	no-alloc	8	2	1	32	16
PowerPC 604	yes	back	alloc?	varies	no	4	32	16
PowerPC 620	yes	either	alloc?	varies	no	8	64	32
Intel Pentium Pro	yes/no	back				2/4	32	8/256
Intel Pentium	yes	back	no-alloc			2	32	8

The DECStation 5000/200 actually has a block size of 4 bytes, but misses fetch 4 lines at a time.

The DECStation 3000/500 uses an Alpha 21064 processor.

The MIPS R5000 and the PowerPC 620 allow the cache to be used as write-through or write-back on a per-page or per-block basis.

Block size

Block sizes typically range between 4 and 128 bytes. The size of the block influences both the likelihood of a miss — the miss rate — and the penalty paid for such a miss. If a program has good spatial locality, increasing the size of the block will reduce the miss rate as it will be more likely that subsequent references will be to addresses in the same block. However, if the block size becomes too large in comparison with overall cache size, and thus the number of blocks in the cache becomes too small (the *pollution point*), cache miss rates may again rise. The penalty incurred in fetching a block from main memory is determined by the time to access the block and the time to transfer it. The latency is independent of block size, but the transfer time depends on the block size. There is a performance trade-off to be made between reducing miss ratios by increasing block size, and increased penalties when a miss does occur.

Associativity

Cache memory can be thought of as associative memory. If a cache were *fully associative* then any block of main memory could be held in any block of the cache. Unfortunately, searching a fully associative cache for a particular block would either be slow or require expensive parallel hardware. Fully associative memory is usually reserved for smaller units, such as the virtual memory subsystem's translation lookaside buffers.

Most caches today are *direct-mapped* — each block of main memory is mapped to a single position in the cache. Although direct-mapped caches are simpler to build and faster to search, they may be more prone to conflicts as frequently used blocks of memory map to the same line in the cache.

Set-associative caches are a compromise between fully associative and direct-mapped caches. Here the cache is divided into *sets*, each of which can contain several blocks; typically two- or four-way sets are used. Blocks of main memory are mapped to a single set (as for a direct mapped cache) but may be placed anywhere within that set. Searching the cache for a particular block requires the tags of the blocks in just one set to be examined. If the search does not reveal the required block, a block in the set is replaced with one fetched from main memory.

Write strategy

As we shall see later, garbage collected programs appear to be particularly sensitive to the way write misses are handled. The cache's behaviour on a write miss is characterised by two design decisions.

Write-through or copy-back

The first is where to send data when a write *hit* occurs. There are two possibilities. A *write-through* cache causes the data to be written to both the block in the cache and the block in the lower level of the memory hierarchy (either main memory or a further level of cache). A *copy-back* (or *write-back*) cache buffers data in the cache block, only flushing it back to the next level when a cache miss forces the replacement of that block. As it is not necessary to write a block back on a miss to the next level of the memory hierarchy if it has not been altered, a *dirty bit* is often associated with each cache block to indicate whether the block has been modified in the cache or not.

Both techniques have their advantages. Copy-back uses less memory bus bandwidth since multiple writes to a single cache block require only the last write to be transferred to the lower level. On the other hand, misses do not cause a block to be displaced from a write-through cache. In particular, read misses do not cause information to be written back to the next level when the block is replaced in the cache since the write has already occurred: the assumption is that reads are more common than writes. It is possible to avoid stalling the CPU while it waits for a write to complete by using a *write-buffer*. The depth of the write-buffer — the number of blocks it can hold — typically varies between four and eight.

Fetch-on-write or write-around

The second decision is whether a block should be allocated in the cache when a write *miss* occurs. *Write-allocate* (or *fetch-on-write*) caches fetch the block into the cache and then treat it as a write hit. *Write-no-allocate* (or *write-around*) caches do not fetch the block into the cache but modify it in the next level of memory. Typically copy-back caches use write-allocate, and write-though caches use write-no-allocate. Table 11.2 shows typical penalties for cache misses [Hennessy and Patterson, 1996].

Table 11.2 Typical cache characteristics [Hennessy and Patterson, 1996]. Reproduced by permission of Morgan Kaufman.

	Level one	*Level two*
Hit time	1–2 cycles	6–15 cycles
Miss penalty	8–66 cycles	30–200 cycles
Miss rate	0.5–20 percent	15–30 percent
Block size	4–32 bytes	32–256 bytes
Cache size	1–128 kilobytes	256–16k kilobytes

Hit time is normally one cycle for the level one cache.

Sub-block placement

The cost of fetching large blocks can be avoided by using *sub-block placement* with direct-mapped, write-through caches. A cache is said to have sub-block placement if a single cache block can be divided into sub-blocks (typically four bytes), each of which has an associated valid bit. The block is no longer the smallest unit of transfer between the cache and main memory, but is the unit associated with an address tag. Whenever a write occurs, the information is written to the sub-block (turning the valid bit on) and through to the next level of memory. If this write would have been a miss, the other sub-blocks in this line are now invalid. They may be either allocated by turning their valid bits off or fetched from memory (for a write-allocate cache) without stalling the CPU. Sub-block placement reduces the cost of writes to one cycle. Read misses on the other hand typically cause the entire block to be fetched.

A *write-validate* policy is equivalent to write-allocate with sub-block placement using one-word sub-blocks. This technique can also avoid fetching memory blocks if every word is written before it is read. Although write-validate can improve the performance of C and Fortran programs [Jouppi, 1993], it has been found to be particularly significant for copying garbage collection. We discuss this further in Section 11.5.

Special cache instructions

A final design possibility is software control of the operation of the cache. Peng and Sohi suggested a special allocate instruction to hint to the cache that it need not bother fetching a block since its contents will be overwritten immediately [Peng and Sohi, 1989]. A similar instruction is provided in higher-end HP 9000 processors. As well as being useful for linear allocation in a compacted heap, as we shall see, this instruction has applications for clearing or copying virtual memory pages (for instance when a parent process forks a child). To the same end, the instruction set of the IBM RS6000 family of processors includes a cache control instruction to allocate and zero a cache line. This too can be used to avoid allocation write misses.

11.3   Patterns of memory access

The effectiveness of the memory hierarchy rests upon certain assumptions about typical patterns of memory access. The strategies at both the virtual memory level and the cache level are similar. The goal of the virtual memory sub-system designer is to ensure that page frames are filled with those pages that are most likely to be used next. Likewise the goal of the cache designer is to fill cache lines with those blocks of main memory that are likely to be used next. The underlying assumption of both systems is that data accesses are typically concentrated on a small subset of the address space of the program or set of programs — the *working set* [Denning, 1968]. It is further assumed that the best estimator for the page or block likely to be touched next is the set of pages already resident in main memory, or the set of blocks already held in the cache. In other words, the spatial proximity of data in memory predicts the temporal proximity of access by the program. Furthermore, the memory hierarchy's replacement algorithms may assume temporal locality. The virtual memory system usually evicts the least recently used (LRU) page when loading a new page, and set-associative caches may also adopt an LRU replacement policy.

If programs do indeed exhibit temporal and spatial locality, such a memory hierarchy, with LRU replacement policies, is effective. But do garbage collected programs, including programs that use compacted heaps (linear allocation, see below in this section), share these locality properties? At first sight, it seems that tracing garbage collection must violate these assumptions. In general, it has necessarily poor spatial and temporal locality since, in its simplest non-generational forms, a tracing collector must visit every active node of the data structure at each collection as its notion of liveness is based on pointer reachability. In order to examine whether garbage collection necessarily interacts poorly with the cache, we shall first classify the typical access patterns of the allocators and collectors. We shall then try to predict how these patterns affect the cache and see whether our predictions are borne out in practice.

Mark-sweep with bitmap and lazy sweep

The memory access pattern of mark-sweep garbage collection depends on its implementation. If a simple collector is used, references to the heap made by the allocator are likely to consist of random reads and writes. The pattern of access is likely to be more predictable if more sophisticated techniques, such as segregated free-lists, mark bitmaps and lazy sweeping (described in Chapter 4), and generational methods (described in Chapter 7) are employed.

The mark phase

The marking phase typically uses a stack to remember branch points (the alternative is to use the pointer reversal technique described in Chapter 4) and a bitmap to mark objects, and accesses heap data to trace pointers. References to the stack are highly localised, for both reads and writes. References to the mark bitmap are also likely to have comparatively good spatial locality, particularly if a two-level organisation is used and the phase behaviour of programs means that objects of the same type, and hence likely to be of the same size, are allocated together. Tracing the graph, on the other hand, generates random but read-only accesses to objects in the heap. If the heap is organised generationally, the range of the references can be constrained to some extent to a limited region of the heap. The overall pattern of access for mark-sweep garbage collection is therefore one of random reads and highly localised writes [Zorn, 1991].

Allocation

If lazy sweep is used, the sweep phase of mark-sweep garbage collection counts against allocation. In any case, the access pattern of the sweep is one of highly sequential reads and writes to mark bits. Using first-fit allocation with separate free-lists for each common object size, the allocation pattern is one of sequential, initialising writes.

Copying garbage collection

We now turn to the behaviour of programs using copying garbage collection. Copying garbage collection compacts the heap (or at least compacts each region of the heap in the case of generational garbage collection). The consequence for the allocator is that allocation is linear — the next object allocated will be placed adjacent to the object last allocated. This has significant implications for the spatial locality of programs.

Copying

A copying garbage collector must scan objects in the grey (copied but not yet updated) region of Tospace. Each pointer-valued word in this region must be read and then updated, causing a pattern of sequential reads and writes. The forwarding address of the Fromspace object to which the pointer refers must also be read. If the Fromspace object has not been copied, the object must be copied to Tospace and its forwarding address updated. Thus, for each live object in Fromspace, the pattern is a read to a random location possibly followed by a write (the forwarding address), and then sequential reads in Fromspace and sequential writes in Tospace (to copy the object). If a Fromspace word is accessed, it is highly likely that its successors will be read too, since most objects are not shared [Clark and Green, 1977; Stoye *et al.*, 1984; Hartel, 1988].

References to Tospace, on the other hand, are concentrated at the address pointed to by `scan` (for read and write) and at the address pointed to by `free` (for write). After a word has been scanned and updated (blackened), it will not be touched by the garbage collector again in this collection cycle. Baker suggests that black data is a good candidate for replacement should it be necessary [Baker, 1991].

Note that, for simplicity, we have ignored the possibility of 'copying' large objects by remapping virtual memory [Moon, 1984]. We have assumed that references to Fromspace are distributed randomly although clustering of objects may increase locality [Hayes, 1991; Hayes, 1993]. We have also ignored the regrouping strategies, discussed in Chapter 6, whose goal was to place related data together on the assumption that the mutator's proximity of access to them would be close. If this strategy were to be successful, the pattern of accesses to Fromspace would be less random than would otherwise be the case.

Allocation

Linear allocation is particularly simple and makes a highly predictable pattern of accesses to Tospace: a sequence of initialising writes. However, it is not uncommon for systems supported by garbage collection to have very high rates of allocation. Computer architects commonly assume that writes are comparatively rare, typically accounting for less than 10 per cent of all instructions executed [Hennessy and Patterson, 1996]. However, the proportion of writes executed by SML/NJ programs has been found to be between 10 and 25 percent, and the overwhelming majority of these writes (up to 96 percent) are due to allocation [Diwan *et al.*, 1994; Gonçalves and Appel, 1995]. Furthermore, copying garbage collection leads to a 'back and forth' pattern of allocation across the two semi-spaces. This pattern may work against the replacement policies of both the virtual memory system and the cache. Thus although linear allocation may be cheap in terms of instructions executed by the allocator itself, it is potentially expensive in cycles.

Incremental garbage collection

Intuition may suggest that incremental garbage collection will worsen the data cache miss rate since it will finely intermingle mutator and collector references. This could be expected to lead to a greater proportion of conflicts as data accessed by the mutator and by the collector are mapped to the same cache line. However, there is some evidence that this is not so [Zorn, 1989]. The style and granularity of incremental collection will also be significant. Read-barriers trap mutator access so the collector will process the same data that the mutator is currently using. This effect is weakened if the granularity of the read-barrier is a page, as it is for some incremental copying collectors that rely on support from the operating system's memory protection system. Write-barriers like Dijkstra's and Steele's, that are not based on virtual memory support, behave similarly to some extent as they similarly mark data subject to mutator writes. Some incremental copying collectors are also designed to improve locality by clustering objects in Tospace according to how they are referenced by the mutator [Courts, 1988]. We are not aware of any studies that have measured the performance of these garbage collectors at the cache level.

Avoiding fetches

For both the mark-sweep and copying styles of garbage collection, existing data stored at a memory location that is about to be allocated is garbage, and thus should be neither paged into main memory nor loaded into the cache. At the level of the virtual memory system, we saw in Chapter 6 that this can be accomplished either by closely coupling the garbage collector with the operating system [Moon, 1984], or by using system calls to 'disclaim' pages of memory [Wang, 1994a]. At the level of the cache, we require a write-miss policy that will allow the collector to allocate new data in the cache without stalling the processor. Preferably the block corresponding to that address should not be fetched from main memory. If the lifetime of this new object is sufficiently short, it may live and die without leaving the cache.

11.4   Standard ways to improve cache performance

Cache performance can be improved in three ways: by reducing the cache miss rate, by reducing the miss penalty, or by reducing the time to hit in the cache [Hennessy and Patterson, 1996]. Conventional programs tend to exhibit a strong locality of reference and data caches are designed to capture this locality. In this section we examine how garbage collection in a garbage collected world affects locality and hence data cache miss rates. In particular we ask how linear allocation affects miss rates. A number of techniques for reducing miss rates are well known. These include the use of larger caches, increasing the size of cache blocks, increasing associativity or prefetching blocks from memory. The miss penalty can be reduced by the use of sub-block placement, second-level caches and other techniques.

Cache size

It is known that increasing cache size reduces miss rates of instruction caches, data caches and unified caches for conventional programs [Hennessy and Patterson, 1996]. For example, Table 11.3 on the following page shows the miss rates for a direct-mapped data cache on the DECStation 5000 for an average of SPEC92 benchmarks [Gee *et al.*, 1993].

Zorn confirms these findings for a range of Lisp programs supported by generational mark-

Table 11.3   Data cache miss rates for the SPEC92 benchmark suite on a DECStation 5000 [Gee *et al.*, 1993]. The cache is direct-mapped with a block-size of 32 bytes.

Cache size (kilobytes)	Miss rate (percent)
1	24·61
2	20·57
4	15·94
8	10·19
16	6·47
32	4·82
64	3·77
128	2·88

sweep garbage collection: caches larger than 512 kilobytes performed substantially better than smaller ones [Zorn, 1991]. Increasing cache size significantly reduced miss rates until the cache was sufficiently large to allow garbage collected programs to 'fit' well. This fit can be achieved by varying the size of the allocation threshold. Rather than assigning a fixed-size region of the heap to the youngest generation and collecting when the region is full, Zorn's collector is invoked when the volume of data allocated since the last collection passes a threshold (see Chapter 4). Each doubling of the size of the cache caused the cache miss rate to be reduced by approximately 1 percent, until a cache of two megabytes almost eliminated cache misses (fewer than 1 percent of memory references missed the cache) provided that the allocation threshold was less than 500 kilobytes.

Diagram 11.2 on the next page shows the overall miss rates (both read and write misses) for Zorn's generational mark-sweep collector against various sizes of direct-mapped cache. The programs are compilers for Lisp and Prolog, written in Common Lisp. Zorn found that the cache performance of the collector was particularly sensitive to the size of the allocation threshold relative to the size of the cache. With a 512-kilobyte cache, the miss rate for the Lisp compiler was three times lower for a 128-kilobyte allocation threshold than it was for a 2-megabyte threshold. The 'knees' in the graphs for the Prolog compiler illustrate particularly clearly how miss rates can be sharply reduced by matching the size of the allocation threshold and the cache.

Similar results are to be expected for copying garbage collection. Wilson *et al.* likewise emphasise the importance of matching the size of the creation region to the size of the data cache for generational copying collectors [Wilson *et al.*, 1992]. Linear allocation's cyclic reuse of space marches the allocation zone through both semi-spaces, which means that the next block of the creation region to be allocated will be precisely the block least recently allocated. Although the cache does not use the same LRU replacement policies as the virtual memory, if the cache is smaller than the creation region, this block is also the one most likely

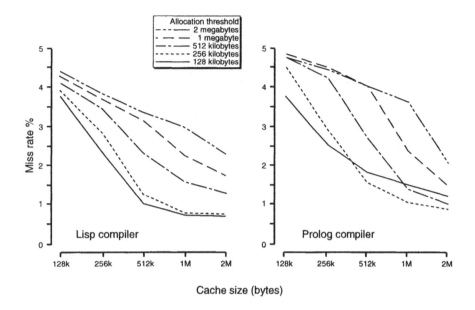

Diagram 11.2 Cache miss rate *vs.* allocation threshold for two large Common Lisp programs. Both programs used mark-sweep collection, and the cache was direct-mapped [Zorn, 1991]. The graphs show the results for a 46,500 line commercial Common Lisp compiler (left) and a much smaller Prolog compiler for a RISC architecture (right). Reproduced with permission.

to have been purged from the cache. Two features of copying garbage collection make matters even worse. First, increasing the size of the cache (or reducing the size of the creation region) should have no effect on caching behaviour until the cache is large enough to hold the reuse queue, i.e. until it can contain both semi-spaces. Second, the write-back rate for copying garbage collection will be worse than that of mark-sweep collection since live data in the heap is dirtied by the collector as it writes forwarding addresses and updates pointers. Mark-sweep collection in contrast does not need to write to heap data at all if a separate bitmap is used for marking.

Gonçalves and Appel confirm these predictions, using Reppy's multi-generational copying collector for SML/NJ [Reppy, 1993]. Diagram 11.3 on the following page shows write-miss rates for a direct-mapped cache [Gonçalves and Appel, 1995]. Again, the write-miss rate increases dramatically once the creation space is larger than the cache. However, although Zorn and Diwan *et al.* found that increasing cache size was beneficial, the benefit was less pronounced than it was for mark-sweep. Other techniques, such as sub-block placement, were more effective [Zorn, 1991; Diwan *et al.*, 1994]. Zorn also found that the miss rates for generational copying collection were consistently higher than those for generational mark-sweep collection. The overall miss rate for copying collection was often twice as high as, and sometimes four times higher than, that for mark-sweep collection. In contrast to mark-sweep

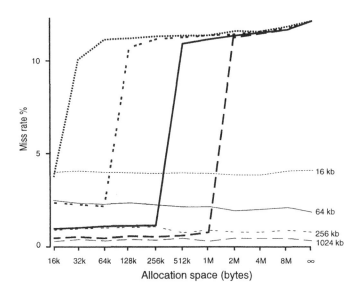

Diagram 11.3   Read and write miss rates *vs.* size of allocation space, for various sizes of direct-mapped data cache [Gonçalves and Appel, 1995]. Write-misses are drawn more boldly than read-misses. FPCA'95, ©1995 Association for Computing Machinery. Reprinted by permission.

collection, varying the allocation threshold had little effect on overall miss rates for copying collection.

Differences in the handling of the youngest generation and reporting of miss rates may explain the discrepancies between the Zorn and the Gonçalves and Appel findings for generational stop-and-copy collection. Two points are worthy of note. First, Reppy's collector used a single 512-kilobyte creation space for the youngest generation, rather than two semi-spaces or an allocation threshold. Zorn points out that use of an allocation threshold, rather than a fixed-size youngest generation, causes the size of the semi-spaces to vary depending on how much data survives a collection. Thus he argues that no single cache size will hold all semi-spaces. If a space grows to the extent that it does not fit in the cache, many conflict misses will arise.

Second, and in contrast to Zorn, Gonçalves and Appel separate write misses from read misses. The effect of cache size on read-miss rates was less sharply pronounced: the miss rate declined smoothly as cache size increased, reflecting the more random pattern of read accesses of mostly functional programs and copying garbage collection. We speculate that this separation of read misses from write misses may be significant. The data for their set of benchmarks show that reads accounted for approximately 23 percent of all instructions whereas writes accounted for 18 percent. This proportion of reads to writes is much lower than that found by Hennessy and Patterson for five SPECint92 programs, where reads similarly accounted for 26 percent of all instructions but writes accounted for only 9 percent [Hennessy and Patterson, 1996]. If both read and write misses are taken into account then the prominent plateau in the Gonçalves and Appel graphs is less pronounced (although still present). If the read:write ratio of Lisp lies somewhere between that of the SPECint92 programs and the SML programs, then the dominance of reads over writes will further mask the sharp knee predicted by Wilson *et al.* and found by Gonçalves and Appel.

However, matching the size of the cache to the size of the creation region means either expanding the cache or shrinking the creation region. We saw in Chapter 7 that reducing the size of the youngest generation diminishes garbage collection pause times but risks earlier promotion. At the virtual memory and cache level, the effect of promotion is to spread the program's working set across more generations. Furthermore, the volume of tenured garbage and the write-barrier overhead will also tend to increase as there may be more old–young pointers. These factors will tend to decrease the mutator's locality of reference and in particular to increase the rate of conflict misses. The problem of cache behaviour does not disappear even if the youngest generation fits inside the cache. There will still be a proportion of references to older generation data and this may range from negligible to significant. These effects were particularly noticeable for Zorn's mark-sweep collector when very small thresholds of 128 kilobytes or less were used with direct-mapped caches since the mark-sweep algorithm's *en masse* promotion policy increased the amount of promoted garbage substantially compared to the generational copying algorithm. Dilution of locality was also noticeable in programs in which a significant proportion of memory references were to objects outside the generation scheme. For example, references to Lisp system objects have been observed to account for up to 28 percent of all data references [Zorn, 1989].

Block size

The second standard method for reducing miss rates is to increase block size. Increasing block size improves miss rate by taking advantage of the spatial locality of programs. Both mark-sweep and copying garbage collection algorithms make sequential, and hence highly predictable, access to certain data structures. Mark-sweep collectors typically use a stack to control the trace, and make a sequential sweep either through the heap or through a mark bitmap. Copying collectors scan the grey region of Tospace linearly to update pointers, and both allocation and evacuation into Tospace are performed linearly. Hence it is not surprising that increasing block size has been found to lead to reduced miss rates [Diwan *et al.*, 1994; Koopman *et al.*, 1992; Wilson *et al.*, 1992]. The benefit is particularly pronounced for write-miss rates (see Diagram 11.4 on the next page).

Associativity

The third technique for reducing conflict miss rates is to increase the associativity of the cache. However, Zorn found that two- and four-way set-associative caches gave little performance gain over direct-mapped caches for mark-sweep collection [Zorn, 1991]. He suggests that this is because few collisions will arise once the cache is large enough to hold the allocation space. Since newly allocated objects remain in the same position in the new space until they are promoted (and this is rare according to the weak generational hypothesis), conflicts will only be between objects in the youngest and older generations. As older generations tend to

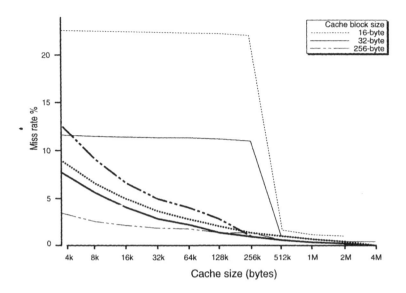

Diagram 11.4 Miss rate *vs.* cache size for different block sizes [Gonçalves and Appel, 1995]. The graphs for the read miss rates are drawn heavier than those for write misses. The cache is direct-mapped, write-allocate, and the creation space is 512 kilobytes. FPCA'95, ©1995 Association for Computing Machinery. Reprinted by permission.

be very much larger than the youngest generation, the site of such conflicts will be random rather than systematic and hence will be less comprehensively controlled by set-associativity.

Similarly, set-associative caches offered little benefit for copying garbage collection if the cache was smaller than the allocation threshold. The cyclic reuse of semi-spaces leads to a large number of conflicts and set-associativity's LRU replacement policy tended to evict most objects before they were reused. Equally, caches gained less from increased associativity if they were sufficiently large to accommodate both semi-spaces. On the other hand, Zorn found that increasing set-associativity reduced miss rates substantially for mid-range cache sizes. The miss rate of a two-way set-associative cache was often half that of a direct-mapped cache and sometimes five times lower.

Zorn's generational copying collector used an allocation threshold to trigger collection rather than a fixed-size creation space. Results from studies of generational copying collectors that used other organisations show different results for increasing the cache's associativity. Results for Scheme-48 and SML/NJ obtained by Wilson *et al.* and by Gonçalves and Appel, respectively, suggest that the miss rates suffered by direct-mapped caches are lower than those suffered by set-associative caches of the same capacity, provided that the size of the cache approximates the size of the creation region [Wilson *et al.*, 1992; Gonçalves and Appel, 1995]. Otherwise the miss rates of direct-mapped caches were higher than those of their set-associative counterparts. Wilson *et al.* presume that this is because at this critical point a direct-mapped cache is able to keep most of creation space in the cache, whereas the LRU policy of set-associative caches tends to evict the next block to be written. Furthermore, higher associativity leads to higher miss ratios.

Outside this sweet spot, both Wilson *et al.* and Gonçalves and Appel found that two- or four-way set-associativity improved miss rates significantly, especially for reads, since it eliminated many conflicts between objects in the creation region and older generations. Four-way associativity was sufficient to eliminate most conflicts in a seven-generation collector, and higher associativities gave comparatively little further benefit. As the size of the cache was increased, the misses suffered by set-associative caches quickly approached the compulsory miss rate as there was room in the cache for older generation blocks without evicting creation-space blocks. Direct-mapped caches, on the other hand, continued to suffer conflict misses even after the capacity misses abated. Conversely, if the cache were smaller than the creation space, set-associative caches suffered fewer conflict misses than direct-mapped ones. Unfortunately one drawback of increasing the associativity of the cache may be to increase the processor's cycle time, and so these gains may not be realised in practice [Hill, 1988]. As a cheaper alternative, Wilson has suggested that the rate of inter-generational conflicts might be reduced by splitting the cache using one high-order bit as well as the low-order bits for cache line indexing [Wilson *et al.*, 1991].

Special instructions

If the cache is very small, it may be impractical to restrict the size of the allocation space to the size of the cache in order to avoid allocation write misses. Eight- or sixteen-kilobyte primary caches are not uncommon (see Table 11.1 on page 281). To set allocation thresholds, or the size of the creation regions, so low would mean increasing the frequency of minor collections and hence increasing the garbage collection overhead. Appel and others have shown that it is possible to use special cache control instructions to avoid allocation write misses [Appel and Shao, 1994; Gonçalves and Appel, 1995]. If the allocator attempts to initialise a block not held in the cache, a write-miss will occur. A write-allocate cache will handle the miss by first fetching the block into the cache and then treating it as a write-hit. Unless some strategy like sub-block placement or early restart is used, the processor may be stalled until this read completes (although many architectures allow certain instructions to be issued and complete while reads are outstanding) [Hennessy and Patterson, 1996].

However, it is unnecessary to fetch the block's data from memory since it will be overwritten before it is read. There are two ways to achieve this with special cache control instructions. The HP PA7100 instruction set includes a cache control hint that a block will be overwritten before it is read, thus avoiding the read when the write misses. Processors such as the IBM Power and Motorola PowerPC provide an instruction to allocate and/or zero a specified cache line. When the heap is allocated linearly, the allocation pointer `free` marches linearly through a direct-mapped cache. If the next line to be allocated is reserved in advance, then the write miss will not occur. This can be achieved by having the compiler insert a cache control instruction to allocate and zero the line containing the address `free + k`, for some suitable `k`, whenever the free space pointer `free` is incremented.

Prefetching

Machines that allow the cache to be directly controlled by software are uncommon. However, it is possible to allocate a cache line in a write-no-allocate cache simply by reading the block. If the result of the read is not required immediately, the read will not stall the processor on many architectures: instructions that do not involve memory accesses may still be issued and completed. For example, the DEC Alpha 21164 processor can accommodate up to six memory references that are waiting to complete without stalling. Thus in the same way as the cache control hint could be used in the RS6000, an instruction can be issued by the compiler to read from the address `free + k` whenever `free` is incremented. The read will have completed without stalling the processor by the time that this address is used for allocation. Koopman *et al.* found that by inserting dummy memory reads, whose results were immediately discarded, before allocating groups of cells, the overall performance of their TIGRE combinator graph reducer could be increased by 20 percent on a VAX 8800, despite the overhead of executing extra instructions [Koopman *et al.*, 1992]. Similar improvements were found by Gonçalves and Appel for SML/NJ on a DECStation 3000/400 and rather smaller improvements (4.5 percent decrease in cycles) by Necula for a more recent version of SML/NJ on a DECStation 3000/600.

11.5   Miss rate and overall cache performance

Most studies of the effect of garbage collection on cache performance have been made in the context of Lisp and mainly functional languages. Most of these studies measured the level of cache misses with cache simulators such as *tycho* [Hill, 1987]. Zorn considered the effects of different cache configurations in the context of large Lisp programs, Wilson *et al.* and Reinhold studied Scheme, Koopman *et al.* measured a combinator graph reducer, and Diwan *et al.*, Appel and Shao, and Gonçalves and Appel investigated SML/NJ [Zorn, 1990b; Zorn, 1991; Wilson *et al.*, 1992; Reinhold, 1994; Koopman *et al.*, 1992; Diwan *et al.*, 1994; Appel and Shao, 1994; Gonçalves and Appel, 1995]. The methodologies used in these studies differ in important respects. Some studies separated read and write misses, others simply counted overall misses; some measured miss rate, others overall performance. We have already noted that styles of programming typically supported by garbage collection exhibit a much higher write rate than conventional programming languages, and that most of these writes are due to allocation. Ignoring differences between the behaviour of reads and writes, or between miss rate and CPI, may lead to a distorted view of cache performance. Actual performance does not simply depend on miss rates: the penalty incurred by misses is also important. Real understanding of the interaction between the memory management and cache strategies must come from analysis of overall performance.

At first sight it appears that garbage collected programs are more likely to interact poorly with the cache than other programs. There are several reasons why this supposition might initially seem attractive.

- Functional and object-oriented programs make more prodigious use of the heap than their conventional counterparts. If the locality of reference to the heap is poorer than it is to stack-allocated data, then programs that make heavier use of the heap should be expected to have poorer cache performance than those that make lighter use of it.

- Functional languages, at least, have high write rates whereas conventional cache designs assume that writes are comparatively uncommon. The performance of programs written in a functional style will be more affected by penalties incurred by cache write misses than those programs with a lower write rate.
- Copying garbage collectors' cyclic use of two semi-spaces may lead to a high rate of cache misses. As we saw above, Wilson *et al.* argue that if the cache is smaller than this frequently reused area then the size of this reuse cycle will defeat caching strategies [Wilson *et al.*, 1992].
- Processors more commonly use direct-mapped rather than set-associative caches (although this appears to be changing). Semi-space allocation may lead to an increase in the number of conflict misses as addresses in each semi-space map to the same cache line.

However, these conjectures assume that higher miss rates necessarily lead to poorer performance. Depending on the design of the cache, this may not be so. We saw in Section 11.2 on page 279 that there are several ways of reducing the penalties for write misses. Several researchers have found that overall miss rates and the performance of rapidly-allocating garbage-collected systems are better than the simplistic expectations above would indicate.

Wilson *et al.* found the capacity miss cost to be only 1.6 percent for Scheme-48, a byte-coded implementation with a generational copying garbage collector, running on a DECStation 5000/200, although they predicted that this cost would rise as CPUs became faster and second-level cache miss penalties rise [Wilson *et al.*, 1992]. Reinhold also found a cache overhead for Scheme of less than 5 percent, again on a DECStation 5000/200, leading him to conclude that many programs written in a functional style, supported by simple linear allocation, are naturally well-suited to direct-mapped caches even without garbage collection [Reinhold, 1994]. Gonçalves and Appel found similarly good cache performance for a suite of SML/NJ programs [Gonçalves and Appel, 1995]. With direct-mapped, write-allocate caches, they found that the ML programs they measured sometimes had a lower overall miss rate than those of the SPEC92 benchmarks.

Why should these programs show good performance with linear allocation even when run on processors with direct-mapped caches? First of all, although the programs exhibited high write rates (particularly SML/NJ) and the caches were write-through, the DEC machines' deep write-buffers were able to absorb the write traffic without stalling the CPU [Koopman *et al.*, 1992; Diwan *et al.*, 1994; Reinhold, 1994; Gonçalves and Appel, 1995]. With a functional style of programming and copying garbage collection, most writes will be allocation writes, and these writes will be bunched as they correspond to the initialisation of newly allocated objects [Diwan *et al.*, 1994]. Write-validate caches (that is, write-allocate with sub-block placement using one-word sub-blocks) can avoid fetching blocks from memory on a write miss. The write-miss penalty for allocation is thus reduced to zero. This organisation solves the problem of initialising write misses, although sub-block placement does not take advantage of any spatial locality when a read misses the cache. There is also evidence that it is unlikely that these newly allocated blocks will be evicted from the cache before they are read. Gonçalves and Appel found that more than 50 percent of reads were to newly allocated objects less than 64 words from the allocation pointer [Gonçalves and Appel, 1995]. Diwan *et al.* found write-validate to be the *most* significant cache design decision in achieving low cache overheads. It consistently out-performed all other configurations, giving a reduction in cycles per instruction of around a sixth for both direct mapped and two-way associative caches [Diwan *et al.*, 1994; Koopman *et al.*, 1992]. A six-deep write-buffer combined with page-mode writes also helped to absorb bursty writes.

If the penalty incurred by write-misses can be reduced substantially then the benefits of employing strategies described in the previous section to reduce the miss rate should be slight. Measurements by Gonçalves and Appel suggest that this is indeed so. For example, the effect of tuning the size of the allocation region for SML/NJ to the size of the cache on the DECStation 5000 was very small, and largely offset by changes in garbage collection overhead (since varying the size of the allocation space varies the frequency of minor collections). On the other hand, for machines that do incur a penalty for write misses, they found that reducing the size of the allocation space to fit the cache could improve performance even though this would increase collection overheads. Reducing the frequency of major collections to compensate for more frequent minor collections further improved performance.

Direct-mapped caches allocate memory blocks by using their lower-order bits to index cache lines. Linear allocation therefore sweeps through the direct-mapped cache. If most objects have very short life-times, they will be dead by the time their cache block is reused for new data, provided that the cache is large enough — the primary caches investigated by Reinhold varied in size between 32 kilobytes and 4 megabytes. He argues it is important not to disturb the allocator's sweep through the direct-mapped cache, from one end to the other. Objects should be afforded the longest possible time to die; linear allocation and infrequent collection spreads objects spatially and temporally throughout the heap; and most objects live and die entirely within the cache. In his words, 'a program written in a mostly-functional style rides the allocation wave, just as a surfer rides an ocean wave'. Long-lived and frequently referenced data may interfere with this pattern, but Reinhold argues that these are rare in programs written in a functional style [Reinhold, 1994]. However, today's machines do not have such large primary caches. It is not clear, for example, that a program's working set could be accommodated within an eight- or sixteen-kilobyte cache without suffering a high rate of capacity misses.

11.6 Special purpose hardware

So far we have considered only conventional cache designs. However, an alternative is to tailor the hardware architecture to support languages that make heavy use of an automatically managed heap. In this section we briefly mention two special-purpose hardware architectures designed in part to improve the cache performance of such languages.

Gehringer and Chang use a co-processor as a second-level cache [Gehringer and Chang, 1993]. The co-processor allocates objects in its cache and manages them with reference counting — an idea first suggested by Peng and Sohi [Peng and Sohi, 1989]. Gehringer's and Chang's simulation studies show that the co-processor can remove up to 70 percent of objects before they age out of the cache, saving a similar amount of bus traffic [Chang and Gehringer, 1993a; Chang and Gehringer, 1993b]. Tracing garbage collection is still necessary, for instance to collect cycles, but reference counting extends the collection interval by approximately 60 percent.

The MUSHROOM architecture is a classical RISC architecture extended with features designed to support dynamic object-oriented languages, such as tagged memory [Williams and Wolczko, 1990; Wolczko and Williams, 1993]. Memory is seen as a fine-grained segmented store, with each segment containing a single object rather than a contiguous address space of words. The primary garbage collector is a generational copying collector with the data cache acting as the youngest generation. This collector is backed up by an incremental, on-the-fly collector in main memory. A particularly elegant feature of this architecture is that the cache/memory boundary acts as a barrier for both collectors. It is a write-barrier for the generational collector and a read-barrier for the incremental collector. The cache is also software-visible: this can be used to avoid redundant bus traffic when allocating objects directly into free cache lines. To avoid mutator/collector cache conflicts, a portion of the cache is dedicated to the collector.

11.7   Issues to consider

We conclude this chapter by summarising the evidence. The functional programming style, in which the overwhelming majority of writes are initialising, combined with linear allocation, appears to result in acceptable cache performance providing the write-miss penalty is negligible. An appropriate architecture might be a large direct-mapped cache, with sub-block placement and a deep write-buffer; caches larger than one megabyte perform particularly well. Such configurations are starting to become available.

If the write-miss penalty is not negligible, the LRU behaviour of copying garbage collection may lead to a high write-miss rate. To avoid this, it is important to match the size of the cache with the size of the youngest generation. Increasing set-associativity to two-way or four-way is effective in dealing with conflict misses, including those between addresses in different generations. Larger block sizes are effective since many garbage collected programs have strong spatial locality. In particular, both the sweep phase of mark-sweep collection and copying collection's scan of the grey region of Tospace make strongly sequential references to the heap. A miss that brings a block into the cache has the side-effect of also loading many other locations that are likely to be accessed soon.

There is evidence that the miss rate of generational mark-sweep garbage collection is lower than that of generational stop-and-copy collection, but published results have only measured overall miss rate; read- and write-misses have not been distinguished, nor has overall performance been measured. Incremental copying collection has a similar cache performance to stop-and-copy collection.

Finally, some researchers have speculated that, far from having an adverse effect on cache performance, programs supported by garbage collection — and particularly mostly functional programs — may have better cache performance, at least for some cache configurations, than conventional programs. Zorn speculates that programs using a generational, highly localised garbage collector may perform better than those with no garbage collection by reusing small areas of space efficiently. In this way the spatial locality of the mutator, and hence its cache performance, might be improved [Zorn, 1991]. Reinhold also notes that, if the cache has a significant effect on performance, a mostly functional style may be more appropriate than the imperative style of programming since updates are comparatively rare, the working set is small, and linear allocation is well-suited to direct-mapped caches with negligible write-miss penalties [Reinhold, 1994]. As the gulf between the relative speeds of processors and main memory continues to widen, and caches play an ever more significant role in guaranteeing overall performance, these arguments may become increasingly powerful.

Gonçalves and Appel offer some evidence to support these conjectures [Gonçalves and Appel, 1995]. Comparisons of a set of small-to-medium size SML/NJ programs with the SPEC92 benchmarks on a direct-mapped, write-allocate cache show the ML programs to have significantly better overall miss rates in very small caches (less than sixteen kilobytes). Providing block size was sufficiently large (64 bytes or more), the miss rates of the SML/NJ programs and those of the SPEC92 benchmarks were broadly similar regardless of cache size [Gonçalves and Appel, 1995].

11.8 Notes

General studies of cache memory design can be found in [Hennessy and Patterson, 1996; Przybylski, 1990]. Most of the studies here used Mark Hill's *tycho* memory subsystem simulator [Hill, 1987]. Diwan *et al.* extended the simulator with a write-buffer simulator [Diwan *et al.*, 1994].

Benjamin Zorn studied the cache behaviour of large Lisp programs in several papers. [Zorn, 1989; Zorn, 1990b] concentrate on comparing the behaviour of generational mark-sweep and generational copying collectors whereas [Zorn, 1991] investigates the effect of different cache parameters more generally. Paul Wilson, Michael Lam and Thomas Moher, and Mark Reinhold simulated different caches in the context of large Scheme programs [Wilson *et al.*, 1992; Reinhold, 1994]. Simulations of the cache behaviour of SML/NJ by Andrew Appel and Zhong Shao, Amer Diwan, David Tarditi and Eliot Moss, and Andrew Appel and Marcelo Gonçalves can be found in [Appel and Shao, 1994; Diwan *et al.*, 1994; Gonçalves and Appel, 1995] respectively. Philip Koopman, Peter Lee and Daniel Siewiorek measured the cache performance for the TIGRE threaded-code combinator-graph reducer [Koopman *et al.*, 1989; Koopman *et al.*, 1992]. They were the first to note the importance of write-validate caches and pre-fetching for linearly allocating programs. However, their results must be treated with some caution, since their benchmark programs were very small and only one allocated enough data to invoke the garbage collector.

The first suggestion that a co-processor acting as a cache could be used for garbage collection was due to Chih-Jui Peng and Gurindar Sohi [Peng and Sohi, 1989]. The reference counting co-processor approach was also taken up by Edward Gehringer and Morris Chang [Gehringer and Chang, 1993; Chang and Gehringer, 1993a; Chang and Gehringer, 1993b]. Details of Manchester University's MUSHROOM hardware design for object-oriented programming by Trevor Hopkins, Ifor Williams and Mario Wolczko can be found in a series of papers [Williams *et al.*, 1987a; Williams *et al.*, 1987b; Williams *et al.*, 1990; Wolczko and Williams, 1990; Williams and Wolczko, 1990; Wolczko and Williams, 1992; Wolczko and Williams, 1993].

12

Distributed Garbage Collection

The old model of a single computer serving all of the computational needs of an organisation is being rapidly superseded by the one in which a large number of separate computers interconnected in a network do the job. Today, machines ranging from personal computers to supercomputers are more likely to be part of a network than not. Networks are no longer an academic curiosity: they have become an essential tool for users in business, government and universities.

As languages are evolving and are freeing users of the burden of doing memory management, so computer networks are evolving into distributed systems. For Tanenbaum

> "The key distinction is that in a distributed system, the existence of multiple autonomous computers is transparent (i.e. not visible) to the user. He can type a command to run a program, and it runs. It is up to the operating system to select the best processor, find and transport all the input files to that processor, and put the results in the appropriate place." [Tanenbaum, 1988]

A distributed system is a special case of a computer network in which a higher-level communication protocol gives a high degree of cohesiveness and transparency, creating a virtual uniprocessor. Nothing has to be done explicitly by the user, but all is automatically done by the system without the user's knowledge.

When one talks about distributed garbage collection the first thing that springs to mind is memory management over a computer network. Is this relevant? The main issue in computer networking is resource sharing. The aim is to make all programs, data and equipment available to anyone on the network without regard to the physical location of the resource and the user. As our ability to gather, process and distribute information grows, the demand for even more sophisticated information processing grows even faster. Algorithms and programs can be split over a distributed system to create finer-grained tasks that communicate somehow to exchange information. Hudak and Keller suggest that there is an 'isomorphism' between *memory* and *process* so that distributed memory management and distributed process management are different ways of addressing the same problem [Hudak and Keller, 1982]. In this scenario objects are active and possess their own thread of control. It makes sense to talk about process collection, recursive (cyclic) processes, and so forth. It is significantly more difficult to manage active objects than passive ones because both reachability and state must be considered. Furthermore, as active objects consume not only memory space but also processing capacity, it is imperative that active garbage objects (processes) are identified quickly. This is one of the reasons why distributed garbage collection is one of the areas that is drawing much attention from the computer science research community.

No doubt this is an area in which one would expect rapid and possibly drastic changes. Network technology is evolving rapidly, yielding everyday more and more sophisticated distributed systems. The World Wide Web is an example today of a complex distributed multi-media database, accessible from all over the world. So far, all information in this kind of distributed database is static; in the near future we envisage the possibility that, amongst many other things, information may migrate to reduce communication costs, or even that the cost of data will be inversely proportional to the number of people who access them. To an extent, Java already addresses this issue. Transparency may be taken to the extreme, allowing powerful distributed systems that will need to run on top of a distributed garbage collection layer of a communication protocol.

It is very difficult to talk about distributed garbage collection without running the risk of being outdated in the near future. On the other hand, it would be impossible to ignore what has been done in this area so far, because any new solution that modern technology may bring will have to be based on the existing knowledge today.

In this chapter we address the main constraints and difficulties in distributed garbage collection, propose a taxonomy to classify algorithms, and present an overview of strategies for distributed garbage collection.

12.1   Requirements

Distributed systems must be analysed at two different levels. The lower level is the network level, and the higher level is the distribution protocol that creates a virtual shared memory. Understanding of both levels is important to allow realistic assumptions to be made, permitting applications to run correctly. In this section, we address some of the features of these two levels and their impact on the requirements of distributed garbage collection.

Network restrictions

A number of factors are relevant in the design of a computer network. The most important of them is possibly the physical distance between machines. If computers are within a short[1] distance from each other, one has a local area network (LAN). Otherwise, one has a wide area network (WAN), also called a long haul network.

---

[1] Distances depend on technology. Tanenbaum considers short distances to be up to about one kilometre [Tanenbaum, 1988].

It is reasonable to assume that in LANs communications are reliable, low-cost and high-speed. There may be real distributed computation involving fine-grained parallelism in which processors will work together, exchanging data towards the solution of a problem. A typical example of a local area network in today's technology is a network of workstations in a laboratory, or spread throughout a university campus or a single-site organisation. Machines interconnected by optical fibres have data transmission rates already of the order of several hundred megabits per second. In LANs one can assume that there is the possibility of some sort of global synchronisation taking place, and that data structures tend to be much smaller in size and interdependent. Migration of passive objects between processors to increase locality of data may be technically viable. LAN distributed garbage collection can be seen as a complex extension of uniprocessor, or more appropriately shared-memory techniques. Although not explicitly mentioned in the literature, it is fair to say that almost all of the existing algorithms for distributed garbage collection are aimed at LANs.

In WANs, communications are unreliable and expensive. Messages may be lost, corrupted, repeated, follow different paths, or be received in a different order from that in which they were sent. Communication costs and data safety may impose the constraint of having replicated information in order to increase locality and thereby reduce the latency of access to data, and increase reliability. The units of data transferred tend to be much larger than in LAN garbage collection and computations tend to be of much coarser grain. In WANs, one would hardly envisage the kind of application in which there is interdependent computation. While the use of a stop-the-world distributed garbage collection algorithm is acceptable in a LAN, it would be unbearably inefficient in a WAN. It is more likely that processes and processors are autonomous and connect themselves for a specific, possibly short-lived task, such as a remote query in a distributed database. Most information and processors are tenured, and an object or process that is not transitively connected to the graph of active processes or cells may become so by sending a message to an active one. Because messages may be pending in the network, the asynchrony of WANs makes it difficult to determine the process (or cell) topology at any given moment. A distributed garbage collection algorithm for WANs has to take all these factors into account. Algorithms such as Maheshwari's *Client-server* [Maheshwari, 1993a; Maheshwari, 1993b], and those of the *Mneme* project [Moss and Sinofsky, 1988; Moss, 1989a; Moss, 1989b; Moss, 1990] handle persistent objects, and can be seen as WAN-suitable algorithms.

As technology evolves machines and networks are becoming faster and more reliable. A computational problem that is addressed by a LAN today may in the near future be running over a WAN. The same evolutionary scale applies to distributed garbage collection protocols.

12.2 Virtually shared memory

Although much effort has been put in hiding message-passing from the programmer, it is difficult to make it entirely transparent. Remote procedure call (RPC) offers a way of hiding communications by making them look like ordinary procedure calls. The programmer, however, still has to be aware that the semantics of RPC are different from those of local procedure calls. Passing pointers as parameters in RPC is difficult, and passing arrays is costly.

The existence of a logical shared memory protocol underneath a distributed garbage collector would permit it to concentrate on garbage collection issues alone, thus behaving in a similar fashion to the relationship between the garbage collector and the operating system in uniprocessors. *Distributed shared memory* (DSM) provides the illusion of a true physical shared memory, in which a number of processes share a single address space. The DSM models make the access protocol consistent with the way sequential applications access data. The simple abstraction provided to the application programmer by the DSM models has made it the focus of recent study.

The two most important approaches to distributed shared memories are the *shared virtual model* (SVM), for which the most widely known algorithm is due to Li [Li, 1986; Li and Hudak, 1989], and the *shared data-object* (SDO) model presented in [Bal *et al.*, 1992]. These two models offer different abstraction.

Shared virtual memory

In the shared virtual memory model the address space is divided into pages, which are distributed amongst the processes, regardless of the structure of the data (objects) stored in them. Processes have either *read*, *write* or *no* access to a page. Read pages can be replicated on multiple processors to increase data locality, reducing access time. A read operation always returns the value of the most recent write to that address. Each process or processor can access any memory location in the shared address space at any time, and read or write values altered by any other process or processor. Mutual exclusion may be implemented by locking pages.

The SVM is a low-level unstructured protocol in which data can only be accessed with primitive operations, such as *load*, *store* and *lock*. No access protection or type-security is enforced by the system. Li's original idea was to allow an easy integration of SVM with the virtual memory management of the host operating system [Li, 1986]. If a shared memory page is held locally at a host, it can be mapped into the application's virtual address space on that host and therefore be accessed using normal machine instructions for accessing memory. An access to a page not held locally triggers a page fault, passing the control to a fault handler, which communicates with a remote host in order to obtain a valid copy of the page before mapping it into the address space of the application. Whenever used on a homogeneous set of hosts SVM can hide communication complexity from the application, achieving complete functional transparency in the sense that a program written for a shared memory multiprocessor system can run on SVM without changes.

Shared data-object model

The shared data-object model was proposed by Bal *et al.* [Bal *et al.*, 1992]. It is a high-level, structured approach to distributed shared memory. In contrast to the SVM model, which is implemented by the kernel using hardware support, the shared data-object model is implemented outside the kernel and completely in software.

The distributed shared memory is not treated as a flat address space that can be accessed in any arbitrary way. Compilers, such as the one for Orca [Bal *et al.*, 1992], provide information to the run-time system, keeping the DSM coherent. The semantics of the language restrict the scope of shared variables. In a shared data-object language, shared data are encapsulated in objects. A shared data-object is an instance of a user-defined abstract data type, and can only be accessed through methods defined in the specification of the object. The run-time system can also replicate objects on more than one processor, to reduce access time. These operations are executed invisibly, and the run-time system ensures that all processes that share the object see the result.

The partitioning of the DSM address space is not defined by the system, as in the SVM approach, but implicitly by the application programmer. A shared object is the unit of programmer-defined sharing, rather than the page. As objects are instances of abstract data types, variables that are independent of each other will typically reside in different objects. Table 12.1 summarises the differences between the SVM and SDO paradigms [Levelt *et al.*, 1992].

Table 12.1 Differences between the SVM and SDO paradigms. From *Software Practice and Experience*, **22**, no. 11, pp. 985–1010, Levelt *et al.*©1992 John Wiley & Sons Ltd. Reprinted by permission of John Wiley & Sons Ltd.

	Shared virtual memory	*Shared data-object*
Implementation	In kernel, hardware support	Completely in software
Unit of sharing	System-defined page	User-defined object
Unit of synchronisation	Machine instruction	Procedure
Data placement	Explicit	Implicit
Address space	Flat	Structured

Garbage collection over distributed shared memory

The use of virtually shared memory protocols may simplify the task of designing garbage collectors in distributed systems by handling message passing protocols in a uniform way. However, in order to be able to perform distributed garbage collection efficiently, the algorithm must try to reduce communication costs by every means. The direct adoption of a shared memory parallel algorithm on top of a virtually shared memory protocol would be unbearably inefficient [Le Sergent and Barthomieu, 1992].

The ideas of virtually shared memory are very recent and their implementation still has to be made more efficient. We envisage that in the near future these ideas will be adopted by most distributed systems and will have a large impact in widening the frontiers of distributed garbage collection.

12.3   Distributed garbage collection issues

Are the requisites for distributed garbage collection the same as for uniprocessor garbage collection or even for shared memory machines? A garbage collection scheme must be able to collect all garbage (*comprehensive*), only garbage must be collected (*correct*), the rate of recycling memory should be sufficient to meet new allocation requests (*expedient*), and space and time overheads should be acceptable (*efficient*). In a distributed system, concurrency is also a constraint to be met. Concurrency allows several processors to change the connectivity of the graph simultaneously in an autonomous way. Besides the distribution issues, some of which were mentioned above, the whole nature of computations may change. An assumption fundamental to many algorithms for uniprocessors or shared memory machines is a certain order in the connectivity of the graph. Cells in use are transitively connected to a root. Cells detached from the graph are garbage cells: the mutator will never access them. In some applications in distributed systems, one can envisage the possibility that a cell that is 'dead' may send a request to a live one connecting itself to the graph, creating a new and more complex scenario.

Taxonomy

As distributed garbage collection algorithms present new difficulties for garbage collection, some classification method seems appropriate.

   We will analyse algorithms depending on the nature of objects managed, their hierarchy, the existence or not of cyclic structures, the way objects are accessed, and their robustness to communication or node failures.

Passive objects

Objects can be either *active* or *passive*. Passive objects hold data but the computational thread of control is external to them. Once a passive object has been disconnected from the graph it is garbage, and its resources are free to be reused. Most of the existing algorithms for distributed garbage collection fall into this category, are suitable for being implemented in LANs, and are based on uniprocessor garbage collection algorithms. The new techniques developed, such as *weighted reference counting* and *generational reference counting* (see Section 12.6 on page 316), try to reduce interprocessor communication.

Active objects

Active objects control their computational thread. They model the behaviour of objects in object-oriented languages, for instance. Their management is more complex than that of passive ones, because reachability and state may need to be analysed simultaneously. A passive garbage object wastes space only, while an active garbage object may consume processing power or drain memory. We restrict the term active to those objects that, if carrying useful computation, are transitively connected to the root of the computation graph. Otherwise, they are garbage and their resources can be automatically recycled.

Actors

Some objects have a behaviour more autonomous than that of active ones, and that allows an object detached from root to come to life by sending a message to a live object. The Actor Model has been used to describe such objects, called *actors* [Hewitt, 1977; Agha, 1986]. Each actor is an entity that has a conceptual location (its *mail* address) and a *behaviour*.

Actors exchange messages amongst each other — this is the only way that one actor can influence the actions of another. Communications between actors are asynchronous, and every message sent will be delivered after some finite delay (fairness of mail delivery). Every actor has its own *mailbox* that queues incoming communications. Actors and their garbage collection are discussed in Section 12.7 on page 317.

Object hierarchy

An important aspect to be analysed is whether all objects are accessible from any other object within the distributed system or not. Interprocessor communication is still far less efficient than local memory access. To avoid communication or space costs, or sometimes to make explicit the kind of operation to be performed by the lower layers of the distributed protocol, objects can be classified as either *local* or *global*. An object is said to be local to a given processor if it lies within its address space. Otherwise, it is said to be global.

Many schemes for distributed garbage collection assume the existence of a local garbage collector running within the processor node and a global garbage collector at the network level. The local and global algorithms cooperate in garbage detection and recycling. In many algorithms, a local object may become a global one. The converse may also happen. A global object may become local by losing all external references to it. Such upgrading and downgrading operations, that change the status of objects, must be carefully handled.

Accessing objects

The main aim of a garbage collection algorithm is to be able to find resources that are no longer needed by the computation, and to recycle them. In indirect methods, the garbage collection algorithm visits all objects forcing communication. Direct checking protocols in distributed systems may yield algorithms that are more communication intensive and less robust to network failures. Direct methods allow information about an object to be stored in other objects in the network. In general, the information about an object is stored in the objects that access it or in tables placed in the node. Indirect checking may allow less intensive communication between processors as the information about a given node is not directly stored in it. This kind of protocol may be more robust to network failures.

Cyclic structures

The same solutions that lead to cyclic structures in uniprocessors also arise in distributed systems. In some distributed garbage collection protocols, a cyclic structure must be confined to a single processor: a *local* cycle. Other distributed algorithms allow cycles to span the network, yielding *global* cycles. Local cycles are dealt with in the same way as in uniprocessors. On the other hand, global cycles may either:

- not be managed by the protocol;
- be managed by the protocol at the network level; or
- be forced to migrate to one single processor where a local garbage collector will eventually take care of it.

Synchronisation

Local information is not always sufficient to determine whether an object is still needed or not. The speculative parallelism model of computation, for instance, initiates several tasks simultaneously in the knowledge that not all of them will be needed ultimately. At some point, somehow, processors need to be reset and the space consumed recycled. In order to allow a decision to be made, processors in the whole (or part) of the network need to interchange messages. At this moment, some sort of synchronisation takes place.

The simplest synchronisation model is by a *stop-the-world* protocol. All processors stop graph mutation, or at least stop making changes to the connectivity of global objects, and collaborate for garbage collection. This process is equivalent to garbage collection pauses in mark-sweep algorithms for uniprocessors. A good representative of the stop-the-world model of garbage collection is distributed mark-sweep, which has been used in practice by the Emerald system, for example [Black *et al.*, 1986; Black *et al.*, 1987; Jul *et al.*, 1988].

Some other algorithms try to weaken the mutator pause restriction by permitting some operations to take place concurrently with garbage collection. In general, this model would not apply to actors. This sort of protocol tends to permit increasing the connectivity of the graph with operations such as New and Update, but seldom allows actual link deletion.

Robustness

Making a network robust to partial failures is far from being a resolved problem. Most of us have already experienced problems even with very basic distributed software such as electronic mail. Sometimes messages arrive more than once, at other times they are delivered unreasonably late or get lost on their way and never find their destination.

The goals of comprehensiveness, concurrency, expediency, efficiency and correctness in distributed garbage collection become much harder to achieve simultaneously when robustness is demanded. Guaranteeing that all garbage is collected, and that there is no memory leakage, under a possibly faulty network of processors requires that the garbage collecting protocol be able to deal with the available parts, while waiting for unavailable parts to become available again. Under all circumstances only garbage must be reclaimed; references to unavailable parts of the network must remain valid. It would be unreasonable to stop the world, and block operations in the whole network just because of a partial failure. The garbage collection protocol must be able to reclaim garbage despite unavailable parts. Failures and their recovery must be handled efficiently. Additional overheads due to robustness must be limited and mainly paid when failures are present [Juul and Jul, 1992].

It is extremely difficult to fulfil all these goals simultaneously. A comprehensive collection depends on all nodes in the distributed system. The presence of communication delays makes the requirements for comprehension and expediency impossible for a single collector. Trading-off comprehension for expediency yields a conservative scheme in which only part of the garbage is collected. One solution is to group nodes together for collection [Mancini *et al.*, 1991; Shapiro *et al.*, 1990; Shapiro, 1991]. The distributed collector proposed in [Lang *et al.*, 1992] eventually reclaims all inaccessible objects. The partitioning and grouping strategies in distributed garbage collection are similar to those used by uniprocessor generational scavengers. Juul and Jul describe a robust and comprehensive algorithm used in the object-based Emerald system [Hutchinson, 1987; Hutchinson *et al.*, 1987; Juul and Jul, 1992].

12.4 Distributed mark-sweep

In the following sections, we present an overview of existing algorithms, and review their main features in the light of the taxonomy presented above. First, we consider mark-sweep garbage collection. Algorithms for distributed mark-sweep form two different families. Some of them are descendants from the original mark-sweep algorithm while some others adapt Dijkstra's on-the-fly mark-sweep garbage collector (discussed in Chapter 8) to work in distributed environments.

Hudak and Keller

The Hudak–Keller mark-tree collector was one of the first distributed algorithms [Hudak and Keller, 1982]. Designed for functional languages, it is based on Dijkstra's on-the-fly scheme. Garbage reclamation is accomplished in parallel with computation, and no central control is necessary other than a logical rendezvous between phases of the collector. It is also capable of finding, and subsequently deleting, active processes that are determined to be no longer relevant to the computation.

The Hudak–Keller architecture is formed by linking together processor nodes. Concurrence is realised at each node either by running the collector on a shared memory processor in parallel with the mutator, or by interleaving the operations of the two processes. There is a virtual addressing scheme whereby a node may reference any other node in the system. Communication between nodes occurs by spawning tasks from one processor to another. A *task* is the smallest autonomous unit of processor activity, and is assumed to be of a much finer granularity than, for example, PL/1 or Ada tasks.

Garbage is defined as nodes unreachable from the root, but there are two other forms of garbage: irrelevant tasks [Friedman and Wise, 1978; Grit and Page, 1981] and dormant subgraphs. *Irrelevant* tasks are created by speculative parallelism and can arise in a number of ways. The eager evaluation of unneeded arguments to a function in a lazy functional language, or the parallel evaluation of conditional branches are instances. A *dormant* computation graph is one for which the semantics of evaluation dictate that no task can ever again propagate work, although that node is still accessible from the root. Irrelevant tasks may be found by tracing and marking nodes from the root. At the end all tasks pointing to unmarked tasks are irrelevant. Dormant subgraphs may be found by tracing from the tasks instead of from the root. These markings may take place either simultaneously (two mark bits are needed) or in alternation. Table 12.2 shows possible outcomes.

Table 12.2   The outcome of marking from roots or tasks [Hudak and Keller, 1982].

		Marked from tasks?	
		yes	no
Marked from root?	yes	active	dormant
	no	irrelevant	garbage

For mutator–collector cooperation, Hudak and Keller use a *mark tree* (hence the name of the algorithm), to which a distributed mutator may add branches. The collapse of the tree indicates that marking is complete. The scheme is best viewed as a parallel implementation of conventional recursive marking, in which each recursive step is replaced by the spawning of a mark task. The mark tree is built to provide mechanisms for cooperation and proper termination. Termination is detected since each mark task eventually spawns an 'uptree' task, which is propagated upward in the mark tree. Spawning an uptree task from the root indicates that marking is complete. In order to provide a way for a mark task to return to its parent once it has been spawned on a node's children, each node is augmented with fields for its parent in the mark tree, and for a count of the number of tasks which have been spawned on its children.

As usual, three colours are used for marking, interpreted for distributed garbage collection. White nodes are those not yet reached by a mark task. Initially all nodes are white, and after marking is complete white nodes are garbage. Grey nodes are those to which marking has been propagated, and from which a mark task has been spawned on each of its children. Once all the mark tasks spawned from a grey node have been 'returned' by uptree tasks, the node is painted black, and an uptree task is spawned on the node's parent in the marking tree. New nodes are also created black.

Initially all nodes are white and their mark task count is zero. The marking phase simply spawns a mark task on the root, with a dummy node as its parent, and then waits for the global flag done to become true. The first mark task to find a white node is the one that shades it grey, makes it a child to its parent in the mark tree, and spawns mark tasks on each of its children, keeping track of how many mark tasks are spawned in its count field. If the node is a leaf, it is painted black and an immediate return is made through an uptree task. Once the marking phase terminates, the sweep phase takes place. At this point, all white nodes are garbage and all tasks pointing to white nodes are irrelevant. The sweep phase first terminates all irrelevant tasks, and collects all white nodes by adding them to the free-list. It then prepares the system for the next collection cycle by flipping the colour the mutator sees as garbage.

Ali's algorithm

Ali presents algorithms that allow each processor to mark-sweep its own heap independently [Mohamed-Ali, 1984]. At the end of a local garbage collection, the processor informs all other processors which remote pointers it retains, and the other processors then treat these as roots that must be marked during their own collections. These algorithms allow each processor to work independently, thus reducing the synchronisation overhead. Ali's algorithms are not real-time since any particular computation may be delayed for a long time while its processor does a garbage collection.

Garbage collection messages can be batched together into large blocks, allowing the communications medium to be used more efficiently. A table stores in-transit references and several message queues are maintained. The issue of lost or in-transit messages is solved by assuming that the communication channel between each pair of nodes is order-preserving (an alternative solution is to keep message counts in each node). Before a garbage collection is completed, a check is made to ensure that the number of reply messages is equal to the message count. The algorithm is unable to collect global cycles.

Hughes's algorithm

Hughes's algorithm is based on Ali's but has lower storage overheads. It is also likely to take longer to recover remotely-referenced garbage, and like Ali's, is not truly real-time, because mutator operation is suspended until garbage collection is over [Hughes, 1985]. Unlike Ali's, it can reclaim global cyclic data structures. Many garbage collections are performed in parallel and each of them marks nodes differently. When the marking phase terminates, unmarked nodes can be deleted. Each processor makes a contribution to all the currently active global garbage collections every time it performs a local garbage collection.

The algorithm assumes the existence of a global clock and that communications are instantaneous, thereby avoiding problems of in-transit messages. These assumptions are reasonable if they are taken to refer to *simulated* time, rather than real time. A global garbage collection marks nodes by stamping them with the time that it started, and counts a node as unmarked if its stamp is less than this time. Nodes created since the garbage collection started are automatically considered marked. Local garbage collections propagate the time-stamps of root nodes on a processor to its leaves, performing part of the mark phase of each currently active garbage collection. At the end of the local garbage collection, marking messages are sent to remote objects whose time-stamps have increased. Each processor keeps track of the earliest global garbage collection for which it has more work to do. When no processor has more work to do for a garbage collection T then all nodes with time-stamp less than T can be collected. Detection of distributed termination is done by an adaptation of Rana's algorithm [Rana, 1983].

The Liskov–Ladin algorithm

Liskov and Ladin take a different approach to distributed memory management [Liskov and Ladin, 1986]. Instead of distributing decision-making, the service is logically centralised but physically replicated in order to achieve high fault-tolerance and availability. All objects and tables are assumed to be backed up in stable storage. Clocks are synchronised and message delivery delay is bounded, allowing the centralised service to build a consistent view of the distributed system. Incoming and outgoing references and their paths are reported by local collectors to the centralised service. Based on the path information collected, the centralised service builds the graph of inter-site (global) references. The centralised service runs a mark-sweep process on this graph and informs the local garbage collectors about the accessibility of their root objects. This information is used by the local mark-sweep collectors to detect garbage.

The adoption of Hughes's algorithm and loosely synchronised local clocks allowed Ladin and Liskov to simplify and correct their original algorithm [Ladin and Liskov, 1992]. There is no need for accurate computation of the paths of incoming and outgoing references for the central service to maintain the graph of global references, because Hughes's algorithm eliminates inter-space cycles of garbage. A termination protocol is no longer necessary, because the central service determines the garbage threshold date.

Augusteijn's algorithm

In order to avoid pauses during mark-sweep, Augusteijn based the garbage collector for the parallel object-oriented language *POOL-T* on Dijkstra's on-the-fly algorithm [Augusteijn, 1987]. POOL-T enables the programmer to describe a distributed program by a collection of cooperating dynamically created processes, called *objects*. The DOOM machine in which POOL-T was supposed to be implemented is really a LAN. Communication between processes follows a rendezvous protocol, with the object sending a message suspended until it receives the result. The message-passing mechanism behaves like a remote procedure call. Since an object can hold a reference to another object anywhere in the system, each collector must be able to communicate with any other collector. This makes the logical communication network between processors fully connected, although the physical network does not need to be. This constraint makes most of the termination detection algorithms unsuitable for Augusteijn's implementation. The solution adopted is not fully distributed, because a special synchronisation object is introduced to establish global invariants.

Vestal's algorithm

Vestal's algorithm is also based on Dijkstra's collector [Vestal, 1987]. Processors cooperate in both phases of the collection and marking proceeds in parallel with mutation. The address space is split into logical areas for which there is no control over site boundary crossing. Each collector performs a global mark starting at the root of an area, which leads to a very high communication overhead.

The Schelvis–Bledoeg algorithm

The distributed Berkeley Smalltalk collector uses a combination of distributed mark-sweep for global objects and a generational scavenger locally [Schelvis and Bledoeg, 1988]. Each processor has its local heap split into areas to be filled with cells of different generations and an additional region that contains all *replicated* objects. This region behaves like the old generation of a generational garbage collector except that it is replicated in every processor. Whenever a local processor runs out of cells in its new space, a scavenge takes place. The roots of the computation graph are the set of new and survivor cells referenced from the replicated spaces on remote nodes.

At the global level, mark-sweep is initiated by traversing and marking the whole graph of living cells. Then, the sweep takes place. According to Abdullahi et al., this algorithm is unable to work properly when not all nodes are able or willing to cooperate [Abdullahi et al., 1992].

The Emerald collector

Emerald is a distributed active-object based system [Hutchinson, 1987; Hutchinson et al., 1987]. Emerald's garbage collection scheme is hierarchical and has been implemented over a LAN of workstations [Jul et al., 1988; Juul and Jul, 1992]. The global collector runs on each node in the system, continuously adapting to the current situation and striving to fulfil the comprehensiveness requirement while giving up on expediency. The local scheme foresees the possibility of failure of many parts of the system by performing an independent and expedient, but not comprehensive, local collection at each node.

Comprehensive collection is achieved by concurrent mark-sweep collectors on each node, which cooperate as a global garbage collector across the entire network. A comprehensive garbage collection can take place while various parts of the distributed system are temporarily unavailable. A second set of collectors does an independent, partial collection on each node. These node-local collectors do a more expedient collection of local garbage without being comprehensive. Both sets of collectors work in parallel with the mutator processes, most of the time. The global collection adds robustness to the garbage collection scheme by waiting for needed, but unavailable, nodes to become available again while progressing the collection in the available parts of the system. Local collectors are able to collect local garbage while the rest of the system is unavailable, adding efficiency and expediency to the scheme, as most objects tend to be short-lived and local [Schelvis and Bledoeg, 1988; Jul et al., 1988; Rudalics, 1986].

During a comprehensive garbage collection, the graph must be traversed from the root set to identify reachable objects. Any node may initiate a global collection cycle and inform the other nodes about that decision. Each collector makes progress independently doing marking locally. External references are handled differently. Non-local objects are seen by mutators as black and by collectors as belonging to a non-local grey set. When the grey set is emptied, non-resident objects are handled by sending a shade request to the node hosting the object. Each shade request is acknowledged to allow the requesting node to remove the reference from its non-resident grey set. Grey references are kept until the node hosting the node guarantees that the object is either grey or black. The mark-phase is finished when the local and non-local grey sets are empty on all nodes. This state can be detected by a two-phase commit protocol or by having a coordinator node.

The cooperating collectors that constitute the global collection may run independently on each node. Cooperation is needed over when to start, i.e. when mutators must be stopped and the local part of the distributed set of root objects constructed; during the mark-phase, i.e. when a non-resident object is shaded; and to determine when the mark-phase is finished. A distributed termination detection protocol must detect that the all grey set is empty in this situation. Any node may decide to start a new cycle of the global collection. By adding the cycle number of a collector to all inter-node messages, every node will become aware of the collection before it engages in the transfer of objects or references with the starting node. During the mark phase, the current cycle number represents the colour black, and the previous collection number the colour white. At the end of the mark phase white objects can be collected by the sweeper, which is interleaved with the allocation routines.

The IK collector

IK is an object-oriented platform intended to simplify the development of distributed and persistent applications [Sousa, 1993]. It runs in user mode on a LAN of heterogeneous Unix machines. IK generalises the notion of volatile and persistent data by considering all objects maintained by the system to be part of the transitive closure of an eternal root. Object invocation is the basic primitive of the system, embodying all of the features required for transparent handling of persistence and distribution. Object faults are triggered solely by intercepting object invocations, and direct access to other objects' member data is not allowed. Faulty objects are either mapped and invoked locally or, if already mapped elsewhere, remotely invoked. IK also provides object migration, but its policy must be defined by application. Three independent garbage collectors are used. Local objects are recycled by a generation-scavenging algorithm. The second garbage collector is a reference counting cluster collector, run off-line by a process running continuously on each storage node. Clusters are locked while being recycled, suspending mutators' access to them. The third garbage collector is a system-wide mark-sweep collector. Initially, a suspending mark-sweep collector was used. It was later replaced by a collector based on the Hudak–Keller algorithm.

12.5   Distributed copying

Rudalics suggested a copying algorithm for a distributed environment [Rudalics, 1986]. This algorithm is a combination of Cheney's copying collector and Baker's real-time algorithm (see Sections 6.1 and 8.5, respectively). Collection is incremental, but each step may take an unbounded amount of time in a processor. The local memory of each processor is divided into three spaces: the *root* space, which stores global objects, and two semi-spaces. Roots are invisible to the programmer, and serve as the second stage in the indirection of references between processors. Each root is an incoming external reference, and contains a local pointer to the actual object and a tag bit for garbage collection. Roots are linked in either of three lists. The first two lists act as semi-spaces for roots, while the third is used to store roots temporarily while a remote object or root is being created. The semi-spaces are used by the collector for moving and compacting local objects. The upper part of each semi-space is reserved for storing remote pointers, which act as indirections to external references, and also have tag bits for garbage collection. Roots and remote pointers establish a two-stage indirection concept, and are similar to inter-area links [Bishop, 1977] and entry/exit pointers [Lieberman and Hewitt, 1983; Plainfossé and Shapiro, 1992].

The algorithm assumes that all objects are reachable from one global root, from which collection starts. Collection consists of a scan phase followed by a flip phase that eventually includes all processors. Rudalics suggests interleaving local collections with global ones in order to reclaim short-lived objects more easily. This protocol is unable to terminate global active objects, but is able to collect them after they exhaust their own resources.

12.6 Distributed reference counting

Reference counting has several advantages over tracing garbage collection that make its application attractive for loosely-coupled multiprocessor architectures. It is performed in small steps interleaved with computation; it has better locality as there is no need to scan global data structures, and it does not degrade with occupancy. Distributed reference counting is a simple extension to uniprocessor reference counting. On a loosely-coupled system the creation of a new reference to an object requires that a message be sent to the object in order to increment its reference count. Likewise, if a remote reference is discarded then a decrement message must be sent. Special care must be taken to prevent an object being reclaimed while references to it still exist. This may happen if messages arrive in an order different from that expected. For instance, if a message deleting the last reference to an object overtakes a copying message, the object will be reclaimed incorrectly.

The Lermen–Maurer protocol

A solution to this problem appears in [Lermen and Maurer, 1986]. Their communication protocol requires that messages between any pair of objects are delivered in the order in which they were sent. Messages must be acknowledged, and objects are only reclaimed if an equal number of copy, acknowledge and delete messages are received for that object. This protocol provides a correct distributed reference counting scheme at the cost of three messages per interprocessor reference.

Indirect reference counting

Piquer's scheme optimises distributed reference counting by avoiding count increment messages [Piquer, 1990b; Piquer, 1991]. The indirect reference count (IRC) algorithm maintains a diffusion tree structure that represents history of pointer copies. This structure is equivalent to the termination trees proposed by Dijkstra and Scholten [Dijkstra and Scholten, 1989]. It uses two extra fields in each pointer: a reference to the pointer's parent in the diffusion tree and a count of its children. The parent pointer serves only distributed garbage collection purposes, and refers either to an object or to another remote pointer. The whole set of remote pointers referencing an object forms a distributed graph which can be traversed using indirect pointers. Creation of new cells or copying of pointers is performed locally without any need for communication. The deletion of a pointer may generate more than one message per reference.

Piquer's scheme is also concerned with object migration between processors. Messages to a migrating object may be flowing in the network and, unless special care is taken, the protocol will behave erroneously. Object migration is performed at a cost of only one interprocessor message. Indirect reference counting communications behave similarly to those of the weighted reference count protocol (see page 316), but its main advantage is that it avoids generating indirection cells, and thus allows access to non-local references in constant time. The IRC protocol, as distributed reference counting, is acyclic and not robust against message loss or duplication.

The Mancini–Shrivastava algorithm

An efficient and fault-tolerant distributed garbage collection algorithm based on reference counting has been proposed by Mancini and Shrivastava [Mancini and Shrivastava, 1991]. Resilience to space or message failures is supported by a remote procedure call mechanism extended to detect and kill orphans. Duplication of remote messages is handled by a special protocol that makes an early short-cut of potential indirections even if they are not used. Two alternatives are proposed to make the protocol cyclic. The first one is distributed mark-sweep. The other alternative is based on a heuristic that allows cells to leak away.

The SPG protocol

The SPG algorithm assumes that interprocessor communication is unreliable and that messages may arrive in a different order from that in which they were sent [Shapiro *et al.*, 1990; Plainfossé and Shapiro, 1992]. Objects may contain references to other objects located in the same or in remote processors, and changes of status are permitted. The SPG protocol relies on any standard local tracing garbage collector. The distributed protocol is based on a conservative extension of reference counting. External references are avoided by migrating objects between processors whenever a local collector discovers that there are no locally held references to the object, thereby allowing garbage cycles to be reclaimed locally (a cyclic extension of the SPG protocol was proposed by Kordale and Ahamad [Kordale and Ahamad, 1993]). Mutators in different spaces communicate via remote procedure call style invocation. The arguments and results in the invocation may contain any mixture of pure data, references, and migrating objects.

Each node maintains entry and exit tables of potential incoming and outgoing references. Both tables are conservative estimates. If two different nodes possibly refer to a single object, each will be assigned an entry item. This differs from reference counting, and in particular from Piquer's approach, because the SPG protocol needs an entry per remote space to tolerate lost or duplicated messages.

When sending a reference, the value of the local clock is stored in the entry item. The same value is used to time-stamp the mutator message. Upon receiving a mutator message, the receiver compares the time-stamp value in the message with the one found in a vector of highest time-stamps. This vector contains a space identifier and an associated time-stamp for each remote node. The time-stamp is increased each time a message is received; if the corresponding entry is not in the vector, the initial value can be taken from the message. Messages carrying the value of the time-stamp vector are sent to the target nodes of a given node. Upon receiving one of these messages, the time-stamp value found in the message is compared with the value in the entry items to detect messages in transit. Message delivery delays may cause improper object reclamation. To guard against duplication or loss of messages, a list of all existing exit items on a node is sent to the nodes referenced: this comparison can deduce entry items that are not reachable, and remove them. To provide fault-tolerance, extra time and ownership information is piggy-backed onto the existing mutator messages. Occasional control messages are exchanged in the background to remove inaccessible entry items.

'Garbage collecting the world'

The 'Garbage collecting the world' paper describes a fault-tolerant, distributed collector that can reclaim distributed cyclic garbage [Lang *et al.*, 1992]. It is a hybrid collector that uses reference counting for global objects, and a tracing collector at each node for local objects. Nodes are organised into groups that are willing to cooperate for garbage collection. Each group gives a unique identifier to each collection cycle, and multiple overlapping group collections can be simultaneously active. If a node fails to cooperate, the group it belongs is reorganised to exclude the node, and collection continues.

A distributed collection begins with group negotiation. All entry objects of nodes within the group are identified and marked as either *hard* or *soft*. An object is hard either if it is referenced from outside the group, or if it is accessible from a root. Other objects reachable only from other nodes in the group are marked soft. The reference counter provides the initial marks of the entry objects of a group, which are propagated towards exit objects by the local collectors. The marks of exit objects are propagated towards the entry objects they reference (if they lie within the group) by the group collector. This process is repeated until marks of entry or exit objects of the group no longer change, at which point the group is disbanded. All objects accessible either from a root or from a node outside the group are now marked hard. Entry objects marked soft must be parts of isolated cycles local to the group and can thus be reclaimed.

Network objects

Birrell *et al.* use reference counting to support distributed object-oriented programming [Birrell *et al.*, 1993]. Objects visible to other nodes are called *network objects*. A process that allocates a network object is called its owner, and the instance of the object in the owner node is called a concrete object. Other client processes may hold indirect references to the concrete object through a *surrogate* object that communicates with the owner through remote procedure calls.

A public network object holds a reference list of identifiers of each process that references it. This set is maintained by communication between processes. When a client first receives a reference to a particular object, it makes a call to the owner and creates a surrogate. When a client's local garbage collector determines that a surrogate is no longer reachable, the client deletes the surrogate and informs the owner that it has done so. Once a network object's reference list is empty, the object can be reclaimed, unless there are local references to it. Network objects face two problems. First, cycle detection is still a problem. Jones and Rodrigues have recently extended the network object system to reclaim cyclic data structures that span the network. Second, although reference lists offer better fault-tolerance than reference counts, the network objects' garbage collector cannot distinguish node failure from long-lasting communication delay. It therefore risks collecting a reachable object if there is a temporary communication failure.

Weighted reference counting

Weighted reference counting is suitable for the management of passive and active objects. This scheme has a low communication overhead of one message per interprocessor reference, with no need for global synchronisation. Each object and each pointer has an associated weight. The algorithm maintains the invariant that the weight of a object is equal to the sum of the weights of all external pointers to it.

New cells are initialised with a predetermined maximum weight, and the weight of the pointer to the new cell is also set to this weight. When a pointer is copied, its weight is divided equally between the two copies of the pointer, thereby maintaining the invariant of the algorithm. An indirection cell is needed if the weight of the original pointer is one. The advantage of this scheme is that no messages need be exchanged with the referent of the pointer.

The only time that communication is needed to maintain the weights is when a pointer is deleted. A message to subtract the weight of the deleted pointer is sent to the remote object. If this causes the object's reference count to drop to zero, the referenced object is freed and its children deleted recursively. As this is the only time that messages are exchanged, the weighted reference count protocol is robust against changes in the order of arrival of messages. The maximum weight is always a power of two to allow for easy division, and the size of its weight field can be reduced by replacing a weight by its logarithm.

Based on Hughes's cyclic reference counting algorithm for uniprocessors (see Chapter 3), Lester proposed an extension of the weighted reference counting protocol that is able to handle cycles in referentially transparent applications, such as pure functional languages [Lester, 1992]. Jones and Lins present general algorithms for weighted reference counting cycles [Lins and Jones, 1993; Jones and Lins, 1993]. These algorithms combine weighted reference counting with Lins's algorithm for cyclic reference counting (discussed in Chapter 3).

Generational reference counting

Generational reference counting is a distributed storage reclamation scheme for loosely-coupled multiprocessors [Goldberg, 1989]. It is suitable for passive and active objects. It is a non-hierarchical scheme, makes indirect access to objects and imposes no global synchronisation. Each reference has an associated *generation*. These should not be confused with generational garbage collection. The original reference to an object is a zero generation reference. Any reference copied from the original reference is a first generation reference, and so on. Each object contains a table, called a *ledger* — an array of the number of outstanding references to a generation. Each pointer contains two additional fields: its generation field and a count of the number of copies of this particular reference. When a pointer is copied, the new pointer has its generation field assigned to the generation of the original pointer plus one, to indicate that it is a descendant of that generation. In a similar way the count field of the original pointer is incremented by one to indicate that it has one more child. Conversely, when a pointer is deleted, the processor holding the reference sends a message containing the address of the referent, the pointer's generation and its count fields. When the target processor receives the message, it adjusts the ledger of the referenced object. If the ledger drops to zero the object is garbage, its children are recursively deleted and the object is placed onto the free-list. Goldberg writes that the major drawback of his algorithm compared with weighted reference counting is its space costs. It is also unable to collect cyclic structures. Because of the complex generation structure, one would hardly envisage the possibility of it becoming cyclic without drastic alterations to its philosophy.

12.7   Garbage collecting actors

The idea of garbage collecting actors was first addressed by Agha, and later refined by Kafura and others [Agha, 1986; Kafura *et al.*, 1990; Puaut, 1992; Venkatasubramanian *et al.*, 1992]. The concept of actor unifies the notions of a process (thread of control), memory (encapsulated variables) and communication (message passing). Actors are currently active objects. There are no passive entities. Each actor is uniquely identified by the address of its single mail queue. Root actors are those actors designated as always running, and those that can interact directly with the external world via I/O devices, external naming, and so forth. An actor B is an *acquaintance* of actor A if B's mail queue address is known to A.

An actor can be considered garbage if its absence from the system cannot be detected by external observation, other than through its consumption of memory and processor resources. Thus, an actor is garbage if it is neither active nor can become active hereafter, or if it cannot send information to, or receive information from a root [Kafura *et al.*, 1990]. The key property of garbage actors is that they cannot become non-garbage. This is because an actor is only determined to be garbage when there is no possibility of communication between it and a root actor. Therefore, once an actor is marked as garbage, there is no possible sequence of transformations which would cause the garbage actor to become non-garbage.

Halstead's algorithm

Halstead's garbage collector uses the concept of an *actor reference tree* — a set of processors and connections between processors such that each processor has a reference to the actor [Halstead, 1978]. Garbage collection is performed by reducing the tree until it contains a single processor. A local garbage collector is then used on each processor to collect garbage actors. A drawback of this scheme is that it cannot reclaim cycles.

Marking algorithms

Nelson's marking algorithm for actors assumes that the mutator is halted, and that all actors in the system reside in the same node [Nelson, 1989]. It uses three colours that, at the end of marking, have the following meanings. White actors are not reachable from a root actor; grey actors are reachable from a root actor but cannot become active; black actors are non-garbage — they are either root actors or both reachable from a root actor and potentially alive.

The *Is-Black* algorithm, also by Kafura and others, uses two colours and a visit field (for cycle detection) [Kafura *et al.*, 1990]. The algorithm starts by colouring all actors white and all roots black. This is followed by painting black the acquaintances of black actors. Then a depth-first search from active actors for a black actor is performed. If a black actor is found, then the originating actor is painted black, together with its acquaintances, and the whole algorithm is repeated. At the termination, all non-black actors are collected.

Washabaugh presents a series of extensions to these algorithms, one of which shows how to adapt them for distributed systems [Washabaugh, 1989]. Two major problems are mentioned, which are the chief difficulties of all the algorithms presented in this chapter. First, the global collector must operate concurrently with the local collectors and mutators, and must synchronise properly with the local collector. Either a snapshot approach or a strategy that time-stamps node acquaintances is suggested. Second, the distributed pieces of the global collector must be able to determine termination. Termination is complicated because a global collector at one node may finish all its work only to be reawakened later by an action taken at another node. Agreement can be achieved by using a rotating token which, if it ever returns to its last owner, signals termination.

Logically centralised collectors

The algorithms proposed by Puaut and by Venkatasubramanian *et al.* merge the ideas from the 'Garbage collecting the world' and the Liskov–Ladin algorithm in order to make Kafura's algorithm distributed and robust [Puaut, 1992; Puaut, 1994a; Puaut, 1994b; Venkatasubramanian *et al.*, 1992]. In both architectures the garbage collectors are hierarchically organised, with local garbage collectors loosely coupled to a logically centralised global garbage collector that maintains a global snapshot of the system. The difference between the two propositions is the way that the global snapshot is obtained: Venkatasubramanian *et al.* use a two-dimensional grid architecture, and properties concerning message-routing on the grid topology are used for detecting a consistent system state. A generational scavenger is used at each node. Puaut uses time-stamping of events to get global information, and no assumption is made of the underlying architecture. Locally, each node runs Nelson's marking algorithm for actors.

12.8 Notes

Surveys of techniques for distributed garbage collection can be found in the proceedings of the International Workshops in Memory Management for 1992 and 1995 [IWMM, 1992; IWMM, 1995]. The survey by David Plainfossé and Marc Shapiro in the latter workshop is particularly good [Plainfossé and Shapiro, 1995].

The distributed shared memory model (DSM) of computation has been studied in [Fleisch, 1989; Forin *et al.*, 1989; Kessler and Livny, 1989; Krieger and Stumm, 1990; Li, 1986; Li and Hudak, 1989; Bennet *et al.*, 1990; Kaashoek *et al.*, 1989; Stumm and Zhou, 1990a; Stumm and Zhou, 1990b; Levelt *et al.*, 1992], and [Stumm and Zhou, 1990a; Bal and Tanenbaum, 1991] provide an overview. [Zhou *et al.*, 1992] studies the design, implementation and performance of shared virtual memory (SVM) in networks of heterogeneous hosts. [Levelt *et al.*, 1992] provides a comparison of the DSM and SVM models. The Actor Model is described in [Hewitt, 1977; Agha, 1986].

POOL-T and DOOM were part of an Esprit project, and most of the references in Augusteijn's paper are to project documents [Augusteijn, 1987]. However, the code for an implementation of his algorithm in POOL-T is provided and the appendix of his paper also presents a brief introduction to that language.

The indirect reference counting algorithm has been implemented on a distributed Lisp system called TransPive, based on LeLisp version 15.2, extended to support remote pointers [Piquer, 1990a].

There is some controversy about the origin of weighted reference counting. The idea was first published in the same conference by Bevan, and Watson and Watson [Bevan, 1987; Watson and Watson, 1987]. The latter attribute it to Weng, but Thomas credits it to Arvind [Weng, 1979; Thomas, 1981]. Piquer discusses the introduction of object migration into weighted reference counting through the use of indirection cells, and through forwarding any messages directed to an object to its new address [Piquer, 1991]. The idea of delaying delete messages in a 'To-Be-Decremented stack' as a way of reducing interprocessor communication in weighted reference counting is presented in [Glaser, 1987; Glaser et al., 1989]. Corporaal uses tables to avoid indirection cells, thereby reducing the access time to objects [Corporaal et al., 1988; Corporaal, 1989; Corporaal et al., 1990]. In [Lester, 1989], Lester proposes combining weighted reference counting with a copying collector for handling local garbage collections. The use of this composite collector in a distributed graph reduction system is described in [Kingdon et al., 1991]. Foster combined weighted reference counting and a local collector for garbage collection in Strand, a single assignment concurrent logic programming language. Dickman [Dickman, 1991] uses a null weight to avoid indirection cells and to improve message failure resilience in weighted reference counting. This makes the total weight in the object always greater than or equal to the sum of the weights of the pointers to it, preventing objects being collected in error. The weak invariant tolerates message re-ordering and loss, network partitions and processor crashes (with or without subsequent recovery), but may cause space leaks. Dickman relies on some other garbage collection strategy to collect cycles and cells that have leaked away.

Glossary

accurate: see **type-accurate**.

activation record: a record that saves the state of computation and return address.

active data: data in use, as opposed to **free** data or **garbage**.

active process: live process.

actor: an entity with an address and a behaviour.

acyclic: structure that contains no cycles; collector unable to manage cyclic data structures.

address, forwarding: a pointer left in a relocated **object** that holds its new location.

address space: the range of values that a pointer may hold.

aging space: a region of a **generation** that holds survivors of collections until they are old enough to be **promoted** to the next generation.

allocation: the acquisition of space from the memory manager.

allocation, heap: allocation of **objects** to an area of memory not subject to the LIFO discipline of **stack allocation**.

allocation, stack: allocation pattern that follows a last-in-first-out order.

allocation, static: allocation pattern in which knowledge of the location and layout of all data can be determined at compile-time, i.e. statically.

barrier, read: a barrier that interrupts reads from an **object**.

barrier, write: a barrier that interrupts writes to an **object**.

bitmap: an array of bits. Typically used by garbage collectors for **marking**, in which case each bit corresponds to a word (or **object**) in the **heap**.

black: colour of an **object** that has been visited by the garbage collector as have its direct descendants.

black-listing: the Boehm–Demers–Weiser **conservative** collector records values that might be misinterpreted as valid pointers in a black-list, and ensures that it does not allocate at these addresses.

block, basic: a code sequence that does not contain any jumps or calls to procedures.

boundary, threatening: a method of **adaptive tenuring** that can retrieve **garbage** that would otherwise remain **tenured**.

break-table: a table that stores relocation information for a **compacting** garbage collector.

bucket: a sub-division of a **generation** by age.

cache block/line: usually the smallest subdivision of a **cache**, (but see **cache, sub-block placement**).

cache, copy-back: write strategy in which data is only written back to the next level when a **cache miss** forces its replacement.

cache, direct-mapped: cache organisation in which each block of memory is mapped to a single **cache block**.

cache, fetch-on-write: see **write-allocate cache**.

cache hit: the CPU has found a needed data or instruction word in the **cache memory**.

cache memory: a small but fast memory between the CPU and the main-memory used to buffer data or instructions.

cache miss: the CPU has not found a needed data or instruction word in the **cache memory**.

cache, miss penalty: the number of cycles for which the processor is stalled after a **cache miss**.

cache, ought to be two: a technique for maintaining the uniqueness of one-bit **reference counts**.

cache, set associative: cache organisation in which each block of memory is mapped to a small set of **cache blocks**.

cache, sub-block placement: cache organisation in which a single **cache block** can be divided into sub-blocks, each of which has an associated valid bit.

cache, write-allocate: strategy for **cache** write **misses** that fetches the block into the cache and then treats it as a write hit.

cache, write-around: see **write-no-allocate cache**.

cache, write-back: see **copy-back** cache.

cache, write buffer: a buffer between the cache and the next level of memory.

cache, write-no-allocate: strategy that does not fetch the block into the **cache** on a write **miss**.

cache, write-through: write strategy in which data is written to both the block in the cache and the block in the next level of the memory.

cache, write-validate: write strategy equivalent to **cache, write-allocate** with **cache, sub-block placement** using one-word sub-blocks.

car: the pointer in a **cons** cell that contains or points to the list element.

card: the division of the **heap** marked by a **write barrier**.

card table: an array of bits or bytes set by the **write barrier** each of which corresponds to a **card** of memory.

cdr: the pointer in a **cons** cell that contains or points to the next *cons* cell in the list.

cell: a number of contiguous memory fields forming a single logical structure.

cell, atomic: an object that contains no pointers.

cell, fixed-size: a **heap** layout in which all **cells** are the same size.

cell, variable-sized: a **heap** layout in which **cells** may have different sizes.

child: a cell B is said to be a child of a cell A if A holds a pointer to B.

closure: a code-environment pair used for later evaluation of the code (used in functional languages, for instance).

closure, transitive referential: the set of **cells** reachable from a given cell by following pointers held in the cells in the set.

collection, major: a **garbage** collection of more than one **generation**.

collection, minor: a **garbage** collection of the youngest **generation** alone.

collector: a process or processor responsible for garbage collection.

collector, copying: a garbage collector that copies all live data to a fresh region of the **heap**.

collector, mark-sweep: a **garbage** collection algorithm that marks each reachable **object** as **live**, and then returns unmarked objects to the storage manager.

collector, moving: a **garbage** collection algorithm that relocates data.

collector, on-the-fly: typically, an **incremental mark-sweep garbage collector**.

collector, tracing: a garbage collector that visits all **live** data.

compacting: the property of a memory management algorithm that moves all **cells** in use to a contiguous region of the workspace.

compaction order, arbitrary: a reordering of **heap objects** that is independent both of their previous ordering and of their kinship relationships.

compaction order, linearising: a reordering of **heap objects** in which objects that originally point to one another occupy adjacent memory positions after relocation.

compaction order, sliding: a reordering of **heap objects** that preserves their original order.

component, strongly-connected: a minimal set of nodes in a graph, each of which is reachable from each other node in the set.

comprehensive: the property of a garbage collection algorithm in which all **garbage** is reclaimed by the end of this collection cycle.

concurrent: two processes are concurrent if they may be executed asynchronously without any pre-defined interleaving.

cons: a spine node in a Lisp list.

conservative: a garbage collection algorithm which may overestimate the amount of **live** data. Especially garbage collectors that expect little cooperation from the compiler (and in particular have no knowledge of which locations contain pointers), and **incremental** and **concurrent** collectors that defer reclamation of some **garbage** until the next cycle.

creation space: a region of a **generation** in which **objects** are created.

crossing map: map of the **heap** showing which **page** boundaries are spanned by **objects**.

cycle: a subset of a linked data structure in which any **cell** in the set can be reached from any other cell in the set by following pointers.

dead: see **garbage**.

deallocation: the return of space to the storage manager.

deallocation, explicit: deallocation under programmer control.

direct: garbage collection method in which **liveness** information is held in the **cells** themselves (for example, reference counting).

dirty-bit: a flag that determines whether a unit of memory has been modified since it was last examined.

environment: a data structure that stores the actual parameters of a procedure.

exit table/vector: a table or vector that stores the pointers that refer to **objects** outside a region of memory.

expediency: the property of a garbage collection algorithm that can reclaim **garbage** despite parts of a distributed system being unavailable.

field: a number of contiguous words in which a single item of information can be stored.

finalisation: a clean-up action performed on an object when it dies.

flip: the action of a **copying collector** in which the rôles of **Fromspace** and **Tospace** are exchanged.

fragmentation: the **heap** is not fully occupied yet does not contain a hole large enough to satisfy an **allocation** request.

frame: a stack- or heap-allocated **activation record**.

free: a **cell** which is available for reuse; to return an unused cell to the storage manager.

freeing, recursive: a **reference counter**'s action of freeing each unshared element of a linked data structure when the head of the data structure is freed.

free-list: a linked list of **free cells**.

free-lists, segregated: an array of **free-lists**, one for each (common) **object** size.

Fromspace: the **semi-space** from which **objects** are copied by a **copying collector**.

garbage: space no longer required by the computation but that has not yet been reclaimed by the memory manager.

garbage collector: an algorithm that automatically recycles **garbage**.

garbage, floating: garbage that is not reclaimed in the current collection cycle.

garbage, tenured: objects that have been promoted to an older **generation** but are now **garbage**.

generation: a division of the **heap** according to the frequency with which it will be collected.

grey: colour of a **object** that has been visited by the garbage collector but whose direct descendants have not.

heap: a region of memory in which the **deallocation** of **objects** follows no specific causal order.

heap occupancy: the proportion of the **heap** occupied by **live** data.

incremental: an algorithm in which computation is performed in small steps, between which it may be suspended.

incremental-update: a **write-barrier** that records changes to the connectivity of the graph.

indirect garbage collection method in which the **liveness** of a **cell** cannot be determined by scrutiny of that cell alone.

large object area: the region of the **heap** in which large **objects** are stored, and which is managed by a separate strategy.

lazy languages: languages in which an expression is evaluated only when its value is required, and then at most once.

live: data that is required by the computation (or at least reachable by following a path of pointers from a **root**).

locality, spatial: the proximity with which related **cells** are stored.

locality, temporal: the proximity with which related **cells** are accessed.

mark-bit: a bit set in an **object** or a **bitmap** to indicate that the object is **live**.

marking: the process of visiting each **live cell** by following pointers from one or more **roots** and whereby a **mark-bit** is set corresponding to each live cell.

memory, virtual: a memory organisation in which the **address spaces** of running processes may be larger than the physical memory of the computer.

mortality: the rate at which **cells** become **garbage**.

multi-processor: an architecture that makes use of several processors.

mutator: the process or processor responsible for executing the user process, in particular changing the connectivity of the graph.

nepotism: the tendency of a **generational garbage collector** to preserve incorrectly the offspring of elderly **dead cells**.

object: a **cell** (unless otherwise explicitly stated).

object, passive: an **object** whose thread of control is external to it.

off-white: typically the colour of a **free cell** in the **heap**.

operation, atomic: an operation that once started will run to completion without interruption.

page: a block of memory used by the virtual memory system (generally of 1024 bytes or small multiples thereof).

page-fault: a **page** required is not found in main memory, forcing the operating system to load it from secondary memory.

pointer, back: a pointer to an earlier member of a linked data structure.

pointer, inter-generational: a pointer from an **object** in one **generation** to an object in another.

pointer, interior: a pointer to the interior of an **object** rather than to its start.

pointer, raw: a pointer of a type supported directly by the language; the opposite of a **smart pointer**.

pointer reversal: a technique for traversing a linked data structure by temporarily changing the direction of its pointers.

pointer, smart: a pointer that is overloaded so that it performs other operations as well as dereferencing.

pointer, weak: a pointer treated specially by the garbage collector. For example, it may not be used in **referential closure** calculations.

promotion: the advancement of an **object** from one **generation** to an older one.

real-time algorithm: an algorithm in which a guaranteed upper bound is placed on the time spent executing any operation. Commonly (but mistakenly) a synonym for **incremental**.

reclamation: the act of returning **garbage** to the storage manager for subsequent reuse.

reference count: a count that stores the number of pointers to an **object**.

reference count, sticky: the maximum value of a **limited-field reference count**. Once attained it cannot be reduced by reference counting alone.

reference counting, cyclic: a reference counting scheme that can reclaim **garbage cycles**.

reference counting, deferred: a reference counting scheme in which the **reference counts** of local variables are not updated.

reference counting, limited-field: a reference counting scheme which uses small **reference count** fields (often only one bit).

reference, dangling: a reference to a **cell** that has been **deallocated**.

regrouping, dynamic: a strategy of clustering **objects** according to the **mutator**'s actual pattern of access.

regrouping, static: a strategy of clustering **objects** according to their topology.

remembered set: a set of addresses of **objects** in an old **generation** that hold references to objects in younger generations.

rendezvous: a synchronisation point.

replication: a non-destructive **copying** algorithm which may create (temporary) replicas of **live objects**.

residency: see **heap occupancy**.

root: a storage location which is always deemed to be **live**.

scavenger: a **copying collector**.

semi-space: each half of (a region of) the **heap** managed by a **copying collector**.

shading: painting a **cell grey**.

shared: a **cell** which is referenced by more than one **object**.

snapshot-at-the-beginning: a **write-barrier** method that records the connectivity of the **heap** as it was at the start of a collection cycle.

space-leak: the situation in which a part of the **heap** is neither in use nor reclaimable by the memory manager.

static-area: an area where permanent **objects** are stored.

sticky: the maximum value that a **reference count** may reach, and once attained, cannot be reduced by **reference counting** alone.

stopping: an algorithm that suspends the computation of the user process while it performs a garbage collection.

stop-the-world: a garbage collection algorithm that suspends **mutators** (for example, in a distributed system).

suspension: see **closure**.

sweep: a linear scan through the **heap** in order to **free cells** that have not been **marked**.

sweep, lazy: a **sweep** interleaved with **allocation** to improve performance and, in particular, locality.

tag: information stored in a **cell** header, or a pointer to a cell, that determines the cell's type.

tenuring: the **promotion** of **objects** to a **generation** not (or infrequently) subject to garbage collection.

tenuring, adaptive: a policy of promoting that allows the **promotion** criterion to vary.

tenuring, demographic feedback-mediated: a form of **adaptive tenuring** that varies the **promotion** rate depending on the volume of survivors.

threading: method of rearranging pointers so all the words that hold pointers to a **cell** can be found from that cell.

tracing: the process of visiting each **live cell** by following pointers from one or more **roots**.

traversal, breadth-first: a traversal of a data structure in which the siblings of a node are visited before its descendants.

traversal, depth-first: a traversal of a data structure in which the siblings of a node are visited after its descendants.

treadmill: a non-moving **tracing** garbage collector; logically a **copying collector**.

tricolour-marking: marking with the **black–grey–white** colour scheme.

Tospace: the **semi-space** to which **objects** are copied by a **copying collector**.

type-accurate: a garbage collector that can determine unambiguously the layout of any **object** including registers and the stack.

white: colour of a **cell** that has not been visited by the garbage collector. At the end of the **tracing** phase, white cells are garbage.

ZCT: a Zero Count Table of **cells** whose **reference-count** has dropped to zero but which have not been reclaimed.

Bibliography

[Abdullahi *et al.*, 1992] S. Abdullahi, Eliot E. Miranda, and Graham Ringwood. Distributed garbage collection. In [IWMM, 1992].

[Abraham and Patel, 1987] Santosh Abraham and J. Patel. Parallel garbage collection on a virtual memory system. In E. Chiricozzi and A. D'Amato, editors, *International Conference on Parallel Processing and Applications*, pages 243–246, L'Aquila, Italy, September 1987. Elsevier-North Holland. Also technical report CSRD 620, University of Illinois at Urbana-Champaign, Center for Supercomputing Research and Development.

[Agha, 1986] G. Agha. *Actors: A Model of Concurrent Computation in Distributed Systems*. MIT Press, 1986.

[Aho *et al.*, 1986] Alfred V. Aho, Ravi Sethi, and Jeffrey D. Ullman. *Compilers: Principles, Techniques and Tools*. Addison-Wesley, 1986.

[Aho *et al.*, 1988] Alfred V. Aho, Brian W. Kernighan, and Peter J. Weinberger. *The AWK Programming Language*. Addison-Wesley, 1988.

[AIX, version 32] *Subroutines Overview*, General Programming Concepts, AIX version 3.2 edition, version 3.2.

[Alonso and Appel, 1990] R. Alonso and Andrew W. Appel. Advisor for flexible working sets. In *Proceedings of the 1990 ACM Sigmetrics Conference on Measurement and Modeling of Computer Systems. Boulder, May 22–25*, pages 153–162. ACM Press, 1990.

[Amamiya *et al.*, 1983] M. Amamiya, R. Hasegawa, and H. Mikami. List processing with a data flow machine. In *Proceedings of RIMS Symposia on Software Science and Engineering, 1980–1982*, volume 147 of *Lecture Notes in Computer Science*, pages 165–190, Kyoto, 1983. Springer-Verlag.

[Andre, 1986] David L. Andre. Paging in Lisp programs. Master's thesis, University of Maryland, College Park, Maryland, 1986.

[ANSI-C, 1989] American National Standards Institute. *American National Standard for Information Systems: Programming Language C*, December 1989.

[ANSI-C++, 1995] ANSI document X3J16/95–0087, ISO document WG21/N0618. *Draft Proposed International Standard for Information SSystems: Programming Language C++*, April 1995.

[Appel and Li, 1991] Andrew W. Appel and Kai Li. Virtual memory primitives for user programs. *ACM SIGPLAN Notices*, 26(4):96–107, 1991. Also in SIGARCH Computer Architecture News 19 (2) and SIGOPS Operating Systems Review 25.

[Appel and Shao, 1994] Andrew W. Appel and Zhong Shao. An empirical and analytic study of stack vs. heap cost for languages with closures. Technical Report CS–TR–450–94, Department of Computer Science, Princeton University, March 1994.

[Appel *et al.*, 1988] Andrew W. Appel, John R. Ellis, and Kai Li. Real-time concurrent collection on stock multiprocessors. *ACM SIGPLAN Notices*, 23(7):11–20, 1988.

[Appel, 1987] Andrew W. Appel. Garbage collection can be faster than stack allocation. *Information Processing Letters*, 25(4):275–279, 1987.

[Appel, 1989a] Andrew W. Appel. Runtime tags aren't necessary. *Lisp and Symbolic Computation*, 2:153–162, 1989.

[Appel, 1989b] Andrew W. Appel. Simple generational garbage collection and fast allocation. *Software Practice and Experience*, 19(2):171–183, 1989.

[Appel, 1992] Andrew W. Appel. *Compiling with Continuations*, chapter 16, pages 205–214. Cambridge University Press, 1992.

[Appleby *et al.*, 1988] Karen Appleby, Mats Carlsson, Seif Haridi, and Dan Sahlin. Garbage collection for Prolog based on WAM. *Communications of the ACM*, 31(6):719–741, 1988.

[ASPLOS, 1991] *Fourth International Conference on Architectural Support for Programming Languages and Operating Systems (ASPLOS IV)*, Santa Clara, CA, April 1991.

[Attardi *et al.*, 1995] Giuseppe Attardi, Tito Flagella, and Pietro Iglio. Performance tuning in a customizable collector. In [IWMM, 1995].

[Augusteijn, 1987] Lex Augusteijn. Garbage collection in a distributed environment. In [PARLE, 1987], pages 75–93.

[Axford, 1990] Thomas H. Axford. Reference counting of cyclic graphs for functional programs. *Computer Journal*, 33(5):466–470, 1990.

[Baden, 1983] Scott B. Baden. Low-overhead storage reclamation in the Smalltalk-80 virtual machine. In [Krasner, 1983], pages 331–342.

[Baecker, 1970] H. D. Baecker. Implementing the Algol–68 heap. *BIT*, 10(4):405–414, 1970.

[Baecker, 1972] H. D. Baecker. Garbage collection for virtual memory computer systems. *Communications of the ACM*, 15(11):981–986, November 1972.

[Baecker, 1975] H. D. Baecker. Areas and record classes. *Computer Journal*, 18(3):223–226, August 1975.

[Baker *et al.*, 1985] Brenda Baker, E. G. Coffman, and D. E. Willard. Algorithms for resolving conflicts in dynamic storage allocation. *Journal of the ACM*, 32(2):327–343, April 1985.

[Baker, 1978] Henry G. Baker. List processing in real-time on a serial computer. *Communications of the ACM*, 21(4):280–94, 1978. Also AI Laboratory Working Paper 139, 1977.

[Baker, 1991] Henry G. Baker. Cache-conscious copying collection. In [OOPSLA-gc, 1991].

[Baker, 1992] Henry G. Baker. The Treadmill, real-time garbage collection without motion sickness. *ACM SIGPLAN Notices*, 27(3), March 1992.

[Baker, 1994] Henry G. Baker. Minimising reference count updating with deferred and anchored pointers for functional data structures. *ACM SIGPLAN Notices*, 29(9), September 1994.

[Bal and Tanenbaum, 1991] Henri E. Bal and Andrew S. Tanenbaum. Distributed programming with shared data. *Computer Languages*, 16(2):129–146, 1991.

[Bal *et al.*, 1992] Henri E. Bal, M. Frans Kaashoek, and Andrew S. Tanenbaum. Orca: A language for parallel programming of distributed systems. *ACM Transactions on Software Engineering*, 18(3):190–205, 1992.

[Barrett and Zorn, 1993a] David A. Barrett and Benjamin Zorn. Garbage collection using a dynamic threatening boundary. Computer Science Technical Report CU-CS-659-93, University of Colorado, July 1993.

[Barrett and Zorn, 1993b] David A. Barrett and Benjamin G. Zorn. Using lifetime predictors to improve memory allocation performance. In [PLDI, 1993], pages 187–196.

[Bartlett, 1988] Joel F. Bartlett. Compacting garbage collection with ambiguous roots. Technical Report 88/2, DEC Western Research Laboratory, Palo Alto, CA, February 1988. Also in Lisp Pointers 1, 6 (April–June 1988), 2–12.

[Bartlett, 1989a] Joel F. Bartlett. Mostly-Copying garbage collection picks up generations and C++. Technical note, DEC Western Research Laboratory, Palo Alto, CA, October 1989. Sources available in ftp://gatekeeper.dec.com/pub/DEC/CCgc.

[Bartlett, 1989b] Joel F. Bartlett. SCHEME->C: a portable Scheme-to-C compiler. Technical report, DEC Western Research Laboratory, Palo Alto, CA, January 1989.

[Bartlett, 1990] Joel F. Bartlett. A generational, compacting collector for C++. In [OOPSLA-gc, 1990].

[Bauer and Wössner, 1982] F. L. Bauer and H. Wössner. *Algorithmic Language and Program Development*. Springer-Verlag, 1982.

[Bawden et al., 1977] A. Bawden, Richard Greenblatt, J. Holloway, T. Knight, David A. Moon, and D. Weinreb. Lisp machine progress report. Technical Report Memo 444, A.I. Lab, MIT, Cambridge, MA, August 1977.

[Bekkers et al., 1992] Yves Bekkers, Olivier Ridoux, and L. Ungaro. A survey on memory management for logic programming. In [IWMM, 1992].

[Ben-Ari, 1982] Mordechai Ben-Ari. On-the-fly garbage collection: New algorithms inspired by program proofs. In M. Nielsen and E. M. Schmidt, editors, *Automata, languages and programming. Ninth colloquium*, pages 14–22, Aarhus, Denmark, July 12–16 1982. Springer-Verlag.

[Ben-Ari, 1984] Mordechai Ben-Ari. Algorithms for on-the-fly garbage collection. *ACM Transactions on Programming Languages and Systems*, 6(3):333–344, July 1984.

[Bennet et al., 1990] J. Bennet, J. Carter, and W. Zwaenepoel. Munin: Distributed shared memory based on type-specific memory coherence. In *ACM Symposium on Principles and Practice of Parallel Programming*, volume 30 of *ACM SIGPLAN Notices*, pages 168–176. ACM Press, March 1990.

[Berkeley and Bobrow, 1974] E. C. Berkeley and Daniel G. Bobrow, editors. *The Programming Language LISP: Its Operation and Applications*. Information International, Inc., Cambridge, MA, fourth edition, 1974.

[Bevan, 1987] David I. Bevan. Distributed garbage collection using reference counting. In *PARLE Parallel Architectures and Languages Europe*, volume 259 of *Lecture Notes in Computer Science*, pages 176–187. Springer-Verlag, June 1987.

[Birrell et al., 1993] Andrew Birrell, David Evers, Greg Nelson, Susan Owicki, and Edward Wobber. Distributed garbage collection for network objects. Technical Report 116, DEC Systems Research Center, 130 Lytton Avenue, Palo Alto, CA 94301, December 1993.

[Bishop, 1977] Peter B. Bishop. *Computer Systems with a Very Large Address Space and Garbage Collection*. PhD thesis, MIT Laboratory for Computer Science, May 1977. Technical report MIT/LCS/TR–178.

[Black et al., 1986] Andrew Black, Norman Hutchinson, Eric Jul, and Henry Levy. Object structure in the Emerald system. In [OOPSLA, 1986], pages 78–86.

[Black et al., 1987] Andrew Black, Norman Hutchinson, Eric Jul, Henry Levy, and Larry Carter. Distribution and abstract types in Emerald. *ACM Transactions on Software Engineering*, 13(1):65–76, January 1987.

[Blau, 1983] Ricki Blau. Paging on an object-oriented personal computer for Smalltalk. In *ACM SIGMETRICS Conference on Measurement and Modeling of Computer Systems Minneapolis*. ACM Press, August 1983. Also appears as Technical Report UCB/CSD 83/125, University of California at Berkeley, Computer Science Division (EECS).

[Bobrow and Clark, 1979] Daniel G. Bobrow and Douglas W. Clark. Compact encodings of list structure. *ACM Transactions on Programming Languages and Systems*, 1(2):266–286, October 1979.

[Bobrow and Murphy, 1967] Daniel G. Bobrow and Daniel L. Murphy. Structure of a LISP system using two-level storage. *Communications of the ACM*, 10(3):155–159, March 1967.

[Bobrow, 1980] Daniel G. Bobrow. Managing re-entrant structures using reference counts. *ACM Transactions on Programming Languages and Systems*, 2(3):269–273, July 1980.

[Boehm and Chase, 1992] Hans-Juergen Boehm and David R. Chase. A proposal for garbage-collector-safe C compilation. *Journal of C Language Translation*, pages 126–141, 1992.

[Boehm and Shao, 1993] Hans-Juergen Boehm and Zhong Shao. Inferring type maps during garbage collection. In [OOPSLA-gc, 1993].

[Boehm and Weiser, 1988] Hans-Juergen Boehm and Mark Weiser. Garbage collection in an uncooperative environment. *Software Practice and Experience*, 18(9):807–820, 1988.

[Boehm *et al.*, 1991] Hans-Juergen Boehm, Alan J. Demers, and Scott Shenker. Mostly parallel garbage collection. *ACM SIGPLAN Notices*, 26(6):157–164, 1991.

[Boehm, 1991a] Hans-Juergen Boehm. Hardware and operating system support for conservative garbage collection. In [IWOOOS, 1991], pages 61–67.

[Boehm, 1991b] Hans-Juergen Boehm. Simple GC-safe compilation. In [OOPSLA-gc, 1991].

[Boehm, 1993] Hans-Juergen Boehm. Space efficient conservative garbage collection. In [PLDI, 1993], pages 197–206.

[Boehm, 1994a] Hans-Juergen Boehm. USENET, April 1994.

[Boehm, 1994b] Hans-Juergen Boehm. Re: Reference counting (was Re: Searching method for incremental garbage collection). USENET, November 1994.

[Boehm, 1995a] Hans-Juergen Boehm. USENET comp.lang.c++, January 1995.

[Boehm, 1995b] Hans-Juergen Boehm. Mark-sweep vs. copying collection and asymptotic complexity. ftp://parcftp.xerox.com/pub/garbage/complexity.ps, September 1995.

[Boehm, 1995c] Hans-Juergen Boehm. Re: Real-time GC (was Re: Widespread C++ competency gap). USENET comp.lang.c++, January 1995.

[Bozman *et al.*, 1984] G. Bozman, W. Buco, T. P. Daly, and W. H. Tetzlaff. Analysis of free storage algorithms — revisited. *IBM Systems Journal*, 23(1):44–64, 1984.

[Branquart and Lewi, 1971] P. Branquart and J. Lewi. A scheme of storage allocation and garbage collection for Algol–68. In J. E. L. Peck, editor, *Algol–68 Implementation*, pages 198–238. North-Holland, Amsterdam, 1971.

[Brent, 1989] R. P. Brent. Efficient implementation of the first-fit strategy for dynamic storage allocation. *ACM Transactions on Programming Languages and Systems*, 11(3):388–403, July 1989.

[Brooks, 1984] Rodney A. Brooks. Trading data space for reduced time and code space in real-time garbage collection on stock hardware. In [LFP, 1984], pages 256–262.

[Brownbridge, 1984] David R. Brownbridge. *Recursive Structures in Computer Systems*. PhD thesis, University of Newcastle upon Tyne, September 1984.

[Brownbridge, 1985] David R. Brownbridge. Cyclic reference counting for combinator machines. In [FPCA, 1985].

[Brus *et al.*, 1987] T. Brus, M. J. C. D. van Eekelen, M. J. Plasmeijer, and H. P. Barendregt. Clean — a language for functional graph rewriting. In [FPCA, 1987], pages 364–384.

[Cann and Oldehoeft, 1988] D. C. Cann and Rod R. Oldehoeft. Reference count and copy elimination for parallel applicative computing. Technical Report CS–88–129, Department of Computer Science, Colorado State University, Fort Collins, CO, 1988.

[Cann *et al.*, 1992] D. C. Cann, J. T. Feo, A. D. W. Bohoem, and Rod R. Oldehoeft. *SISAL Reference Manual: Language Version 2.0*, 1992.

[Cardelli *et al.*, 1988] Luca Cardelli, James Donahue, Lucille Glassman, Mick Jordan, Bill Kalsow, and Greg Nelson. Modula-3 report (revised). Research Report PRC–131, DEC Systems Research Center and Olivetti Research Center, 1988.

[Cardelli *et al.*, 1992] Luca Cardelli, James Donahue, Lucille Glassman, Mick Jordan, Bill Kalsow, and Greg Nelson. Modula-3 language definition. *ACM SIGPLAN Notices*, 27(8):15–42, August 1992.

[Caudill and Wirfs-Brock, 1986] Patrick J. Caudill and Allen Wirfs-Brock. A third-generation Smalltalk-80 implementation. In [OOPSLA, 1986], pages 119–130.

[CenterLine, 1992] CenterLine Software, Cambridge, MA. *CodeCenter, The Programming Environment*, 1992.

[Chailloux, 1992] Emmanuel Chailloux. A conservative garbage collector with ambiguous roots, for static type checking languages. In [IWMM, 1992].

[Chambers *et al.*, 1989] Craig Chambers, David M. Ungar, and Elgin Lee. An efficient implementation of SELF, a dynamically-typed object-oriented language based on prototypes. In *OOPSLA'89 ACM Conference on Object-Oriented Systems, Languages and Applications*, volume 24(10) of *ACM SIGPLAN Notices*, pages 48–70, New Orleans, LA, October 1989. ACM Press.

[Chambers *et al.*, 1991] Craig Chambers, David M. Ungar, and Frank Jackson. An efficient implementation of SELF, a dynamically-typed object-oriented language based on prototypes. *Lisp and Symbolic Computation*, 4:243–281, 1991.

[Chambers, 1992] Craig Chambers. *The Design and Implementation of the SELF Compiler, an Optimizing Compiler for an Objected-Oriented Programming Language.* PhD thesis, Stanford University, March 1992.

[Chang and Gehringer, 1993a] J. Morris Chang and Edward F. Gehringer. Evaluation of an object-caching coprocessor design for object-oriented systems. In *Proceedings of IEEE International Conference on Computer Design.* IEEE Press, October 1993.

[Chang and Gehringer, 1993b] J. Morris Chang and Edward F. Gehringer. Performance of object caching for object-oriented systems. In *Proceedings of International Conference on Very Large Scale Integration, VLSI'93, Grenoble, France*, September 1993.

[Chase, 1987] David R. Chase. Garbage collection and other optimizations. Technical report, Rice University, August 1987.

[Chase, 1988] David R. Chase. Safety considerations for storage allocation optimizations. *ACM SIGPLAN Notices*, 23(7):1–10, 1988.

[Cheney, 1970] C. J. Cheney. A non-recursive list compacting algorithm. *Communications of the ACM*, 13(11):677–8, November 1970.

[Cheong, 1992] Fah-Chun Cheong. Almost tag-free garbage collection for strongly-typed object-oriented languages. Technical Report CSE-TR-126-92, University of Michigan, 1992.

[Chikayama and Kimura, 1987] T. Chikayama and Y. Kimura. Multiple reference management in Flat GHC. In *4th International Conference on Logic Programming*, pages 276–293, 1987.

[Christopher, 1984] T. W. Christopher. Reference count garbage collection. *Software Practice and Experience*, 14(6):503–507, June 1984.

[Clark and Green, 1977] Douglas W. Clark and C. Cordell Green. An empirical study of list structure in Lisp. *Communications of the ACM*, 20(2):78–86, February 1977.

[Clark, 1975] Douglas W. Clark. A fast algorithm for copying binary trees. *Information Processing Letters*, 9(3):62–63, December 1975.

[Clark, 1976] Douglas W. Clark. An efficient list moving algorithm using constant workspace. *Communications of the ACM*, 19(6):352–354, June 1976.

[Clark, 1978] Douglas W. Clark. A fast algorithm for copying list structures. *Communications of the ACM*, 21(5):351–357, May 1978.

[Clark, 1979] Douglas W. Clark. Measurements of dynamic list structure in Lisp. *ACM Transactions on Software Engineering*, 5(1):51–59, January 1979.

[Codewright's Toolworks, 1993] Codewright's Toolworks, San Pedro, CA. *Alloc-GC: The Garbage Collecting Replacement for malloc()*, 1993.

[Cohen and Nicolau, 1983] Jacques Cohen and Alexandru Nicolau.   Comparison of compacting algorithms for garbage collection. *ACM Transactions on Programming Languages and Systems*, 5(4):532–553, 1983.

[Cohen and Trilling, 1967] Jacques Cohen and Laurent Trilling.   Remarks on garbage collection using a two level storage. *BIT*, 7(1):22–30, 1967.

[Collins, 1960] George E. Collins.   A method for overlapping and erasure of lists. *Communications of the ACM*, 3(12):655–657, December 1960.

[Coplien, 1992] James Coplien. *Advanced C++ Programming Styles and Idioms*. Addison-Wesley, 1992.

[Corporaal *et al.*, 1988] H. Corporaal, T. Veldman, and A. J. van de Goor. Reference weight-based garbage collection for distributed systems. In *Proceedings of the SION Conference on Computing Science in the Netherlands*, Utrecht, November 1988.

[Corporaal *et al.*, 1990] H. Corporaal, T. Veldman, and A. J. van de Goor. Efficient, reference weight-based garbage collection method for distributed systems. In *PARBASE-90: International Conference on Databases, Parallel Architectures, and Their Applications*, pages 463–465, Miami Beach, 7–9 March 1990. IEEE Press.

[Corporaal, 1989] H. Corporaal. Garbage collection in distributed systems. Internal report, Technical University, Delft, 1989.

[Courts, 1988] Robert Courts.   Improving locality of reference in a garbage-collecting memory management-system. *Communications of the ACM*, 31(9):1128–1138, 1988.

[Cridlig, 1992] Regis Cridlig. An optimising ML to C compiler. In David MacQueen, editor, *ACM SIGPLAN Workshop on ML and its Applications*, San Francisco, June 1992. ACM Press.

[Davies, 1984] D. Julian M. Davies.   Memory occupancy patterns in garbage collection systems. *Communications of the ACM*, 27(8):819–825, August 1984.

[Dawson, 1992] Jeffrey L. Dawson. Improved effectiveness from a real-time LISP garbage collector. In [LFP, 1992], pages 159–167.

[Demers *et al.*, 1990] Alan Demers, Mark Weiser, Barry Hayes, Daniel G. Bobrow, and Scott Shenker.   Combining generational and conservative garbage collection: Framework and implementations. In *Conference Record of the Seventeenth Annual ACM Symposium on Principles of Programming Languages*, ACM SIGPLAN Notices, pages 261–269, San Francisco, CA, January 1990. ACM Press.

[Denning, 1968] P. J. Denning.   The working set model for program behaviour. *Communications of the ACM*, 11:323–333, 1968.

[Detlefs and Kalsow, 1995] Dave Detlefs and Bill Kalsow. Debugging storage management problems in garbage-collected environments. In *USENIX Conference on Object-Oriented Technologies*. USENIX Association, June 1995.

[Detlefs *et al.*, 1993] David L. Detlefs, Al Dosser, and Benjamin Zorn. Memory allocation costs in large C and C++ programs. Computer Science Technical Report CU-CS-665-93, Digital Equipment Corporation and University of Colorado, 130 Lytton Avenue, Palo Alto, CA 94301 and Campus Box 430, Boulder, CO 80309, August 1993.

[Detlefs *et al.*, 1994] David Detlefs, Al Dosser, and Benjamin Zorn. Memory allocation costs in large C and C++ programs. *Software Practice and Experience*, 24(6), 1994.

[Detlefs, 1990] David L. Detlefs. Concurrent garbage collection for C++. Technical Report CMU–CS–90–119, Carnegie Mellon University, Pittsburgh, PA, May 1990.

[Detlefs, 1991a] David L. Detlefs. *Concurrent, Atomic Garbage Collection*. PhD thesis, Department of Computer Science, Carnegie Mellon University, Pittsburgh, PA, 15213, November 1991.

[Detlefs, 1991b] David L. Detlefs. Concurrent garbage collection for C++. In Peter Lee, editor, *Topics in Advanced Language Implementation*. MIT Press, 1991.

[Detlefs, 1992] David L. Detlefs. Garbage collection and runtime typing as a C++ library. In *USENIX C++ Conference*, Portland, Oregon, August 1992. USENIX Association.

[Detlefs, 1993] David L. Detlefs. Empirical evidence for using garbage collection in C and C++ programs. In [OOPSLA-gc, 1993].

[DeTreville, 1990a] John DeTreville. Experience with concurrent garbage collectors for Modula-2+. Technical Report 64, DEC Systems Research Center, Palo Alto, CA, August 1990.

[DeTreville, 1990b] John DeTreville. Heap usage in the Topaz environment. Technical Report 63, DEC Systems Research Center, Palo Alto, CA, August 1990.

[Deutsch and Bobrow, 1976] L. Peter Deutsch and Daniel G. Bobrow. An efficient incremental automatic garbage collector. *Communications of the ACM*, 19(9):522–526, September 1976.

[Deutsch, 1983] L. Peter Deutsch. The Dorado Smalltalk-80 implementation: Hardware architecture's impact on software architecture. In [Krasner, 1983], pages 113–125.

[Dewar and McCann, 1977] Robert B. K. Dewar and A. P. McCann. MACRO SPITBOL — a SNOBOL4 compiler. *Software Practice and Experience*, 7(1):95–113, 1977.

[Dickman, 1991] Peter Dickman. Effective load balancing in a distributed object-support operating system. In [IWOOOS, 1991].

[Dijkstra and Scholten, 1989] Edsgar W. Dijkstra and C. S. Scholten. Termination detection for diffusing computations. *Information Processing Letters*, 11, August 1989.

[Dijkstra *et al.*, 1976] Edsgar W. Dijkstra, Leslie Lamport, A. J. Martin, C. S. Scholten, and E. F. M. Steffens. On-the-fly garbage collection: An exercise in cooperation. In *Lecture Notes in Computer Science, No. 46*. Springer-Verlag, New York, 1976.

[Dijkstra et al., 1978] Edsgar W. Dijkstra, Leslie Lamport, A. J. Martin, C. S. Scholten, and E. F. M. Steffens. On-the-fly garbage collection: An exercise in cooperation. *Communications of the ACM*, 21(11):965–975, November 1978.

[Dijkstra, 1975] Edsgar W. Dijkstra. Notes on a real-time garbage collection system. From a conversation with D. E. Knuth (private collection of D. E. Knuth), 1975.

[Diwan et al., 1992] Amer Diwan, J. Eliot B. Moss, and Richard L. Hudson. Compiler support for garbage collection in a statically typed language. In *Proceedings of SIGPLAN'92 Conference on Programming Languages Design and Implementation*, volume 27 of *ACM SIGPLAN Notices*, pages 273–282, San Francisco, CA, June 1992. ACM Press.

[Diwan et al., 1994] Amer Diwan, David Tarditi, and J. Eliot B. Moss. Memory subsystem performance of programs using copying garbage collection. In [POPL, 1994].

[Diwan, 1991] Amer Diwan. Stack tracing in a statically typed language. In [OOPSLA-gc, 1991].

[Doligez and Gonthier, 1994] Damien Doligez and Georges Gonthier. Portable, unobtrusive garbage collection for multiprocessor systems. In [POPL, 1994].

[Doligez and Leroy, 1993] Damien Doligez and Xavier Leroy. A concurrent generational garbage collector for a multi-threaded implementation of ML. In *Conference Record of the Twentieth Annual ACM Symposium on Principles of Programming Languages*, ACM SIGPLAN Notices, pages 113–123. ACM Press, January 1993.

[Douglis, 1993] Fred Douglis. The compression cache: Using on-line compression to extend physical memory. In *1993 Winter USENIX Conference*, pages 519–529, San Diego, CA, January 1993. USENIX Association.

[Dwyer, 1973] B. Dwyer. Simple algorithms for traversing a tree without an auxiliary stack. *Inf Process. Lett.*, 2(5):143–145, December 1973.

[Eckart and Leblanc, 1987] J. Dana Eckart and Richard J. Leblanc. Distributed garbage collection. *ACM SIGPLAN Notices*, 22(7):264–273, 1987.

[Edelson and Pohl, 1990] Daniel R. Edelson and Ira Pohl. The case for garbage collection in C++. In [OOPSLA-gc, 1990]. Also University of California Santa Cruz technical report UCSC-CRL-90-37.

[Edelson and Pohl, 1991] Daniel R. Edelson and Ira Pohl. A copying collector for C++. In *Usenix C++ Conference Proceedings*, pages 85–102. USENIX Association, 1991.

[Edelson, 1990] Daniel R. Edelson. Dynamic storage reclamation in C++. Master's thesis, University of California at Santa Cruz, June 1990.

[Edelson, 1992a] Daniel R. Edelson. A mark-and-sweep collector for C++. In [POPL, 1992].

[Edelson, 1992b] Daniel R. Edelson. Precompiling C++ for garbage collection. In [IWMM, 1992].

[Edelson, 1992c] Daniel R. Edelson. Smart pointers: They're smart, but they're not pointers. In *USENIX C++ Conference*. USENIX Association, 1992.

[Edelson, 1993a] Daniel R. Edelson. Comparing two garbage collectors for C++. Technical Report UCSC-CRL-93-20, University of California, Santa Cruz, January 1993.

[Edelson, 1993b] Daniel Ross Edelson. *Type-Specific Storage Management*. PhD thesis, University of California, Santa Cruz, May 1993.

[Ellis and Detlefs, 1993] John R. Ellis and David L. Detlefs. Safe, efficient garbage collection for C++. Technical report, Xerox PARC, Palo Alto, CA, 1993.

[Ellis and Stroustrup, 1990] Margaret A. Ellis and Bjarne Stroustrup. *The Annotated C++ Reference Manual*. Addison-Wesley, 1990.

[Ellis, 1993] John R. Ellis. Put up or shut up. In [OOPSLA-gc, 1993].

[Ellis, 1995] John Ellis. Re: GC, and objects finalization (was: GC, again). USENET comp.lang.misc, January 1995.

[Engelstad and Vandendorpe, 1991] Steven L. Engelstad and James E. Vandendorpe. Automatic storage management for systems with real time constraints. In [OOPSLA-gc, 1991].

[Explorer, 1987, 1987] *Explorer (tm) System Software Design Notes*, June 1987. Texas Instruments part number 2243208–0001*A.

[Fenichel and Yochelson, 1969] Robert R. Fenichel and Jerome C. Yochelson. A Lisp garbage collector for virtual memory computer systems. *Communications of the ACM*, 12(11):611–612, November 1969.

[Fernandez and Hanson, 1992] Mary F. Fernandez and David R. Hanson. Garbage collection alternatives for Icon. *Software Practice and Experience*, 22(8):659–672, August 1992.

[Ferrari, 1990] Domenico Ferrari. Improving locality by critical working sets. *Communications of the ACM*, 17(11):612–620, November 1990.

[Ferreira, 1991] Paulo Ferreira. Garbage collection in C++. In [OOPSLA-gc, 1991].

[Fisher, 1974] David A. Fisher. Bounded workspace garbage collection in an address order preserving list processing environment. *Information Processing Letters*, 3(1):25–32, July 1974.

[Fisher, 1975] David A. Fisher. Copying cyclic list structure in linear time using bounded workspace. *Communications of the ACM*, 18(5):251–252, May 1975.

[Fitch and Norman, 1978] John P. Fitch and Arthur C. Norman. A note on compacting garbage collection. *Computer Journal*, 21(1):31–34, February 1978.

[Fiterman, 1995] Charles Fiterman. An incremental reflexive garbage collector for C++. USENET comp.lang.c++, January 1995.

[Fleisch, 1989] B. D. Fleisch. Mirage: A coherent distributed shared memory design. In *Proceedings of 12th ACM Symposium on Operating Systems Principles*, pages 211–213. ACM Press, December 1989.

[Foderaro and Fateman, 1981] John K. Foderaro and Richard J. Fateman. Characterization of VAX Macsyma. In *1981 ACM Symposium on Symbolic and Algebraic Computation*, pages 14–19, Berkeley, CA, 1981. ACM Press.

[Foderaro *et al.*, 1985] John K. Foderaro, Keith Sklower, Kevin Layer, *et al. Franz Lisp Reference Manual*. Franz Inc., 1985.

[Forin *et al.*, 1989] A. Forin, J. Barrera, M. Young, and R. Rashid. Design, implementation, and performance evaluation of a distributed shared memory server for Mach. In *Proceedings of the 1989 Winter USENIX conference*. USENIX Association, January 1989.

[Foster, 1989] Ian Foster. A multicomputer garbage collector for a single-assignment language. *International Journal of Parallel Programming*, 18(3):181–203, 1989.

[FPCA, 1985] Jean-Pierre Jouannaud, editor. *Record of the 1985 Conference on Functional Programming and Computer Architecture*, volume 201 of *Lecture Notes in Computer Science*, Nancy, France, September 1985. Springer-Verlag.

[FPCA, 1987] Gilles Kahn, editor. *Record of the 1987 Conference on Functional Programming and Computer Architecture*, volume 274 of *Lecture Notes in Computer Science*, Portland, Oregon, September 1987. Springer-Verlag.

[Francez, 1978] Nissim Francez. An application of a method for analysis of cyclic programs. *ACM Transactions on Software Engineering*, 4(5):371–377, September 1978.

[Franz, 1992, 1992] Franz Inc. *Allegro CL User Guide, Version 4.1*, revision 2 edition, March 1992.

[Friedman and Wise, 1978] Daniel P. Friedman and David S. Wise. Aspects of applicative programming for parallel processing. *IEEE Transactions on Computers*, 27(4):289–296, April 1978.

[Friedman and Wise, 1979] Daniel P. Friedman and David S. Wise. Reference counting can manage the circular environments of mutual recursion. *Information Processing Letters*, 8(1):41–45, January 1979.

[Furusou *et al.*, 1991] Shinichi Furusou, Satoshi Matsuoka, and Akinori Yonezawa. Parallel conservative garbage collection with fast allocation. In [OOPSLA-gc, 1991].

[Gabriel, 1985] Richard P. Gabriel. *Performance and Evaluation of Lisp Systems*. MIT Press Series in Computer Science. MIT Press, Cambridge, MA, 1985.

[Ganesan, 1994] Ravichandran Ganesan. Local variable allocation for accurate garbage collection of C++. Master's thesis, Iowa State University, July 1994. Technical report ISUTR 94–12.

[Gee *et al.*, 1993] Jeffrey D. Gee, Mark D. Hill, Dionisios N. Pnevmatikatos, and Alan J. Smith. Cache performance of the SPEC92 benchmark suite. *IEEE Micro*, 13(4):17–27, 1993.

[Gehringer and Chang, 1993] Edward F. Gehringer and Ellis Chang. Hardware-assisted memory management. In [OOPSLA-gc, 1993].

[Gelernter *et al.*, 1960] H. Gelernter, J. R. Hansen, and C. L. Gerberich. A Fortran-compiled list processing language. *Journal of the ACM*, 7(2):87–101, April 1960.

[Gerhart, 1979] S. L. Gerhart. A derivation oriented proof of Schorr–Waite marking algorithm. *Lecture Notes in Computer Science*, 69:472–492, 1979.

[Ginter, 1991] Andrew Ginter. Cooperative garbage collection using smart pointers in the C++ programming language. Master's thesis, University of Calgary, December 1991. Technical report 91/451/45.

[Girard, 1987] J.-Y. Girard. Linear logic. *Theoretical Computer Science*, 50:1–102, 1987.

[Glaser and Thompson, 1987] Hugh W. Glaser and P. Thompson. Lazy garbage collection. *Software Practice and Experience*, 17(1):1–4, January 1987.

[Glaser *et al.*, 1989] Hugh W. Glaser, Michael Reeve, and S. Wright. An analysis of reference count garbage collection schemes for declarative languages. Technical report, Department of Computing, Imperial College, London, 1989.

[Glaser, 1987] Hugh W. Glaser. On minimal overhead reference count garbage collection in distributed systems. Technical report, Department of Computing, Imperial College, London, 1987.

[Goldberg and Gloger, 1992] Benjamin Goldberg and Michael Gloger. Polymorphic type reconstruction for garbage collection without tags. In [LFP, 1992], pages 53–65.

[Goldberg and Robson, 1983] Adele Goldberg and D. Robson. *Smalltalk-80: The Language and its Implementation*. Addison-Wesley, 1983.

[Goldberg, 1989] Benjamin Goldberg. Generational reference counting: A reduced-communication distributed storage reclamation scheme. In [PLDI, 1989], pages 313–320.

[Goldberg, 1991] Benjamin Goldberg. Tag-free garbage collection for strongly typed programming languages. *ACM SIGPLAN Notices*, 26(6):165–176, 1991.

[Goldberg, 1992] Benjamin Goldberg. Incremental garbage collection without tags. In *Proceedings ESOP92 — European Symposium on Programming*, 1992.

[Gonçalves and Appel, 1995] Marcelo J. R. Gonçalves and Andrew W. Appel. Cache performance of fast-allocating programs. In *Record of the 1995 Conference on Functional Programming and Computer Architecture*, June 1995.

[Goto *et al.*, 1988] Atsuhiro Goto, Y. Kimura, T. Nakagawa, and T. Chikayama. Lazy reference counting: An incremental garbage collection method for parallel inference machines. In *Proceedings of Fifth International Conference on Logic Programming*, pages 1241–1256, 1988. Also ICOT Technical Report TR-354, 1988.

[Greenblatt, 1984] Richard Greenblatt. The LISP machine. In D. R. Barstow, H. E. Shrobe, and E. Sandewall, editors, *Interactive Programming Environments*. McGraw-Hill, 1984.

[Gries, 1977] David Gries. An exercise in proving parallel programs correct. *Communications of the ACM*, 20(12):921–930, December 1977.

[Gries, 1979] David Gries. The Schorr–Waite graph marking algorithm. *Acta Informatica*, 11(3):223–232, 1979.

[Grit and Page, 1981] Dale H. Grit and Rex L. Page. Deleting irrelevant tasks in an expression-oriented multiprocessor system. *ACM Transactions on Programming Languages and Systems*, 3(1):49–59, January 1981.

[Grunwald *et al.*, 1993] Dirk Grunwald, Benjamin Zorn, and Robert Henderson. Improving the cache locality of memory allocation. In [PLDI, 1993], pages 177–186.

[Guggilla, 1994] Satish Kumar Guggilla. Generational garbage collection of C++ targeted to SPARC architectures. Master's thesis, Iowa State University, July 1994. Technical report ISUTR 94-11.

[Gupta and Fuchs, 1988] Aloke Gupta and W. K. Fuchs. Reliable garbage collection in distributed object oriented systems. In *Proceedings of the Twelfth Annual International Computer Software Applications Conference (COMPSAC 88)*, pages 324–328, Chicago, October 1988. IEEE Press.

[Haddon and Waite, 1967] B. K. Haddon and W. M. Waite. A compaction procedure for variable length storage elements. *Computer Journal*, 10:162–165, August 1967.

[Halstead, 1978] Robert H. Halstead. Multiple-processor implementations of message passing systems. Technical Report TR–198, MIT Laboratory for Computer Science, April 1978.

[Halstead, 1984] Robert H. Halstead. Implementation of Multilisp: Lisp on a multiprocessor. In [LFP, 1984].

[Hansen, 1969] Wilfred J. Hansen. Compact list representation: Definition, garbage collection, and system implementation. *Communications of the ACM*, 12(9):499–507, September 1969.

[Hanson, 1977] David R. Hanson. Storage management for an implementation of Snobol 4. *Software Practice and Experience*, 7(2):179–192, 1977.

[Hart and Evans, 1974] Timothy P. Hart and Thomas G. Evans. Notes on implementing LISP for the M–460 computer. In [Berkeley and Bobrow, 1974], pages 191–203.

[Hartel, 1988] Pieter H. Hartel. *Performance Analysis of Storage Management in Combinator Graph Reduction*. PhD thesis, Department of Computer Systems, University of Amsterdam, Amsterdam, 1988.

[Hartel, 1990] Pieter H. Hartel. A comparison of 3 garbage collection algorithms. *Structured Programming*, 11(3):117–127, 1990.

[Hayes, 1990] Barry Hayes. Open systems require conservative garbage collectors. In [OOPSLA-gc, 1990].

[Hayes, 1991] Barry Hayes. Using key object opportunism to collect old objects. In [OOPSLA, 1991], pages 33–46.

[Hayes, 1992] Barry Hayes. Finalization of the collector interface. In [IWMM, 1992].

[Hayes, 1993] Barry Hayes. *Key Objects in Garbage Collection*. PhD thesis, Stanford University, March 1993.

[Hederman, 1988] Lucy Hederman. *Compile-time Garbage Collection Using Reference Count Analysis*. PhD thesis, Rice University, August 1988. Also Rice University Technical Report TR88–75 but, according to Rice University's technical report list, this report is no longer available for distribution.

[Hennessey, 1993] Wade Hennessey. Real-time garbage collection in a multimedia programming language. In [OOPSLA-gc, 1993].

[Hennessy and Patterson, 1996] John L. Hennessy and David A. Patterson. *Computer Architecture: A Quantitative Approach*. Morgan Kaufman, second edition, 1996.

[Hewitt, 1977] Carl Hewitt. Viewing control structures as patterns of passing messages. *Journal of Artificial Intelligence*, 8(3):323–364, June 1977.

[Hickey and Cohen, 1984] Tim Hickey and Jacques Cohen. Performance analysis of on-the-fly garbage collection. *Communications of the ACM*, 27(11):1143–1154, November 1984.

[Hill, 1987] Mark D. Hill. *Aspects of Cache Memory and Instruction Buffer Performance*. PhD thesis, University of California, Berkeley, November 1987. Also UCB/CSD Technical report 87/381.

[Hill, 1988] Mark D. Hill. A case for direct-mapped caches. *IEEE Computer*, 21(12):25–40, December 1988.

[Hölzle, 1993] Urs Hölzle. A fast write barrier for generational garbage collectors. In [OOPSLA-gc, 1993].

[Hosking and Hudson, 1993] Antony L. Hosking and Richard L. Hudson. Remembered sets can also play cards. In [OOPSLA-gc, 1993].

[Hosking *et al.*, 1992] Anthony L. Hosking, J. Eliot B. Moss, and Darko Stefanović. A comparative performance evaluation of write barrier implementations. In Andreas Paepcke, editor, *OOPSLA'92 ACM Conference on Object-Oriented Systems, Languages and Applications*, volume 27(10) of *ACM SIGPLAN Notices*, pages 92–109, Vancouver, British Columbia, October 1992. ACM Press.

[Hudak and Keller, 1982] Paul R. Hudak and R. M. Keller. Garbage collection and task deletion in distributed applicative processing systems. In *Conference Record of the 1982 ACM Symposium on Lisp and Functional Programming*, pages 168–178, Pittsburgh, PA, August 1982. ACM Press.

[Hudak *et al.*, 1992] Paul Hudak, Simon L. Peyton Jones, and Phillip Wadler. Report on the programming language Haskell, a non-strict purely functional language (version 1.2). *ACM SIGPLAN Notices*, 27(5), May 1992.

[Hudak, 1986] Paul R. Hudak. A semantic model of reference counting and its abstraction (detailed summary). In [LFP, 1986], pages 351–363.

[Hudson and Diwan, 1990] Richard L. Hudson and Amer Diwan. Adaptive garbage collection for Modula-3 and Smalltalk. In [OOPSLA-gc, 1990].

[Hudson and Moss, 1992] Richard L. Hudson and J. Eliot B. Moss. Incremental garbage collection for mature objects. In [IWMM, 1992].

[Hudson *et al.*, 1991] Richard L. Hudson, J. Eliot B. Moss, Amer Diwan, and Christopher F. Weight. A language-independent garbage collector toolkit. Technical Report COINS 91-47, University of Massachusetts at Amherst, Department of Computer and Information Science, September 1991.

[Hudson, 1991] Richard L. Hudson. Finalization in a garbage collected world. In [OOPSLA-gc, 1991].

[Huelsbergen and Larus, 1993] Lorenz Huelsbergen and James R. Larus. A concurrent copying garbage collector for languages that distinguish (im)mutable data. In *Fourth Annual ACM Symposium on Principles and Practice of Parallel Programming*, volume 28(7) of *ACM SIGPLAN Notices*, pages 73–82, San Diego, CA, May 1993. ACM Press.

[Hughes, 1982] R. John M. Hughes. A semi-incremental garbage collection algorithm. *Software Practice and Experience*, 12(11):1081–1084, November 1982.

[Hughes, 1983] R. John M. Hughes. Reference counting with circular structures in virtual memory applicative systems. Internal paper, Programming Research Group, Oxford, 1983.

[Hughes, 1985] R. John M. Hughes. A distributed garbage collection algorithm. In [FPCA, 1985], pages 256–272.

[Hughes, 1987] R. John M. Hughes. Managing reduction graphs with reference counts. Departmental Research Report CSC/87/R2, University of Glasgow, March 1987.

[Hutchinson *et al.*, 1987] Norman Hutchinson, R. K. Raj, Andrew P. Black, Henry M. Levy, and Eric Jul. The Emerald programming language report. Technical Report 87–10–07, University of Washington, October 1987.

[Hutchinson, 1987] Norman Hutchinson. *Emerald: An Object-Based Language for Distributed Programming*. PhD thesis, University of Washington, January 1987.

[Ichisuki and Yonezawa, 1990] Yuuji Ichisuki and Akinori Yonezawa. Distributed garbage collection using group reference counting. In [OOPSLA-gc, 1990].

[IWMM, 1992] Yves Bekkers and Jacques Cohen, editors. *Proceedings of International Workshop on Memory Management*, volume 637 of *Lecture Notes in Computer Science*, St Malo, France, 16–18 September 1992. Springer-Verlag.

[IWMM, 1995] Henry Baker, editor. *Proceedings of International Workshop on Memory Management*, volume 986 of *Lecture Notes in Computer Science*, Kinross, Scotland, September 1995. Springer-Verlag.

[IWOOOS, 1991] Luis-Felipe Cabrera, Vincent Russo, and Marc Shapiro, editors. *International Workshop on Object Orientation in Operating Systems*, Palo Alto, CA, October 1991. IEEE Press.

[Johnson, 1988] Douglas Johnson. Trap architectures for Lisp systems. Technical Report UCB/CSD/88/470, University of California, Berkeley, November 1988.

[Johnson, 1991a] Douglas Johnson. The case for a read barrier. *ACM SIGPLAN Notices*, 26(4):279–287, 1991.

[Johnson, 1991b] Douglas Johnson. Comparing two garbage collectors. In [OOPSLA-gc, 1991].

[Johnson, 1992] Ralph E. Johnson. Reducing the latency of a real-time garbage collector. *Letters on Programming Languages and Systems*, 1(1):46–58, March 1992.

[Johnsson, 1987] Thomas Johnsson. *Compiling Lazy Functional Languages*. PhD thesis, Chalmers University of Technology, 1987.

[Jones and Lins, 1992] Richard E. Jones and Rafael D. Lins. Cyclic weighted reference counting without delay. Technical Report 28–92, Computing Laboratory, The University of Kent at Canterbury, December 1992.

[Jones and Lins, 1993] Richard E. Jones and Rafael D. Lins. Cyclic weighted reference counting without delay. In Arndt Bode, Mike Reeve, and Gottfried Wolf, editors, *PARLE'93 Parallel Architectures and Languages Europe*, volume 694 of *Lecture Notes in Computer Science*. Springer-Verlag, June 1993.

[Jonkers, 1979] H. B. M. Jonkers. A fast garbage compaction algorithm. *Information Processing Letters*, 9(1):25–30, July 1979.

[Jouppi, 1990] Norman P. Jouppi. Improving direct-mapped cache performance by the addition of a small fully-associative cache and prefetch buffers. In *17th Annual International Symposium on Computer Architecture*, pages 346–373, May 1990.

[Jouppi, 1993] Norman P. Jouppi. Cache write policies and performance. In *20th Annual International Symposium on Computer Architecture*, pages 191–201, San Diego, CA, May 1993. IEEE Press.

[Jul *et al.*, 1988] Eric Jul, Henry Levy, Norman Hutchinson, and Andrew Black. Fine-grained mobility in the Emerald system. *ACM Transactions on Computer Systems*, 6(1):109–133, January 1988.

[Juul and Jul, 1992] Neils-Christian Juul and Eric Jul. Comprehensive and robust garbage collection in a distributed system. In [IWMM, 1992].

[Kaashoek *et al.*, 1989] M. Frans Kaashoek, Andrew Tanenbaum, S. Hummel, and Henri E. Bal. An efficient reliable broadcast protocol. *Operating Systems Review*, 23(4):5–19, October 1989.

[Kafura *et al.*, 1990] Dennis Kafura, Doug Washabaugh, and Jeff Nelson. Garbage collection of actors. In Norman Meyrowitz, editor, *OOPSLA'90 ACM Conference on Object-Oriented Systems, Languages and Applications*, volume 25(10) of *ACM SIGPLAN Notices*, pages 126–134, Ottawa, Ontario, October 1990. ACM Press.

[Kakuta *et al.*, 1986] K. Kakuta, H. Nakamura, and S. Iida. Parallel reference counting algorithm. *Information Processing Letters*, 23(1):33–37, 1986.

[Kennedy, 1991] Brian Kennedy. The features of the object oriented abstract type hierarchy (OATH). In *Proceedings of the Usenix C++ Conference*, pages 41–50. Usenix Association, April 1991.

[Kessler and Livny, 1989] Richard E. Kessler and M. Livny. An analysis of distributed shared memory algorithms. In *Proceedings of the 9th International Conference on Distributed Computing Systems*, June 1989.

[Kingdon *et al.*, 1991] H. Kingdon, David R. Lester, and Geoffrey L. Burn. The HDG-machine: A highly distributed graph reducer for a transputer network. *Computer Journal*, 34:290–301, September 1991.

[Knight, 1974] Tom Knight. CONS. Working Paper 80, MIT AI Laboratory, November 1974.

[Knuth, 1973] Donald E. Knuth. *The Art of Computer Programming*, volume I: Fundamental Algorithms, chapter 2. Addison-Wesley, second edition, 1973.

[Koopman *et al.*, 1989] Philip J. Koopman, Peter Lee, and Daniel P. Siewiorek. Cache performance of combinator graph reduction. In [PLDI, 1989], pages 110–119.

[Koopman *et al.*, 1992] Philip J. Koopman, Peter Lee, and Daniel P. Siewiorek. Cache behavior of combinator graph reduction. *ACM Transactions on Programming Languages and Systems*, 14(2):265–297, April 1992.

[Kordale and Ahamad, 1993] R. Kordale and Mustaque Ahamad. A scalable cyclic garbage detection algorithm for distributed systems. In [OOPSLA-gc, 1993].

[Kowaltowski, 1979] T. Kowaltowski. Data structures and correctness of programs. *Journal of the ACM*, 26(2):283–301, April 1979.

[Krasner, 1983] Glenn Krasner, editor. *Smalltalk-80: Bits of History, Words of Advice.* Addison-Wesley, 1983.

[Kriegel, 1993] E. Ulrich Kriegel. A conservative garbage collector for an EuLisp to ASM/C compiler. In [OOPSLA-gc, 1993].

[Krieger and Stumm, 1990] O. Krieger and Michael Stumm. An optimistic approach for consistent replicated data for multicomputers. In *Proc. HICCSS*, 1990.

[Kung and Song, 1977] H. T. Kung and S. W. Song. An efficient parallel garbage collection system and its correctness proof. In *IEEE Symposium on Foundations of Computer Science*, pages 120–131. IEEE Press, 1977.

[Kurokawa, 1981] T. Kurokawa. A new fast and safe marking algorithm. *Software Practice and Experience*, 11:671–682, 1981.

[Ladin and Liskov, 1992] Rivka Ladin and Barbara Liskov. Garbage collection of a distributed heap. In *International Conference on Distributed Computing Systems*, Yokohama, June 1992.

[Lam and others, 1991] Monica S. Lam *et al.* The cache performance and optimizations of blocked algorithms. In [ASPLOS, 1991], pages 63–74.

[Lam *et al.*, 1992] Michael S. Lam, Paul R. Wilson, and Thomas G. Moher. Object type directed garbage collection to improve locality. In [IWMM, 1992].

[Lamport, 1976] Leslie Lamport. Garbage collection with multiple processes: an exercise in parallelism. In *Proceedings of the 1976 International Conference on Parallel Processing*, pages 50–54, 1976.

[Lamport, 1991] Leslie Lamport. The temporal logic of actions. Research Report 79, DEC Systems Research Center, Palo Alto, CA, 1991.

[Lang and Dupont, 1987] Bernard Lang and Francis Dupont. Incremental incrementally compacting garbage collection. In *SIGPLAN'87 Symposium on Interpreters and Interpretive Techniques*, volume 22(7) of *ACM SIGPLAN Notices*, pages 253–263. ACM Press, 1987.

[Lang and Wegbreit, 1972] Bernard Lang and B. Wegbreit. Fast compactification. Technical Report 25–72, Harvard University, Cambridge, MA, November 1972.

[Lang *et al.*, 1992] Bernard Lang, Christian Quenniac, and José Piquer. Garbage collecting the world. In [POPL, 1992], pages 39–50.

[Le Sergent and Barthomieu, 1992] Thierry Le Sergent and Bernard Barthomieu. Incremental multi-threaded garbage collection on virtually shared memory architectures. In [IWMM, 1992].

[Lee *et al.*, 1979] S. Lee, W. P. De Roever, and S. Gerhart. The evolution of list copying algorithms. In *6th ACM Symposium on Principles of Programming Languages*, pages 53–56, San Antonio, Texas, January 1979. ACM Press.

[Lee, 1980] K. P. Lee. A linear algorithm for copying binary trees using bounded workspace. *Communications of the ACM*, 23(3):159–162, March 1980.

[Lermen and Maurer, 1986] C.-W. Lermen and Dieter Maurer. A protocol for distributed reference counting. In [LFP, 1986], pages 343–350.

[Lester, 1989] David Lester. An efficient distributed garbage collector algorithm. In Eddy Odijik, M. Rem, and Jean-Claude Sayr, editors, *PARLE'89 Parallel Architectures and Languages Europe*, volume 265/366 of *Lecture Notes in Computer Science*, Eindhoven, The Netherlands, June 1989. Springer-Verlag.

[Lester, 1992] David Lester. Distributed garbage collection of cyclic structures. In *4th International Workshop on the Parallel Implementation of Functional Languages*, Aachen, September 1992. Available from Herbert Kuchen, Lehrstuhl Informatik II, RWTH Aachen, Ahornstr. 55, W-51000 Aachen. Also Glasgow Functional Programming Workshop 1993.

[Levelt *et al.*, 1992] Willem G. Levelt, M. Frans Kaashoek, Henri E. Bal, and Andrew Tanenbaum. A comparison of two paradigms for distributed shared memory. *Software Practice and Experience*, 22(11):985–1010, November 1992.

[LFP, 1984] Guy L. Steele, editor. *Conference Record of the 1984 ACM Symposium on Lisp and Functional Programming*, Austin, TX, August 1984. ACM Press.

[LFP, 1986] *Conference Record of the 1986 ACM Symposium on Lisp and Functional Programming*, ACM SIGPLAN Notices, Cambridge, MA, August 1986. ACM Press.

[LFP, 1992] *Conference Record of the 1992 ACM Symposium on Lisp and Functional Programming*, San Francisco, CA, June 1992. ACM Press.

[Li and Hudak, 1989] Kai Li and Paul Hudak. Memory coherence in shared virtual memory systems. *ACM Transactions on Computer Systems*, 7(4):321–359, November 1989.

[Li, 1986] Kai Li. *Shared Virtual Memory on Loosely Coupled Multiprocessors*. PhD thesis, Yale University, 1986.

[Lieberman and Hewitt, 1983] Henry Lieberman and Carl E. Hewitt. A real-time garbage collector based on the lifetimes of objects. *Communications of the ACM*, 26(6):419–29, 1983. Also report TM–184, Laboratory for Computer Science, MIT, Cambridge, MA, July 1980 and AI Lab Memo 569, 1981.

[Lindstrom, 1973] Gary Lindstrom. Scaning list structures without stacks or tag bits. *Information Processing Letters*, 2(2):47–51, June 1973.

[Lindstrom, 1974] Gary Lindstrom. Copying list structures using bounded workspace. *Communications of the ACM*, 17(4):199–202, April 1974.

[Lins and Jones, 1993] Rafael D. Lins and Richard E. Jones. Cyclic weighted reference counting. In K. Boyanov, editor, *Procedings of WP & DP'93 Workshop on Parallel and Distributed Processing*. North Holland, May 1993. Also Computing Laboratory Technical Report 95, University of Kent, December 1991.

[Lins and Vasques, 1991] Rafael D. Lins and Márcio A. Vasques. A comparative study of algorithms for cyclic reference counting. Technical Report 92, Computing Laboratory, The University of Kent at Canterbury, August 1991.

[Lins, 1991] Rafael D. Lins. A shared memory architecture for parallel cyclic reference counting. *Microprocessing and Microprogramming*, 34:31–35, September 1991.

[Lins, 1992a] Rafael D. Lins. Cyclic reference counting with lazy mark-scan. *Information Processing Letters*, 44(4):215–220, 1992. Also Computing Laboratory Technical Report 75, University of Kent, July 1990.

[Lins, 1992b] Rafael D. Lins. A multi-processor shared memory architecture for parallel cyclic reference counting. *Microprocessing and Microprogramming*, 35:563–568, September 1992.

[Liskov and Ladin, 1986] Barbara Liskov and Rivka Ladin. Highly available distributed services and fault-tolerant distributed garbage collection. In J. Halpern, editor, *Proceedings of the Fifth Annual ACM Symposium on the Principles on Distributed Computing*, pages 29–39, Calgary, August 1986. ACM Press.

[Llames, 1991] Rene Lim Llames. *Performance Analysis of Garbage Collection and Dynamic Reordering in a LISP System*. PhD thesis, University of Illinois at Urbana-Champaign, 1991.

[Lomet, 1975] D. B. Lomet. Scheme for invalidating references to freed storage. *IBM Journal of Research and Development*, pages 26–35, January 1975.

[Lyon, 1988] G. Lyon. Tagless marking that is linear over subtrees. *Information Processing Letters*, 27(1):23–28, 1988.

[Madany *et al.*, 1992] Peter W. Madany, Nayeem Islam, Panos Kougiouris, and Roy H. Campbell. Reification and reflection in C++: An operating systems perspective. Technical Report UIUCDCS–R–92–1736, Department of Computer Science, University of Illinois at Urbana-Champaign, March 1992.

[Maeder, 1992] Roman E. Maeder. A provably correct reference count scheme for a symbolic computation system. In unpublished form, cited by Edelson, 1992.

[Maheshwari, 1993a] Umesh Maheshwari. Distributed garbage collection in a client–server persistent object system. In [OOPSLA-gc, 1993].

[Maheshwari, 1993b] Umesh Maheshwari. Distributed garbage collection in a client–server, transactional, persistent object system. Technical Report MIT/LCS/TR–574, MIT Press, February 1993.

[Mancini and Shrivastava, 1991] Luigi V. Mancini and S. K. Shrivastava. Fault-tolerant reference counting for garbage collection in distributed systems. *Computer Journal*, 34(6):503–513, December 1991.

[Mancini *et al.*, 1991] Luigi V. Mancini, Vittoria Rotella, and Simonetta Venosa. Copying garbage collection for distributed object stores. In *Proceedings ot the Tenth Symposium on Reliable Distributed Systems, Pisa*, September 1991.

[Martin, 1982] Johannes J. Martin. An efficient garbage compaction algorithm. *Communications of the ACM*, 25(8):571–581, August 1982.

[Martinez *et al.*, 1990] A. D. Martinez, R. Wachenchauzer, and Rafael D. Lins. Cyclic reference counting with local mark-scan. *Information Processing Letters*, 34:31–35, 1990.

[McBeth, 1963] J. Harold McBeth. On the reference counter method. *Communications of the ACM*, 6(9):575, September 1963.

[McCarthy, 1960] John McCarthy. Recursive functions of symbolic expressions and their computation by machine. *Communications of the ACM*, 3:184–195, 1960.

[McCarthy, 1981] John McCarthy. History of LISP. In Richard L. Wexelblat, editor, *History of Programming Languages*, chapter IV, pages 173–197. ACM Monograph, 1981.

[McIlroy, 1976] M. Douglas McIlroy. Mass-produced software components. In J. M. Buxton, Peter Naur, and Brian Randell, editors, *Software Engineering Concepts and Techniques (1968 NATO Conference of Software Engineering)*, pages 88–98, 1976.

[Metropolis *et al.*, 1980] N. Metropolis, J. Howlett, and Gian-Carlo Rota, editors. *A History of Computing in the Twentieth Century*. Academic Press, 1980.

[Meyer, 1988] Bertrand Meyer. *Object-oriented Software Construction*. Prentice-Hall, 1988.

[Miller and Rozas, 1994] James S. Miller and Guillermo J. Rozas. Garbage collection is fast, but a stack is faster. Technical Report AIM-1462, MIT AI Laboratory, March 1994.

[Minsky, 1963] Marvin L. Minsky. A Lisp garbage collector algorithm using serial secondary storage. Technical Report Memo 58 (rev.), Project MAC, MIT, Cambridge, MA, December 1963.

[Mogul and Borg, 1991] Jeffrey C. Mogul and Anita Borg. The effect of context switches on cache performance. In [ASPLOS, 1991], pages 75–84.

[Mohamed-Ali, 1984] Khayri A. Mohamed-Ali. *Object Oriented Storage Management and Garbage Collection in Distributed Processing Systems*. PhD thesis, Royal Institute of Technology, Stockholm, December 1984.

[Moon, 1984] David A. Moon. Garbage collection in a large LISP system. In [LFP, 1984], pages 235–245.

[Moon, 1985] David A. Moon. Architecture of the Symbolics 3600. In *Proceedings of the 12th Annual International Symposium on Computer Architecture*, pages 76–83, Boston, MA, June 1985.

[Morris, 1978] F. Lockwood Morris. A time- and space-efficient garbage compaction algorithm. *Communications of the ACM*, 21(8):662–5, 1978.

[Morris, 1979] F. Lockwood Morris. On a comparison of garbage collection techniques. *Communications of the ACM*, 22(10):571, October 1979.

[Morris, 1982] F. Lockwood Morris. Another compacting garbage collector. *Information Processing Letters*, 15(4):139–142, October 1982.

[Moss and Sinofsky, 1988] J. Eliot B. Moss and S. Sinofsky. Managing persistent data with Mneme: Designing a reliable, shared object interface. In *Advances in Object-oriented Database Systems*, volume 334 of *Lecture Notes in Computer Science*, pages 298–316. Springer-Verlag, 1988.

[Moss, 1989a] J. Eliot B. Moss. Addressing large distributed collections of persistent objects: The Mneme project's approach. In *Second International Workshop on Database Programming Languages*, pages 269–285, Glenedon Beach, OR, June 1989. Also available as Technical Report 89-68, University of Massachusetts Department of Computer and Information Science, Amherst, MA, 1989.

[Moss, 1989b] J. Eliot B. Moss. The Mneme persistent object store. COINS Technical Report 89–107, University of Massachusetts, Department of Computer and Information Science, 1989.

[Moss, 1990] J. Eliot B. Moss. Garbage collecting persistent object stores. In [OOPSLA-gc, 1990]. Also in SIGPLAN Notices 23(1):45–52, January 1991.

[Müller, 1976] Klaus A. G. Müller. *On the Feasibility of Concurrent Garbage Collection*. PhD thesis, Tech. Hogeschool Delft, March 1976.

[Nagle, 1995] John Nagle. Re: Real-time GC (was Re: Widespread C++ competency gap). USENET comp.lang.c++, January 1995.

[Nelson, 1989] Jeffrey E. Nelson. Automatic, incremental, on-the-fly garbage collection of actors. Master's thesis, Virginia Polytechnic Institute and State University, 1989.

[Nettles and O'Toole, 1993] Scott M. Nettles and James W. O'Toole. Real-time replication-based garbage collection. In [PLDI, 1993].

[Nettles *et al.*, 1992] Scott M. Nettles, James W. O'Toole, David Pierce, and Nicholas Haines. Replication-based incremental copying collection. In [IWMM, 1992].

[Nettles *et al.*, 1993] Scott M. Nettles, James W. O'Toole, and David Gifford. Concurrent garbage collection of persistent heaps. Technical Report MIT/LCS/TR–569 and CMU–CS–93–137, Computer Science Department, Carnegie-Mellon University, April 1993. The same paper as [O'Toole *et al.*, 1993].

[Nilsen and Gao, 1995] Kelvin Nilsen and H. Gao. The real-time behaviour of dynamic memory management in C++. In *IEEE Real-Time Technologies and Applications Symposium*, pages 142–153, Chicago, May 1995. IEEE Press.

[Nilsen and Schmidt, 1990a] Kelvin D. Nilsen and William J. Schmidt. Hardware support for garbage collection of linked objects and arrays in real-time. In [OOPSLA-gc, 1990].

[Nilsen and Schmidt, 1990b] Kelvin D. Nilsen and William J. Schmidt. A high-level overview of hardware assisted real-time garbage collection. Technical Report TR90-18a, Iowa State University, Department of Computer Science, October 1990.

[Nilsen and Schmidt, 1992a] Kelvin D. Nilsen and William J. Schmidt. Hardware-assisted general-purpose garbage collection for hard real-time systems. Technical Report ISU TR92-15, Iowa State University, Department of Computer Science, October 1992.

[Nilsen and Schmidt, 1992b] Kelvin D. Nilsen and William J. Schmidt. Preferred embodiment of a hardware-assisted garbage collection system. Technical Report ISU TR92-17, Iowa State University, Department of Computer Science, November 1992.

[Nilsen and Schmidt, 1994] Kelvin D. Nilsen and William J. Schmidt. A high-performance hardware-assisted real time garbage collection system. *Journal of Programming Languages*, 2(1), 1994.

[Nilsen, 1993] Kelvin D. Nilsen. Reliable real-time garbage collection of C++. In [OOPSLA-gc, 1993].

[Nilsen, 1994a] Kelvin D. Nilsen. Cost-effective hardware-assisted real-time garbage collection. In *Workshop on Language, Compiler, and Tool Support for Real-Time Systems, PLDI94*, June 1994.

[Nilsen, 1994b] Kelvin D. Nilsen. Reliable real-time garbage collection of C++. *Computing Systems*, 7(4), 1994.

[Nilsen, 1995] Kelvin Nilsen. Progress in hardware-assisted real-time garbage collection. In [IWMM, 1995].

[North and Reppy, 1987] S. C. North and John H. Reppy. Concurrent garbage collection on stock hardware. In [FPCA, 1987], pages 113–133.

[Oldehoeft, 1994] Rod Oldehoeft. Re: ref counting vs. heavy GC. USENET comp.functional, September 1994. Parallel SISAL on Sequents optimises away most RCs.

[OOPSLA-gc, 1990] Eric Jul and Niels-Christian Juul, editors. *OOPSLA/ECOOP '90 Workshop on Garbage Collection in Object-Oriented Systems*, Ottawa, October 1990.

[OOPSLA-gc, 1991] Paul R. Wilson and Barry Hayes, editors. *OOPSLA/ECOOP '91 Workshop on Garbage Collection in Object-Oriented Systems*, October 1991.

[OOPSLA-gc, 1993] Eliot Moss, Paul R. Wilson, and Benjamin Zorn, editors. *OOPSLA/ECOOP '93 Workshop on Garbage Collection in Object-Oriented Systems*, October 1993.

[OOPSLA, 1986] Norman Meyrowitz, editor. *OOPSLA'86 ACM Conference on Object-Oriented Systems, Languages and Applications*, volume 21(11) of *ACM SIGPLAN Notices*. ACM Press, October 1986.

[OOPSLA, 1991] Andreas Paepcke, editor. *OOPSLA'91 ACM Conference on Object-Oriented Systems, Languages and Applications*, volume 26(11) of *ACM SIGPLAN Notices*, Phoenix, Arizona, October 1991. ACM Press.

[O'Toole and Nettles, 1993] James W. O'Toole and Scott M. Nettles. Concurrent replicating garbage collection. Technical Report MIT–LCS–TR–570 and CMU–CS–93–138, MIT and CMU, 1993. Also LFP94 and OOPSLA93 Workshop on Memory Management and Garbage Collection.

[O'Toole *et al.*, 1993] James W. O'Toole, Scott M. Nettles, and David Gifford. Concurrent compacting garbage collection of a persistent heap. In *Proceedings of the Fourteenth Symposium on Operating Systems Principles*, volume 27(5) of *Operating Systems Review*, pages 161–174, Asheville, North Carolina, December 1993. ACM Press. Also MIT/CMU Technical report MIT–LCS–TR–569. The same paper as [Nettles *et al.*, 1993].

[Owicki and Lamport, 1982] Susan Owicki and Leslie Lamport. Proving liveness properties of concurrent programs. *ACM Transactions on Programming Languages and Systems*, 4(3):455–495, July 1982.

[PARLE, 1987] Jacobus W. de Bakker, L. Nijman, and Philip C. Treleaven, editors. *PARLE'87 Parallel Architectures and Languages Europe*, volume 258/259 of *Lecture Notes in Computer Science*, Eindhoven, The Netherlands, June 1987. Springer-Verlag.

[Peng and Sohi, 1989] Chih-Jui Peng and Gurindar S. Sohi. Cache memory design considerations to support languages with dynamic heap allocation. Technical Report 860, Computer Sciences Department, University of Wisconsin-Madison, July 1989.

[Pepels *et al.*, 1988] E. J. H. Pepels, M. C. J. D. van Eekelen, and M. J. Plasmeijer. A cyclic reference counting algorithm and its proof. Technical Report 88–10, Computing Science Department, University of Nijmegen, 1988.

[Peyton Jones, 1992] Simon L. Peyton Jones. Implementing lazy functional languages on stock hardware: The Spineless Tagless G-machine. *Journal of Functional Programming*, 2(2):127–202, April 1992.

[Piquer, 1990a] José M. Piquer. Sharing date structures in distributed Lisp. In *Proceedings of High Performance and Parallel Computing in Lisp Workshop*, London, November 1990.

[Piquer, 1990b] José M. Piquer. Un GC parallèle pour un Lisp distribué. *Journées francophones des langages applicatifs*, January 1990. Also Bigre 69, July 1990.

[Piquer, 1991] José M. Piquer. Indirect reference counting: A distributed garbage collection algorithm. In Aarts *et al.*, editors, *PARLE'91 Parallel Architectures and Languages Europe*, volume 505 of *Lecture Notes in Computer Science*. Springer-Verlag, June 1991.

[Pixley, 1988] C. Pixley. An incremental garbage collection algorithm for multi-mutator systems. *Distributed Computing*, 3(1):41–50, 1988.

[Plainfossé and Shapiro, 1992] David Plainfossé and Marc Shapiro. Experience with fault-tolerant garbage collection in a distributed Lisp system. In [IWMM, 1992].

[Plainfossé and Shapiro, 1995] David Plainfossé and Marc Shapiro. A survey of distributed garbage collection techniques. In [IWMM, 1995].

[PLDI, 1989] *Proceedings of SIGPLAN'89 Conference on Programming Languages Design and Implementation*, volume 24(7) of *ACM SIGPLAN Notices*, Portland, Oregon, June 1989. ACM Press.

[PLDI, 1993] *Proceedings of SIGPLAN'93 Conference on Programming Languages Design and Implementation*, volume 28(6) of *ACM SIGPLAN Notices*, Albuquerque, NM, June 1993. ACM Press.

[PLDI, 1994] *Proceedings of SIGPLAN'94 Conference on Programming Languages Design and Implementation*, volume 29 of *ACM SIGPLAN Notices*, Orlando, FL, June 1994. ACM Press. Also Lisp Pointers VIII 3, July–September 1994.

[Pollack *et al.*, 1982] F. J. Pollack, G. W. Cox, D. W. Hammerstein, K. C. Kahn, K. K. Lai, and J. R. Rattner. Supporting Ada memory management in the iAPX–432. In *Second International Conference on Architectural Support for Programming Languages and Operating Systems (ASPLOS)*, volume 12(4) of *ACM SIGPLAN Notices*, pages 117–131. ACM Press, 1982.

[POPL, 1992] *Conference Record of the Nineteenth Annual ACM Symposium on Principles of Programming Languages*, ACM SIGPLAN Notices. ACM Press, January 1992.

[POPL, 1994] *Conference Record of the Twenty-first Annual ACM Symposium on Principles of Programming Languages*, ACM SIGPLAN Notices. ACM Press, January 1994.

[Przybylski, 1990] Steven A. Przybylski. *Cache and Memory Hierarchy Design: A Performance-Directed Approach*. Morgan Kaufman, Palo Alto, CA, 1990.

[Puaut, 1992] Isabelle Puaut. Distributed garbage collection of active objects with no global synchronisation. In [IWMM, 1992].

[Puaut, 1994a] Isabelle Puaut. A distributed garbage collector for active objects. In *PARLE'94 Parallel Architectures and Languages Europe*, Lecture Notes in Computer Science. Springer-Verlag, 1994. Also INRIA UCIS-DIFUSION RR 2134.

[Puaut, 1994b] Isabelle Puaut. A distributed garbage collector for active objects. In *OOPSLA'94 ACM Conference on Object-Oriented Systems, Languages and Applications*, volume 29 of *ACM SIGPLAN Notices*, pages 113–128. ACM Press, October 1994.

[Purify, 1992] Pure Software, Los Altos, CA. *Purify*, 1992.

[Queinnec *et al.*, 1989] Christian Queinnec, Barbara Beaudoing, and Jean-Pierre Queille. Mark DURING Sweep rather than Mark THEN Sweep. *Lecture Notes in Computer Science*, 365:224–237, 1989.

[Ramesh and Mehndiratta, 1983] S. Ramesh and S. L. Mehndiratta. The liveness property of on-the-fly garbage collector — a proof. *Information Processing Letters*, 17(4):189–195, November 1983.

[Rana, 1983] S. P. Rana. A distributed solution to the distributed termination problem. *Information Processing Letters*, 17:43–46, July 1983.

[Reingold, 1973] E. M. Reingold. A non-recursive list moving algorithm. *Communications of the ACM*, 16(5):305–307, May 1973.

[Reinhold, 1994] Mark B. Reinhold. Cache performance of garbage-collected programs. In [PLDI, 1994]. Also Lisp Pointers VIII 3, July–September 1994.

[Reppy, 1993] John H. Reppy. A high-performance garbage collector for Standard ML. Technical memorandum, AT&T Bell Laboratories, Murray Hill, NJ, December 1993.

[Robson, 1973] J. M. Robson. An improved algorithm for traversing binary trees without auxiliary stack. *Information Processing Letters*, 2(1):12–14, March 1973.

[Robson, 1977] J. M. Robson. A bounded storage algorithm for copying cyclic structures. *Communications of the ACM*, 20(6):431–433, June 1977.

[Röjemo, 1992] Niklas Röjemo. A concurrent generational garbage collector for a parallel graph reducer. In [IWMM, 1992].

[Ross, 1967] D. T. Ross. The AED free storage package. *Communications of the ACM*, 10(8):481–492, August 1967.

[Rovner, 1985] Paul Rovner. On adding garbage collection and runtime types to a strongly-typed, statically-checked, concurrent language. Technical Report CSL–84–7, Xerox PARC, Palo Alto, CA, July 1985.

[Rudalics, 1986] M. Rudalics. Distributed copying garbage collection. In [LFP, 1986], pages 364–372.

[Russinoff, 1994] David M. Russinoff. A mechanically verified incremental garbage collector. *Formal Aspects of Computing*, 6:359–390, 1994.

[Russo, 1991] Vincent F. Russo. Garbage collecting and object-oriented operating system kernel. In [OOPSLA-gc, 1991].

[Salkild, 1987] Jon D. Salkild. Implementation and analysis of two reference counting algorithms. Master's thesis, University College, London, 1987.

[Samples, 1992] A. Dain Samples. Garbage collection-cooperative C++. In [IWMM, 1992].

[Sansom and Peyton Jones, 1993] Patrick M. Sansom and Simon L. Peyton Jones. Generational garbage collection for Haskell. In R. John M. Hughes, editor, *Record of the 1993 Conference on Functional Programming and Computer Architecture*, volume 523 of *Lecture Notes in Computer Science*, University of Glasgow, June 1993. Springer-Verlag.

[Sansom, 1991] Patrick M. Sansom. Dual-mode garbage collection. Technical Report CSTR 91–07, Department of Electronics and Computer Science, University of Southampton, June 1991. *Proceedings of Third International Workshop on Implementation of Functional Languages on Parallel Architectures.*

[Sansom, 1992] Patrick M. Sansom. Combining copying and compacting garbage collection. In Simon L. Peyton Jones, G. Hutton, and C. K. Hols, editors, *Fourth Annual Glasgow Workshop on Functional Programming*, Workshops in Computer Science. Springer-Verlag, 1992.

[Satishkumar, 1994] S. Satishkumar. Register allocation for accurate garbage collection of C++. Master's thesis, Iowa State University, July 1994. Technical report ISUTR 94–12.

[Saunders, 1974] Robert A. Saunders. The LISP system for the Q–32 computer. In [Berkeley and Bobrow, 1974], pages 220–231.

[Schelter and Ballantyne, 1988] W. F. Schelter and M. Ballantyne. Kyoto Common Lisp. *AI Expert*, 3(3):75–77, 1988.

[Schelvis and Bledoeg, 1988] M. Schelvis and E. Bledoeg. The implementation of a distributed Smalltalk. *Lecture Notes in Computer Science*, 322:212–232, 1988.

[Schorr and Waite, 1967] H. Schorr and W. Waite. An efficient machine independent procedure for garbage collection in various list structures. *Communications of the ACM*, 10(8):501–506, August 1967.

[Seliger, 1990] Robert Seliger. Extending C++ to support remote procedure call, concurrency, exception handling and garbage collection. In *Usenix C++ Conference Proceedings*, pages 241–264. USENIX Association, 1990.

[Shapiro *et al.*, 1990] Marc Shapiro, Olivier Gruber, and David Plainfossé. A garbage detection protocol for a realistic distributed object-support system. Rapports de Recherche 1320, INRIA-Rocquencourt, November 1990. Superseded by [Shapiro, 1991].

[Shapiro, 1991] Marc Shapiro. A fault-tolerant, scalable, low-overhead distributed garbage collection protocol. In *Proceedings of the Tenth Symposium on Reliable Distributed Systems*, Pisa, September 1991.

[Sharma and Soffa, 1991] Ravi Sharma and Mary Lou Soffa. Parallel generational garbage collection. In [OOPSLA, 1991], pages 16–32.

[Shaw, 1987] Robert A. Shaw. Improving garbage collector performance in virtual memory. Technical Report CSL–TR–87–323, Stanford University, March 1987. Also Hewlett-Packard Laboratories report STL–TM–87–05, Palo Alto, 1987.

[Shaw, 1988] Robert A. Shaw. *Empirical Analysis of a Lisp System.* PhD thesis, Stanford University, 1988. Technical Report CSL–TR–88–351.

[Siklossy, 1972] L. Siklossy. Fast and readonly algorithms for traversing trees without an auxiliary stack. *Information Processing Letters*, 1(4):149–152, June 1972.

[Sobalvarro, 1988] Patrick Sobalvarro. A lifetime-based garbage collector for Lisp systems on general-purpose computers. Technical Report AITR-1417, MIT AI Lab, February 1988. Bachelor of Science thesis.

[Sousa, 1993] Pedro Sousa. Garbage collection of persistent objects in a distributed object-oriented platform. In [OOPSLA-gc, 1993].

[Stamos, 1982] James W. Stamos. A large object-oriented virtual memory: Grouping strategies, measurements, and performance. Technical Report SCG-82-2, Xerox PARC, Palo Alto, CA, May 1982.

[Stamos, 1984] James W. Stamos. Static grouping of small objects to enhance performance of a paged virtual memory. *ACM Transactions on Computer Systems*, 2(3):155–180, May 1984.

[Standish, 1980] Thomas A. Standish. *Data Structures Techniques.* Addison-Wesley, 1980.

[Steele, 1975] Guy L. Steele. Multiprocessing compactifying garbage collection. *Communications of the ACM*, 18(9):495–508, September 1975.

[Steele, 1976] Guy L. Steele. Corrigendum: Multiprocessing compactifying garbage collection. *Communications of the ACM*, 19(6):354, June 1976.

[Steenkiste and Hennessy, 1987] Peter Steenkiste and John Hennessy. Tags and type checking in LISP: Hardware and software approaches. In *Second International Conference on Architectural Support for Programming Languages and Operating Systems (ASPLOS II)*, pages 50–59, Palo Alto, CA, October 1987.

[Steenkiste, 1987] Peter Steenkiste. *Lisp on a Reduced-Instruction-Set Processor: Characterization and Optimization.* PhD thesis, Stanford University, Also appears as Technical Report CSL-TR-87-324, Stanford University Computer System Laboratory, Palo Alto, CA, March 1987.

[Steenkiste, 1989] Peter Steenkiste. The impact of code density on instruction cache performance. In *Proceedings of Sixteenth Annual International Symposium on Computer Architecture*, pages 252–259, May 1989.

[Stoye *et al.*, 1984] Will R. Stoye, T. J. W. Clarke, and Arthur C. Norman. Some practical methods for rapid combinator reduction. In [LFP, 1984], pages 159–166.

[Stroustrup, 1991] Bjarne Stroustrup. *The C++ Programming Language*. Addison-Wesley, second edition, December 1991.

[Stumm and Zhou, 1990a] M. Stumm and Songnian Zhou. Algorithms implementing distributed shared memory. *IEEE Computing*, 23(5), May 1990.

[Stumm and Zhou, 1990b] Michael Stumm and Songnian Zhou. Fault tolerant distributed shared memory. In *Proceedings of IEEE International Conference on Parallel Distributed Computing*. IEEE Press, December 1990.

[Swanson, 1986] M. Swanson. An improved portable copying garbage collector. OPnote 86–03, University of Utah, February 1986.

[Swinehart *et al.*, 1986] Daniel C. Swinehart, Polle T. Zellweger, Richard J. Beach, and Robert B. Hagmann. A structural view of the Cedar programming environment. Technical Report CSL–86–1, Xerox Corporation, 1986.

[Tanenbaum, 1988] Andrew S. Tanenbaum. *Computer Networks*. Prentice-Hall, second edition, 1988.

[Taylor *et al.*, 1986] George S. Taylor, Paul N. Hilfinger, James R. Larus, David A. Patterson, and Benjamin G. Zorn. Evaluation of the SPUR Lisp architecture. In *Proceedings of the Thirteenth Symposium on Computer Architecture*, June 1986.

[Terashima and Goto, 1978] Motoaki Terashima and Eiichi Goto. Genetic order and compactifying garbage collectors. *Information Processing Letters*, 7(1):27–32, January 1978.

[Thomas and Jones, 1994] Stephen P. Thomas and Richard E. Jones. Garbage collection for shared environment closure reducers. Technical Report 31–94, University of Kent and University of Nottingham, December 1994.

[Thomas, 1981] R. E. Thomas. A dataflow computer with improved asymptotic performance. Technical Report MIT/LCS/TR–265, MIT Laboratory for Computer Science, 1981.

[Thomas, 1993] Stephen P. Thomas. *The Pragmatics of Closure Reduction*. PhD thesis, The Computing Laboratory, University of Kent at Canterbury, October 1993.

[Thomas, 1995] Stephen P. Thomas. Having your cake and eating it: Recursive depth-first copying garbage collection with no extra stack. Personal communication, May 1995.

[Thompson and Lins, 1988] Simon J. Thompson and Rafael D. Lins. Cyclic reference counting: A correction to Brownbridge's algorithm. Unpublished notes, 1988.

[Thorelli, 1972] Lars-Erik Thorelli. Marking algorithms. *BIT*, 12(4):555–568, 1972.

[Thorelli, 1976] Lars-Erik Thorelli. A fast compactifying garbage collector. *BIT*, 16(4):426–441, 1976.

[Tolmach, 1994] Andrew Tolmach. Tag-free garbage collection using explicit type parameters. In [PLDI, 1994], pages 1–11. Also Lisp Pointers VIII 3, July–September 1994.

[Topor, 1979] R. Topor. The correctness of the Schorr–Waite list marking algorithm. *Acta Informatica*, 11(3), 1979.

[Turner, 1979] David A. Turner. A new implementation technique for applicative languages. *Software Practice and Experience*, 9, 1979.

[Turner, 1981] David A. Turner. Recursion equations as a programming language. In John Darlington, Peter Henderson, and David Turner, editors, *Functional Programming and its Applications*, pages 1–28. Cambridge University Press, January 1981.

[Turner, 1985] David A. Turner. Miranda — a non-strict functional language with polymorphic types. In [FPCA, 1985], pages 1–16.

[Ungar and Jackson, 1988] David M. Ungar and Frank Jackson. Tenuring policies for generation-based storage reclamation. *ACM SIGPLAN Notices*, 23(11):1–17, 1988.

[Ungar and Jackson, 1991] David M. Ungar and Frank Jackson. Outwitting GC devils: A hybrid incremental garbage collector. In [OOPSLA-gc, 1991].

[Ungar and Jackson, 1992] David M. Ungar and Frank Jackson. An adaptive tenuring policy for generation scavengers. *ACM Transactions on Programming Languages and Systems*, 14(1):1–27, 1992.

[Ungar, 1984] David M. Ungar. Generation scavenging: A non-disruptive high performance storage reclamation algorithm. *ACM SIGPLAN Notices*, 19(5):157–167, April 1984. Also published as ACM Software Engineering Notes 9, 3 (May 1984) — Proceedings of the ACM/SIGSOFT/SIGPLAN Software Engineering Symposium on Practical Software Development Environments, 157–167, April 1984.

[Ungar, 1986] David M. Ungar. *The Design and Evaluation of a High Performance Smalltalk System*. ACM distinguished dissertation 1986. MIT Press, 1986.

[van de Snepscheut, 1987] Jan van de Snepscheut. Algorithms for on-the-fly garbage collection revisited. *Information Processing Letters*, 24(4):211–216, March 1987.

[Veillon, 1976] G. Veillon. Transformations de programmes recursifs. *R.A.I.R.O. Informatique*, 10(9):7–20, September 1976.

[Venkatasubramanian *et al.*, 1992] Nalini Venkatasubramanian, Gul Agha, and Carolyn Talcott. Scalable distributed garbage collection for systems of active objects. In [IWMM, 1992], pages 134–147.

[Vestal, 1987] Stephen C. Vestal. *Garbage Collection: An Exercise in Distributed, Fault-Tolerant Programming*. PhD thesis, University of Washington, Seattle, WA, 1987.

[Wadler, 1976] Philip L. Wadler. Analysis of an algorithm for real-time garbage collection. *Communications of the ACM*, 19(9):491–500, September 1976.

[Wakeling, 1990] David Wakeling. *Linearity and Laziness*. PhD thesis, University of York, November 1990.

[Wall and Schwartz, 1991] Larry Wall and Randal L. Schwartz. *Programming Perl*. O'Reilly and Associates, Inc., 1991.

[Wallace and Runciman, 1993] Malcolm Wallace and Colin Runciman. An incremental garbage collector for embedded real-time systems. In *Proceedings of the Chalmers Winter Meeting*, pages 273–288, Tanum Strand, Sweden, 1993. Published as Programming Methodology Group, Chalmers University of Technology, Technical Report 73.

[Wang, 1989] Thomas Wang. The MM garbage collector for C++. Master's thesis, California State Polytechnic University, October 1989.

[Wang, 1994a] Thomas Wang. Better C: An object-oriented C language with automatic memory manager suitable for interactive applications. *ACM SIGPLAN Notices*, 29(11):104–111, December 1994.

[Wang, 1994b] Thomas Wang. Eliminate memory fragmentation through holes in the heap. *ACM SIGPLAN Notices*, 29(11):112–113, December 1994.

[Warren, 1983] David H. D. Warren. An abstract Prolog instruction set. Technical Note 309, SRI International, 1983.

[Washabaugh, 1989] Douglas Markham Washabaugh. Real-time garbage collection of actors in a distributed system. Master's thesis, Virginia Polytechnic Institute and State University, 1989.

[Watson and Watson, 1987] Paul Watson and Ian Watson. An efficient garbage collection scheme for parallel computer architectures. In [PARLE, 1987], pages 432–443.

[Wegbreit, 1972a] B. Wegbreit. A generalised compactifying garbage collector. *Computer Journal*, 15(3):204–208, August 1972.

[Wegbreit, 1972b] B. Wegbreit. A space efficient list structure tracing algorithm. *IEEE Transactions on Computers*, pages 1098–1010, September 1972.

[Weizenbaum, 1963] J. Weizenbaum. Symmetric list processor. *Communications of the ACM*, 6(9):524–544, September 1963.

[Weizenbaum, 1969] J. Weizenbaum. Recovery of reentrant list structures in SLIP. *Communications of the ACM*, 12(7):370–372, July 1969.

[Weng, 1979] K.-S. Weng. An abstract implementation for a generalised dataflow language. Technical Report MIT/LCS/TR228, MIT Laboratory for Computer Science, 1979.

[Wentworth, 1990] E. P. Wentworth. Pitfalls of conservative garbage collection. *Software Practice and Experience*, 20(7):719–727, 1990.

[While and Field, 1992] R. Lyndon While and Tony Field. Incremental garbage collection for the Spineless Tagless G-machine. In Evan Ireland and Nigel Perry, editors, *Proceedings of the Massey Functional Programming Workshop 1992*. Department of Computer Science, Massey University, 1992.

[White, 1980] Jon L. White. Address/memory management for a gigantic Lisp environment, or, GC Considered Harmful. In *Conference Record of the 1980 Lisp Conference*, pages 119–127, Redwood Estates, CA, August 1980.

[White, 1990] Jon L. White. Three issues in objected-oriented garbage collection. In [OOPSLA-gc, 1990].

[Wholey and Fahlman, 1984] Skef Wholey and Scott E. Fahlman. The design of an instruction set for Common Lisp. In [LFP, 1984], pages 150–158.

[Wilkes, 1964a] Maurice V. Wilkes. An experiment with a self-compiling compiler for a simple list-processing language. *Annual Review in Automatic Programming*, 4:1–48, 1964.

[Wilkes, 1964b] Maurice V. Wilkes. Lists and why they are useful. In *Proceedings of the ACM 19th National Conference*. ACM Press, August 1964.

[Williams and Wolczko, 1990] Ifor W. Williams and Mario I. Wolczko. An object-based memory architecture. In Alan Dearle, Gail M. Shaw, and Stanley B. Zdonik, editors, *Implementing Persistent Object Bases: Principles and Practice (Proceedings of the Fourth International Workshop on Persistent Object Systems)*, pages 114–130, Martha's Vineyard, MA, September 1990. Morgan Kaufman.

[Williams et al., 1987a] Ifor W. Williams, Mario I. Wolczko, and T. P. Hopkins. Realisation of a dynamic grouped object-oriented virtual memory hierarchy. In *Second International Workshop on Persistent Object Systems*, pages 298–308, Appin, Scotland, August 1987. Persistent Programming Research Report, Universities of Glasgow and St Andrews, number PPRR–44–87.

[Williams et al., 1987b] Ifor W. Williams, Mario I. Wolczko, and Trevor P. Hopkins. Dynamic grouping in an object-oriented virtual memory hierarchy. In J. Bézivin, J.-M. Hullot, P. Cointe, and Henry Lieberman, editors, *Proceedings of 1987 European Conference on Object-Oriented Programming*, volume 276 of *Lecture Notes in Computer Science*, pages 79–88. Springer-Verlag, June 1987.

[Williams et al., 1990] Ifor Williams, Mario I. Wolczko, and Trevor Hopkins. Realization of a dynamically grouped object-oriented memory hierarchy. Technical report, University of Manchester Department of Computer Science, Manchester, 1990.

[Wilson and Johnstone, 1993] Paul R. Wilson and Mark S. Johnstone. Truly real-time non-copying garbage collection. In [OOPSLA-gc, 1993].

[Wilson and Moher, 1989a] Paul R. Wilson and Thomas G. Moher. A card-marking scheme for controlling intergenerational references in generation-based garbage collection on stock hardware. *ACM SIGPLAN Notices*, 24(5):87–92, 1989.

[Wilson and Moher, 1989b] Paul R. Wilson and Thomas G. Moher.   Design of the opportunistic garbage collector. *ACM SIGPLAN Notices*, 24(10):23–35, 1989.

[Wilson *et al.*, 1991] Paul R. Wilson, Michael S. Lam, and Thomas G. Moher. Effective static-graph reorganization to improve locality in garbage collected systems.   *ACM SIGPLAN Notices*, 26(6):177–191, 1991.

[Wilson *et al.*, 1992] Paul R. Wilson, Michael S. Lam, and Thomas G. Moher. Caching considerations for generational garbage collection. In [LFP, 1992], pages 32–42.

[Wilson *et al.*, 1995] Paul R. Wilson, Mark S. Johnstone, Michael Neely, and David Boles. Dynamic storage allocation: A survey and critical review. In [IWMM, 1995].

[Wilson, 1989] Paul R. Wilson.   A simple bucket-brigade advancement mechanism for generation-based garbage collection. *ACM SIGPLAN Notices*, 24(5):38–46, May 1989.

[Wilson, 1990] Paul R. Wilson. Some issues and strategies in heap management and memory hierarchies. In [OOPSLA-gc, 1990]. Also in SIGPLAN Notices 23(1):45–52, January 1991.

[Wilson, 1991] Paul R. Wilson. *Heap Management and Memory Hierarchies*. PhD thesis, University of Illinois at Chicago, December 1991.

[Wilson, 1992a] Paul R. Wilson.   Operating system support for small objects.   In Luis-Felipe Cabrera, Vince Russo, and Marc Shapiro, editors, *International Workshop on Object Orientation in Operating Systems*, Paris, September 1992. IEEE Press.

[Wilson, 1992b] Paul R. Wilson. Uniprocessor garbage collection techniques. In [IWMM, 1992].

[Wilson, 1994] Paul R. Wilson.   Uniprocessor garbage collection techniques.   Technical report, University of Texas, January 1994. Expanded version of the IWMM92 paper.

[Wilson, 1995] Paul R. Wilson. Re: Real-time GC (was Re: Widespread C++ competency gap). USENET comp.lang.c++, January 1995.

[Wise and Friedman, 1977] David S. Wise and Daniel P. Friedman. The one-bit reference count. *BIT*, 17(3):351–9, 1977.

[Wise *et al.*, 1994] David S. Wise, Brian Heck, Caleb Hess, Willie Hunt, and Eric Ost. Uniprocessor performance of a reference-counting hardware heap. Technical Report TR-401, Indiana University, Computer Science Department, May 1994.

[Wise, 1979] David S. Wise.   Morris' garbage compaction algorithm restores reference counts. *ACM Transactions on Programming Languages and Systems*, 1:115–120, July 1979.

[Wise, 1985] David S. Wise. Design for a multiprocessing heap with on-board reference counting. In [FPCA, 1985], pages 289–304.

[Wise, 1993] David S. Wise. Stop and one-bit reference counting. Technical Report 360, Indiana University, Computer Science Department, March 1993.

[Withington, 1991] P. Tucker Withington. How real is "real time" garbage collection? In [OOPSLA-gc, 1991].

[Wolczko and Williams, 1990] Mario I. Wolczko and Ifor Williams. Garbage collection in high performance system. In [OOPSLA-gc, 1990].

[Wolczko and Williams, 1992] Mario I. Wolczko and Ifor Williams. Multi-level GC in a high-performance persistent object system. In *Fifth International Workshop on Persistent Object Systems*, Pisa, Italy, September 1992. Springer-Verlag.

[Wolczko and Williams, 1993] Mario I. Wolczko and Ifor Williams. An alternative architecture for objects: Lessons from the MUSHROOM project. In [OOPSLA-gc, 1993].

[Yelowitz and Duncan, 1977] L. Yelowitz and A. G. Duncan. Abstractions, instantiations and proofs of marking algorithms. *ACM SIGPLAN Notices*, 12(8):13–21, August 1977.

[Yip, 1991] G. May Yip. Incremental, generational mostly-copying garbage collection in uncooperative environments. Technical Report 91/8, Digital, Western Research Laboratory, June 1991. Masters Thesis — MIT, Cambridge, MA, 1991.

[Yuasa and Hagiya, 1985] Taiichi Yuasa and Masumi Hagiya. Kyoto Common Lisp report. Technical report, Teikoku Insatsu Publishing, Kyoto, 1985.

[Yuasa, 1990] Taichi Yuasa. Real-time garbage collection on general-purpose machines. *Journal of Software and Systems*, 11(3):181–198, 1990.

[Zave, 1975] Derek A. Zave. A fast compacting garbage collector. *Information Processing Letters*, 3(6):167–169, July 1975.

[Zhou *et al.*, 1992] Songnian Zhou, Michael Stumm, Kai Li, and David Wortman. Heterogeneous distributed shared memory. *IEEE Transactions on Parallel and Distributed Systems*, 3(5):540–554, September 1992.

[Zorn and Grunwald, 1992] Benjamin Zorn and Dirk Grunwald. Evaluating models of memory allocation. Computer Science Technical Report CU-CS-603-92, University of Colorado, July 1992.

[Zorn, 1989] Benjamin G. Zorn. *Comparative Performance Evaluation of Garbage Collection Algorithms*. PhD thesis, University of California at Berkeley, March 1989. Technical Report UCB/CSD 89/544.

[Zorn, 1990a] Benjamin Zorn. Barrier methods for garbage collection. Technical Report CU-CS-494-90, University of Colorado, Boulder, November 1990.

[Zorn, 1990b] Benjamin Zorn. Comparing mark-and-sweep and stop-and-copy garbage collection. In *Conference Record of the 1990 ACM Symposium on Lisp and Functional Programming*, Nice, France, June 1990. ACM Press.

[Zorn, 1991] Benjamin Zorn.   The effect of garbage collection on cache performance. Technical Report CU–CS–528–91, University of Colorado at Boulder, May 1991.

[Zorn, 1992] Benjamin Zorn.   The measured cost of garbage collection.   Technical Report CU–CS–573–92, University of Colorado at Boulder, Department of Computer Science, Boulder, Colorado, April 1992.

[Zorn, 1993] Benjamin Zorn. The measured cost of conservative garbage collection. *Software Practice and Experience*, 23:733–756, 1993.

Index

Printed and bound by CPI Group (UK) Ltd, Croydon, CR0 4YY

27/10/2024

14580374-0001